D1047373

Alternatives in Assessment of Achievements, Learning Processes and Prior Knowledge

Evaluation in Education and Human Services

Editors:

George F. Madaus, Boston College,
  Chestnut Hill, Massachusetts, U.S.A.
Daniel L. Stufflebeam, Western Michigan
  University, Kalamazoo, Michigan, U.S.A.

Alternatives in Assessment of Achievements, Learning Processes and Prior Knowledge

edited by

Menucha Birenbaum

Tel Aviv University
Israel

and

Filip J.R.C. Dochy

University of Heerlen
The Netherlands

KLUWER ACADEMIC PUBLISHERS
Boston/Dordrecht/London

Distributors for North, Central and South America:
Kluwer Academic Publishers
101 Philip Drive
Assinippi Park
Norwell, Massachusetts 02061 USA
Telephone (781) 871-6600
Fax (781) 871-6528
E-Mail <kluwer@wkap.com>

Distributors for all other countries:
Kluwer Academic Publishers Group
Distribution Centre
Post Office Box 322
3300 AH Dordrecht, THE NETHERLANDS
Telephone 31 78 6392 392
Fax 31 78 6546 474
E-Mail services@wkap.nl>

 Electronic Services <http://www.wkap.nl>

Library of Congress Cataloging-in-Publication

Alternatives in assessment of achievements, learning processes, and
prior knowledge / edited by Menucha Birenbaum and Filip J.R.C.
Dochy.
    p.   cm. --(Evaluation in education and human services)
Includes bibliography and index.
ISBN 0-7923-9615-4 (alk.paper)
1. Academic achievement --Evaluation. 2. Learning--Evaluation.
3. Educational tests and measurements. I. Birenbaum, Menucha.
II. Dochy, F. J.R.C. (Filip J.R.C.)   III. Series
  LB3051.A5675   1995   95-34913
  371.27--dc20   CIP

Contents

I
ALTERNATIVES IN ASSESSMENT
OF ACHIEVEMENT (cont.)

II
ASSESSMENT OF PRIOR KNOWLEDGE
AND LEARNING PROCESSES

Contributing Authors

Carmen Aragonés
Dept. of Psychology, University of Madrid, Campus de Cantoblanc 28049,
Madrid, Spain

Gail P. Baxter
School of Education, University of Michigan, 610 E. University, 4115 SEB
Ann Arbor, MI 48109-1259, USA

Isabel Bermejo
Dept. of Psychology, University of Madrid, Campus de Cantoblanc 28049,
Madrid, Spain

Menucha Birenbaum
School of Education, Tel Aviv University, Ramat Aviv 69978, Israel

Leone Burton
School of Education, The University of Birmingham, Edgbaston, Birmingham
B15 2TT, UK

Marta del Castillo
Dept. of Psychology, University of Madrid, Campus de Cantoblanc 28049,
Madrid, Spain

David J. Clarke
Dept. of Science and Mathematics Education, University of Melbourne, Doug
McDonell Science Education Building, Parkville, Victoria 3052, Australia

Filip J. R. C. Dochy
Center for Educational Technology, University of Heerlen, P O Box 2960, 6401
DL Heerlen, The Netherlands

Noel Entwistle
Center for Research on Learning and Instruction, University of Edinburgh, 10/12
Buccleuch Place, Edinburgh EH8 9JT , Scotland, UK

Xiaohong Gao
American College Testing. 2210 N. Dodge St., Iowa City, IA 52243, USA

Teresa Garcia
Dept. of Educational Psychology, University of Texas at Austin, SZB 5-4,
Austin, TX 78712, USA

Elke Geisler-Brenstein
Dept. of Educational Psychology, Southern Illinois University at Carbondale,
Carbondale, Il. 62901, USA

Piet J. Janssen
University of Leuven, Center for School Psychology, Tiensestraat 102, B-3000
Leuven, Belgium

Alexander Minnaert
Center for School Psychology, Dept. of Psychology, University of Leuven,
Tiensestraat 102, B-3000 Leuven, Belgium

Paul R. Pintrich
School of Education, University of Michigan, 610 E. University, 1225 SEB,
Ann Arbor, MI 48109-1259, USA

Gissi Sarig
Academic Literacy Center, Kibbutzim Teachers' College, 149 Namir Rd., Tel-
Aviv 62507, Israel

Ronald R. Schmeck
Dept. of Educational Psychology, Southern Illinois University at Carbondale,
Carbondale, Il. 62901, USA

Mien S. R. Segers
Dept. of Educational Development and Research, University of Maastricht, P O
Box 616, 6200 MD Maastricht, The Netherlands

Richard J. Shavelson
School of Education, Stanford University, Stanford, CA 94305-3096, USA

Elana Shohamy
School of Education, Tel Aviv University, Ramat Aviv 69978, Israel

Carol Speth
Center for Research on Learning and Instruction, University of Edinburgh, 10/12
Buccleuch Place, Edinburgh EH8 9JT , Scotland, UK

Max Stephens
Victorian Board of Studies, 15 Pelham Street, Carlton, Victoria 3053, Australia

Hilary Tait
Center for Research on Learning and Instruction, University of Edinburgh, 10/12
Buccleuch Place, Edinburgh EH8 9JT , Scotland, UK

Pinchas Tamir
The Amos De-Shalit Science Teaching Center, Hebrew University of Jerusalem,
Jerusalem 91904, Israel

Carmen Vizcarro
Dept. of Psychology, University of Madrid, Campus de Cantoblanc 28049,
Madrid, Spain

Preface

This book was initiated during the 5th Conference of the European Association for Research on Learning and Instruction (EARLI), held in Aix-en Provence, France in the summer of 1993. At this conference the Special Interest Group on Assessment and Evaluation decided to publish a series of books discussing contemporary issues in that area, based on papers presented by its members in the present and future EARLI conferences. This book is on alternatives in assessment, reflecting the role of education at the beginning of the 21st century, and is the result of efforts by many SIG members.

We owe thanks to many people for making this book possible. First and foremost we wish to express our gratitude to the authors of these chapters who contributed their expertise and energy to this project, making our job as editors professionally and personally rewarding. Preparation of this book was facilitated by a small grant from the School of Education at Tel Aviv University and by the great help provided to us by its professional publishing team. Particular thanks are due to Mirjam Hadar who skillfully copy-edited the manuscripts, to Alice Zilcha who patiently formatted them and to Lisa Amdur who provided administrative support. Their conscientious commitment and effort are greatly appreciated.

Menucha Birenbaum
Filip J. R. C. Dochy

Introduction

The area of achievement assessment has been undergoing major changes during the past few years. A shift has taken place from what some call a "culture of testing" to a "culture of assessment". A strong emphasis is now put on integrating assessment and instruction, on assessing process rather than just products and on evaluating individual progress relative to each student's starting point. The position of the student with regard to the evaluation process has also been changing from that of a passive, powerless, often oppressed subject who is mystified by the process, to that of an active participant who shares responsibility in the process, practices self evaluation, reflection, and collaboration and conducts a continuous dialogue with the teacher. The assessment itself takes many forms and functions. Usually there is less time pressure, and a variety of tools, which are used in real life for performing similar tasks, are allowed. The task is often interesting, meaningful, authentic and challenging. Reporting practices have shifted from a single score to a profile -- from a snapshot to an overall screening. All these changes are part of a school restructuring process, meant to develop self-motivated and self-regulated learners and intended to make learning a more mindful and meaningful experience which is responsive to individual differences among the learners. This shift reflects an "overall assessment prophecy" which holds that it is no longer possible to consider assessment only as a means of determining which individuals are already adapted to, or have the potential for adapting to, mainstream educational practice. A conceivable alternative goal is to reverse this sequence of adaptation: Rather than requiring individuals to adapt to means of instruction, the desired objective is to adapt the means of instruction to individuals in order to maximize their potential for success. As contemporary views of assessment consider it to be an integral part of instruction, the new assessment alternatives being developed enhance the possibilities for adaptation. Examples of such alternatives include portfolios, progress tests, assessments of prior knowledge, reflective journals, etc.

The present book addresses assessment issues related to this new state of affairs. In its first part new alternatives in assessment of achievement in various subject matter areas are discussed, focusing on agenda, practice, impact and evaluation of the assessment. In the second part issues related to the shift towards assessment of the learning process are discussed, specifically questions concerning the assessment of individual differences in prior knowledge, learning skills and strategies. This book is intended for researchers in the areas of assessment and evaluation, teaching, and learning; for teacher educators and their students in university departments of education and in teacher colleges; for school administrators and those involved in framing assessment policy, and for teachers in all school levels who are looking for alternative methods for assessing their students' learning process and progress, as they prepare them to become self-regulated learners. Following is a brief overview of the book's chapters.

PART I: ALTERNATIVES IN ASSESSMENT OF ACHIEVEMENT

In Chapter 1, Menucha Birenbaum presents a general overview of alternative assessment, its rationale, characteristics, and devices, focusing on the portfolio and describing its various forms, its uses and judgment. She then discusses the criteria for assessing the assessment and the lessons to be learned from some current high-stakes applications of alternative assessment . Finally, she presents a rationale for a pluralistic approach to assessment. In Chapter 2, Leone Burton discusses assessment in mathematics in relation to current theories of learning and teaching of this subject. She argues that curriculum developments predicated on a social constructivist epistemology do not only affect the design and choice of assessment tasks but are set within a view of the curriculum as a coherent whole. She then compares alternative assessment approaches from four countries with respect to content, effects on particular groups and impact on mathematics education. In Chapter 3, David Clarke and Max Stephens describe a systematic three-stage investigation of the impact on instructional practices in mathematics at all high school levels of the introduction of performance assessment into a statewide, mandated assessment of senior high school mathematics in Victoria, Australia. Pinchas Tamir, in Chapter 4, discusses the basic goals for the science curriculum in relation to learning theories, and describes the variety of approaches, strategies, and means used to assess the extent to which these goals are attained. Chapter 5 by Richard Shavelson, Xiaohong Gao, and Gail Baxter deals with content validity of performance assessment in science and demonstrates empirically the importance of accurate specification of a subject matter domain in the development of performance assessment. A case in which a science domain was misspecified is presented and the consequences -- overestimation of the number of tasks needed to reach minimum generalizability and underestimation of systematic differences in students' performances -- are discussed. Chapter 6 by Elana Shohamy deals with second language assessment, discussing the close link between the definitions of language knowledge and the procedures used to measure it. She identifies and describes four eras in language testing, each reflecting a different definition of language knowledge of the time, and the specific measurement procedures that matched it. In conclusion she describes an innovative multidimensional assessment battery which has been recently introduced in Israel for assessing Hebrew language acquisition by immigrant children in a school context. In Chapter 7, Gissi Sarig focuses on assessment of academic literacy. She first outlines a theoretical rationale for assessing literacy in general and academic literacy in particular from a semiotic-epistemic perspective. She then presents a model of academic literate learning goals, followed by a description of one specific assessment instrument, namely the reflective journal. She suggests assessment rubrics for it and discusses the complexities involved in the assessment. To conclude this part of the book, Mien Segers, in Chapter 8, tackles a key problem in designing valid assessments, namely that of making assessment procedures congruent with educational and instructional principles. For this purpose the instructional key features are translated into different specific requirements for the assessment system which include: assessment based on authentic problems, assessment of knowledge acquisition and assessment of knowledge application. She then compares students' performance on two types of tests: a factual knowledge test, and a problem solving overall test, administered in a problem-based curriculum in economics at the university level.

PART II: ASSESSMENT OF PRIOR KNOWLEDGE AND LEARNING PROCESSES

In Chapter 9, Filip Dochy focuses on the definition and assessment of prior knowledge, noting that a key to developing an integrated and generative knowledge base is to build upon the learner's prior knowledge as a part of an assessment system. Taking into account the starting level of a student will thus facilitate the learning process. Dochy then presents a model that maps the structure of knowledge into four types of dimensions, and offers a methodology for their assessment, which leads to the construction of knowledge profiles. Finally he presents results of an empirical study designed to examine the validity of domain specific knowledge profiles with respect to expertise in the field of economics. In Chapter 10, Alexander Minnaert and Piet Janssen discuss the relationships between domain specific prior knowledge and study skills in predicting success in undergraduate studies of psychology. The results of their longitudinal study show significant effects of domain-specific prior knowledge on the speed and accuracy of study behaviors and study processes, such as speed of reading and accuracy of summarizing, synthesizing and memorizing. Their model confirms the hypothesis that prior knowledge as well as study skills are both necessary prerequisites for success in higher education. Chapter 11 by Elke Geisler-Brenstein and Ronald Schmeck deals with the subtle manifestation of individuality in the ways students approach learning. They describe the development history of the Inventory of Learning Processes (ILP) and discuss substantive and methodological improvements in its recently revised version. Finally they discuss underlying assumptions about the conceptual and behavioral stability of individual differences in learning with special emphasis on the role self-concept plays in the development of a viable learning style. Chapter 12 by Teresa Garcia and Paul Pintrich deals with the assessment of student motivation and learning strategies in the classroom setting. Noting the importance of considering both motivational and cognitive components of academic performance, the authors discuss the problems related to the assessment of those components in the classroom setting using self report measures. They then present the Motivated Strategies for Learning Questionnaire (MSLQ), describing its development and the content of each scale. Finally they discuss the psychometric properties of the questionnaire and its practical utility. In Chapter 13, Carmen Vizcarro and her colleagues Isabel Bermejo, Marta del Castillo and Carmen Aragonés describe the process of developing their inventory to measure learning strategies (LS) of secondary and university students. Results of an empirical study involving a large sample of students are presented and issues related to reliability and discriminant validity of the scales are discussed. Finally, in Chapter 14, Noel Entwistle, Hilary Tait and Carol Speth describe three main areas of activity in a project designed to develop a computer-based package to identify students in higher education, who are at risk due to ineffective study skills and strategies, and then to advise them. They first describe their continuing work on the inventory of assessing study methods and strategies, and then describe the development of a computer-based visualization tool used to provide university departments with information about the nature and extent of their students' study difficulties. Finally they describe the development of a computer system which will provide advice to students on study skills and strategies.

I

ALTERNATIVES IN ASSESSMENT OF ACHIEVEMENT

Assessment 2000:
Towards a Pluralistic Approach
to Assessment

Menucha Birenbaum

INTRODUCTION

The title Assessment 2000 would have sounded like science fiction a few decades ago, an opportunity to use my imagination in making creative and wild speculations about assessment in a distant future. However, less than half a decade before the due date, this chapter entails more modest and careful speculations, based on contemporary theories and on lessons gained from current practice. Indeed, it starts by introducing the most generic term currently used in educational literature with respect to assessment, i.e., *alternative assessment*. It briefly explains to what and why an alternative is sought and describes the main features of this type of assessment, as it is currently viewed. Of the various devices subsumed under the alternative assessment umbrella a focus is put on the portfolio describing its various types, uses and criteria for judgment. Next, criteria for evaluating alternative assessment and lessons to be learnt from current practice are discussed, and finally, a rationale for a pluralistic approach to assessment is presented.

The new era in assessment, which can be traced back to the mid 80's, has enriched the assessment literature with many new terms, such as performance assessment, authentic assessment, direct assessment, constructive assessment, incidental assessment, informal assessment, balanced assessment, curriculum-embedded assessment, curriculum-based assessment, and possibly a few more. When a concept is very salient in a particular culture it usually accrues a rich terminology that distinguishes its subtle nuances, (or, as we like to point out: in the Eskimo language there are numerous terms for describing snow). On the other hand, a variety of terms may indicate an incoherent, vague concept that has not gained an established terminology, perhaps due to its novelty. The richness of terms in such cases represents confusion among the users and a need for crystallization of that concept. It seems that the current conception of assessment illustrates the second of these possibilities.

Contemporary Goals and Objectives of Instruction

In choosing a method for assessment we have to first ask: What is it we want to assess? In order to answer this question we have to take into consideration the goals for instruction in the context of which the assessment takes place. Goals and objectives of instruction can be classified along dimensions that vary from specific to general. The most general one, which seems to fit any educational system, is to prepare the student to function successfully both in school and outside it, in the present and in the future. The question that arises in any particular period is what is needed for successful functioning at that point in time. Thus, in the second half of the 19th century, schools served as an agency of socialization aimed at providing the necessary skills for functioning in the industrial society to members of social classes that had previously been deprived of formal education. Hence to function successfully in the era of the industrial revolution required that a skillful worker be capable of performing the specific tasks he/she was trained to perform. Information in this era was assumed to be finite. *Education for the masses* stressed the acquisition of basic skills while higher order thinking and intellectual pursuits were reserved for the elite ruling class.

However, what characterizes the era following the technological revolution, sometimes referred to as the "information age", and which leads us into the 21st century, is pluralism and continual, dynamic changes. As information is no longer considered finite and static but rather infinite and dynamic, the well-functioning person is likely to have to acquire new knowledge independently and use it to solve new unforeseen problems. Hence, successful functioning in this era demands an adaptable, thinking, autonomous person, who is a self-regulated learner, capable of communicating and cooperating with others. The specific competencies that are required of such a person include a) cognitive competencies such as problem solving, critical thinking, formulating questions, searching for relevant information, making informed judgments, efficient use of information, conducting observations, investigations, inventing and creating new things, analyzing data, presenting data communicatively, oral and written expression; b) meta-cognitive competencies such as self-reflection, or self-evaluation; c) social competencies such as leading discussions and conversations, persuading, cooperating, working in groups, etc. and d) affective dispositions such as for instance perseverance, internal motivation, initiative, responsibility, self-efficacy, independence, flexibility, or coping with frustrating situations. The need to develop these competencies expands the scope of education and thus creates a challenging enterprise for educators.

THE NATURE OF CHANGE IN INSTRUCTION AND ASSESSMENT

The differences between the goals of education in the two eras mentioned above are reflected in the kinds of instruction and assessment that have been implemented for achieving those goals.

The Traditional Approach

The type of instruction aimed at achieving the goals of education in the traditional context is characterized by Freire through the "banking concept" (Freire, 1972); he describes this as follows:

> Narration (with the teacher as narrator) leads the students to memorize mechanically the narrated content. Worse still, it turns them into 'containers', into receptacles to be filled by the teacher. The more completely he fills the receptacles, the better a teacher he is. The more meekly the receptacles permit themselves to be filled, the better students they are. Education thus becomes an act of depositing, in which the students are depositories and the teachers the depositor. Instead of communication, the teacher issues communiqués and 'makes deposits' which the students patiently receive, memorize, and repeat. This is the 'banking' concept of education, in which the scope of action allowed to the students extends only as far as receiving, filing, and storing the deposits. (pp. 45-46)

The assessment approach that suits this teaching conception concentrates mainly on the testing of basic skills, supposedly acquired through tedious drill and practice experiences, rehearsals and repetitions of what was taught in class or in the textbook. During the past three decades, the development of tests for accountability purposes, as well as their scoring and interpretation has been dominated by measurement experts using sophisticated psychometric models. In the western world, especially in the United States, their work was guided by the demand for objectivity and fairness in testing, requiring a high level of standardization because of the high stakes attributed to test scores. Under such circumstances, tests, mainly of the choice response format, such as multiple-choice, true/false or matching items, became the common tools for assessment. These types of items, that best measure low level cognitive competencies, have been publicly criticized for their negative consequences which include inflated test scores, i.e., the "Lake Wobegon" effect (Cannell, 1989), and deteriorated instruction which resulted from promoting those cognitive levels addressed by the tests at the expense of higher order competencies. Moreover, test pollution became a serious problem as teachers were accused of teaching to the test or even teaching the test . This undesired phenomenon gave rise to the call for measurement driven instruction (MDI), which required higher cognitive levels to be addressed by standardized tests and to promote their systemic validity (Frederiksen, 1984; Frederiksen & Collins, 1989).

The paradigm that has guided the development of psychometric theory and practice assumes the universality of achievement test scores. Thus, a certain score on a specific standardized test is assumed to bear the same meaning for all examinees receiving that score. Such an assumption stems from the view that a consensus can be reached regarding the meaning of educational goals and objectives. Another psychometric paradigm implies that goals can be separated from the means for their attainment. Hence, psychometric experts are regarded as the qualified agencies for the development of achievement tests and the analysis of their results, instead of the teachers who actuate the instructional process. Such an approach supports the need for centralized control in the education system.

An assessment system that develops in such an environment and is sometimes referred to as a *testing culture* (Kleinsasser, Horsch, & Tastad, 1993; Wolf, Bixby, Glenn, & Gardner, 1991) has the following characteristics: Instruction and assessment are considered separate activities, the former being the responsibility of the teacher and the latter the responsibility of the measurement expert. This distinction has raised serious doubts regarding the validity of those tests that are not directly related to the actual instruction that takes place in class. Furthermore, the test plan, the item writing as well as the development of criteria for evaluating test performance and the scoring process, are not usually shared with the students and remain a mystery to them. The items/tasks are often synthetic in as much as they are unrelated to the student's life experience. Moreover, the majority of the test items are of the choice format, examining knowledge of decontextualized, discrete units of the subject matter. The tests are usually of the paper and pencil type, administered in class under time constraints and forbidding the use of helping materials and tools. In other words, the first draft of the student's work produced under stressful conditions, and unrealistic constraints is often used for determining high stake consequences. What is being evaluated is merely the product, with no regard to the process, and the reporting of the results usually takes the form of a single total score.

The Alternative Approach

As opposed to the traditional approach to instruction, which is based on the behavioristic theory of learning, the instructional approach aimed at achieving the goals of education in the information age is based on the cognitive learning theory. Basic to this theory are the modern views of intelligence which emphasize the multidimensional nature of this construct (Gardner, 1983, 1993; Gardner & Hatch, 1989; Sternberg, 1985). Unlike traditional conceptions that viewed intelligence as a fixed trait which is normally distributed in the population and is the source of individual differences, the current view stresses the nonfixed nature of intelligence, also referred to as *mind* (Wolf et al., 1991). The message is that one can learn how to learn and that there is no one best way to teach all learners. Moreover, the current conception is that thinking involves a meta-cognitive component in addition to the cognitive one, and that the development of intelligence results from developing the meta-cognitive component, either naturally or through direct instruction. Furthermore, the mental processes are believed to be dependent upon the social and cultural context in which they occur and to be shaped as the learner interacts with the environment.

The cognitive learning theory postulates that all learning involves thinking (Perkins, 1992; Perkins & Blythe, 1994; Resnick & Klopfer, 1989; Resnick & Resnick, 1992), so that memorization, without the development of a conceptual model or a global view of the activity, is anticipated to impair the retrieval, application and generalization of the material. Hence, the atomization and sequencing approach, also referred to as the *bricks method*, which assumes that the material has to be broken into small hierarchically related pieces (bricks) and transmitted to the learners, and which expects that the latter will put one brick after another into their mind until the entire unit is built up, is doomed to fail. As claimed by the constructivists, learning involves the learner's active construction of schemes in order to understand the material, making it a process whereby the learner is engaged in creating meaning. Effective instruction, according to this view, entails a change in the teacher's role whereby s/he becomes a mentor or a coach who provides opportunities for the learners to use what they already know in order to understand new material. The teacher is expected to supply meaningful tasks which are related to the learner's experience and can improve his/her learning strategies and understanding. In their efforts to convince educators to bring thinking up front in the instructional process, Perkins and Blythe (1994) define understanding as "being able to carry out a variety of 'performances' that show one's understanding of the topic and, at the same time, advance it" (p. 6). They call such performances "understanding performances" and emphasize the role of ongoing assessment in learning for understanding. The three common factors they identify among various approaches to ongoing assessment are: "shared and public criteria, regular feedback, and frequent reflection throughout the learning process" (p. 7).

According to Freire (1972), the dialogue between the teacher and the students has a central role within what he calls the problem-posing or liberating education. Freire argues that

> through dialogue, the teacher-of-students and the students-of-the-teacher cease to exist and a new term emerges: teacher-student with students-teachers. The teacher is no longer merely the-one-who teaches, but one who is himself taught in dialogue with the students, who in their turn while being taught also teach. They become jointly responsible for a process in which all grow. (p. 53)

Freire further argues that unlike the "banking" approach to education, the "problem-posing education regards dialogue as indispensable to the act of cognition which unveils reality", and he states that this kind of education "bases itself on creativity and stimulates true reflection and action upon reality, thereby responding to the vocation of men as beings who are authentic only when engaged in inquiry and creative transformation" [p. 56].

The assessment approach that suits this teaching conception, and is sometimes called an *assessment culture* (Wolf et al., 1991; Kleinsasser et al., 1993), strongly emphasizes the integration of assessment and instruction. In this culture the perceived position of the student with regard to the evaluation process changes from that of a passive, powerless, often oppressed, subject who is mystified by the process, to an active participant who shares responsibility in the process, practices self-evaluation, reflection, and collaboration, and conducts a continuous dialogue with the teacher. The assessment itself takes many forms, all of which are generally referred to by psychometricians as "unstandardized assessments embedded in instruction" (Koretz, Stecher, Klein & McCaffrey, 1994). Usually there is no time pressure, and a variety of tools which are used in real life for performing similar tasks are permitted. The tasks are often interesting, meaningful, authentic, challenging and engaging, involving investigations of various kinds. Students participate in the development of the criteria and the standards for evaluating their performance while both the process and the product are being assessed. Students document their reflections in a journal and use portfolios to keep track of their academic/vocational growth. Finally, reporting practices shift from a single score to a profile, i.e., from quantification to portrayal.

It is interesting to note that the term test, which was recently replaced by the term assessment, originated from the Latin *testum* -- a tool for examining the purity of metals, whereas the origin of the word assessment is in the Latin verb *assidere* --

meaning sitting alongside someone. Thus, the substantial differences between the testing and the assessment cultures are also marked semantically.

In summary, as we approach the 21st century, the contemporary view of education, is as follows: *Instruction-wise*, teaching as a method of depositing knowledge in the heads of the students is being replaced by an approach that promotes the development of a thinking self-regulated learner; *learning-wise*, memorizing as a way of acquiring knowledge is being replaced by a constructivist approach which stresses the student's active role in making use of knowledge, investigating and constructing meaning; finally, *assessment-wise*, the psychometric - quantitative approach is being challenged by a contextual - qualitative approach.

Alternative Assessment Devices

A variety of methods and devices are subsumed under the alternative assessment umbrella; these include: authentic performance tasks, simulations, portfolios, journals, group projects, exhibitions, observations, interviews, oral presentations, self evaluation, peer-evaluation, etc. Most of these methods are described in other chapters in this book. Here I chose to focus on the portfolio which is a device that is well suited for accomplishing the goals of alternative assessment. Although, in the past, various professions have used portfolios to demonstrate competence, skills and accomplishments (e.g., painters, architects, models, writers, journalists, etc.) they have only recently been introduced as educational assessment devices (Arter & Spandel, 1992; Paulson, Paulson & Meyer, 1991; Shulman, 1988; Wolf Palmer, 1989).

The following is the most quoted definition of a student portfolio in an assessment context:

> A purposeful collection of student work that tells the story of the student's efforts, progress, or achievement in (a) given area(s). This collection must include student participation in the selection of portfolio content; the guidelines for selection; the criteria for judging merit; and evidence of student self-reflection. (Arter & Spandel, 1992, p. 36)

As this definition implies, a portfolio compiled for assessment purposes is neither a container that holds every item the student has produced during his/her studies of the subject, nor is it, on the other hand, a random selection of items. The entries contained in the portfolio should have been carefully selected to serve as evidence that learning has occurred, indicating what the student knows and can do in a particular subject, and what his/her accomplishments and progress are. The freedom of choice regarding the entries can vary from unrestricted to restricted, i.e., from letting the student choose whatever s/he considers as relevant evidence, to letting him/her choose only according to prespecified categories. Students should also be aware of what qualifies as appropriate evidence. The development of such guidelines can be shared with them. Similarly, as the students assemble their portfolios for the purpose of assessment, they should be aware of the criteria and standards for judging the merit of each entry as well as of the portfolio as a whole. Deciding upon the criteria (i.e., what is valued in a student's performance) and the standards (i.e., what is considered exemplary performance on each criterion for a particular normative group) is, in itself, a valuable learning experience. It is therefore recommended that criteria and standards be jointly developed by the teacher and the students. Finally, an indispensable component of a portfolio is evidence of self-reflection. The students are required to reflect on each piece included in the portfolio, explaining why they consider it relevant evidence, how they created it , what their difficulties were, how they overcame them, what they learnt from working on the task, etc. They are also expected to compare more effective and less effective pieces, explaining how they differ. In addition, when the portfolio is ready for assessment, the students must attach a cover letter explaining the purpose of the portfolio and its organizing theme, taking into consideration the perspectives of their audience. The cover letter should summarize the student's reflection on the portfolio as a whole, thus providing a complete story, or portrait, of the student as a reflective learner. It should be noted that the content of the portfolio reflects the emphasis of the taught curriculum. Based on that curriculum the students develop a sense of what is valued and it guides their choices of the entries for their portfolios. Thus, if the instruction in a given class emphasizes rote memorization over higher order processes this will be reflected in the content of the portfolios produced in that class.

Portfolio seems to be a generic term that can address various assessment purposes, can encompass a wide range of uses and contents, and can take many different forms. Purposes for implementing a portfolio system include monitoring student progress, grading, high-school credit, college admission, program evaluation, etc. The audiences to whom the portfolio is presented also vary. A list of possible audiences may include parents, school-board members, next year's teacher, assessment staff of the district and of the state, and the general public. Subject-wise, portfolios are being used in a wide variety of areas, either in one specific content area or combining areas in an interdisciplinary endeavor. They can be used at all educational levels, from kindergarten (Koppert, 1991) to higher education (Hamp-Lyons & Condon, 1993; Larsen, 1991; Valeri-Gold, Olson, & Deming, 1991). Extensive use of portfolios in language is evident in communication (writing) or integrated language arts (writing, reading, speaking and listening) and in first and second/foreign language classes (Blake-Yancey, 1992; Belanoff & Dickson, 1991; Camp, 1991, 1992; Hansen, 1992; Tierney, Carter, & Desai, 1991; Valencia, 1990). Recently mathematics portfolios have also become widely used (Asturias, 1994; Knight, 1992; Mumme, 1991) as have science portfolios (Collins, 1991; Hamm & Adams, 1991). Similarly, portfolios have been increasingly used for teacher evaluation (Collins, 1993; Leiva, 1995; Shulman, 1988). Portfolios also vary in their content. They can contain items presented in a variety of forms: written, visual, auditory or other multimedia presentations. Being a carefully selected collection the portfolio can contain complete works, rough drafts, outlines, performance on a timed test, samples of comments on the student's work made by the teacher, by peers, by community members or by external experts; comments made by the student on his/her classmate's work; summaries of assessment conferences between the student and the teacher, and any other information the student considers to be important evidence of what s/he knows and can do, and of how much s/he has progressed in that subject matter area. Following are examples of possible entries for portfolios in mathematics and in literacy: *Mathematical portfolio*s can contain examples of a mathematical investigation requiring data collection, data-analysis, presentation of the results, their interpretation, and conclusions; examples of creative problem solving; of a practical mathematics application; of a linkage between mathematics and another content area; diagrams, graphs, figures; computer-printouts produced for solving a problem; audio/video taped presentation by student of a mathematical topic; drafts from various stages of a problem solving process; solution to a mathematical riddle, etc. *Literacy portfolios* can contain samples of a short story, a poem, an expository piece, a persuasive piece, an essay, an article, a literary analysis, a timed writing sample; a list of books read outside of school, a series of revisions, a personal response to a book/ movie/ TV program/ social event/ scientific phenomenon/ mathematical problem; a reading comprehension test, etc.

Portfolios can be used for internal as well as external evaluation and at various levels of aggregation (i.e., class, school, district). Currently portfolios are being used for classroom assessment as well as for large-scale assessment (Koretz et al., 1994). Yet, several unresolved problems have been encountered during current implementations of portfolios for large-scale high-stakes assessments, a few of which will be discussed later in this chapter.

D'Aoust (1992) identifies three distinctive types of portfolios: An *exemplary folio*, which is a collection of examples accumulated over time presenting the best and most representative works of the student; a *process folio,* which includes examples of the developmental process of the student's learning. It consists of complete as well as incomplete works, more effective and less effective pieces, rough drafts and other pieces of evidence regarding the learning process the student has been undergoing with respect to that subject; a *combined folio,* which includes two subfolios, each including selected entries from the other two types of portfolios. Another distinction is made between two ways of reviewing the portfolio: One, an inquiry reading and the other, a reading for grading. The first is employed for formative assessment purposes whereas the second is commonly employed for formal summative assessment purposes, usually in large-scale assessment programs.

Special attention is given to the organization and content of the portfolio. There are many ways in which a portfolio can be organized, for instance: by topics, by objectives or goals, according to the chronological order of production of the items, by the type of product, by the level of the student's satisfaction with the product , etc. Whatever the organizing criterion may be it should be stated clearly in the cover letter attached to the portfolio and specified in the table of contents.

Common to the various types and uses of the portfolio as an assessment device are the following features: It is a device that integrates instruction and assessment and is used for a longitudinal assessment of processes and products. It advances the dialogue and cooperation between the student and the teacher, in which the two collaborate in assessing the student's accomplishments and development with respect to the subject matter. The portfolio enables a wide view of the student's learning outcomes across a wide range of contents, thus providing a method for comprehensively portraying, or telling the story of the student as a learner, pointing out his/her strengths and weaknesses. Hence, portfolios fulfill the requirements demanded of good assessment, i.e., authenticity, dynamism, longitudinality, multidimensionality, interactivity and richness of evidence. Furthermore, the production of a portfolio encourages students to participate in and take responsibility for their learning. A unique attribute of the portfolio is the choice it enables the student to make with respect to the pieces s/he would like to include as evidence of growth. Moreover, it helps the student develop personal dispositions that are considered essential for effective learning, namely, self-regulation, self-efficacy, self-discipline, and self-assessment, as well as intrinsic motivation, persistence, and flexibility.

Because the portfolio, taken as a whole, is expected to provide more information than the sum of its entries, the assessment of a portfolio should include criteria for judging the merit of the portfolio as a whole as well as of its pieces. The development of the two sets of criteria is not an easy task and the judging process is a problematic one, as will be discussed in the next section. Of the two sets of criteria, the one for assessing the portfolio as a whole seems to have gained much less attention than that for the individual entries which is subsumed under the more general category of judging performance-based assessment (see Herman, Aschbacher, & Winters, 1992). Following is an example of a rubric for assessing the portfolio as a whole (based in part on a draft by Paulson & Paulson, 1992). It addresses the standards to be met in order to earn each of these holistic 4-point-scale scores.

A Rubric for Judging a Portfolio as a Whole:

4 = The entries are carefully chosen to render a coherent picture of the student as a reflective learner, of what s/he knows and can do, and of how much s/he has progressed in the subject. The entries bear a clear relationship to each other and to a central organizing theme. The rationale for the choice of the entries has been defined and clearly stated, reflecting a well grounded self-assessment. The student is well aware of the audience's perspectives as is evident in the organization and the presentation of the portfolio.

3 = There is evidence that the student has thought about the selection of the entries. Each entry is justified by an argument and reflected upon. More effective and less effective entries are compared. The student seems to be aware of his/her learning process and accomplishments. Yet the portfolio lacks a central purpose and the pieces do not add up to a coherent picture of the student as a learner. There is insufficient evidence that the student is aware of the audience's perspectives.

2 = There is some evidence of intentional selection of entries but the reason is not clearly stated beyond shallow statements such as "I selected this piece because I like it very much". The portfolio lacks an organizing theme and a central purpose. Although there is some evidence of self-reflection the portfolio lacks sufficient information to afford a picture of the student as a learner.

1 = The portfolio is simply a haphazard collection of works or tests. There is no evidence of intentional selection of entries. No attempts are made to compare between entries or to organize the entries according to a central theme. The portfolio does not even sketch a vague picture of the student as a reflective learner.

ASSESSING ALTERNATIVE ASSESSMENT

Issues related to the evaluation of alternative assessment will be discussed in this section, beginning with those related to the two criteria by which educational and psychological assessment measures are commonly evaluated, namely, validity and reliability, followed by a summary of the lessons learned from current implementations of high-stakes alternative assessment programs.

The meaning of validity and reliability has recently been expanded since their inclusion in the standards for educational and psychological testing developed a decade ago (AERA, APA, & NCME, 1985) prior to the introduction of alternative assessment (Linn, Baker, & Dunbar, 1991; Linn, 1994, Messick, 1989,1994; Shepard, 1993). Yet, there are still those who stress the need to identify new criteria to fully capture the unique nature of alternative assessment (Delandshere & Petrosky,

1994; Moss, 1994, in press; Wolf et al., 1991). This dissatisfaction with the available criteria, which were originally developed to evaluate indirect measures of performance, is attributed to their insensitivity to the characteristics of a direct assessment of performance. On the available criteria alternative assessment seems to compare unfavorably with standardized tests. Following is a summary of the main issues addressed with respect to validity and reliability of alternative assessment. In this discussion, only the most demanding role of alternative assessment, namely, high-stakes assessment, will be considered. Assessments are referred to as "high-stakes" when they bear critical consequences for the individual (e.g., certification of competence) or can cause a wholescale change in a school program, thereby affecting all students. Such assessments therefore require control of a type and rigor not always needed for classroom assessment.

Validity Related Issues

Being a direct assessment of performance, unlike traditional tests which measure indicators, alternative assessment appears to be potentially highly valid. However, an assessment cannot be judged by its appearances but must rather be supported by empirical evidence and demonstrate technical adequacy. A pivotal aspect of validity is construct validity which is viewed as a unified concept because it is difficult to disentangle its many, highly intertwined facets (Messick, 1994, Shepard, 1993, Cronbach, 1988). Nevertheless, for reasons of simplicity, issues related to validity of alternative assessment will be discussed in this section with respect to each facet separately.

Messick (1994) claims that interpretation and use of all kinds of assessment should be validated in terms of content, substantive, structural, external, generalizability, and consequential, aspects of construct validity. For utilizing alternative assessment in high stakes assessment programs, the following aspects of construct validity seem to be of special relevance:

Content/domain specification. Due to the fact that they are complex and therefore time consuming, authentic tasks tend to compare unfavorably with choice-response items with respect to domain coverage. Moreover, because authentic tasks are often loosely structured an important question arises concerning the domains about which inferences are to be drawn on the basis of the assessment. It is therefore important to clearly specify the domains and design the assessment rubrics so that they clearly cover those domains. Shavelson, Gao, and Baxter (this volume) empirically demonstrate the importance of accurate specification of a subject matter domain in the development of performance assessment. It should be noted that there is a trade-off between breadth of the domain and the reliability of the assessment. A well known effect of narrowing the domain to which the results generalize, by increasing the specificity of the tasks, is the increment in the reliability of the assessment. However, increasing the specificity of the tasks undermines validity as the inferences become too narrow to matter. Thus, by employing loosely structured tasks inferences may be kept broad enough to be important but reliability will decrease. A related concern regarding the construction or selection of performance tasks is raised by Messick (1994) who cautions against a task-driven approach if the performance is viewed as the vehicle, not the target, of assessment. Instead he advises to adopt a construct-driven approach so that the meaning of the construct will guide the construction or selection of relevant tasks and the development of scoring criteria and rubrics. He further emphasizes that a construct-driven approach also makes salient the issue of construct underrepresentation and construct-irrelevant variance, which he considers as the two main threats to validity. An additional concern regarding the content of the direct assessment pertains to its quality. The content should be consistent with the best current understanding in the field and subject matter experts must approve the tasks as being contextualized, meaningful, and worthy of the time invested in them (Linn et al., 1991).

Equity. Because of its authenticity, alternative assessment appears to have the potential of being more equitable than traditional tests (Darling-Hammond, 1995). Yet empirical studies in the United States, comparing the gap in achievement between white and minority groups on multiple-choice items versus performance-based tasks, have yielded inconclusive results. Badger (1995) reports that students in Low Advantaged schools in the State of Massachusetts performed better on open-ended questions than they did on multiple-choice ones. She points out that this finding was reflected throughout the grades and the subject matter areas tested. On the other hand, there is evidence that the racial/ethnic gap in performance on indirect assessment is maintained in the same order of magnitude, or grows even larger with respect to direct assessment (Dunbar, Koretz & Hoover, 1991; Linn et al., 1991). The differences in achievement between white and minority students can be explained, according to Darling-Hammond (1995), by unequal access to high quality curriculum and instruction. She argues that "the quality of education made available to many students has been undermined by the nature of the testing program used to monitor and shape their learning" (p. 97). This conclusion is based on research findings showing that students in lower tracks or remedial programs -- disproportionately populated by minority and economically disadvantaged students -- experience instruction geared only to multiple-choice tests, that is, promoting rote memorization and emphasizing superficial and shallow understanding at the expense of higher order thought processes. Therefore, when implementing alternative assessment for accountability purposes substantial changes are required in instructional strategy and practice, in resource allocation, and teacher training in order to ensure that all students are adequately prepared for this kind of assessment. According to Nettles and Bernstein (1995), the requirements for ensuring equitable assessment include the following: ensuring that all students are able to relate to the content of the assessment and that it is relevant and useful for their own educational and occupational goals; eliminating bias, language- and content-wise, against racial and gender groups; ensuring fairness, and opening to public scrutiny the various processes related to the development, administration, scoring and reporting of the assessment results.

Consequential validity. Validity is construed as a characteristic of inferences, not of the measures themselves (Messick, 1989). It has therefore been suggested that the consequential basis of validity be given much greater prominence amongst the criteria of judging assessment (Linn et al., 1991). As stated by Messick (1994) "evidence of intended and unintended consequences of test interpretation and use should be evaluated as an integral part of the validation process" (p. 22). Recent applications of alternative assessment carry both good and bad news in this respect. The good news is that since its introduction in high-stakes assessment programs more teachers have been introducing tasks designed to measure higher order cognitive processes (Clarke & Stephens, this volume; Koretz, McCaffrey, Klein, Bell & Stecher, 1992; Koretz, et al., 1994). However, the bad news is that in some classes students memorized those tasks without developing the type of thinking and problem solving skills that are intended. Thus, the unintended effect of test pollution, observed in the results of standardized tests, where teaching to the test resulted in increasing test scores much more than improved achievement, is beginning to be evident in some classes with respect to alternative assessment as well. In order to ensure the intended consequences of alternative assessment it is therefore suggested that evidence be required that the performance is not a result of memorization but is indicative of the complexity of the cognitive process students employ for solving the problem. Relevant sources for judging the merit of the performance include information regarding the duration of students' engagement with the task, the amount of help provided them, as well as documentation of the process of solving the task and self reflection.

Reliability Related Issues

Members of the psychometric community attach great importance to the criteria of reliability and comparability of scores in judging the quality of an assessment device. In order to make inferences and use of high-stake assessments, considerable consistency is required across raters and across tasks that are designed to measure the same domain. Also necessary is considerable stability within subjects in performing the same tasks across different occasions. The unique nature of alternative assessment has affected the traditional conception of reliability, much as it has affected the conception of validity, resulting in the expansion of its scope and a change in the weights attached to its various components.

Following are research findings and controversial issues regarding the various aspects of reliability as pertaining to alternative assessment.

Interrater reliability or reproducibility. Alternative assessment tends to compare unfavorably to traditional assessment when conventional criteria of interrater reliability are employed. Portfolio assessment is the most troublesome with respect to this kind of reliability. Lack of standardization of tasks, resulting from the freedom of choice given to students regarding the selection of entries to their portfolios, decreases reliability of scores as it requires raters to stretch general-purpose rubrics to cover a wide variety of tasks. Although improvements can be made by providing more detailed rubrics for judging performance, better trained raters, and a smaller number of points on the scale score, dissatisfaction with this criterion, based on philosophical grounds, is still in evidence. For instance, Moss (1994) argues that the nature of alternative assessment, especially portfolio assessment, does not lend itself to judgment according to the reliability criterion. She asserts that a hermeneutic approach to making and warranting interpretations of human performance, which produces "integrative interpretations based on all the relevant evidence", is more appropriate for alternative assessment than the psychometric approach that limits human judgment "to single performances, the results of which are then aggregated and compared with performance standards" (p. 8). Operationally, Moss suggests an alternative to the use of rubrics for guiding the judgment wherein independent evaluations are prepared by experts who then meet as a committee and discuss their reviews till an agreement is reached. Comparing the psychometric to the hermeneutic approach Moss (1994) states:

> In a very real sense, attention to reliability actually works against critical dialogue, at least at one phase of inquiry. It leads to procedures that attempt

to exclude, to the extent possible, the value and contextualized knowledge of the reader and that foreclose on dialogue among readers about the specific performances being evaluated. A hermeneutic approach to assessment encourages such dialogue at all phases of the assessment. (p. 9)

It should be noted that when dealing with complex judgments committees in a number of professional disciplines are common practice . In medicine, for example, a medical board meeting is convened in serious cases where high-stakes diagnoses are required. Similarly, three judges preside in supreme courts (in juridical systems which do not include a jury) and a verdict is reached according to a majority ruling, under the assumption that in complex cases it is quite unlikely that all judges will reach the same verdict. These examples reflect the understanding that integrating evidence into a consistent and a defensible evaluation is a creative process that can result in different solutions, even when done by experts, and therefore cannot be prespecified by clear-cut rubrics. However, employing assessment committees, appealing as it may seem, is quite impractical for large-scale assessments of educational achievement. Moreover, the factors and dynamics of decision making in a committee are not yet well understood. A more practical solution is suggested by Delandshere & Petrosky (1994) who require the rater to prepare the review according to leading questions referring to relevant dimensions of the subject matter and to accepted standards for performance. They thus conceptualize reliability as confirmation of the first rater's review by a second rater, indicating the extent to which to his/her opinion the first review is consistent with the existing evidence.

Response consistency and stability. The assumption underlying generalizability theory is that scores on a single task or on a specific collection of tasks are of little interest in and of themselves. Their potential importance depends on the extent to which they lead to valid generalizations about achievements on the broader domain they represent. Hence the demand for justifying the generalization from the specific assessment tasks to the broader domain of achievement. In order to ensure a high level of generalizability the following types of consistency are commonly examined: Consistency on a single occasion across parallel tasks and across tasks that vary in content or format but still assess the same domain, as well as stability of performance on the same tasks across occasions. Research findings show that correlations among tasks drop sharply as the tasks become more heterogeneous (Dunbar et al., 1991; Linn et al., 1991). It was therefore concluded that performance is highly task-dependent, so that interpretations that are not task-centered but rather construct-centered have to be justified (Linn, 1994). Furthermore, it has been shown that the variance component for sampling of tasks tends to be larger than that for the sampling of raters (Dunbar et al., 1991; Hieronymus & Hoover, 1987; Shavelson, Baxter, & Gao, 1993). Shavelson and his colleagues (1993) estimated that between 10 and 23 tasks would be needed to achieve absolute G coefficients of approximately 0.80. Yet, when school is the object of measurement matrix sampling of tasks can greatly reduce the contribution of tasks to the error of measurement (Linn, 1994). It is asserted that score reliability tends to be lower than rater reliability because of the variability of students' performance inherent even in tasks of the same format. Shavelson and his colleagues have further demonstrated that there is also lack of stability within subjects in the procedures used to perform the same tasks across occasions (Ruiz-Primo, Baxter, & Shavelson, 1993). However, it should be noted that for lower stakes uses of student-level results, lower levels of generalizability can be accepted. As emphasized by Linn (1994), the claims that are made for an assessment, the specific uses and interpretations intended are central to determining the level of generalizability that is needed.

Lessons from Implementations of High-Stakes Alternative Assessment Programs

Discussed in this section are lessons from two types of high-stakes assessment implementations: large-scale assessment for accountability purposes and school-based assessment for graduation.

a. Large-scale Assessment

In summarizing their conclusions from the evaluation of the Vermont portfolio assessment program Koretz and his associates (1994) state that this experience "highlights the need for caution and moderate expectations" (p. 15). Following are several of the main issues that emerged as a result of state-wide implementations of alternative assessment.

Efficiency. Those who implemented alternative assessment programs have acknowledged that such programs are highly expensive, time consuming and labor intensive compared to traditional testing programs. As is estimated by Maeroff (1991) "expenses and time may turn out to be the brakes on the alternative assessment movement" (p. 281). Expenses of developing performance assessment include designing authentic tasks and developing rubrics for assessing each task, which, in turn, involves identifying the appropriate dimensions, defining the criteria within each dimension, and setting the standards, i.e., the performance levels, that are represented by various achievements. This is a labor intensive endeavor that requires a high level of expertise. The assessment of performance using the rubrics is also time consuming even for trained teachers. It includes grading constructed responses such as essay type responses, project-papers and portfolios. Also included in this category are observing hands-on performances, group discussions, and conducting interviews. It seems that due to the great weight placed on efficiency amongst policy makers and test users, alternative assessment once again compares unfavorably to traditional standardized tests.

Teacher training. A conclusion that has been drawn repeatedly in reviews of various implementations of alternative assessment programs is that teachers need to be adequately trained to assess direct performances. The variation in the interrater reliability across various evaluation reports [compare the reports of the Vermont project (Koretz, et al., 1992, 1994) to those of NAEP (Gentile, 1992) and Pittsburgh (LeMahieu, 1993)], is due, in part, to the intensity of guidance provided to the participating teachers. The more intensive the training provided, the higher the interrater reliabilities.

Task disclosure. A positive correlation between the number of years an assessment device is available and the scores on the assessment has been documented with respect to publisher's standardized achievement tests. The same effect, albeit more noticeable, is evident with respect to direct assessment tasks. The fact that performance assessment consists of fewer tasks than assessment of the choice response makes it easier to coach to the test, thus making the problem of test pollution even more serious.

Quality of comparative data. As noted by Koretz and his associates (1994) classrooms or schools greatly varied from one another with respect to the implementation of the portfolio program. Differences were observed with respect to levels of novelty and complexity of tasks, to limits placed on help seeking, to rules for revision of portfolio entries and their selection, to amount of structure built into tasks for students of different ability levels, etc. All these differences which result from the instruction-embedded nature of the portfolio, affect the quality of the performance data, thus threatening the validity of comparisons based on these scores.

Effect on instruction. The better news regarding the implementation of alternative assessment for large-scale assessment is related to its effect on instruction. Koretz and his associates (1992) report that about 80% of the mathematics teachers in their sample claimed that they put more emphasis on problem solving as a result of the new state-wide assessment program and that students spent more time working in pairs or small groups. Moreover, roughly half of the sample schools reported they had extended the use of portfolios beyond the grades and subjects participating in the state program. Similarly, Clarke and Stephens (this volume), based on their experience in Victoria, Australia, report on what they term the *ripple effect*, whereby the introduction of mathematics performance assessment in high-schools affected the instruction of mathematics in the lower grades.

b. School-based portfolios for graduation

Davis and Felknor (1994) conducted a case study on a school which was among the first public high schools in the United States to base graduation entirely on a portfolio assessment. The authors focused on one subject -- history -- and described the changes which resulted from the implementation of the portfolio program along three years. They observed the following changes: The teacher's role changed from a presenter to a coach; a dramatic increase took place in collegial conversations and collaborations related to instruction; a refocusing of instruction occurred whereby the portfolio inclusions were used as a conceptual framework to structure teachers' instruction. As described by the researchers:

> When teachers finally began truly to internalize a finite set of goals for students that centered on conceptual understanding and the relating of history to the present, their instruction became coherent and intentional in ways that they had not previously experienced. Teachers found this conceptual clarity exciting. When talking about their previous teaching, the five teachers used words like 'fragmented' and 'hit and miss'; in contrast, they described their subsequent teaching as 'focused', and 'tied together'. (p. 24)

As to students' performance, the following effects were observed: The distribution of grades changed from a bell shaped distribution with the majority of scores being mediocre, to a bimodal one with more high and low scores than mediocre ones. It became obvious that not all students worked diligently or effectively on the loosely-structured tasks which required more than one day to complete. More students transferred or dropped out of school than previously, as they were not able to cope with the requirements of the new graduation program. The public was not enthusiastic either. The board of education questioned the validity of the demonstrations of learning included in the portfolios and criticized them for focusing excessively on process skills rather than content knowledge. Consequently, the board did not support the program and after two and a half years voted to rescind the portfolio system and return to course credit as the basis for graduation. In reviewing the consequences the researchers concluded that the link to graduation was absolutely essential for the portfolio system to succeed. They argue that because such a system makes enormous demands on the faculty and requires extraordinary efforts of teachers and administrators it can only be justified and successful if required for graduation -- high-school's most valued currency.

The Dilemma

Proponents of alternative assessment in general and portfolio assessment in particular, are faced with the dilemma that although this assessment has the attributes that suit the goals of instruction geared at preparing the students to function successfully in the information age, the use of portfolios in large-scale high-stakes assessment programs is still fraught with obstacles both psychometric- and practice-wise. Skeptics even claim that the conflict between the instructional and measurement goals is fundamental, implying that it may not be satisfactorily resolved (Koretz et al., 1994). In order to avoid these serious pitfalls it has been suggested to reserve portfolio and other instruction-embedded forms of assessment for classroom assessment and to use multiple-choice standardized tests for high-stakes large-scale assessment programs (Worthen, 1993). However, experience has taught us that only what is examined in high-stakes tests actually gets taught and practiced in class. Thus, if we acknowledge the importance of the portfolio as a tool that integrates instruction and assessment, it is essential that it be used in large-scale assessment programs and that further research be directed toward investigating ways to ensure quality control of such assessment. This is not to say that portfolio assessment should replace all other assessment methods and tools. As will be discussed in the next section, a variety of assessment tools is preferable to a single tool as it enables a triangulation based on a wide-range of evidence, thus increasing the quality and validity of the inferences drawn on the basis of the assessment.

FROM ALTERNATIVE ASSESSMENT TO ALTERNATIVES IN ASSESSMENT: TOWARDS A PLURALISTIC APPROACH TO ASSESSMENT

Although often presented as stemming from two contradictory cultures, traditional and alternative assessments can be viewed as playing complementary rather than contradictory roles. It can therefore be argued that we cannot and should not relinquish the traditional and more standardized assessment techniques in favor of alternative assessment. The reason why we cannot relinquish traditional assessment techniques is implied by the difficulties discussed in the previous section. The reason why we should not be doing so will be discussed in this section. The proposition on which this section is centered states that the right assessment technique is the one that fits its purpose, is suited to the characteristics of the learner and is linked to the taught curriculum. Each of these requirements is further elaborated below.

Adapting the Assessment Technique to its Purpose

The need to adapt the assessment technique to its purpose is based on the assumption that no single assessment technique can satisfy all assessment purposes and needs. Madaus & Kellaghan (1993) list the following functions being currently proposed for a national testing system in the United States:

> Improving instruction and learning, monitoring progress toward the national goals, holding institutions and individuals accountable, certifying the successful completion of a given level of education, assisting in decisions about college admission or entry-level employment, and motivating students by having real rewards for success and real consequences for failure. (p. 459)

To illustrate that different assessment techniques are suitable for different purposes and needs, the following four facets of the assessment context and their elements will be considered:

A The status of the assessment: 1) Low-stakes vs. 2) High-stakes
B The type of the assessment: 1) Formative vs. 2) Summative
C The level of aggregation of the results: 1) Individual student vs. 2) Group (class/ school/ district/ state)
D The decision maker: 1) Classroom teacher, 2) Institute authorities, 3) Curriculum designer, 4) Policy decision makers.

The various combinations of elements from these facets result in different requirements from the assessment device. Several examples are given below:

1. The combination A1,B1,C1,D1 (low-stakes formative assessment, of the individual student's achievements, done by the classroom-teacher) can indicate a diagnostic test for remedial instruction. The domain covered by such a test is limited but the coverage is thorough. A relatively low level of standardization is required for such assessment. If one is to choose between choice and constructed-response items, then, based on earlier findings, the latter would be the recommended ones for this type of assessment (Birenbaum & Tatsuoka, 1987; Birenbaum, Tatsuoka & Gutvirtz, 1992).

2. The combination A2,B2,C1,D2 (high-stakes summative assessment, of the individual student's achievements, done by the institute authorities) can indicate a college admission test. Such a test covers a large domain but not thoroughly. If one is to choose between choice and constructed-response items, then, based on earlier findings, the former would be the recommended ones for this type of assessment (Lukhele, Thissen & Wainer, 1994).

3. The combination A2,B2,C2,D4 (high-stakes summative assessment the results of which are aggregated at the school level for the purpose of policy decision making) can indicate an assessment for accountability purposes which entails the comparison of various schools and therefore requires a high level of standardization. If portfolios are to be used in this case, then the students cannot be allowed complete freedom of choice in selecting the entries as it puts the standardization in jeopardy.

4. The combination A1,B2,C1,D1 (low-stakes summative assessment of the individual student's achievements done by the classroom teacher) can indicate an end-

of-the year assessment, which requires a comprehensive view of how the student has progressed during the entire school year. If the purpose of the assessment is to report individual relative progress and if portfolios are to be used in this case, then the students can be allowed complete freedom of choice in selecting the entries as this assessment does not require a high level of standardization.

It should be noted that the facets mentioned above do not include the cognitive level required for performing the task. Such a facet has major implications for the choice of the assessment form because some forms are more effective than others in assessing particular levels (e.g., items of the choice format are more effective in assessing lower cognitive levels whereas items of the construction format are more effective in assessing higher-order levels). Nevertheless, by examining the combinations of the elements from those four facets it can be concluded that one assessment type does not suit all of them. (For a mapping sentence that includes all these facets and others see Birenbaum, 1994a). Summarizing the British experience with *authentic* testing, Madaus and Kellaghan (1993) concluded that "the context of use is critical in evaluating the potential impact of any assessment technique, 'authentic' or not" (p. 459), and that "the life of 'authentic' testing, designed to serve a multiplicity of purposes, may not be a very long one" (p. 469). Hence the need to adapt the assessment technique to the purpose of the assessment.

Adapting the Assessment Technique to the Learner's Characteristics

As many would admit, in assessment, like often elsewhere, one size does not fit all. Thus, trying to impose the same assessment technique on all students may result in a bias which could render the assessment results of some students invalid and useless. Potential factors that can jeopardize assessment validity are subsumed under the terms *assessment bias* or *construct-irrelevant variance*, which refer to systematic differences in individual characteristics, other than the ability/achievement tested, that affect performance. Among the sources of construct-irrelevant variance are differences in cognitive, affective and conative characteristics of the examinees. In his discussion of the construct validity of constructed versus choice responses, Snow (1993) notes that "If the two test designs evoke different motivational structures, effort investments, expectations for success, feelings of self-efficacy, or worries, that is as major an implication for test score interpretation as any cognitive difference" (p. 46).

Several studies investigated the effects of biasing factors such as cognitive style (field-dependence/independence), test anxiety and gender on performance. Field-independent subjects were found to perform substantially better than did field-dependent subjects on performance-based assessment (Lu & Suen, 1993) and on cloze tests (Chapelle, 1988; Chapelle & Roberts, 1986; Hansen, 1984; Hansen & Stansfield, 1981). High test-anxious students performed better on the conventional multiple-choice format whereas low test-anxious students performed better on the open-ended format (Crocker & Schmitt, 1987). High test-anxious low-achievers performed better on a take-home exam than on a conventional classroom test given under time limit and without support materials (Zoller & Ben-Chaim, 1988). Studies of gender differences in multiple-choice test performance indicated that girls were more reluctant than boys to guess on such items and were more likely to leave items blank (Ben-Shakhar & Sinai, 1991; Grandy, 1987; Linn, De Benedictis, Delucchi, Harris & Stage, 1987).

Obviously, the results of these studies call for adapting the assessment to the examinee's affective, as well as cognitive characteristics, in order to enhance the validity of his/her test score interpretation. However, an attempt to assess the many potential biasing factors before choosing the appropriate assessment technique seems both a complicated and an impractical endeavor. An alternative approach is to let the student choose his/her preferred type of assessment. Studies have shown that examinees are capable of accurately choosing the appropriate difficulty level of test items that best suit their ability/achievement level (Rocklin & O'Donnell, 1987; Wise, Plake, Johnson & Roos, 1992). It has also been shown that such self adaptive testing resulted in reduced test anxiety and higher performance level as compared to computerized adaptive testing (Wise et al., 1992). It remains to be seen if students are also capable of choosing the appropriate assessment format that will eliminate the effects of biasing factors, thus reflecting more precisely their true achievement level.

In light of the effect assessment has on students, both as performers and as the subjects (and often victims) of the decisions based on the assessment results, it is surprising to witness the paucity of research regarding students' assessment attitudes and preferences (Zeidner, 1987; Zoller & Ben-Chaim, 1988, 1990). Moreover, most of the studies that did investigate this issue did not relate it to students' personal characteristics, such as those that were shown to be potential sources of test bias. Recent studies in this direction indicate significant relations between dimensions of assessment preferences and personal characteristics such as test anxiety, self-efficacy, intrinsic motivation, cognitive strategy use, and self-regulation (Birenbaum, 1994b; Birenbaum & Feldman, 1995; Birenbaum & Gutvirtz, 1995).

Given these findings it seems that the question concerning assessment preferences ought to be "Who prefers what?" rather than "What is preferred by most?" Stated differently, the question of interest is "Which personal characteristics affect students' assessment preferences and how?" It can be expected that if we provide the students with the assessment types they prefer, it will motivate them to perform their best, and it will reduce bias due to debilitating factors, consequently reflecting the students' true achievements/ accomplishments, hence increasing the validity of the assessment results and the inferences based upon them. It is therefore suggested that further research regarding assessment preferences focus on other psychological constructs (in addition to test-anxiety, self-regulation and field dependence/ independence), which may turn out to be potential causes of bias in alternative assessment, such as tolerance of ambiguity, procrastination, locus of control, etc. In addition, psychometric studies need to be directed toward exploring new models and techniques for preparing equitable assessments that differ in item type or mode.

Linking Assessment to the Taught Curriculum

Although alternative assessment is often presented as being interwoven with instruction and is even termed instruction-embedded assessment, in practice this is not always the case. Imposing alternative assessment for accountability purposes will most probably ensure that students will be engaged in performance tasks because this is the long known effect of MDI (measurement driven instruction) and indeed this effect has already been witnessed with respect to alternative assessment in several places, e.g., Vermont (Koretz et al., 1994), Victoria (Clarke & Stephens in this volume). Yet, being engaged in a performance task does not necessarily mean that the task assesses what it was intended to assess. We shall presently describe a real case to illustrate this point.

In a graduate course in alternative assessment the students -- all in-service teachers in the various school-levels -- developed a performance task in their respective subject matter areas. One of the students, who teaches in grade five, developed a task in geography in which the students, who at that point in time studied how to use an atlas, were asked to plan a rescue operation for a group of scouts that had lost its way in a certain location defined by the teacher in terms of the intersection of two coordinates. The class was divided into small groups and each group was assigned a different location. The students were given ten days for this task. A careful examination of several papers indicated that they concentrated on standard equipment for a rescue operation such as a map of the area, binoculars, a compass, a flashlight, etc. Several students even suggested to rent a helicopter and quoted the rental price per hour. No one justified the choice of the equipment in relation to the particular area where the rescue operation was supposed to take place. One paper that was submitted by a high achiever in that class was especially representative. She and her friend opened the atlas, found their assigned location -- a town in China; they did not take the trouble to write down its name but just mentioned it was in east China. To show the route a rescue team from Israel would have to take in order to reach to its destination in China, they drew a "map" which was really just a "squiggly line", at one end of which they had written "Israel" and at the other "China". The paper itself looked neat and it was evident from the colorful title page and the tidy hand-writing that they spent some time working on the project. After the students had handed in the paper they were asked to answer several questions designed to prompt reflection regarding their work on that task. In one question they were asked if there was something that they did not like about the project. The answer these two students gave to this question was that they were annoyed by the fact that the teacher did not tell them on which page of the atlas to look in order to find the assigned destination. To the question how they divided the work between the two of them they answered that the work was equally divided, one wrote one page and the other wrote the next, and so on.

This "squiggly line" example illustrates the point made earlier that engaging students in performance tasks does not necessarily mean that they are learning and creating meaning. Similarly, Perkins & Blythe (1994) cautioned that not all engaging activities involve performances of understanding, "typically they do not press the learner to think well beyond what they already know" (p. 7). It was clear from the papers examined in our case that they did not contain evidence that the students were using geographic knowledge for performing the particular task. It is interesting to note that the same students who produced the "squiggly line" paper scored high on a multiple-choice test given at the conclusion of the unit dealing with the uses of an atlas. Call it lack of tacit knowledge (Wagner & Sternberg, 1986) or lack of thoughtfulness (Perkins, 1992), the fact remains that the performance-based assessment in this case was not linked to the taught curriculum in that class, which, to use Perkins phrasing, "trained the students' memories rather than their minds". Students in this class were not prepared to work on such tasks nor on any others that required self-regulation, thoughtful problem-solving and cooperation. They were not taught reflection and thinking strategies -- skills that, as is often stressed, need to be explicitly taught and cannot be expected to develop without intervention (Arter & Spandel, 1992; Perkins, 1986, 1992; Swartz & Perkins, 1991). Moreover, the criteria and standards for assessing such a task should have been known to the students before they started their work on the task, or even have been developed together with them. When all these instructional components are missing, alternative assessment becomes just an attractive wrapping for an empty box. The consequences of such practices can even be more harmful than if the traditional method of "teaching by telling" were used because in the former students were found to have spent their time on performing activities in which their understanding of the geographical topic was neither being demonstrated nor advanced. It can therefore be concluded that an attempt to embark on alternative assessment, expecting it to motivate the desired change in instruction, may turn out to be a fruitless effort in some cases, much like looking for a missing coin under the streetlight just because it is dark everywhere else. Similarly, Perrone (1994) cautions that "without a growing discourse about curriculum purposes, student understandings, and ways teachers can foster student learning, assessment measures such as portfolios and exhibitions will not have a very long or inspiring history" (p. 13).

CONCLUSION

This chapter began with an overview of the conditions that gave rise to the demand for alternative assessment. This assessment was portrayed as a means for measuring the extent to which the goals of instruction, which is responsive to the requirements for appropriate functioning in the information age, have been reached. The main features of an *assessment culture* as opposed to those of a *testing culture* were specified, enumerating various devices subsumed under the alternative assessment umbrella. Special attention was given to the portfolio, describing the features that make it a useful instructional and assessment device which, when properly implemented, may also become a means for achieving those instructional goals. Issues related to the assessment of alternative assessment were then discussed, pointing to the fact that alternative assessment tends to compare unfavorably with traditional assessment devices when evaluated with respect to traditional conceptions of validity and reliability. Hence the need to expand the scope of those concepts. Lessons learned from two types of high-stakes alternative assessment programs -- a large scale assessment for accountability purposes and school based assessment for graduation -- were discussed pointing to the conflicting goals of measurement and instruction. The dilemma resulting from this conflict was discussed considering the implications of a suggestion to reserve portfolios and other instructional-embedded forms of assessment for classroom assessment and to use choice-response standardized tests for high-stakes large-scales assessment programs.

Subsequently, the need for multiple assessment types was stressed, based on two arguments: the acknowledgment that one assessment type cannot serve a multitude of purposes and audiences, and the findings regarding the effect of the assessment format on performance, which indicate that one assessment type does not fit all students. The desired type of assessment tasks was further discussed pointing to the fact that in order for the tasks to be in accordance with contemporary instructional goals they need to be of the kind Perkins and his associates call "understanding performances" (Perkins & Blythe, 1994; Simmons, 1994) i.e., tasks that provide evidence regarding the extent to which the student has generated knowledge and has appropriately used it for problem solving. Performance on such tasks, coupled with demonstration of communicative competencies and metacognitive awareness, constitutes the relevant evidence for assessing educational attainments that fits the contemporary goals of instruction. The appropriateness of the portfolio as a device for maintaining these attainment records was stressed along with the need for well grounded dimensions, criteria and standards for designing useful assessment rubrics. The danger of using such tasks for assessment when the link to instruction is missing was also discussed.

Once sufficient evidence has been gathered, a question arises regarding the scoring and reporting methods to be employed. Several such methods could be used in order to serve the various purposes of assessment and its multiple audiences. When a complete portrayal of a student as a reflective learner is required an integrated interpretative evaluation based on the multiple types of evidence could be generated. Such an evaluation should be non-intuitive but rather sound, defensible and reproducible. Judgment of this kind could be reached by an evaluation committee, as suggested by Moss (1994), or, as suggested by Delandshere & Petrosky (1994), by a review of an evaluation report by a second expert, indicating the extent to which to his/her opinion the first review is consistent with the existing evidence. An alternative reporting method could take the form of a profile (verbal or numerical) where students' performance is rated on several essential dimensions related to performance standards in a specific subject matter. The rating on each dimension can take any one of the following forms: Student-referenced rating (i.e., a rating relative to the student's personal progress); criterion-referenced rating (an absolute rating), or a norm-referenced rating (i.e., a rating relative to the group's performance). In the case of the norm-referenced rating, an external monitoring system is required for score calibration. If needed, an additional single weighted score could be computed based on the profile's multidimensional scores.

In summary, evidence collected using a variety of devices seems to be the aim of a comprehensive assessment of achievement that is valid, generalizable, and equitable, an assessment that is responsive to a variety of purposes and audiences and sensitive to individual differences in response bias. Understanding performances constitute the targeted kind of assessment tasks that can provide relevant information regarding students' attainments, and that are in accordance with the goals set for education towards the beginning of the 21st century. Achieving these aims and ensuring appropriate implementation is a challenging endeavor educators, curriculum designers, and measurement experts are already engaged in.

REFERENCES

American Educational Research Association, American Psychological Association, & National Council on Measurement in Education. (1985). *Standards for educational and psychological testing.* Washington, DC: National Education Association.

Arter, J. A., & Spandel, V. (1992). Using portfolios of student work in instruction and assessment. *Educational, Measurement: Issues and Practice, 11* (1), 36-44.

Asturias, H. (1994). Using students' portfolios to assess mathematical understanding. *Mathematics Teacher, 87* (9), 698-701.

Badger, E. (1995). The effect of expectations on achieving equity in state-wide testing: Lessons from Massachusetts. In: Nettles, M. T., & A. L Nettles, *Equity and excellence in educational testing and assessment.* (pp. 289-308). Boston: Kluwer.

Belanoff, P., & Dickson, M. (Eds.). (1991). Portfolios: Process and product. Portsmouth: Boynton/ Cook.

Ben-Shakhar, G., & Sinai, Y. (1991). Gender differences in multiple-choice tests: The role of differential guessing tendencies. *Journal of Educational Measurement, 28,* 23-35.

Birenbaum, M. (1994a). Toward adaptive assessment -- the student's angle. *Studies in Educational Assessment., 20,* 239-255.

Birenbaum, M. (1994b). *Effects of gender, test anxiety, and self regulation on students' attitudes toward two assessment formats.* Unpublished Manuscript. School of Education Tel Aviv University.

Birenbaum, M., & Feldman, R. (1995, July). *Relationships between learning patterns and attitudes toward two assessment formats.* Paper prepared for presentation at the 16th International Conference of the Stress and Anxiety Research Society. Prague: Czech Republic.

Birenbaum, M., & Gutvirtz, Y. (1995, January). *Relationships between assessment preferences, cognitive style, motivation and learning strategies.* Paper presented at the 11th conference of the Israeli Educational Research Association. Jerusalem.

Birenbaum, M., & Tatsuoka, K. K. (1987). Open-ended versus multiple-choice response format -- it does make a difference. *Applied Psychological Measurement, 11,* 385-395.

Birenbaum, M., Tatsuoka, K. K., & Gutvirtz, Y. (1992). Effects of response format on diagnostic assessment of scholastic achievement. *Applied Psychological Measurement, 16,* 353-363.

Blake Yancey, K. (Ed.). (1992). *Portfolios in the writing classroom.* Urbana, Il: National Council of Teachers of English.

Camp, R. (1991). Portfolios evolving. Background and variations in sixth-through twelfth - grade classrooms. In P. Belanoff, & M. Dickson (Eds.), *Portfolios process and product* (pp. 194-205). Portsmouth, NH: Boyton/Cook Heineman.

Camp, R. (1992). The place of portfolios in our changing views of writing assessment. In R. Bennett, & W. Ward (Eds.), *Construction versus choice in cognitive measurement.* Hillsdale, NJ: Erlbaum.

Cannell, J. J. (1989). *The "Lake Wobegon" report. How public educators cheat on standardized achievement tests.* Albuquerque, NM: Friends for Education.

Chapelle, C. (1988). Field independence: A source of language test variance. *Language Testing, 5,* 62-82.

Chapelle, C., & Roberts, C. (1986). Ambiguity tolerance and field dependence as predictors of proficiency in English as a second language. *Language Learning, 36,* 27-45.

Clarke, D., & Stephens, M. (1995). The ripple effect: The instructional implications of the systemic introduction of performance assessment in mathematics. In M. Birenbaum, & F.J.R.C. Dochy (Eds.), *Alternatives in assessment of achievement, learning processes and prior knowledge.* Boston: Kluwer.

Collins, A. (1991). Portfolios for biology teacher assessment. *Journal of Personnel Evaluation in Education, 5,* 147-169.

Collins, A. (1993). Performance-based assessment of biology: Promises and pitfalls. *Journal of Research in Science Teaching, 30,* 1103-1120.

Crocker, L., & Schmitt, A. (1987). Improving multiple-choice test performance for examinees with different levels of test anxiety. *Journal of Experimental Education, 55*, 201-205.

Cronbach, L. J. (1988). Five perspectives on validation argument. In H. Wainer, & H. Braun (Eds.), *Test validity* (pp. 3-17). Hillsdale, NJ: Erlbaum.

D'Aoust, C. (1992). Portfolios: Process for students and teachers. In K. Blake Yancey (Ed.), *Portfolios in the writing classroom.* (pp. 39-48). Urbana, Il: National Council of Teachers of English.

Darling-Hammond, L. (1995). Equity issues in performance-based assessment. In M. T. Nettles, & A. L Nettles, *Equity and excellence in educational testing and assessment.* (pp. 89-114). Boston: Kluwer.

Davis, A., & Felknor, C. (1994). *Graduation by exhibition: The effects of high stakes portfolio assessments on curriculum and instruction on one high school.* Paper presented at the Annual Meeting of the American Educational Research Association. New Orleans, LA.

Delandshere, G., & Petrosky, A. R. (1994). Capturing teachers' knowledge: Performance assessment. *Educational Researcher, 23* (5), 11-18.

Dunbar, S. B., Koretz, D. M., & Hoover, H. D. (1991). Quality control in the development and use of performance assessments. *Applied Measurement in Education, 4,* 289-303.

Frederiksen, J. R., & Collins A. (1989). A systems approach to educational testing. *Educational Researcher, 18* (9), 27-32.

Frederiksen, N. (1984), The real test bias: Influences of testing on teaching and learning. *American Psychologist, 39*, 193-202.

Freire, P. P. (1972). *Pedagogy of the oppressed.* Harmondsworth, Middlesex UK: Penguin Books.

Gardner, H. (1983). *Frames of mind.* New York: Basic Books.

Gardner, H. (1993). *Multiple intelligences: The theory in practice.* New York: Basic Books

Gardner, H., & Hatch, T. (1989). Multiple intelligences go to school. Educational implications of the theory of multiple intelligences. *Educational Researcher, 18*, (8), 4-10.

Gentile, C. (1992). *Exploring new methods for collecting students' school-based writing: NAEP's 1990 portfolio study.* Washington, DC: National Center for Education Statistics.

Grandy, J. (1987). *Characteristics of examinees who leave questions unanswered on the GRE general test under rights-only scoring.* ETS Research Report 87-38. Princeton, NJ: Educational Testing Service.

Hamm, M., & Adams, D. (1991). Portfolio assessment. *The Science Teacher, 58* (5) 18-21.

Hamp-Lyons, L., & Condon, W, (1993). Questioning assumptions about portfolio-based assessment. *College Composition and Communication, 44* (2), 176-190.

Hansen, J. (1984). Field dependence-independence and language testing: Evidence from six pacific island cultures. *TESOL Quarterly, 18,* 311-324.

Hansen, J. (1992). Literacy portfolios: Helping students know themselves. *Educational Leadership, 49,* 66-68.

Hansen, J., & Stansfield, C. (1981). The relationship between field dependent-independent cognitive styles and foreign language achievement, *Language Learning, 31*, 349-367.

Herman, J. L., Aschbacher, R., & Winters, L. (1992). A practical guide to alternative assessment. Alexandria, VA: Association for Supervision and Curriculum Development.

Hieronymus, A. N., & Hoover, H. D. (1987). *Iowa tests of basic skills: Writing supplement teacher's guide.* Chicago: Riverside.

Kleinsasser, A., Horsch, E., & Tastad, S. (1993, April). *Walking the talk: Moving from a testing culture to an assessment culture.* Paper presented at the Annual Meeting of the American Educational Research Association. Atlanta, GA.

Knight, D. (1992). How I use portfolios in mathematics. *Educational Leadership, 49,* 71-72.

Koppert, J. (1991). *Primary performance assessment portfolio.* Mountain Village, AK: Lower Yukon School District.

Koretz, D., McCaffrey, D., Klein, S., Bell, R., & Stecher, B. (1992). *The reliability of scores from the 1992 Vermont portfolio assessment program.* Interim Report. Santa Monica, CA: RAND Institute of Education and Training.

Koretz, D., Stecher, B., Klein, S, & McCaffrey, D. (1994). The Vermont portfolio assessment program: Findings and implications. *Educational Measurement; Issues and Practice, 13* (3), 5-16.

Larsen R, L. (1991). Using portfolios in the assessment of writing in the academic disciplines. In P. Belanoff, & M. Dickson (Eds.). *Portfolios: Process and product.* Portsmouth, NH: Boynton/Cook.

LeMahieu, P. (1993, April). Data from the Pittsburgh writing portfolio assessment. In J. Herman (Chair), *Portfolio assessment meets the reality of data.* Symposium conducted at the Annual Meeting of the American Educational Research Association, Atlanta, GA.

Leiva, M. (1995). Empowering teachers through the evaluation process. *Mathematics Teacher, 88,* (19), 44-47.

Linn, M. C. , De Benedictis, T., Delucchi, K., Harris, & A., Stage, E. (1987). Gender differences in National Assessment of Educational Progress in science items.: What does 'I don't know' really mean? *Journal of Research on Science Teaching, 24,* 267-278.

Linn, R. L. (1994). Performance assessment: Policy promises and technical measurement standards. *Educational Researcher, 23,* (9), 4-14.

Linn, R. L., Baker, E., & Dunbar, S. (1991). Complex, performance-based assessment: Expectations and validation criteria. *Educational Researcher, 16.* 15-21.

Lu, C., & Suen, H. K. (1993, April). *The interaction effect of individual characteristics and assessment format on the result of performance-based assessment.* Paper presented at the Annual Meeting of the American Educational Research Association. Atlanta, GA.

Lukhele, R., Thissen, D., & Wainer, H. (1994). On the relative value of multiple-choice, constructed response, and examinee-selected items on two achievement tests. *Journal of Educational Measurement, 31,* 234-250.

Madaus, G. F., & Kellaghan, T. (1993). The British experience with 'authentic' testing. *Phi Delta Kappan, 74*(6), 458-469.

Maeroff, G. I. (1991). Assessing alternative assessment. *Phi Delta Kappan. 72,* 272-281.

Messick, S. (1989). Validity. In R. L. Linn (Ed.), *Educational Measurement* (3rd ed., pp. 13-103). New York: Macmillan.

Messick, S. (1994). The interplay of evidence and consequences in the validation of performance assessments. *Educational Researcher, 23* (2) 13-23.

Moss, P. A. (1994). Can there be validity without reliability? *Educational Researcher, 23,* (2) 5 -12.

Moss, P. A. (in press). Rethinking validity: Themes and variations in current theory. *Educational Measurement: Issues and Practice.*

Mumme, J. (1991). *Portfolio assessment in mathematics.* Santa Barbara: California Mathematics Project. University of California, Santa Barbara.

Nettles, M. T., & Bernstein A. (1995). Introduction: The pursuit of equity in educational testing and assessment. In: Nettles, M. T., & A. L Nettles, *Equity and excellence in educational testing and assessment.* (pp. 3-21). Boston: Kluwer.

Paulson, F. L., & Paulson, P. R. (1992, October). A draft for judging portfolios. Draft prepared for use at the NWEA Fifth Annual October Institute on Assessment Alternatives. Portland OR.

Paulson, F. L., Paulson, P. R. , & Meyer, C. A. (1991). What makes a portfolio a portfolio? *Educational Leadership, 48,.* 60-63.

Perkins, D. N. (1986). Thinking frames: An integrative perspective on teaching cognitive skills. In J. B . Baron, & R. S. Sternberg (Eds.), *Teaching thinking skills: Theory and practice* (pp. 41-61). New York: W. H. Freeman.

Perkins, D. N. (1992). Smart schools. New York: The Free Press.

Perkins, D. N., & Blythe, T. (1994). Putting understanding up front. *Educational Leadership, 51,* (5), 4-7.

Perrone, V. (1994). How to Engage students in learning. *Educational Leadership, 51*(5), 11-13.

Resnick, L. B., & Klopfer, L. E. (Eds.). (1989). *Toward the thinking curriculum: Current cognitive research. Alexandria,* VA: ASCD.

Resnick, L. B., & Resnick, D. P. (1992). Assessing the thinking curriculum: New tools for educational reform. In B. R. Gifford, & C. O'Connor (Eds.), *Changing assessments: Alternative views of aptitude, achievement and instruction* (pp. 37-75). Boston, MA: Kluwer.

Rocklin, T., & O'Donnell, A. M. (1987). Self adapted testing: A performance-improving variant of computerized adaptive testing. *Journal of Educational Psychology, 79,* 315-319.

Ruiz-Primo, M. A., Baxter, G. P., & Shavelson, R. J. (1993). On stability of performance assessments. *Journal of Educational Measurement, 30,* 41-53.

Shavelson, R., J., Baxter, G. P., & Gao, X. (1993). Sampling variability of performance assessments. *Journal of Educational Measurement, 30,* 215-232.

Shavelson, R., J., Gao, X., & Baxter, G. P. (1995). On the content validity of performance assessments: Centrality of domain specification. In M. Birenbaum, & F.J.R.C. Dochy (Eds.), *Alternatives in assessment of achievement, learning processes and prior knowledge.* Boston: Kluwer.

Shepard, L. A. (1993). Evaluating test validity. *Review of Research in Education, 19,* 405-450.

Shulman, L. S. (1988). A union of insufficiencies: Strategies for teacher assessment in a period of educational reform. *Educational Leadership, 45,* 36-14.

Simmons, R. (1994). The horse before the cart: Assessing for understanding. *Educational Leadership, 51* (5), 22-23.

Snow, R. E. (1993). Construct validity and constructed-response tests. In R. E. Bennett, & W. C. Ward (Eds.), *Construction versus choice in cognitive measurement* (pp. 45-60). Hillsdale NJ: Erlbaum.

Sternberg, R. J. (1985). *Beyond IQ: A triarchic theory of human intelligence.* New York: Cambridge University Press.

Swartz, R. J., & Perkins, D. N. (1991). *Teaching thinking: Issues and approaches.* Pacific Grove, CA: Midwest Publications.

Tierney, R. J., Carter, M. A., & Desai, L. E. (1991). *Portfolio assessment in the reading writing classroom.* Norwood, AM: Christopher Gordon.

Valencia, S. (1990). A portfolio approach to classroom reading assessment: The whys, whats and hows. *The Reading Teacher, 44,* 338-340.

Valeri-Gold, M., Olson, J. R., & Deming, M. P. (1991-2). Portfolios: Collaborative authentic assessment opportunities for college developmental learners. *Journal of Reading, 35* (4), 298-305.

Wagner, R. K., & Sternberg, R. J. (1986). Tacit knowledge and intelligence in the everyday world. In R. J. Sternberg, & R. K. Wagner (Eds.), Practical intelligence: Nature and origins of competence in the everyday world (pp. 51-83). New York: Cambridge University Press.

Wise, L. S., Plake, B. S., Johnson, P. L., & Roos, L. L. (1992). A comparison of self-adapted and computerized adaptive tests. *Journal of Educational Measurement, 29,* 329-339.

Wolf Palmer, D. (1989). Portfolio assessment: Sampling student work. *Educational Leadership, 46,* 35-39.

Wolf, D., Bixby, J., Glenn III, J., & Gardner, H. (1991). To use their minds well: Investigating new forms of student assessment. *Review of Research in Education, 17,* 31-73.

Worthen, B. R. (1993). Critical issues that will determine the future of alternative assessment. *Phi Delta Kappan, 74,* 444-456.

Zeidner, M. (1987). Essay versus multiple-choice type classroom exams: The student's perspective. *Journal of Educational Research, 80,* 352-258.

Zoller, U., & Ben-Chaim, D. (1988). Interaction between examination-type anxiety state, and academic achievement in college science; An action-oriented research. *Journal of Research in Science Teaching, 26,* 65-77.

Zoller, U., & Ben-Chaim, D. (1990). Gender differences in examination-type performances, test anxiety, and academic achievements in college science education - A case study. *Science Education, 74,* 597-608.

Assessment of Mathematics - What is the Agenda?

Leone Burton

INTRODUCTION

The pervading international paradigm within which classroom learning, teaching and assessing of mathematics is set is of an "objective" discipline which is "best" taught by transmission. Indeed, when it is decided what mathematics young people *should* learn, the most efficient, and preferred, style for that learning is seen by many to be, first, to tell the facts, or show the skill, and then, to practice. "Increasingly over the past few decades it has been argued that schools are preoccupied with 'putting knowledge into the child's mind'" (Davis, 1986, p. 274). Not only in schools, but also in higher education the same approach often holds for both mathematics and science. Speaking of university physics, Kim Thomas wrote: "the teaching tended to be conventional and hierarchical, very much like school, with students being given a body of information to absorb" (1990, p. 58).

Two assumptions lie behind this view. The first is that each element of mathematics to be learnt is fixed and that interpretations other than that being offered are not possible. The second is that the teacher's role is to transfer the "given" knowledge into the heads of the students. The implications of these two assumptions include that meaning lies within the knowledge, and not within the students who are not meaning-makers but dependent upon the teacher/text for meaning, and expected to be unquestioning in their reception of it. Understanding is seen to come about through meeting the new knowledge and then practicing it. The epistemology is consequently predicated on reproduction and is consistent with a behaviourist stance on the psychology of learning. Such a knowledge paradigm has important implications for curricular decisions.

The curriculum can be considered as a combination of syllabus (what should pupils learn?), pedagogy (how should they learn?), and assessment (how do we/they know they have learnt?) (see Burton, 1992a). A view of the mathematics curriculum as consisting of the reproduction and transmission of "objectively" defined knowledge and skills has the following effects. It:

- reifies and essentialises the syllabus content into a hierarchy;
- leads directly towards didactic teaching;
- promotes receptive learning, i.e., static pupil roles in the classroom;
- emphasises individualisation;
- prefers an "objective" testing mode of assessment (see ibid.).

This epistemology governs choices for mathematics learning, teaching and assessing in many classrooms.

However, there is an alternative paradigm which has achieved widespread acceptance among mathematics educators along with the education community in other disciplines. This springs from the work of Piaget and Vygotsky and emphasises the construction of knowing in a socio-cultural context. Curriculum development projects around the world have been operating within this frame of reference and the widespread acceptance of *investigational* styles of learning mathematics is a testimony to its influence. Despite the governmental emphasis in England and Wales, for example, on the hierarchy of received knowledge in the mathematics national curriculum, materials which have been written for teachers to support their pedagogical practices use social constructivist language to talk in terms of networks of knowledge, pupils' constructing their own understanding, the negotiation of meaning, the social context of learning, and so on. Elsewhere (Burton, 1992b), I have pointed to the conflict induced in the mathematics teaching community by this paradigmatic clash especially when the "objective" paradigm has statutory power. Nonetheless, there is evidence from many countries with very different approaches to education of the power of the social constructivist conception to affect views on learning, teaching and assessing. Tom Romberg said it succinctly:

> The assessment challenge we face is to give up old assessment methods to determine what students know which are based on behavioural theories of learning and develop authentic assessment procedures that reflect current epistemological beliefs both about what it means to know mathematics and how students come to know. (1993, p. 109)

Such curriculum developments predicated on a social constructivist epistemology do not only affect the design and choice of assessment tasks but are set within a view of the curriculum as a coherent whole. The activities undertaken by students within the mathematics classroom contribute to, and are part of, the totality of their learning. This leads to a re-definition of the nature of mathematics learning which fundamentally affects syllabus and pedagogy as well as assessment.

> *Authentic performance assessment* (Lajoie, 1992), based on constructivist notions, begins with complex tasks which students are expected to work on for some period of time. Also, their responses are not just answers; instead, they are arguments which describe conjectures, strategies, and justifications. (Ibid., p. 109; original emphasis)

From the "objective"-knowledge perspective it appears to be possible to assess learning by constructing a behaviourist, norm-referenced test independently of the classroom experiences of the pupils who are being assessed in this way, and then to believe that the results are informative. A growing body of voices, however, speaks against such practices.

> Traditional examinations and tests have few friends. Though there are often deep reasons for the dislike and fear of formal examinations, they are open to criticism on several grounds: their artificiality (too limited a basis for judgement), unreliability (variation between markers and in pupils' performance), lack of validity (over-dependence on examination technique, memory and writing skill) and primarily the limiting influence of examinations on learning and teaching. (Nisbet, 1993, pp. 31-32)

Changing the epistemological view on mathematics, for example adopting a social constructivist perspective on learning and on styles of assessment, appears to offer more consistency of practice in a richer environment which acknowledges the complexity of all the factors involved, the mathematics but also the learning and the social context. And, asking students to work at complex tasks over time, with a different set of learning parameters and expectations, is clearly a nonsense if this style of working has not been central to their learning experience. The synchronicity between the epistemological and the curricular paradigm is clearly exposed from this perspective, helping to explain the frequent assertion that assessment 'drives' the curriculum. An epistemological stance on knowing mathematics which is objectivist appears to support an apparently simple relationship between a fact/skill based syllabus, a didactic pedagogy and norm-referenced tests whereas adopting a different epistemology demands a re-thinking of the purposes and the practices of learning and assessment.

In this chapter, I outline some examples of attempts to articulate theories of learning and bring them more closely together with the practice of assessment of mathematics. These examples are drawn from the Netherlands, England and Wales, Australia and Portugal. Social constructivism is permeating thinking about mathematics learning in many countries of the world but not everywhere has this led to innovation, whether at the curricular project level, or at the system level. In choosing the countries on which to focus, therefore, I had many possibilities. I begin with the Netherlands, a country which has been at the forefront of development undertaken slowly and carefully, with the involvement of teachers, and with an attempt to construct practices which are consistent with the theory base on which they depend. By contrast, in England and Wales with which I am most familiar, developments were driven by political considerations, speed, and conflicting and poorly articulated positions. Victoria, in Australia, introduced systemic assessment-led changes, a different model to that in the Netherlands. Portugal is an example of project-led development. Two English-speaking and two non-English speaking case studies seemed like a good cultural compromise.

The four country studies are followed by a consideration of what, under these changed conditions, is assessed and who is affected. A short section then raises some systemic issues with respect to assessment of mathematics. Finally, what is particularly noticeable about much of the writing in this area is that it tends to challenge the nature of mathematical behaviour while leaving unexamined the nature of mathematics itself. Hence mathematics students are expected to engage with a question, undertake an enquiry, justify their choices and present arguments to sustain their conclusions. This, in itself, is novel and innovative for many mathematics classrooms. However, it leaves unresolved questions about what mathematics is, the relationship between process and product, the impact of technology, and equity concerns, which are raised in the conclusion.

ALTERNATIVE APPROACHES TO ASSESSMENT

In presenting "snapshots" of assessment systems in seven different countries, Jim Ridgway and Don Passey (1993, pp. 57-61) showed that assessment was predominantly examination or test-based for the purpose of certification and access. In many countries, these tests have a multiple-choice format. As the authors point out:

> Assessment is a murky business. It raises fundamental issues about our beliefs on the nature of mathematics and knowledge in general, teaching and the educational process, and the relationships between the individual, school and society ... Attempts to use improved assessment practices to drive desirable educational change are laudable, but likely to be difficult in practice. (Ibid., p. 72)

In fact, by no means all of the four such attempts reported below drove curricular change by changes in assessment practices. In the first, the Netherlands, the interdependence between change in syllabus, pedagogy and assessment is demonstrated.

The Netherlands

Between 1971 and 1993, mathematics education in the Netherlands underwent what has been termed a revolution (de Lange, 1992) but it has been a revolution driven by clearly articulated theoretical considerations.

- "Educational development is more than curriculum development. It is an integrated activity, integrated meaning that the development takes place longitudinally, simultaneously at all levels, including teacher training, and *in* the schools, *with* the schools and *for* the schools." (Ibid., p. 305, original emphasis)
- An *innovation philosophy* was articulated: "there is no separation between research-development and diffusion activities and thus no ordering of these activities" (Treffers, 1986 quoted in de Lange, 1992, p. 306).
- A theory for mathematics education was labelled "realistic mathematics education" (Treffers, 1986).
- Three areas, curriculum and product development, research, and teacher/pupil/social change, were seen to support each other and, usually, cyclically not linearly.

Because of the cyclical nature of the developments, starting in 1971 with early work at primary level in one school over a considerable length of time, leading to open consultation, experimentation and discussion and not extending into two schools in the secondary sector until 1981, the philosophy, as well as the pragmatics, of the development grew out of the process. Examining the changes, it is possible to identify four central ideas:

1. Context:

> the start of any subcurriculum takes place in some real world situation. This real world is not restricted to the physical and social world. The 'inner' reality of mathematics and the real world of the students' imagination also provide sources for developing mathematical concepts. The context's second role is in the applications: students uncover reality as the source and domain of application. (de Lange, 1992, p. 308)

2. Conceptual mathematisation:

> The real-world situation or problem is explored in the first place intuitively, with a view to mathematising it. This means organising and structuring the problem, trying to identify the mathematical aspects of the problem, trying to discover regularities (which) should lead to the development, discovery or (re)invention of mathematical concepts. (Ibid., p. 308)

3. Reflection:

> "reflection on the process of mathematisation is essential" (ibid., p. 309). By engaging students in the construction of their own learning through a wide range of outcomes "the student is forced to reflect on the path he or she has taken in his or her learning process and, at the same time, to anticipate its continuation" (ibid., p. 310).

4. Active engagement of learners within a learning community:

> Our classroom observations showed that the students did, sooner or later, extract mathematical concepts from real situations, using such factors as interaction between students, interaction between students and teachers, the social environment and the ability to formalise and abstract. (Ibid., p. 308)

Assessment styles did not become an issue in these developments until the work at the secondary level was well under way. But the original secondary innovation was aimed at the higher achieving pupils in the educational system so the

> designers were confronted with a serious problem; restricted-time written tests ... were unsuitable for proper testing, especially for the higher levels...When designing tests was left to the teacher the results were disappointing ... So we started developmental research to devise new test formats. (Ibid., p. 314)

Five principles were enunciated:
1. Tests should improve learning.
2. Tests should enable students to show what they know (positive testing).
3. Tests should operationalise all goals.
4. The most important quality of the test is not its potential for objective scoring.
5. Tests should fit into the constraints of usual school practice (see de Lange, 1987; 250-251).

A typical final examination in mathematics takes over three hours and usually consists of five large problems with 20 shorter questions (approximately). In Figure 1, "The examination for non-specialist mathematicians", one shorter problem is shown.

If no fish are caught, they will increase in the coming years. The graph in figure 14.6 models the growth of the total weight of fish.

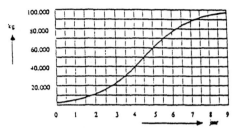

Figure 14.6 Graph showing the growth of the weight of fish

• Draw an increase diagram, with intervals of a year, starting with the interval 1-2 years.

The fish farmer will wait some years before he catches or harvests the fish. After the first catch he wants to take the same amount of fish each year as in the first year, and he wants as much fish as possible. After every catch the weight of fish increases again according to the graph.

Give advice to the fish farmer about:
• the number of years he has to wait after stocking the fish;
• the amount of fish that he will catch every year.

Give convincing arguments to explain your answers.

The reader should know, when looking at this exercise, that the curriculum does not cover the subject 'differentiation of functions' but studies the changes of real phenomena in a discrete way. This is an excellent preparation for calculus. Instead of the graph of the derivative of a function, the students are accustomed to the discrete apparatus called an 'increase diagram'. So the first question is very straightforward and uses only the lowest level. The other question was a new, desired and long awaited addition.

Communicating mathematics, drawing conclusions, and finding convincing arguments are activities that all too often are not very visible in mathematics tests and examinations. Many teachers were surprised and did not know what to think of this new development, although they were prepared; the experiments had given fair indication of the new approach. Students seemed less surprised (as usual), although they gave a wide variety of responses:

I would wait for four years and then catch 20 000 kg per year. You can't loose that way, man.

If you wait till the end of the fifth year then you have a big harvest every year: 20 000 kg of fish: that's certainly no peanuts. If you can't wait that long, and start to catch one year earlier you can catch only 17 000 kg, and if you wait too long (one year) you can only catch 18 000 kg of fish.

So you have the best results after waiting for five years. Be patient; wait those years. You won't regret it.

Source: de Lange, J. (1992). Critical factors for real changes in mathematics learning. In G. Leder (Ed.), *Assessment and Learning of Mathematics*, Hawthorn, Vic.: A.C.E.R. (pp.318-320). Reprinted by permission of the publisher.

Figure 1: The Examination for Non-Specialist Mathematicians.

Figure 2, "The examination for the specialist students", shows a problem example.

The exterior beams in the building shown in figure 14.7(a) are constructed in such a way that the roof is hung by means of steel cables. In figure 14.7(b) the building has been drawn from an oblique perspective, so that the square roof is represented in its true form. In figure 14.7(c) the measurements of the three main directions, x, y, and z are all shown on the same scale: 1 cm in the drawing corresponds to about 2 m. The roof consists of 25 squares of 3 m x 3 m.

- How long is the cable? Give an accurate answer.

If you walk around the building at a good distance from it, you will see it in a nearly parallel projection. At certain viewing points, various cables will appear to converge.

- Does a viewing point exist where cables a and b appear to converge?
- Does a viewing point exist where the cables a and c will appear to converge?
- Draw, using figure 14.7(b), a view of the building from the x-direction showing the beams and cables.

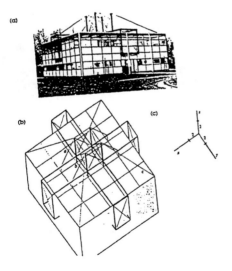

Source: de Lange, J. (1992). Critical factors for real changes in mathematics learning. In G. Leder (Ed.), Assessment and learning of Mathematics (pp. 320-321). Hawthorn, Vic.: Australian Council for Educ. Research. Reprinted by permission of the publisher.

Figure 2: The Examination for the Specialist Students

Innovatory styles of testing have also been developed for use in schools by teachers wanting to monitor the progress of their students using the same principles of teaching and design. One example from a school test is shown in Figure 3.

The test results of two mathematics classes are presented in a stem-and-leaf display:

Class A		Class B
7	1	
7	2	3 4
4	3	
5 5	4	
4	5	
1	6	5
1	7	1 2 3 4 4 6 6 8
9 9 6 6 5 5 5	8	1 1 4
9 7	9	1

• Does this table suffice to judge which class performed best?

This example is typical in the sense that it shows that a very simple problem may not have a very simple solution. The teacher has to consider carefully the different arguments and has to accept a variety of solutions.

At first glance, many students, and teachers as well, tended to find class A better than class B because of the many scores in the 80s. However, some students argued that class B is definitely better because only two students did poorly. On the other hand some argued that you cannot say anything because the average of both classes seems to be the same. But the median is definitely better for class A and how about the mode? So it boils down to the question: What do you mean by 'better'?

Source: de Lange, J. (1992). Critical factors for real changes in mathematics learning. In G. Leder (Ed.), *Assessment and Learning of Mathematics* (pp.323-324). Hawthorn, Vic.: Australian Council for Educ. Research. Reprinted by permission of the publisher.

Figure 3: A School Test Problem with Possibilities

Other developments were:
• The two-stage task: the first stage is a conventional timed written test. The tests are marked and returned to the students by the teacher. The students then have the opportunity, at home, to review their test, and improve their work but without time restrictions.
• The essay: students are provided with a magazine article with information in numbers and tables. They are asked to re-write the article making use of graphical representations.
• The test task: students are asked to design a one-hour test for their classmates on a just completed section of work, showing all the expected working and answers.

Figure 4 represents the response of one student to a task on content about the mean, median, boxplots and histograms.

- In 1968, the United States was the first and the Soviet Union was second in machine tool production. In 1988, Japan was the first

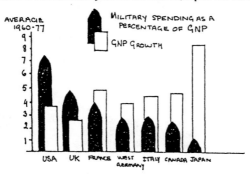

Figure 14.11 Illustration included in student's test

and West Germany was second. Compare the difference in dollars between the two sets.
The difference in 1968 is roughly 3 billion dollars and in 1988, it's 2 billion dollars. This could mean that in 1988, the amounts of the production of machine tools are more evenly spread.

- Why are data collected like this?
Data are collected to learn who is the leading producer of machine tools. For the United States it is also helpful to know what to improve in the economy.

- Would a line graph represent these data better?
No, I didn't think so, because line graphs are primarily used to show sudden changes in connected things. A bar graph is better for this information because each country is separate and not connected in any specific way besides machine tool production.

- What is the average for each of the sets separately and combined?
For both of the sets, the average is about 3.92 billion dollars. Its only an approximation because you can't tell the exact numbers from the 1968 bars. For 1968 alone, it's about 2.74 billion dollars. For 1988 alone, the numbers average 5.02 billion dollars.

- Is there any way to tell the averages besides computing?
Yes, I think so because if you look at the length of the bars themselves and not the actual numbers, you can tell pretty closely for each of the individual sets. For both sets combined, it gets harder because you have to balance them.

(De Lange et al. 1991)

Source: de Lange, J. (1992) 'Critical factors for real changes in mathematics learning' in Leder, G. (Ed) *Assessment and Learning of Mathematics*, Hawthorn, Vic.:   Australian Council for Educ. Research (pp.325-326) Reprinted by permission of the publisher.

Figure 4: Write Your Own Test with Answers

Of course the Netherlands' developments should not be taken out of the social context within which they were derived, although there is a current collaboration between the Freudenthal Institute in Utrecht and the University of Wisconsin in the USA to apply appropriate approaches and develop new ones. But two lessons are worth learning. One is the power of designing new curricula in a theory-rich context. The second is that robust development was neither test-driven, nor test-responsive. It was integrative of syllabi, pedagogy and assessment, and that means, of the various communities who were affected by or involved in it.

England and Wales

Many developments in mathematics education in England and Wales resulted from the Cockcroft Report (1982) which included the following assessment recommendations:
*   Assessment methods should enable pupils to demonstrate what they know.
*   Examinations should not undermine pupil confidence.
*   Assessment should enable demonstration not only of those aspects of mathematics accessible to examination by written papers, but also of those which respond best to other styles.
*   Teacher assessment should be a necessary part of the public judgment of attainment, in order to encourage good classroom practice. (Cockcroft Report 1982, Chapter 10).

One outcome was that, in 1988, when a new examination framework, the General Certificate of Secondary Education (GCSE), common to all pupils aged 16, replaced the former two-tier system, it incorporated two new features. One was a proportion of *coursework*, which is class-based and teacher assessed and usually consists of extended investigations in mathematics. The second new feature was oral examinations in mathematics, formerly unknown in the English system. (Coursework only became a compulsory feature in 1991.) Another innovation was the identification of national criteria (see Cockcroft Report, 1982), to establish what was seen as an essential link between classroom practice and pupil achievement. The emphases were taken from paragraph 243 of the Report:

Mathematics teaching at all levels should include opportunities for exposition by the teacher; discussion between teacher and pupils and between pupils themselves; appropriate practical work; consolidation and practice of fundamental skills and routines; problem solving, including the application of mathematics to everyday situations and investigational work (ibid.).

The national criteria represented an attempt to criterion-reference the skills and understandings to be expected of a student of mathematics. However, as Jim Ridgway (1988) pointed out:

The whole notion of the criterion-referencing of process skills and conceptual understanding is problematic. Objectives which use words and phrases like 'interpret', 'understand', 'form generalizations', 'select a suitable strategy', 'discuss mathematical ideas' cannot be considered to be criteria in the sense implied by 'criterion-referenced testing'. While these are all desirable objectives, they do not say what it is that pupils who have satisfied such criteria have been able to do. (1988, p. 75)

The national curriculum introduced into the law in 1991, after a development process of less than one year, incorporated the criteria as statements of attainment which have come to represent the means through which achievement is measured throughout the years of schooling. Since its introduction, and possibly because of the haste with which it was originally devised, the national curriculum has undergone two reconstructions, the second of which has recently, at the time of writing, been made public. During this time, teachers have had to continue to work within its (current) prescriptions.

Assessment styles which, in 1988 in the GCSE were intended to "provide a balance of techniques for assessment which cover both written aspects and other aspects including practical work, investigations, mental mathematics, and oral work" (Ridgway, 1988, p. 69) and to offer evidence of positive achievement to a broader constituency of pupils, are being pushed back towards paper and pencil, unseen, timed tests, within the national curriculum framework.   These, inevitably, concentrate on reproductive, algorithmic behaviour despite the evidence which now exists that the introduction of coursework into the GCSE appears to correlate with improved achievement, especially of girls, for whom the greater the proportion of coursework, the more noticeable the improvement.

> Added support to the coursework-is-better argument are the statistics from another examination board that offers end of course examination with either 20% or 40% coursework. Both proportionally and in actual numbers, the girls attained better in the 40% coursework across the higher grades than in the 20% coursework option. (Nickson & Prestage, 1994, p. 57)

The government has now ruled that, "in future, there will be a maximum of 20% coursework for any mathematics syllabus and that syllabuses without coursework will be available for any school department that wishes to adopt one" (Ridgway, 1988, p. 59).

Nonetheless, there has been curriculum development work focussing upon the necessary teaching, learning and assessment styles which support the introduction of extended pieces of investigatory work in the mathematics classroom. Much of this work, at the secondary level, was done at the Shell Centre for Mathematical Education, Nottingham, and is reported upon in Ridgway (1988). For example, in "The Language of Functions and Graphs" (Joint Matriculation Board/Shell Centre for Mathematical Education, 1985) pupils are expected to:

> interpret and use information presented in a variety of mathematical and non-mathematical forms ...It focuses on the representation of meaning in a variety of ways and on ways of translating between these different representations ...Active processing of materials via such activities as discussing, translating and explaining, are all likely to lead to the development of elaborated conceptual structures. (Ridgway, 1988, p. 83)

In order to be able to meet these objectives, there are necessary pedagogic shifts to be made in the classroom. Most obviously, groupwork is intended. But teachers and pupils also have to learn what constitutes the writing of a report, or a mathematical essay, and by what criteria to assess this work. Figure 5 provides a specimen examination question included in the module which demonstrates this novelty:

Example 5:   The Hurdles Race

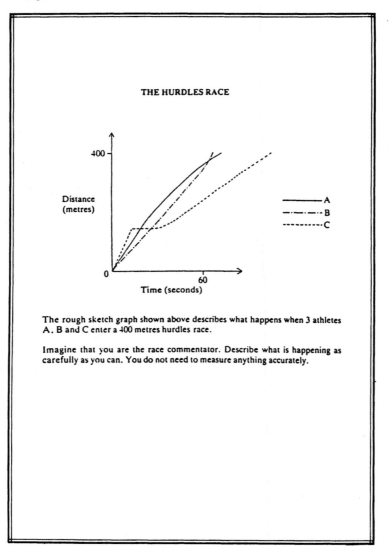

THE HURDLES RACE

The rough sketch graph shown above describes what happens when 3 athletes A, B and C enter a 400 metres hurdles race.

Imagine that you are the race commentator. Describe what is happening as carefully as you can. You do not need to measure anything accurately.

Source: Ridgway, J. (1988). *Assessing Mathematical Attainment*. Windsor, Berkshire: NFER-Nelson, (p. 106). Reprinted by permission of the author.

Figure 5: The Hurdles Race

Figure 6 is self-explanatory.

THE HURDLES RACE...MARKING SCHEME

Interpreting a mathematical representation using words.

1 mark	for 'C takes the lead'
1 mark	for 'C stops running'
1 mark	for 'B overtakes A'
1 mark	for 'B wins'
2 marks	for any four of the following:

A and B pass C

C starts running again

C runs at a slower pace

A slows down (or B speeds up)

A finishes 2nd (or C finishes last)

Part mark: 1 mark if any two (or three) of the above points are mentioned.

2 marks   for a lively commentary which mentions hurdles.

Part mark: 1 mark for a lively commentary which does not mention hurdles, or for a 'report' which mentions hurdles.

A total of 8 marks are available for this question.

Source: Ridgway, J. (1988). *Assessing Mathematical Attainment.* Windsor, Berkshire: NFER-Nelson, (p. 107). Reprinted by permission of the author.

Figure 6: The Marking Scheme

Figure 7 provides three examples of pupils' responses.

Martin

And they were off. C increased speed very rapidly for the
first 150 m and covered a big distance in a very short
time. B took it calmly and paced himself to his limits he
went reasonably fast and A went faster than B but
slower than C at the start, but then C stopped for a
rest and carried on slowly coming in last A went faster
and kept going, but was overtaken by B who beat A and
came first, B won, A was second, and C was third.

Stephen

Here at the start of the race the three athletes are ready to start.
There off. Athlete C takes an early lead. Athlete A is close in second
and athlete B win the race after a bad start. They're approaching the
100m mark. Its out C leading from B A and B is catching up C h no.
C as fell. He's getting up and chasing A and B. At half way A has a
small lead but B is gradually catching him and it looks like C won't
much chance of wining. There now in the final 100m A and B are
neck and neck, C has just passed halfway. Athlete A crosses
the line first B is only just behind him. C is about 100m out.
I think C might have won if he didn't fell.

Wendy

Athlete A came 2nd - He started off
fairly fast and got slightly slower during
the race
Athlete B came 1st - He started off at
a steady rate and picked up speed all
the way through the race.
Athlete C came 3rd - He started off
going fast, then he fell over and didn't
run for a few seconds, then he started
running again, gradually getting slower and slower

Source: Ridgway, J. (1988). *Assessing Mathematical Attainment*. Windsor, Berkshire:
NFER-Nelson, (p. 108). Reprinted by permission of the author.

Figure 7: Some Pupils' Responses

Figure 8 shows how the above work was scored:

Marking the descriptions

Martin has mentioned all of the first 4 factors and also 3 of the additional ones. For this he scored 5 marks. Martin's commentary reads more like a report than a commentary, and since he does not mention the hurdles, he was not awarded any "commentary" marks. Therefore, Martin obtained a total of 5 marks out of the possible 8.

Stephen has only mentioned 2 of the first 4 factors and 2 of the additional ones, thus scoring 3 marks. However, Stephen's commentary is lively and interesting although he has ignored the fact that it is a hurdles race. He was awarded one "commentary" mark, making a total of 4 out of the possible 8.

Wendy has also mentioned 2 of the first 4 points, as well as 3 of the additional ones. She was awarded 3 marks for these. Wendy does not, however, obtain any "commentary" marks, since she has described each athlete's run separately, rather than giving a commentary on the race as a whole.

Source: Ridgway, J. (1988). *Assessing Mathematical Attainment*. Windsor, Berkshire: NFER-Nelson, (p. 109). Reprinted by permission of the author.

Figure 8: Applying the Marking Scheme

An example of a different approach to investigational work is shown in Figure 9.

8 VILLAGE STREETS

NUMERICAL, SPATIAL

In a village there are three streets. All the streets are straight. One lamp-post is put up at each crossroads.

What is the greatest number of lamp-posts that could be needed? Now try four streets and five streets. Predict the answer for six streets then check it. Can you see a pattern? Why does the pattern work?

FOR THE TEACHER

Help the children to get started by encouraging the use of representations. Suggest they look for a pattern by drawing up a table connecting the number of streets with the number of lamp-posts.

Make them aware of how and why the pattern works by seeing what happens to the number of intersections with existing streets, each time a new street is added.

Vary the problem by allowing streets to cross at any angle.

EXTENSIONS

1 What if the streets are either parallel or perpendicular?

2 Triangular numbers occur in quite a number of contexts and problems.

See for example Problem 30 and Extensions for Problems 12 and 13.

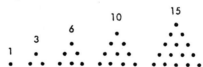

Source: Burton, L. (1984). *Thinking Things Through.* Oxford: Basil Blackwell, (pp. 78-79). Reproduced by permission of the author.

Figure 9: Village Streets

The English and Welsh experience is of slow development sustained through considerable expenditure on teacher education and support which, over the period 1982 - 1988 and culminating in the introduction of the GCSE, led to many teachers reconsidering their views on mathematics, its learning and teaching and consequently their practices. This has been followed by rapid governmental educational changes re-asserting the primacy of an assessment-led system in a highly dogma-driven environment which has induced confusion and low morale in teachers. Interestingly, while the government constrains the shifts which had taken place in schools towards a greater proportion of oral and extended writing in the learning and assessing of mathematics, parallel pressure in the opposite direction is operating on higher education. University mathematics departments are being encouraged to consider (and incorporate), for example, project work, comprehension exercises, group-solving and modelling, use of posters as alternatives to the domination of timed, unseen, written examinations.

Australia - the Victorian Certificate of Education

Education in Australia is state-, not federal-, controlled so that, in practice, national developments in Australia are restricted to the publication of material of an advisory nature. The new Australian mathematical profiles fall into this category. They support a national mathematics statement meant to provide a framework for curriculum development within each state (Australian Education Council, 1990). The profile documents provide teachers with *"rich exemplification* of the descriptions or pointers to assist teachers in making consistent judgements about student achievement ...[and] reflect the achievements of *well taught students"* (Ferguson, 1992, p. 10) The examples are heavily contextualised to make clear that there can be no general expectation of a pupil response to an activity, each response being affected by the student's background, experience, knowledge, preferences, and so on. (For further details, see Burton, 1994a.)

When it comes to particular assessment arrangements within each of the seven Australian states, these vary from one in which there is saturation state-wide testing on 'objective' items to another where for more than twenty years, all assessment has been in the hands of classroom teachers (and universities set their own entry examinations). Perhaps the state which has achieved greatest recent publicity is Victoria which in 1990, introduced a new school leaving examination in years 11 and 12 (the Victorian Certificate of Education, VCE).

> By the end of the 1980s, sweeping changes to curriculum and assessment in the senior secondary years were introduced in response to a changed agenda for secondary schooling, in all Australian States, where it is now assumed that the vast majority of young people will complete Year 12 before moving on to further study, work , or a combination of both. As a result there has been an extensive top-down reform of curriculum and assessment arrangements across all subjects in the senior secondary years.   In mathematics, these reforms have given effect to many of the changes which had been urged for many years by the mathematics education community. (Stephens & Money, 1993, p. 156)

The examination system was recognised as a means through which practice in mathematics classrooms could be transformed. As a result, assessment strategies were devised to value such aspects of mathematical behaviour involved in enquiring and reporting, in contrast to simple knowledge or skill reproduction. Max Stephens and Robert Money make the point, however, that "related innovations in the assessment of mathematics in the senior secondary years are taking place in several other Australian States and Territories" (ibid., p. 170).

The VCE includes reports of mathematical investigations and problem solving activities both as part of the *work requirements* and the *common assessment tasks*.

> Work requirements are intended to be used by teachers in planning and managing each course, and to provide a clear link between what students do

in each course and how their work is assessed. Three work requirements apply to each course of study in mathematics:

Projects: extended independent investigations involving the use of mathematics.

Problem solving and modelling: the creative application of mathematical knowledge and skills to solve problems in unfamiliar situations, including real life situations.

Skills practice and standard applications: the study of aspects of the existing body of mathematical knowledge through learning and practicing mathematical algorithms, routines and techniques, and using them to find solutions to standard problems.

The Mathematics Study Design for the VCE stipulates that at least 20% of class time must be devoted to each work requirement. (Stephens, 1993, p. 165.)

Additional to the work requirements, there are centrally set and monitored common assessment tasks (CAT) of which CAT 1 is an investigative project to be carried out over a designated 12 week period, partly in school, partly outside. "CAT 1 is intended to enable students to demonstrate their ability to carry out an extended piece of independent work in mathematics" (Stephens & Money, 1993, p. 159). Classroom teachers are expected to ensure that the centrally set theme task and starting points for the investigation are well embedded into their mathematics curriculum and that the criteria for assessment are well understood by the pupils. Teachers also assist students in undertaking and reporting on their investigation. The example in Figure 10 makes clear how one student gets started on a theme.

In a report based on the theme *Describing variations in the weather,* and on the starting point *Accuracy of forecasts,* a student discusses in the main text the methods chosen and clearly relates them to them to the theme and particular starting point

A measure of accuracy can be obtained by subtracting the forecast (temperature) from the observed temperature on any particular day. If the result is positive then the forecast was too low. If it is negative the forecast is too high. If it is zero then the forecast is correct within the limits of accuracy imposed by the number of (decimal) places used. Forecasts are given with no decimal places and if the observed temperature is recorded to no decimal places then the error could be anything up to one degree.

The forecast accuracy for longer periods could be determined by averaging the separate 'observed' forecast results. If the absolute values were used the end result would indicate the average amount the forecast was inaccurate by. If non-absolute values were used the end result would indicate any overall bias. By using a box plot of non-absolute temperatures both the overall bias and the spread of results would be indicated. Forecasts which were a long way off would become the outliers on the box plot. In an ideal situation the box plot would become a single vertical line above the zero mark. In practice the box plot is clearly defined as having a median line, an upper and lower quartile, a minimum and a maximum, and sometimes outliers. Box plots of all of the months in 1990 have been included in the Appendix....

Figure 10 (cont.)

Another method of visually analysing the accuracy is using a scatter plot of forecast against observed temperature. These can be useful for determining a subjective measure of a forecast accuracy but are difficult to use in calculations.

These points illustrate at a high level an understanding, interpretation and evaluation of the mathematics used. They provide a mathematical formulation of the problem being investigated, and at the same time identify important information and show how it will be collected and analysed.

Source: Stephens, M. (1993). Valuing and Fostering Mathematical Writing in the Victorian Certificate of Education. In M. Stephens, A. Waywood, D. Clarke, & J. Izard, (Eds.), *Communicating Mathematics: Perspectives from Classroom Practice and Current Research* (p. 171). Hawthorn, Vic.: ACER. Reprinted by permission of the publisher.

Figure 10: A Student Interprets a Problem

Figure 11 illustrates how a student develops the argument and shows the kind of writing being encouraged:

In a report, based on the theme *Determining Curves*, one possible starting point was *Approximating a complicated function with simpler functions*, students were asked to choose a function and a domain for a function such as sin x or e^x. They were then asked to 'find a cubic curve that is as close as possible to the graph of your function, over your chosen domain'. Then they were asked 'How did you measure *as close as possible*? You will have to invent your own method for this and describe it clearly. Is the cubic you have found the closest cubic there is?'

A student who investigated the graph of sin x over the domain $-\pi$ to π explained what needed to be done by referring to two methods and by giving reasons for choosing one of these:

I then decided how I was going to measure 'as close as possible'. One method I thought of but decided against involved finding the difference between the y-values for x values at regular intervals in the domain and then averaging them. The curve with the least distance would be the closest.
The reason I rejected this method was because it would take a long time to work out and it could be inaccurate....
The method I decided upon would show up any problem such as the one I mentioned above. The method of integration (involved finding the) area between curves

Source: Stephens, M. (1993). Valuing and Fostering Mathematical Writing in the Victorian Certificate of Education. In M. Stephens, A. Waywood, D. Clarke, & J. Izard, (Eds.), *Communicating Mathematics: Perspectives from Classroom Practice and Current Research* (p. 171-172). Hawthorn, Vic.: ACER. Reprinted by permission of the publisher.

Figure 11: A Student Develops the Argument

CAT 2, the Challenging Problem:

> takes place early in the second semester. Students undertake a problem-solving and/or modeling task ...selected in consultation with the teacher from a list of four externally set problems, and are required to complete a written report of their solution according to the format specified. Students are given two weeks for this task ... CAT 2 is intended to enable students to demonstrate their ability to read and understand a problem; formulate and interpret problems mathematically; use problem-solving and/or modeling strategies; try simple cases; find patterns and formulate hypotheses; simplify complex situations; define important variables; find proofs and explanations; and interpret solutions. (Stephens & Money, 1993, p. 160)

A sample task is shown in Figure 12.

The following question was posed to a group of mathematics students.

"Are there any shapes for which the numerical value of the length of the perimeter is the same as the numerical value of the area?"

One student quickly saw that a square is a shape with this property because a square which has a side length of 4 units has a perimeter of 16 units and an area of 16 square units. The student could also easily show that there could only be one square with this property.

After looking at families of shapes like triangles, circles, rectangles and other polygons the students made the following conjecture.

"For every family of shapes there is at least one of these shapes for which the numerical value of the area and the numerical value of the perimeter are the same."

By "family of shapes" the students meant all shapes which are similar to a given shape. For example there is only one family of squares, but there is an infinite number of families of rectangles.

You are required to find the following.

o   For which shapes does the conjecture hold?
o   For each class of shapes for which the conjecture holds, give a method for finding an actual shape for which the numerical value of the area is the same as the numerical value of the perimeter.

Source: Stephens, M. & Money, R. (1993). New Developments in Senior Secondary Assessment in Australia. In Niss, M. (Ed.), *Cases of Assessment in Mathematics Education* (p. 163). Dordrecht: Kluwer. Reprinted by permission of the publisher.

Figure 12: A Challenging Space and Number

As the students engage in a task such as the one in Figure 12, they are required to discuss the assessment criteria with their teacher. The criteria are grouped under three major headings as shown in Figure 13. These can be used as indicators for dialogue between teacher and students, or supportive activities.

Max Stephens makes the point that such work requires a student to demonstrate "a sustained ability for mathematical thinking and a capacity to describe how a mathematical investigation or problem solving task was conducted and its related findings or solutions" (1993, Stephens, p. 175).

An evaluation of the VCE, three years after it was first introduced, showed that there had been a trickle-down effect so that different work practices were being used in years 7 to 10 although difficulties still remained. An important component of the new assessment style was its reliance on teacher-based assessment which left a component of professional choice and judgement in the teachers' hands (Blane, 1992).

Defining the problem
- ° clear definition of what is required
- ° definition of important variables, assumptions and constraints
- ° identification of nature of solution sought

Solution and justification
- ° production of a solution which adresses the problem
- ° degree of mathematical formulation of problem
- ° appropriate use of mathematical language, symbols and conventions
- ° accuracy of mathematics
- ° interpretation of mathematical results
- ° depth of analysis of problem
- ° quality of justification of solution

The solution process
- ° usefulness of questions asked
- ° relevance of mathematics used
- ° generation and analysis of appropriate information
- ° recognition of the relevance of fndings
- ° refinement of definition of problem

Source: Stephens, M. & Money, R. (1993). New Developments in Senior Secondary Assessment in Australia. In M. Niss (Ed.), Cases of Assessment in Mathematics Education (pp. 166-167). Dordrecht: Kluwer. Reprinted by permission of the publisher.

Figure 13: Assessment Criteria

Portugal - a local curriculum development

A much smaller scale curriculum development in Portugal nonetheless provides an example of the spread of a similar constructivist epistemology outside the

English-speaking world.   From 1988 to 1992, an innovative mathematics curriculum for pupils aged 12-15 was implemented in four classes in Lisbon.

> According to the perspective of the Project, mathematics education should develop in students a positive attitude of self-confidence, as well as an understanding of the role and importance of this science in his or her life, and in society. The learning process should be oriented essentially toward construction (not 'absorption'), in such a way that transmission and repetition mechanisms play only a secondary role. This construction should appear naturally in appropriate contexts, the concepts being built by students as the proposed activities develop. In this sense, a given problem situation is not presented merely to motivate or to introduce a new concept, or to apply one; it provides a context for students' work. (Leal & Abrantes, 1993e, p. 173)

The authors draw attention to a number of principles which were adopted by the project. These were as follows:

1.   Assessment should be an intrinsic part of learning.
2.   Methods and instruments for assessing should be consistent with those used in instruction.
3.   Assessment should value what students know and can do.
4.   Adopting a form of assessment should not depend on its possibilities for quantitative scoring; qualitative information is just as valuable.
5.   Assessment must take place in an environment which is comfortable and where argument and critique are natural.

The similarities between these principles and those adopted in the Netherlands are not surprising given that the team designing the Portuguese project drew heavily upon the Dutch work.

The following forms of assessment were developed:

Two-Stage Tests in which a time-limited test is given in the classroom. After marking the test, indicating the more serious errors, and challenging the pupil to develop the work, the teacher returns the test to the pupils who re-work it at home over a pre-arranged period of time. A new evaluation is made after the second stage. A question from a two-stage test for 12/13 year olds provides an example.

> You may know three different methods to determine the greatest common denominator of two numbers. In earlier grades you have learned how to do it from corresponding sets of divisors. This year you did it in the classroom using a process based on the prime factors of the numbers. In your booklet about natural numbers another method, Euclid's algorithm, is described.
>
> Try to answer the following questions: In which situation does it seem to you more convenient to use one or another of these methods? Do the experiments you find necessary to form a personal opinion and present them together with your answer. (Leal & Abrantes, 1993, p. 176)

Leonor Leal and Paulo Abrantes comment:

As would be expected, some interesting answers were given at the first stage because most pupils took it as a question to be developed for the second stage. The diversity was enormous, going from simple randomly chosen examples for each method without further comments to some very elaborate answers (for this age level), for example: 'The algorithm of Euclid will be adequate when numbers are like 'a' and 'something' times 'a' because one single division is enough' (ibid., p. 177).

Essay-Type Questions and Short Reports have been used either individually or in groups, over different time periods and either related to, or independently of, previous work. Three examples of such questions follow:

- A personal comment on a newspaper article about the system of car license plates (considering the size of our population, other countries' systems and their development, as well as other aspects you may find relevant, is our system a good one for the future and what are some practical suggestions?) - 12/13 year olds.
- A group report about the tourism conditions of a given region, considering data about temperature and precipitation for an extended period of time (imagine you work for a travel agency and you have to write recommendations for vacations during the various months) - 12/14 year olds.
- An individual report on a computer program explored by the pupils in the classroom, where they describe the general functioning of the program as well as their strategies to solve the proposed problem (to estimate the time spent by a car to go a given distance using different rates of speed) - 13/15 year olds. (Leal & Abrantes, 1993, p. 179)

The work is assessed using both an evaluation of the whole and criteria-referencing applying such foci as

the structure of the work, the extent to which the subject has been explored deeply and developed, the correctness of the content, the quality of the communication, and the originality of the work (if it exists). A qualitative score is given to each task and the teacher comments on it to the individual pupil or to the group. (Ibid, p. 179)

Project work is done over a longer period of time scale of three to four weeks and requires time to be spent both inside and outside the classroom. An example given by Leonor Leal and Paulo Abrantes is of an 8th grade class of 13/14 year olds who:

focused on the way the school's cafetaria functioned ... based on the opinions of the students of the school. The pupils developed a questionnaire, selected the sample, collected the answers, and worked on the data with the support of a computer. Finally, they discussed the main results and organized posters for an exhibition. There was no assessment of specific products, yet the work made it possible for the teacher to collect information, beyond other aspects, about pupils' attitudes, especially their sense of responsibility and personal commitment. (ibid., p. 181)

In reflecting upon the results of their work, Leonor Leal and Paulo Abrantes draw attention to the pleasure expressed by the pupils at the changed style of assessing. But:

> more importantly, pupils showed an increasing capacity to evaluate their own work, making balanced observations about their personal involvement in different tasks...One relevant result of our work was the positive change in the classroom atmosphere. Anxiety is very commonly associated with school mathematics, and assessment methods play a decisive role in creating anxiety...It (also) required a lot of reflection on the goals of the curriculum and the intentions and nature of each activity. (ibid., p. 181)

This particular project is being run independently of the Ministry of Education at the present time. However, it represents the permeation of a model for change into the Portuguese educational system. Similar developments have taken place in Spain where, in 1990, the Catalan Government commissioned a complete curricular mathematics project for 12-16 year old pupils. This has generated an assessment package integrated with teaching activities (see Fortuny, Gimenez, & Alsina, 1994).

WHAT AND WHO IS BEING ASSESSED BY THE NEW APPROACHES?

The perpetuation, in many countries, of a model of assessing mathematics which is entirely dependent upon 'objective' tests is, rationally, hard to sustain especially given governmental appeals for raised standards across a broader constituency of learners and evidence which exists as to their lack of efficacy. In a recent electronic conference on assessment, one American professor of educational psychology wrote: "Each stakeholder sees a different purpose for assessment - all are legitimate from a limited perspective. The mistake has been the general attempt to meet all these diverse purposes with a single standardized test." Another American researcher wrote: "The reason standardized tests take the form they do is because it is a cheap ... way to assign comparative numbers across large and varied groups of individuals. Admittedly, the numbers are essentially worthless." Although cost is a major factor in using these tests, it is administrative costs, rather than costs to teacher and student time, effort and self-image, which are calculated. In the recent case of the English and Welsh national curriculum and national testing developments, large sums have been spent in order to put into place something which, almost immediately, has had to be changed and which, in the long run, might (I personally would say will) prove a futile way of meeting governmental objectives. The problem with these objectives of raising standards and broadening the educational base is that the former remain undefined, except subjectively in terms of numerical comparisons, and the latter is unaddressed by the implications of the systems put in place ostensibly to address the raising of standards.

I believe that we have accumulating, although not yet substantial, evidence that changing the nature of engagement with mathematics, and consequently changing the evaluation demands which are levied on teachers and pupils, does affect the learners' views of the discipline and, consequently, their achievement. However, such changes are neither cosmetic, nor small, nor easy. We also have evidence that where they have been so regarded, little actually changes. Adding an occasional investigation to the mathematics timetable without interrogating how this impacts upon teacher and pupil views of the nature of mathematics and its learning, and without valuing it in a public way, demonstrates that it is perceived as irrelevant by the teacher and/or the system, and ensures that it falls outside the scope of the learner's agenda. Taking an investigational stance to all learning, raising questions about the meaning of some mathematics which was formerly regarded as unnegotiable, and treating those questions with respect as the basis of a learning agenda is to take a major pedagogical step. Many of those teachers who take that step claim astonishment at what happens in their mathematics classrooms.

An emphasis on content-driven teaching, learning and assessing was questioned in the Introduction to this chapter from the perspective of its epistemological bias but also because of the impact that stance has on learning experiences. Reports from many countries demonstrate the poverty of attitudes, skills and understandings that years of compulsory mathematics education can create in learners. At the same time, out-of-school studies show learners' mathematical competency which conflicts with in-school poor performance (see, for example, Millroy, 1992, Nunes, Schliemann, & Carraher, 1993, Rogoff & Lave,1984). Changing the classroom epistemology but maintaining the 'objective' public assessment strategies induces conflict and is, in any case, ineffective. Shifting to a different epistemological stance on all aspects of the mathematics curriculum is more challenging but, ultimately, might be the only way of addressing the need to broaden the constituency of learners of mathematics and positively affect their performance.

To make such changes requires long-term thinking and discussion about the values which are attributed to the *subjective* syllabus choices in each society. These syllabus choices reflect the pervading powerful cultures so that a re-consideration of them is a product of thinking about who makes up the society, what society needs those people to know and what those people themselves need to know, and about how society might be affected by a re-distribution of its (mathematical) power. At the present time, mathematics acts as a gatekeeper to many opportunities and hence is a major site of power. Close attention to how it is constituted, which aspects of mathematics are valued, which disregarded, what mathematising behaviours are valued and how this value is accorded and recognised demonstrates that we are living with extremely biased choices. It therefore comes as no surprise to find that we also have biased products of the system. Investing the decisions about mathematics curricula in schools with the outcomes of a dialogue and debate about the different answers to these questions will consequently affect the outcomes of the schooling process.

SYSTEMIC ISSUES

Most assessment systems have two distinct aims. One is to monitor individuals, sometimes to support their progress through the educational system, but more usually to certify them on completion. However, assessment is also used to monitor the health of educational systems. In England and Wales, for example, as in Victoria, Australia, innovation in assessment was initially proposed because of the failure of simplistic, pencil-and-paper, formal, timed tests in both validity and reliability terms. Additionally, teachers had shown that external tests had the power to influence them to teach to the test, which defeated their purpose. Claims were made that teaching and learning styles would not change until they were informed by the outcomes of changes in assessing styles. To move towards this end, teachers needed to shift their expectations and understanding about the links between learning and assessing, and innovatory assessments appeared to encourage such shifts. So, the decision was taken to introduce innovative assessment because the practices within the system were not seen as meeting systemic needs. In this way, the two aims become inextricably intertwined.

It is clear that a new assessment system, and especially one which is innovative, requires considerable resources for in-service development. Expenditure on experimental tasks must be matched by expenditure on teachers who are crucial to the implementation, as well as to the resultant measurement of the tasks themselves. Teachers in England and Wales showed themselves interested and, often, very willing to be part of such developments but their major professional loyalties were to their pupils and many felt unsupported by the resources available to help in coming to terms with the new demands. After an extremely brief foray into innovation, and despite the evidence provided by what little research was done on the results, the Government has now chosen to return to paper-and-pencil testing. Part of the rationale for that decision is to do with the ease of processing of simplistic, 'objective' tests, despite the concerns and criticisms expressed in the international literature with respect to the judgments that tend to be made on results of this kind.

In making system-type judgments, it is difficult to unpick the many different components that influence the success, or otherwise, of an assessment process. Raw numbers can, and do, hide results which differentiate by race, sex and class. Pencil-and-paper tests affirm a particular curricular paradigm which is antagonistic to the development of independent, autonomous, enquiring young people since it rewards learning behaviours which are contrary to those required to support personal meaning-making. They also deny professional recognition to teachers as they negate the power of evaluation to contribute to the learning of their pupils and site power in the authority which sets and marks the tests. An outcome of this is teaching to the tests, and consequent de-professionalisation in terms of both content and pedagogical style.

One alternative is being tried in the UK, the USA and elsewhere:

> The Balanced Assessment (BA) project is funded by the US National Science Foundation. It involves three sites in the USA, in California (based at the University of California at Berkeley), Michigan (based at Michigan State University), and Massachusetts (based at Harvard University), in collaboration with the Shell Centre for Mathematical Education at the University of Nottingham, England, and with consultants from assessment projects in a number of other countries...All are trying to implement, or support, a vision of mathematics instruction that is consistent with, and extends, the vision in recent curricular documents. (Ridgway & Schoenfeld, 1994, p. 2)

It consists of developing personal pupil profiles, or portfolios, which would constitute an account of the learning of that pupil over a specified period. An analogy is drawn with the portfolios which, for example, aspiring artists present to art colleges when applying for entry. The difference in the learning paradigm here is obvious. A portfolio is collected over time, demonstrates development, can exemplify a wide range of activities and interests, and is particular to, and owned by, the student.

A 'Balanced Assessment' produces a 'body of evidence' or portfolio representing a student's work. The evidence is balanced with regard to:
(a) the coverage of content (e.g., 'important mathematics')
(b) process (exploring, conjecture, proof, abstraction, reflection, ...)
(c) type of task (short exercise to extended project)
(d) format of task (short answer to major report). (Ibid., p. 1)

"One of the ambitions of the BA project is to develop tasks which, like Target, are open in all three respects - response, method, and end points. (Target asks students to create the numbers from 1 through 10 using only the keys 3, 4, x, -, and = on a calculator.)" (ibid: 7)   Jim Ridgway and Alan Schoenfeld point to a number of questions in the context of this development. For example, What constitutes an appropriate body of evidence in a portfolio? Does that evidence include information on how that student sustains and develops some mathematics? Should progress in mathematics be quantified by answering the question How much? As freedom of choice increases how does a teacher, and the system, deal with issues of monitoring and control?

The Balanced Assessment Project has been exploring a scheme with four top-level categories, and with more fine-grained elaborations. In short, the top-level category questions are these:
* What does the student know? (content descriptors)
* Can the student think mathematically? (process descriptors)
* What can the student produce?
  (products: reports, investigations, models, etc.)
* How much has the student learned this year? (growth) (Ridgway & Schoenfeld, 1994, p. 16)

Using portfolios in part to demonstrate system health, as well as monitor individual progress, requires a very different set of criteria than simply asking questions about numbers and grades. However, that does not mean that it cannot, and should not, be done. Indeed, in the Australian example given above where assessments are in the hands of teachers, Max Stephens and Robert Money point out that:

Teachers' decisions about the award of grades have to be defensible to their students, and credible across schools. The verification process requires teachers within a school to confer with one another about the application of the assessment criteria, and subsequently to share their assessment with teachers from other schools. This is to ensure that the assessment criteria are consistently applied by each school, and also to ensure the credibility of assessments themselves and their comparability across schools. (1993, p. 168)

Many European countries have similar systems of teacher-based asessments which are monitored regionally across schools (for more detail, see Burton, 1994b). What these systems demonstrate is that valuable system state information can be gathered in ways other than widespread 'objective' testing. What is clear is the way in which quality judgments are embedded in value positions. If those positions remain hidden, the resultant judgments pretend at an objectivity which must be spurious. (For a discussion of the links between quality and equality, see Riley, 1994.)

CONCLUSION

What the evidence offered in this chapter demonstrates is that internationally there is increasing concern about the failure of conventional, traditional systems of teaching mathematics to meet the current needs of individuals and societies. "Over the past decade a remarkable consensus has arisen internationally about the need for change in mathematics instruction at all levels, and about the role that assessment might play in influencing curricula to move in appropriate directions" (Ridgway & Schoenfeld, 1994, p. 2). In some countries, serious attempts are being made to change these traditional systems of mathematics education. With increasing knowledge about how people learn, we are in a stronger and stronger position to make adjustments to systems that in the past have served only a small percentage of the population. The costs of not innovating can be counted at both levels, individually and societially. Many so-called developing countries, eager to emulate their developed neighbours, have rushed to put educational systems in place that are now reproducing the same effects and the same costs as have been regularly reported in Australia, Europe and the USA.

However, the pull of the traditional is extremely strong. For example, with each new technological advance, we slide back into reproductive learning strategies before becoming aware of how the technology can release powerful learning if used differently. Thus, when calculators first appearerd in schools, they were used for checking and providing a quick means of dealing with 'nasty' numbers. Only recently has work in classrooms demonstrated that calculators used as a resource for young children's learning of mathematics are powerful tools to affect their attitudes towards, and knowledge of numbers (see Shuard, Walsh, Goodwin, & Worcster, 1991). Likewise, as computers develop and become more available as learning tools, so their use can change and affect the acquisition and demonstration of mathematical ideas. But this only happens in classrooms which reject the use of computers for making mathematical drill and practice slightly more pupil-friendly or as electronic testers. The technology is a variable in the extremely complex function which describes the links between the learner, their pedagogical environment, and their acquisition of knowledge and skills (see Burton & Jaworski, 1995).

Behind all of this lies the continued lack of resolution of the paradigmatic clash which I described in the Introduction. Not only does this clash remain unresolved by practising mathematicians and teachers of mathematics but it fuels a perception of the discipline by those outside it of an absolute body of knowledge the components of which, once established, are fixed and unchanging. Such misconceptions support those in decision-making roles in maintaining the very structures which sustain the malfunctions which they decry.

> We must attack the naive realism of formal mathematics in quite the same way that we attack naive realism in the sciences in general. Human agency (mathematicians) create a world of objects; a *culture* then applies itself (that is, a network of mathematicians with shared values etc. moves into that world and goes to work) to understanding and explaining those objects. The mathematician creates a world, then gets "born" into and raised in it as a member of a culture; this is a world of chaos for him or her. There are no immediately known, a priori rules. The mathematician now sets about unraveling the nature of that world. (Restivo, 1992, pp. 167-168)

The learner has exactly the same experiences as described above, attempting to make order and 'unravel the nature' of the world of mathematics that s/he is encountering. Pretence at objectivity whether in the content of the learning, or in its assessment, not only damages but fundamentally misrepresents the mathematics to the learner. The work to which reference has been made in this chapter has not dealt, in an overt way, with the problematics of the mathematics curriculum itself. In many ways which are both innovative and creative, attempts are being made to address the pedagogical failures of mathematics, even at higher education level. Such attempts tend to leave entangled performance in mathematics, with attitudes and behaviours that support learning generally (e.g., Does the student work well in a group?). Leal and Abrantes (1993), for example, make clear that their "defined goals not only contemplate the cognitive aspects, but also include affective or social attitudes [so] assessment must also consider these areas." (p.175) If the objective is to change pedagogical style, it is not surprising that these goals are included, if only because of the frequently reported positive attitudinal changes that accompany such curriculum developments. But there is little discussion about the nature of the discipline and of the objects within it which are so revered within curricula. Neither are connections made between the lack of that discussion and the maldistribution of success in mathematics across class, race and sex.

A reasonable agenda for assessment of mathematics education in the coming century cannot be separated, in my view, from an integrated approach to the curriculum, its content and pedagogical context. We must make an attempt to unravel some of the questions raised here about that social content and context but also to develop strategies whereby learners become instrumental in their own learning instead of being seen as the objects of assessment by other agencies.

REFERENCES

Australian Education Council. (1990). *A national statement on mathematics for Australian schools*, Canberra: Curriculum Corporation.

Blane, D. (1992). Curriculum planning, assessment and student learning in mathematics: A top-down approach. In G. Leder (Ed.), *Assessment and learning of mathematic*. Hawthorn, Vic.: Australian Council for Educational Research.

Burton, L. (1984). *Thinking things through*. Oxford: Basil Blackwell.

Burton, L.(1992a). Who assesses whom and to what purpose? In M. Stephens & J. Izard, (Eds.), *Reshaping assessment practices: Assessment in the mathematical sciences under challenge*. Hawthorn, Vic.: Australian Council for Educational Research.

Burton, L. (1992b). Becoming a teacher of mathematics. *Cambridge Journal of Education, 22* (3), 377-386.

Burton, L. (1994a). Clashing epistemologies of mathematics education - Can we see the 'wood' for the 'trees'? *Curriculum Studies, 2* (2), 203-219.

Burton, L.(Ed.). (1994b). *Who counts? Assessing mathematics in Europe*. Stoke-on-Trent: Trentham.

Burton, L., & Jaworski, B. (Eds.). (1995). *Technology - A bridge between teaching and learning*. Bromley, UK: Chartwell-Bratt,

Cockcroft, W.H. (1982). *Mathematics counts*. London: Her Majesty's Stationery Office.

Davis, R.B. (1986). Conceptual and procedural knowledge in mathematics: A summary analysis. In J. Hiebert (Ed.), *Conceptual and procedural knowledge: The case of mathematic.* London: Lawrence Erlbaum.

de Lange, J. (1992). Critical factors for real changes in mathematics learning. In G. Leder (Ed.), *Assessment and learning of mathematics.* Hawthorn, Vic.: Australian Council for Educational Research,

de Lange, J. (1987). *Mathematics, insight and meaning.* Utrecht: OW & OC.

Ferguson, S. (1992). Mathematics profiles. In M. Stephens & J. Izard, (Eds.), *Reshaping assessment practices: Assessment in the mathematical sciences under challenge.* Hawthorn, Vic.: Australian Council for Educational Research.

Fortuny, J.M., Gimenez, J., & Alsina, C. (1994). Integrated assessment of mathematics 12-16. *Educational Studies in Mathematics, Special Issue on Assessment, 27*(4), 401-412.

Joint Matriculation Board/Shell Centre for Mathematical Education. (1985) *The language of functions and graphs: An examination module for secondary schools.* Manchester: Joint Matriculation Board.

Lajoie, S. (1992). A framework for authentic assessment in mathematics. *NCRMSE Research Review, 1* (1), 6-12.

Leal, L. C., & Abrantes, P.(1993). Assessment in an innovative curriculum project for mathematics in grades 7-9 in Portugal. In M. Niss (Ed.), *Cases of assessment in mathematics education.* Dordrecht: Kluwer.

Millroy, W.L. (1992). An ethnographic study of the mathematical ideas of a group of carpenters. *Journal for Research in Mathematics Education Monograph No. 5.* Reston, Va.: NCTM,

Nickson, M., & Prestage, S. (1994). England and Wales. In L. Burton (Ed.), *Who counts? Assessing mathematics in Europe.* Stoke-on-Trent: Trentham.

Nunes, T., Schliemann, A.D., & Carraher, D. (1993). *Street mathematics and school mathematics.* Cambridge: Cambridge University Press,.

Nisbet, J. (1993). Introduction. In: *Curriculum reform: Assessment in question.* Paris: OECD and the Centre for Educational Research and Innovation.

Restivo, S. (1992). *Mathematics in society and history.* Dordrecht: Kluwer.

Ridgway, J. (1988). *Assessing mathematical attainment.* Windsor, Berks: NFER-Nelson.

Ridgway, J., & Passey, D. (1993). An international view of mathematics assessment - through a class, darkly. In M. Niss (Ed.), *Investigations into assessment in mathematics education.* Dordrecht: Kluwer.

Ridgway, J., & Schoenfeld, A. (1994, February). *Balanced Assessment: Designing Assessment Schemes to promote desirable change in mathematics education.* Paper given to the European Electronic Conference on Assessment and Evaluation.

Riley, K. (1994). *Quality and equality.* London: Cassell.

Rogoff, B., & Lave, J. (Eds.). (1984). *Everyday cognition: Its development in social context.* London. Harvard University Press.

Romberg, T.A. (1993). How one comes to know: Models and theories of the learning of mathematics. In M. Niss (Ed.), *Investigations into assessment in mathematics education.* Dordrecht: Kluwer.

Shuard, H., Walsh, A., Goodwin, J., & Worcester, V. (1991). *Calculators, children and mathematics.* London: Simon & Schuster.

Stephens, M. (1993). Valuing and fostering mathematical writing in the Victorian certificate of education. In M. Stephens, A. Waywood, D. Clarke, & J. Izard (Eds.), *Communicating mathematics: Perspectives from classroom practice and current research.* Hawthorn, Vic.: Australian Council for Educational Research.

Stephens, M., & Money, R. (1993). New developments in senior secondary assessment in Australia. In M. Niss (Ed.), *Cases of assessment in mathematics education.* Dordrecht: Kluwer.

Thomas, K. (1990). *Gender and subject in higher education.* Buckingham: Open University Press.

Treffers, A. (1986). *Three dimensions.* Dordrecht: Reidel.

The Ripple Effect:
The Instructional Impact of the
Systemic Introduction of
Performance Assessment in Mathematics

David Clarke and
Max Stephens

INTRODUCTION

Mathematics assessment recently has been primarily directed towards increasing the degree of correspondence between the intended curriculum, the taught curriculum, the learned curriculum, and the assessed curriculum. In the past, countries such as Australia, in attempting to assess the taught curriculum, have limited their assessment to timed and written tests, where the major focus has been on facts or skills. It is becoming increasingly evident that exclusive reliance on this form of testing is inappropriate: misrepresenting mathematics, at odds with contemporary curricula, misleading in the information it provides teachers, and potentially destructive in its effects on some learners (Clarke, 1992).

Internationally, we find many initiatives in the area of assessment. The criteria by which changes to assessment are advocated vary. Niss (1993), for example, points to recently established changes in curricular content and to changes in forms of student work in school mathematics, and asserts that these changes have not been matched by corresponding developments in the forms of assessment. Van Reeuwijk (1993) has associated traditional mathematics education with a product orientation, in which mathematical knowledge is defined as skills and facts to be tested. The form of assessment advocated by van Reeuwijk and his colleagues at the Freudenthal Institute (The Netherlands) derives its principles from a conception of *realistic mathematics education* which can be traced back to the work of Freudenthal (Streefland, 1991). The tasks which characterise this perspective are typically purposeful, contextually-specific, and to some extent open-ended, and they provide a vehicle for the demonstration and development of problem solving, communication, reasoning, making connections, and other higher order skills.

Swan (1993), by contrast, imposes the criteria of *balance* and *curriculum validity* on the design of assessment tasks. Swan's notion of balance finds its echo in many international attempts to model mathematics through multi-component assessment packages. His use of curriculum validity is more idiosyncratic and demands that "assessment tasks themselves must represent activities of high educational value so that significant time spent on them will represent a benefit rather than a loss of pupils' learning" (Swan, 1993, p. 199). The demand that assessment should be educational imposes new burdens on those responsible for developing assessment tasks and on those who must act on the information such tasks provide.

Recent American interest in *performance assessment* underlines a view of what it is to know and do mathematics and seeks through assessment to model the types of performances which constitute the goals of the new curriculum (NCTM, 1992). This view is supported by Amit and Hillman (1994):

> Performance assessment activities encourage students to demonstrate their knowledge. Open-ended, real-world problems allow for multiple levels and types of solutions with the potential to provide information about students' higher order thinking. (p.4)

Within this vision, it is expected that student responses will encompass more than just "answers", but will include conjectures, strategies and justifications which have been used in the solution of complex mathematical problems.

The alternative visions of mathematical behaviour, which can be found in the writing referred to above and in contemporary curriculum documents (AEC, 1991; NCTM, 1989), demand alternative forms of assessment. The realization of the new assessment agenda requires tasks which provide pupils with the opportunity to engage in mathematical thinking in a variety of forms and contexts, and at different levels of sophistication.

THE VICTORIAN CERTIFICATE OF EDUCATION

Assessment is being conceived both in Australia and internationally as a catalyst for systemic reform in mathematics education. Experiences in Britain and Australia support this view; there it has been suggested that changes in mathematics assessment at the senior secondary level have been associated with extensive changes in instructional and assessment practices throughout the school system. This curricular "ripple effect" has yet to be demonstrated by any systematic study. Attempts to model mathematical behaviour in assessment systems have recently led to the development of multiple-component systems, such as the senior secondary mathematics assessment in most Australian states. In the various Australian states and territories, a range of prototype assessment tasks is emerging for use in primary and secondary schools, including multiple choice questions in simple and enhanced formats, questions which require explicit responses, open-ended questions in specified content domains, questions which require extended answers with different degrees of explicit cueing and guidance to students, as well as more open-ended investigative tasks and problem solving activities (Stephens, 1992). Application of the "ripple effect" argument is predicated on a belief that curriculum, teaching practice, and forms of assessment in the junior and middle secondary years will replicate practices arising from the implementation of changed assessment at the senior secondary level. However, the question remains as to whether teachers of junior and middle secondary mathematics find in this expanded range of assessment practices and the instructional correlates an opportunity to increase the effectiveness of their teaching, or simply additional administrative and organizational burdens, which increase their workload in ways that ultimately reduce rather than enhance the quality of their instruction.

In the Victorian Certificate of Education, which forms the focus of this study, students complete a multiple-choice skills test, an extended answer analytic test, a 10-hour *Challenging Problem*, and a 20-hour *Investigative Project* (Victorian Curriculum and Assessment Board, 1990). Each of these components is weighted equally in its contribution to the final grade, and all are intended in their totality to model mathematical behaviour in a variety of contexts and forms. Similar innovations in assessment have been introduced in other Australian States and Territories. The Challenging Problem and the Investigative Project components best characterise the shift in curriculum and assessment embodied in the VCE Mathematics. Two examples illustrate these two task types.

Example 1. The Investigative Project

This task, presented in Figure 1, is one of three *Starting Points* from which students were required to select one as the topic for their Investigative Project. All parts of the problem were to be answered.

**MATHEMATICAL METHODS 1994
INVESTIGATIVE PROJECT**

PROBLEM 1

1. x^α and beyond
In this starting point you will explore the behaviour of functions of the form $y = x^\alpha$ defined on their maximum real domain and for different values of α where α is a rational number. In particular, you will be required to identify key points such as maxima or minima or points of inflexion. You will then try to extend your investigation to the sums of such functions.
a.
i. First consider positive integer values of $\alpha, \alpha = 1, 2, 3, \ldots$ In general, for which values of α does the curve have a minimum value at $x = 0$? Sketch the general shape of such a curve.

ii. For which values of α does the curve $y = x^\alpha$ have a point of inflexion? Sketch the general shape of such a curve. (Note: A point of inflexion is a point where a curve crosses its tangent without doubling back on itself. Alternatively, a point of inflexion can be thought of as the point where a curve changes the direction of its concavity — see the diagram below. A stationary point of inflexion is a special case of a point of inflexion.)

Figure 1 (cont.)

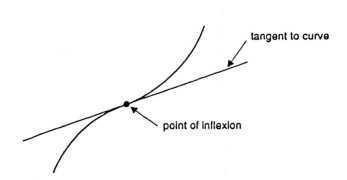

tangent to curve

point of inflexion

b.
i.   Now consider the reciprocals of the positive integer values: 1/2, 1/3, 1/4, ... For which values of α is the function $y = x^\alpha$ defined for all x? Describe the behaviour of the tangent to $y = x^\alpha$ at $x = 0$. For which values of α does $y = x^\alpha$ have a minimum at $x = 0$?

ii.   Sketch graphs of $y = x^\alpha$ for other positive fractional values of α, for example $\alpha = \frac{2}{3}$ or $\alpha = \frac{3}{4}$. What is the domain of each of these functions? (Note: Some computer packages may not graph these functions over their whole domain.) How can you predict the type of graph or the domain of the function from the value of α? Does it matter whether $x^{\frac{2}{3}}$ is interpreted as $\left(x^{\frac{2}{3}}\right)$ or $\left(x^2\right)^{\frac{1}{3}}$? Consider this question for other values of α. There are curves $y = x^\alpha$ where a minimum at $x = 0$ is not detected by the condition $\frac{dy}{dx} = 0$. Identify and sketch several such curves. What is the value of $\frac{dy}{dx}$ at $x = 0$ in these cases?

c.   Extension
i.   Consider how the behaviour of $y = x^\alpha$ at a minimum or inflexion point is affected by adding or subtracting another function $y = x^\beta$, to get $x^\alpha \pm x^\beta$. Investigate integer values of α and β first. Can maxima or minima or points of inflexion be created or destroyed by this process? Give several examples which justify your answer. Explain how a point of inflexion may be recognised from the graph of $\frac{dy}{dx}$.

Figure 1 (cont.)

---

ii. Some curves $y = x^\alpha$ have a cusp at $x = 0$, a sharp point like the spine on a holly leaf as shown in the diagram below.

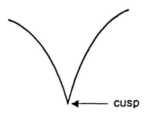

Give several examples of curves which have this property. If a function $y = x^\alpha$ has a cusp, what can you say about $y = x^\alpha + x, y = x^\alpha + x^2$? Devise a curve that has cusps at $x = 0$ and $x = 1$, and sketch its graph.

iii. Devise and sketch another curve of the form $y = x^\alpha \pm x^\beta$ with another combination of features, for example, a cusp and a point of inflexion.

Figure 1: The Investigative Project

The three *Starting Points* for the Investigative Project were centrally designed. The selected Project was undertaken by students over a four-week period, using a mix of in-class and out-of-class time. Students' Project Reports were then graded by their teachers using assessment criteria provided with the Project. During the four-week period, students were required to submit a first draft of their Report and to revise this in the light of critical comment provided by the class teacher.

Example 2.   The Challenging Problem

This task, presented in Figure 2, was one of four centrally-designed problems from which students were required to select one for completion over a period of two weeks.

SPACE AND NUMBER 1990
CHALLENGING PROBLEM

PROBLEM 3   Linkages

There are a number of different ways in which rigid bars can be linked in order to produce straight line motion. The diagrams below show two sets of linked bars. For each of these linkages to produce straight line motion, the hinged joints at **A** and **C** have to be fixed to the plan a fixed distance apart. The other joints are hinged, but are not fixed to the plane.

Figure 3 contains five bars **AB**, **BP**, **PD**, **DC** and **EF**. Relationships between the different bars are shown.

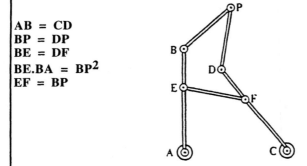

AB = CD
BP = DP
BE = DF
BE.BA = BP^2
EF = BP

Figure 3

Which point moves in a straight line? Where is this line? What distance between **A** and **C** will result in straight line motion?

Figure 4 contains seven bars **AO**, **BO**, **AR**, **QR**, **PQ**, **BR** and **BC**. Relationships between the different bars are shown.

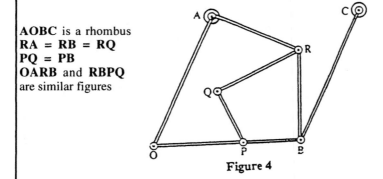

AOBC is a rhombus
RA = RB = RQ
PQ = PB
OARB and **RBPQ**
are similar figures

Figure 4

Which point moves in a straight line? Where is this line?

Figure 2: The Challenging Problem

The selected Challenging Problem was undertaken by students using a mix of in-class and out-of-class time. It was required that students' Problem Solving Reports be organized under three main headings: Defining the problem; Solution and justification; Solution process. These Problem Solving Reports were then graded by their teachers using assessment criteria and solution notes provided with the Challenging Problem. During the two week period, students were required to submit a first draft of their Report and to revise this in the light of critical comment provided by the class teacher.

THE RIPPLE EFFECT

This study employs the imagery of the Ripple Effect metaphor in seeking to identify the mechanisms whereby the mathematical performances demanded by new *high-stakes* assessment tasks, which unquestionably lead to a restructuring of instructional practice at those levels at which the new assessment is implemented, trigger changes in instruction and assessment at grade levels prior to those immediately subject to the new assessment. If the hypothesized Ripple Effect is observed in Years 7 to 10, should the motivation for the change be attributed to:

- a desire on the part of teachers and school administrators to commence the preparation of students for the new assessment as early as possible (given its high-stakes nature);
- a desire on the part of school administrators for curricular uniformity, taking the mandated elements as a base;
- a reconceived notion of mathematical activity (redefined in the new assessment tasks), endorsed and adopted by mathematics teachers;
- a reconceived notion of mathematical assessment, implemented at the policy and practice levels;
- the creation of a *climate of change* as a consequence of the mandated assessment changes, which then facilitates change in areas other than those involving the new assessment;
- a paradigm shift in the mathematics education community as a whole, such that both the changes to mandated assessment and the chances to instructional and assessment practice elsewhere in the school should be seen simply as symptoms of an underlying movement for change?

It is not suggested that the above alternatives are mutually exclusive. The goal of this study was to establish the existence (or otherwise) of the Ripple Effect and to identify the mechanisms and motivations which characterize it. This characterization will be empirical rather than theoretical in nature, and should inform the activities of those seeking to change the curriculum. In their evaluation of the VCE implementation after three years, Northfield et al. (1992) report that:

> Almost without exception teachers of Year 7 to 10 indicated that there were changes in work practices of junior students as a result of the VCE. Many schools were introducing the terminology of VCE. Work requirements were being specified commonly in Years 9 to 10. Some extreme cases have seen work requirements and even CATs [Common Assessment Tasks] introduced as far down as Year 7, although one suspects that, in many instances, this is little more than renaming an end of term test as a CAT. (pp. 31-32)

Our study suggests that the extent of change in instruction and assessment practices is much more than the "nominal change" (Romberg & Price, 1984) implied by Northfield et al. The principal thesis encapsulated in the Ripple Effect is that the introduction of new assessment practices into existing high stakes assessment creates a climate of change which has immediate and direct consequences for policy and instruction at the level of school and classroom. This change climate functions to stimulate and support the introduction of specific practices. The emergent hypothesis is that unless a term or practice receives the explicit sanction of inclusion in high stakes assessment it is unlikely to influence school policy or classroom practice. In all schools participating in this study the end of term tests were no longer the only form of assessment. In all schools, assessment through substantial problem solving activities or investigations had become a significant component of a much more elaborate assessment scheme than had been in operation prior to the introduction of the VCE. In some schools, end of term tests had disappeared altogether, although the assessment of conventional mathematical skills and applications continued through various forms of continuous (that is, progressive) assessment, alongside the assessment of problem solving and investigations.

The research discussed in this report comprises a study into the instructional effects in Year 7 to 10 mathematics classes of changed assessment practices in the senior secondary years. It is anticipated that the findings and the methodology employed in this study will be applied in similar studies in other Australian states where similar changes in assessment practices have occurred, and that the study itself could be replicated elsewhere.

Sample

Schools were selected by a process of theoretical sampling to include the following characteristics: rural and metropolitan, government and non-government schools, and social demographic characteristics (including ethnicity and language). The variation in Victorian schools with respect to these characteristics has been encompassed effectively in a sample of eleven schools. Only schools providing instruction for Years 7 to 12 were included in the sample.

The Three-Stage Design

Stage One

Stage one of the study involved the analysis of documents relating to the mathematics curriculum, teaching practice, and assessment and reporting in mathematics from eleven Victorian high schools. This revealed extensive adoption of the distinctive features of the VCE *Mathematics Study Design* (VCAB, 1990), and its multi-component assessment scheme. The document analysis charted the impact of these changes in nomenclature on the structure and practice of the mathematics curriculum in Years 7 to 10. This first stage of the study strongly confirmed the impact of changed assessment practices in Years 11 and 12 on curriculum policy and practice, and on how mathematics is taught and assessed throughout secondary school. This impact was investigated with respect to the following areas: school policy, curriculum and teaching, assessment, and reporting.

Stage Two

In stage two, the detail of changes in practice which had been inferred from the document analysis were reassessed through questionnaire and interview. In particular, the second stage documented respondents' perceptions of the changes in administration, curriculum planning, classroom instruction, and assessment in the junior and middle secondary years, which were perceived as being linked to the curriculum and assessment practices of VCE mathematics.

In stage two, teachers on selected school sites throughout Victoria completed questionnaires related to their current teaching practices at Years 7 to 10, their involvement in the VCE, and their reports of valued teaching practices and the frequency of use of these. The essential purpose of stage two was to address the question: Is the documentary evidence of changed classroom practice sustained in teachers' accounts of their instruction?

Stage Three

Stage 3 investigated teachers' articulation of the value systems that distinguished the rationale underlying teachers' introduction of the new practices. It was also intended to associate teacher characteristics and beliefs with actual differences in classroom implementation, where possible.

Methodology

Document analysis

Stage one of the study involved the analysis of documents relating to the mathematics curriculum, teaching practice, as well as to assessment and reporting in mathematics from eleven Victorian high schools. This revealed extensive adoption of the distinctive features of the VCE *Mathematics Study Design* (VCAB, 1990), and its multi-component assessment scheme. The document analysis charted the impact of these changes in nomenclature on the structure and practice of the mathematics curriculum in Years 7 to 10.

This phase of the study centres on the analysis of relevant school documents. The aim of the study is to obtain sufficient data to adequately portray current practice on each of the school sites, and also to document the recent origins of current practice, and the immediate consequences of the introduction of the VCE. This document analysis is intended to reveal both professed practice and structural change.

Document characteristics
The following sources of information were requested from the participating schools in order to indicate significant aspects of mathematics teaching in Years 7 - 10 which could be associated with changed assessment practices in senior mathematics:

- course planning documents (e.g., course outlines, syllabuses)
- information to parents/students regarding course options and requirements
- sample assessment tasks
- sample of student assignments and project work

- school report forms
- teaching notes
- other school-developed support material for teachers

In addition, school communications with the researchers provided further valuable data on the practical implementation of assessment-related curricular changes.

Content analysis

Each document was analyzed with respect to the occurrence of key terms (words or phrases). For the purposes of this study, a term was considered significant if it met either one of two criteria:

- the term represented a change in practice
- the term matched a corresponding term found in VCE documentation

Lists were compiled of such significant terms, grouped initially according to the source document. Within the compiled lists of terms, it was possible to distinguish three categories of curricular change:

1. Change in nomenclature (terminology)

For inclusion in this category, the use of a term in a school document was taken to represent change at the level of description, without necessarily implying a consequent change in practice.

2. Change in structure

Some terms could be taken as indicative of new structures for assessment and instruction. For example, the specific inclusion of investigative projects and problem solving tasks as separate components within school-based course planning documents and reports to parents represented a structural change in the school mathematics curriculum. The degree of change at the level of teacher or student practice could not be inferred necessarily from the structural inclusion of such elements.

3. Change in practice

The inclusion in sample tasks of terms such as *predict, model, draft and re-draft,* and *format* (in relation to the writing of students' reports of extended projects or problem solving activity) indicated changes in both teacher and student classroom practice. Likewise, the use of criteria specifically derived from the assessment of problem solving and investigations within VCE mathematics indicates a significant qualitative change in the conception of desired mathematical behaviours in the junior secondary school.

Questionnaire design

Teachers on selected school sites throughout Victoria completed questionnaires related to their current teaching practices at Years 7 to 10, their involvement in the VCE, and their reports of valued teaching practices and the frequency of use of these. The essential purpose of stage two was to address the following question: Is the documentary evidence of changed classroom practice sustained in teachers' accounts of their instruction?

The second stage documented respondents' perceptions of the changes in administration, curriculum planning, classroom instruction, and assessment in the junior and middle secondary years, which were perceived as being linked to the curriculum and assessment practices of VCE mathematics

Sample selection

In writing to the eleven schools, the researchers asked each head of department to nominate several teachers of mathematics who would be invited to respond to the questionnaire. In addition to the head of department, it was suggested that other teachers invited to participate in the questionnaire phase should include those with current or previous teaching experience of VCE mathematics and those with no current or previous teaching experience of VCE mathematics in Years 11 or 12. This split in the sample was intended to allow the researchers to test the hypothesis that VCE-derived practices might be more evident or more clearly affirmed in teaching and assessment of mathematics in Years 7 to 10 among those who had personal experience of implementing related practices in Years 11 or 12 than among those who had no direct experience of teaching VCE mathematics.

Questionnaire analysis

Respondents were required to indicate the degree of importance they attached to each of several specific teaching, assessment and reporting practices. The questionnaire included practices specifically derived from VCE documents (for example, work requirements and investigative projects), but it also included other practices of current interest or advocacy within the mathematics education community (for example, student mathematics journals and student self-assessment). A four-point scale was used: *highly important, of some importance, beneficial but not essential, of little importance.* Variation in the degree of importance attached to each of these was analyzed with repect to:
- current VCE teaching
- previous VCE teaching
- nature of teaching responsibility
- level of teaching experience

Interviews

Stage 3 investigated teachers' articulation of the value systems that distinguished the rationale underlying teachers' introduction of the new practices. It was also possible to associate teacher characteristics and beliefs with actual differences in classroom implementation. Two questions were uppermost in the design of the interviews:

To what degree did teachers hold shared meanings of the key elements of the assessment and teaching practices identified in the first two stages of this study as consequences of the Ripple Effect?
What consistency of meaning was attached to other elements of assessment and teaching practice, reported in the first two stages, but which were not formally sanctioned by inclusion in the VCE Study Design?

Interview data facilitated the elaboration of the differences between groups such as experienced teachers and those relatively new to the profession in their implementation of changed assessment and instructional practices and in the value they attached to these new practices.

Content validity

How is the Ripple Effect characterized in terms of reported classroom practice? The essential criteria by which a specific practice was taken to constitute evidence of the hypothesized Ripple Effect were:

- That a specific term introduced through VCE documentation was replicated in either school documents, questionnaire responses or interview statements in relation to instruction or assessment at Years 7 to 10.
- The form in which a particular instructional or assessment practice was embodied in Years 7 to 10 closely resembled the form in which that practice had been introduced through the VCE.
- Statements were made by teachers on questionnaires or in interviews which explicitly linked these practices to those advocated within the VCE; in particular, statements indicating that particular assessment and instructional practices in Years 7 to 10 were derived or adapted from corresponding practices in Years 11 and 12.

A Descriptive Framework for the Ripple Effect Study

In documenting the form taken by the Ripple Effect, data analysis was organized around the following three domains. The relevant data source from each phase of the study is indicated by the coding D (Document Analysis), Q (Questionnaire), I (Interview).

Impact on School Policy
To what extent does school policy for the teaching and assessment of mathematics in Years 7 to 10 replicate the structural elements of the new VCE?
[D, Q]

Evidence of the Adoption of VCE-derived Practices
To what extent are teaching and assessment practices inherent in VCE mathematics evident in the teaching of mathematics in Years 7 to 10?
[D, Q, I]

Attribution by teachers of classroom practice in Years 7 to 10 to those practices inherent in the VCE.
[Q, I]

Is there evidence of the widespread use of a new vocabulary, demonstrably derived from the VCE, by which mathematical activity at Years 7 to 10 is described?
[D, Q, I]

Evidence of Shared Beliefs and Common Values Underpinning Changed Practice
Is there evidence of congruency of meaning and purpose in the way assessment and instruction is conceived in the VCE and in Years 7 to 10?
[Q, I]

RESULTS

Stage One Results: The Document Analysis

Documented Change

The results of the document analysis can be reported as indicative of change in four key areas: Policy; Curriculum and Teaching; Assessment; and Reporting. Analysis of the occurrence of *Work Requirements* in the various documents is used in the following discussion as an illustrative example both of the methodology used in this document analysis and of the manner in which elements characteristic of VCE mathematics assessment find their embodiment in each of these four key areas.

Changes in Policy

The VCE *Mathematics Study Design* frames a curriculum in terms of specific Work Requirements. These prescribe the sorts of activities in which students must engage for the satisfactory completion of classwork. In their course planning for Years 11 and 12, teachers are required to allocate significant proportions of classtime to all of the work requirements. There is also a direct correspondence between the work requirements and the components of assessment. In mathematics, three Work Requirements are specified: Investigative Projects, Problem Solving and Modelling Activities, and Skills Practice and Standard Applications. In their policy documents for Years 7 to 10, all eleven participating schools had adopted the VCE practice of using the three work requirement categories of extended mathematical projects, problem solving and skills practice to describe their mathematics courses. The actual term *work requirements* was used in the policy documents of eight of the eleven schools. The absence of this term from the policy documents of the other three schools should not be taken as indicative of reduced importance attached to investigative projects and problems in those schools. Two non-government schools, while omitting the term work requirements itself, paid very clear attention to problem solving and investigations in their policy documents. The third school, which has a background in technical and vocational education, included in its course objectives for Years 7 and 8 a focus on analysing and solving practical problems, as well as work on basic mathematical skills and concepts. The description of the mathematics program for Year 9 at this school spoke of "focussing more on problem solving and practical applications". In this school's course description for Year 10, "skills of investigation, problem solving and modelling" were explicitly stated. The point being made is that whether or not the term work requirements was employed in school documents, all eleven schools had recognized an extended range of mathematical performance derived from the VCE.

By way of example, the "Year 7 Information Booklet and Course Details" from one school specifically listed as "work requirements in order to achieve satisfactory completion of a unit" such activities as: "set exercises", "project work", "problem solving", "a written summary of work covered", and a "self assessment". The impact of the work requirements for VCE Mathematics is therefore quite direct in the sense that work requirements are intended to specify what will be included in the school mathematics curriculum and what will be assessed. Whether work requirements are reported on separately, as in the case of VCE, in terms of their satisfactory or non-satisfactory completion will be discussed later in this report.

Changes in Curriculum and Teaching

Within course documents produced by the mathematics departments in all participating schools, problem solving tasks and investigative projects were elaborated for teachers and students in very specific terms strongly resembling those used in VCE curriculum documents. The mathematics department in one non-government school had even developed "Problem Solving Teaching Notes" with subsections such as "Some suggestions on how to teach problem solving", and "Problem Solving Students Notes" aimed at clarifying the nature of mathematical problem solving for students and with specific attention to the demands of non-routine mathematical tasks. In the majority of schools problem solving and investigations were clearly distinguished in the documents provided. However, in three of the eleven schools, head teachers of mathematics reported that there could be some blurring in practice between problem solving and investigations. The school with a technical/vocational emphasis reported that their problem solving tasks were drawn from technical studies and the emphasis was on applying a mathematical justification to problems drawn from these contexts. In a second school, the head of mathematics was unsure whether problem solving tasks and investigations were being included in all classes. In this school there were no formal checks as to whether individual teachers were implementing these elements to the same degree. In the third school, common assessment tasks at each year level ensured that extended non-routine mathematical tasks formed a significant part of the curriculum in Years 7 to 10. Based on the documents provided, these common assessment tasks favoured independent investigations rather than problem solving as conceived within the VCE. On the basis of evidence provided by these three schools, it is possible that the distinction between problem solving and investigative project work is more difficult to embody in the curriculum of Years 7 to 10 than within the more sophisticated mathematics of the VCE.

Six schools provided samples of problem solving tasks and investigative projects. These activities are substantial, ranging from those which require short one-page reports of a problem solving activity in Year 7 to those which require more extended reports in Years 9 and 10. In these years, the procedures for developing a report, and the suggested format for reports, more closely resemble those required for the VCE. At one school, "Consultations and evidence of drafting" were required to be recorded by those students in Years 9 and 10 submitting reports of problem solving or investigative project work. A sample of an investigative project used in Year 8 in one of the study schools is provided in Figure 3.

The Surface Area of a Person's Skin

The skin area of the human body is important particularly in cases of skin damage associated with severe burns. Medical doctors assess the area of skin loss by the 'rule of nine', whereby the body is divided into nine main areas, making up 99% of the skins surface area. A burns patient has a poor chance of survival if more than 33% of their body skin is burnt.

Your task in this project is to determine the surface area of your own skin, and that of at least two other people. It would be better to choose people of various stages of physical development, e.g., say a 10 year old, say somebody over 20 years, etc.

Figure 3 (cont.)

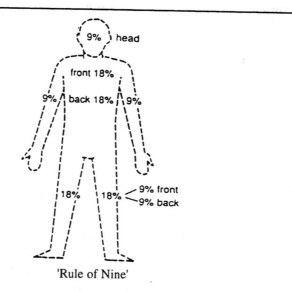

'Rule of Nine'

You will need to calculate skin areas using - (1) the surface area of the palm of a hand, which represents 1% of body skin area. And (2) the surface area of the arm, which represents 9% of body skin area.

Your detailed calculations should be shown in your report, as should any explanations of your workings.

You should comment on the two values of your skin area, and suggest which value may be more accurate, giving any reasons why. This should also be done for the other people you have measured.

Extension

How many times can your skin area fit onto the area of a Volley Ball court?

Figure 3. An Investigative Project

The above task is structured, contextualized, and open-ended. Students are not directed as to what method should be used. Rather, students are expected to devise a suitable method to represent and quantify an area of skin and to meet the other mathematical demands of the task. The expected components of the report to be submitted are made clear, but in general terms. The conclusion of one student's report, together with the teacher's grading of the report are provided in Figure 4. The teacher's assessment criteria are clearly shown. These criteria were discussed with students upon commencement of the project. There is a high level of similarity between these criteria and those provided to teachers for use in grading the VCE "Investigative Project" Common Assessment Task. The similarity is evident in both the criteria used and the three-point grading scale applied to each criterion in the following example, Student Work and Teacher's Assessment Criteria:

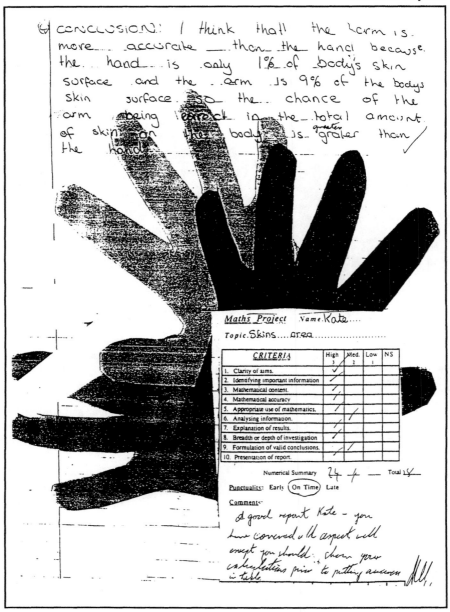

Figure 4. Sample of Student Work (Conclusion) and Teacher's Assessment Criteria

Documentary evidence of the kind provided by these samples can only be illustrative and suggestive of what might be general practice. A key factor in shaping teachers' practice with regard to problem solving and investigative project work is how these tasks are assessed and whether they are included as separate items within term or semester reports to parents.

The question remains as to whether teachers in their classroom practice make a firm distinction between problem solving tasks and extended mathematical investigations. This issue was discussed with the head of mathematics in each school, and was probed in several items of the questionnaire administered in the next stage of the study.

Changes in Assessment

Changed assessment practices were evident in:
- the tasks which comprised a school assessment package;
- what students were expected to do in those tasks; and
- how the tasks themselves were assessed.

In all eleven schools, course documents outlined the clear expectation that the assessment of problem solving and investigative projects, together with the assessment of standard mathematical skills and applications, should contribute to students' overall assessment in mathematics. It was essential to establish whether the implementation of this assessment policy was uniform or a matter for the discretion of the individual teacher. One way of ascertaining the importance attached to problem solving tasks and investigative projects is to determine whether they have been incorporated into the school's formal structures of assessment and reporting. A first step was to examine whether a school's assessment practices had changed as a consequence of inclusion of a broadened range of mathematical performance.

In our analysis, the eleven schools could be divided into three subgroups:
Group 1.   School assessments based solely on descriptive reports.
Group 2.   School assessments which formally include reference to "satisfactory/non-satisfactory completion", sometimes together with other elements such as grades.
Group 3.   School assessments based primarily on grades, with the avoidance of the terms "satisfactory/non-satisfactory".

Only in one school was it difficult to infer the degree of change from the documentation provided and from discussion with the head of mathematics. This school, along with the other Group 1 school, continued to use descriptive reporting with the responsibility for gathering assessment information left to individual teachers. In the latter school, descriptive assessments continued to be used, but the head of mathematics reported that his department was "trying to upgrade assessment so that there is a gradual transition from Year 7 to 10 in picking up the language and criteria of the VCE". Six other schools (Group 2) used the VCE-derived term "satisfactory or non-satisfactory completion" with regard to problem solving tasks and investigations, together with descriptive assessments. In four of these six schools, grades (such as A, B, C, D) were not used at all. However, in two of these four schools the head of department reported that, while individual pieces of student work were not graded, teachers provided comments "for improvement". Such qualitative feedback on specific pieces of students' work was described by one head of department as a "subtle use of VCE criteria". This appeared to be especially true for those teachers who had experience of assessing students' work in Years 11 and 12. In the remaining two schools of this sub-group, grades were assigned to problem solving tasks and investigations, and these grades were based on modifications of the criteria used in the VCE for these assessment tasks. The three schools in Group 3 used grades and, in one case, percentage marks, interpreted as a five-point letter-grade scale, to assess problem solving tasks and investigations. In this third school it was not clear whether the criteria used for assessment in VCE Mathematics were influential in determining actual scores. In the other two schools, the VCE criteria were modified and applied to common assessment tasks for each year level.

Other features of assessment in VCE Mathematics were also evident. A key feature of the Investigative Project CAT is the use of the project report format, which sets out not only the headings under which the report should be prepared but also key mathematical elements that are to be included. The project report format at one school specified key mathematical considerations to be included in the various sections. For example, in the section labelled "Conclusions" we find the following:

> In this section, the results of the project should be brought together, evaluated and related to the stated aims. The conclusions should include discussion of the more important limitations of the investigation and possible further investigation suggested by the results.

In preparing a report of a problem solving activity, students at this school are required to present not only a solution, but to give explicit attention to a statement of the problem, the solution process which they have followed, and to carefully justify both the solution and the steps which have led to it. The similarity with VCE assessment requirements is obvious and quite deliberate.

In assessing reports of problem solving activities and investigative projects, teachers almost without exception have adapted the criteria for assessment of the corresponding components in the VCE. The number of separate criteria is frequently reduced, and they are sometimes tailored to suit a specific problem solving assignment. For example, in the assessment of a Year 8 project on Pick's Rule, eight criteria were used, each being graded, as in the VCE, as *not shown, low, medium* and *high*. The use of the VCE coding *not shown, low, medium* and *high* appeared to be quite general among the schools sampled.

Changes in Reporting

In this final phase of the document analysis, we sought further evidence that the assessment of problem solving tasks and investigations had been incorporated into the formal structures of assessment and reporting. Had separate space been given in end of term or semester reports for reporting assessments of students' completion and performance in these two areas? In all but two schools, this was the case. In one school, teachers were free to report on whatever assessment information they had considered appropriate. This appeared to be the case in a second school, except that, for reports in Year 10 mathematics, explicit attention to problem solving was required. Among the nine schools where problem solving and investigations were specifically included in term or semester reports, there were differences in how these components were to be reported upon. As discussed earlier, five schools used the VCE-derived term, *satisfactory completion*, to report on problem solving tasks and investigations as set out in course handbooks. In two of these five schools, letter grades were also used to report on student performance in each of these areas. In the remaining three schools of this sub-group, which incidentally were all non-government schools, letter grades were used to report separately on problem solving and investigations.

One example serves to convey a picture of changed reporting practices. Among the schools participating in this study, one reported to parents on "Group investigation and oral reports to class". Evaluative and numerical grades were provided on the "Oral presentation", the "Prepared written presentation", "Research undertaken - depth, breadth and appropriateness", "Explanations and answers to questions", and "Use of mathematics and conventions" in the pro-forma employed in reporting to parents. This explicit acknowledgement of aspects of student mathematical activity which had not previously formed a part of school communication to parents can be explicitly linked to the VCE.

In summary, the significant changes in reporting appeared to include:
- report format;
- the nature of the student activities reported upon; and,
- the manner in which the information was conveyed.

A new vocabulary of assessment and reporting was in evidence, and this could be traced directly to VCE terminology and practice.

Stage Two Results: The Questionnaire

The questionnaire sample

The total sample comprised fifty teachers, with the number of teachers per site ranging from 2 to 6 with a median of of 5. The sample of teachers across all eleven schools included 13 teachers who responded as heads of department, the greater number being due to the fact that in one school the section of Years 7 to 12 was divided into a junior, middle and senior secondary structure with three teachers assuming responsibility for mathematics at each level. There were 37 other respondents who were not heads of department, all of whom were teaching in Years 7 to 10. It should be noted that not all heads of department were currently teaching at Years 7 to 10, and for that reason they did not complete a section of the questionnaire dealing with current teaching practice in Years 7 to 10. The final sample included 15 teachers without previous VCE experience. The sample included comparable proportions teaching each of Years 7, 8, 9, and 10. Within the sample, it was possible to access a wide range of teaching experience (from those comparatively new to teaching to some with over 25 years of teaching experience). The sample included 34 teachers currently teaching VCE mathematics, either at Year 11 or at Year 12 level. Thirty-five teachers, currently teaching in Years 7 to 10 across the eleven sites had current or recent experience in teaching VCE mathematics. Fifteen teachers currently teaching mathematics in Years 7 to 10 had no experience of teaching VCE mathematics. For the purposes of statistical analysis, three categories of teaching experience were created: New (6 years or less), Established (7 to 15 years), and Veteran (over 15 years). In all, there were 6 teachers in the first category , 15 in the second, and 29 in the third. For those teachers with previous experience of teaching VCE mathematics, the mean number of years of teaching VCE at Year 11 was 2.4 years, and 1.6 years at Year 12. For two teachers, previous experience went back to 1989 when VCE mathematics was first accredited in Year 11, and to 1990 for Year 12.

Problem solving activities and investigations

The proportion of classtime which teachers reported giving to small scale investigations and to problem solving activities at Years 7 to 10 is recorded in Table 1.

Table 1
Proportion of Classtime Reported by Teachers as Being Given to Small Scale Investigations and Problem Solving Activities in Years 7 to 10

Proportion of classtime reported as given to the activity type(%)	Small scale investigations No. respondents (percentage of sample)	Problem solving activities No. respondents. (percentage of sample)
0 to < 10	7(16)	6(14)
10 to < 20	21(49)	20(45)
20 to < 30	12(28)	15(34)
30 to < 40	3(7)	3(7)

Respondents were asked to indicate the degree of importance they attached to each of the aspects described below. A four-point scale was used (*highly important, of some importance, beneficial but not essential, of little importance*) to allow teachers to indicate their purposes in using problem solving activities and investigations with respect to the following aspects. The percentage responses of teachers who indicated that a particular aspect of problem solving or investigation was *highly important* is given alongside each item.

Students developing investigative skills (74%)
The use of different mathematical skills in combination (72%)
Teaching problem solving skills (69%)
Presenting problems which require a range of problem solving techniques (67%)
As preparation for these work requirements for the VCE (66%)
The application of mathematics to real world contexts (66%)
Developing students' report writing skills (55%)
Using problem solving to develop mathematical skills (54%)
Presenting problems spanning a range of content areas in mathematics (45%)
Using problems specific to the topic being taught (45%)
Providing students with substantial written comment on their problem solving attempts (36%)
Students undertaking an extended mathematical activity (32%)
Students undertaking open-ended mathematical activities (30%)
Students posing their own problems (22%)
The regular completion of student mathematical journals (18%)

The list itself reflected different ways in which problem solving and investigations *could* be valued and used by teachers. The majority of items in the list were those which had been clearly endorsed by the manner in which problem solving and investigations had been assessed in VCE mathematics, or which were directly drawn from reference to problem solving and investigations within the VCE Mathematics study, or which could be seen by teachers as a direct preparation for VCE. Two items were intentionally included in the list which, while potentially valuable for the teaching and learning of mathematics, lacked one or more forms of endorsement stated above. These were: Students posing their own problems, and The regular completion of student mathematical journals.

Consistently high levels of approval (> 50%) were given by those with VCE experience and by those without VCE experience to those aspects which were strongly endorsed by VCE curriculum advice and assessment practice. The two items which were not derived from VCE practice received the smallest proportion of "highly important", 22% and 18% respectively. Variation in the degree of importance attached to each of these was analysed with respect to: current VCE teaching; previous VCE teaching; nature of teaching responsibility; level of teaching experience. In general, no significant difference was found in the evaluations attaching to the above items between those teachers with VCE experience and those with no direct experience of teaching VCE; between those who were heads of department and those who were not; or according to the level of teaching experience using the categories "new", "established" and "veteran" as defined above. There were some exceptions to this general pattern which are now discussed.

While considered "highly important" overall by 66% of respondents, there was a substantially stronger degree of endorsement for *the application of mathematics to real world contexts* by new and established teachers than by veteran teachers. Significant differences did emerge on several items which were less well supported by the sample as a whole. These are *presenting problems spanning a range of content areas in mathematics* (45%), and *using problems specific to the topic being taught* (45%). Significant differences (p = .0055) were found between level of experience and the use of problems spanning a range of content areas. The use of problems spanning a range of content areas was valued inversely with teaching experience. These strategies for integrating problem solving and the content of the mathematics program have not been explicitly advocated in the course documents for VCE Mathematics. This may account for the lower percentage of "highly important" evaluations. Established and veteran teachers were substantially more likely than new teachers to value the use of problems specific to the topic being taught.

There was a significant difference (p = .039) in the degree of support for *providing students with substantial written comment on their problem solving attempts*. This was one of the two items for which a statistically significant difference emerged between those with current VCE experience and those without current VCE experience. In all, 88% of those with current VCE experience considered this practice to be "of some importance" or "highly important" in contrast to only 57% of those without current VCE experience. The practice of providing comments on students' drafts of reports of problem solving projects is well established in Years 11 and 12, especially in Year 12 where for the Investigative project Common Assessment Task (CAT) students are required to submit a first draft of their report to their teacher for comment at least one week before the completion date.

There was a lower percentage of teachers who rated as "highly important" *students undertaking extended mathematical activities* (32%) and *students undertaking open-ended mathematical activities* (30%) in Years 7 to 10, although these elements are clearly evident within VCE curriculum and assessment practice. Among teachers who considered open-ended mathematical activities to be "highly important", teachers with current VCE experience were more likely to strongly endorse these practices (p = .0426) than those without current VCE experience.

Assessment and Reporting Practices

Respondents were asked to indicate which formal assessment strategies they employed, and whether their use was a consequence of VCE influence (see Table 2). The formal strategies presented were:

A. *Tests or exams*   B. *Project reports*
C. *Student problem solving reports*   D. *Student self-assessment*

Table 2
Current VCE Teaching and Types of Formal Assessment Strategies Employed
(percentages of column totals)

| | Formal strategies | | | | | | | |
| | A | | B | | C | | D | |
	empl.	infl.	empl.	infl.	empl.	infl.	empl.	infl.
non-VCE	100	41.7	92.9	81.8	90.9	75	16.7	20
VCE	100	34.5	93.8	92.6	93.5	85.7	48.4	13.6

empl.=employed by respondent; infl.=reported to be a consequence of VCE influence

Consistently high levels of use and attribution to VCE were reported for *Project reports* and *Student problem solving* regardless of VCE experience. However, teachers with current VCE experience were more likely to employ student self assessment than those without, as Table 3 shows.

Table 3
Current VCE Teaching and Employment of Student Self-Assessment
(table entries are percentages of column totals)

| Student self assessment | Current VCE teaching | |
	Yes (%)	No (%)
Yes	48	17
No	52	83

(n=43, Chi square=3.641, DF=1, p=.0564)

The extent to which teachers currently teaching the VCE were more likely to employ student self assessment than were non-VCE teachers, is worthy of note. Current VCE teachers were more likely to identify the VCE as an influence on their use of student self assessment (see Table 4).

Table 4
Current VCE Teaching and the Influence of the VCE on the Use of Student Self-Assessment
(table entries are percentages of column totals)

Employment of student self-assessment	Current VCE teaching	
	Yes (%)	No (%)
Yes	41	10
No	59	90

(n=37, Chi square=3.147, DF=1, p=.0761)

This attributed influence is particularly interesting. While student self assessment is not explicitly referred to in VCE documents such as the Mathematics Study Design (VCAB, 1990), the question can be asked whether the use of student self assessment may be derived from the practice of VCE assessment of students' reports? The greater endorsement of student self assessment by current VCE teachers could well be linked to the use of specific criteria to assess students' reports for investigative projects and problem solving activities in Years 11 and 12, and the importance given by VCE teachers to having students know how to apply and interpret these criteria in regard to their own work. However, it is worthy of note that a substantial proportion of veteran teachers, regardless of VCE experience, did not employ student self assessment strategies at Years 7 to 10 (see Table 5).

Table 5
Level of Teaching Experience and the Use of Student Self-Assessment
(table entries are percentages of column totals)

Student self-assessment	Level of teaching experience		
	New	Established	Veteran
Yes	57	57	22
No	43	43	77

(n=43, Chi square=5.324, DF=2, p=.0698)

Taken together with the document analysis, the second phase of this study substantiated the hypothesised Ripple Effect in Years 7 to 10 of changed assessment practices at Years 11 and 12. In addition to its confirmatory value, the second phase of the study has provided a more detailed characterisation of this Ripple Effect in terms of teachers reported classroom practices in Years 7 to 10. In particular, specific terminology and practices associated with the VCE were consistently given high levels of endorsement in mathematics instruction at every level of the secondary school. Other practices, such as student self assessment and the use of student journals, while endorsed by the informed community, did not have the explicit sanction of inclusion in high stakes assessment. As a consequence, the uneven occurrence (and widely different interpretations and implementation) of these non-VCE practices in the sample schools is taken as significant confirmation of our research hypothesis. It is a specific finding of this study that teachers are reluctant to embrace new assessment and instructional practices unless these are policy driven, that is, have the endorsement of inclusion in high stakes assessment.

Teaching experience and current involvement in the VCE were both associated with significant variance in the valuing and use of certain teaching practices, particularly with respect to the perceived value of problem solving activities. However, with respect to teachers' actual experience in teaching VCE mathematics, there was a general lack of variance in the reported practices and beliefs among teachers of Years 7 to 10 mathematics. This suggests that the extent of change documented in stage one is less attributable to the actual experience of teaching VCE mathematics than it is to the creation of a climate of change associated with the introduction of the new assessment practices.

Stage Three Results: The Interviews

Analysis of documentary evidence and the questionnaire data supported the existence of a Ripple Effect, whereby changes to high-stakes assessment were associated with changes at the level of policy and practice which made use of structures, terminology, task types, and grading and report formats adapted or adopted from the new assessment. The uneven adoption of some practices, advocated by the informed community but not incorporated in the VCE assessment, was taken as evidence that the nature of the influence of the VCE was more specific than the creation of a climate of change. Explanatory detail beyond these points was sought by interview. In particular, it was important that the study reveal whether or not participating teachers held shared meanings of the terms and practices documented in phases one and two.

Shared meanings

Despite the modelling of advocated practice within the Victorian Certificate of Education, teachers in this study provided different interpretations, and examples, and attached different significance to the many VCE curricular practices. It is a significant finding of this study that teacher interviews revealed a substantial commonality of meaning for those terms and practices integral to VCE mathematics. This was particularly true of the nomenclature related to structural elements within the VCE Study Design such as Work Requirements, Skills and Applications, and Problem Solving. Problem Solving, for instance, was consistently associated with open-ended mathematical activity, rather than merely "textbook problems". None of the teachers in this study saw the completion of routine problems from a textbook as constituting engagement in problem solving activity. Whether related or not to a topic currently being taught, good problem solving activities were seen as requiring the application of pre-existing mathematical skills, having students complete a written report based on how they went about solving the problem as well as their answer, and being assessed in ways which give credit not only to solutions but also to a process of solution and justification of findings.

It might be argued that the inclusion of problem-solving in the curriculum of Years 7 to 10 can hardly be attributed to the influence of the VCE when it has received such wide endorsement from the wider educational community. Clearly, the inclusion of problem solving in itself is not evidence of the impact of the VCE. Our argument is based rather on the particular emphasis given to problem solving in the participating schools, and the consistently shared beliefs among teachers about how problem solving activities are to be implemented. It is because these particular beliefs and practices are so consistent with, and so closely reflect, the practices and approaches to problem solving endorsed by VCE Mathematics that the Ripple Effect argument is strongly supported by the data. In the interview data, teachers consistently employed similar language to describe classroom problem solving activity, its structure and the means by which it was assessed. In particular, the terminology employed was predominantly the terminology of the VCE problem solving assessment guidelines. In the following interview excerpts, some of these key terms have been italicized.

T1: At the end I write two or three sentences about the level of *analysis* or *evaluation* that they could have done on their work. *(School 1)*

T2: (In commenting on problem solving reports) Have they written out their *aim* clearly, and that doesn't mean using the words that were in the problem, ... rewriting it for themselves? [I] expect to see the *aim* and *information* given or any *assumptions*...and then *solution* and *justification*...why the *solution* should be accepted ... how they've reached the answers. *(School 1)*

T3: Overall we look for the *clarity of understanding* and the *argument*. We look for *logical presentation* ...for *accurate use of mathematical language and symbols* and appropriate use of them, and we look for *accuracy in mathematics*. *(School 2)*

T4: The first thing that we would encourage would be like good graphs, those sort of skills, in the *presentation of mathematical information*. Then we would look for the application of an appropriate scheme ... and then some discussion of the *reasonableness of answers*. ... And along with that, providing students with the *criteria for assessment* before the task. *(School 3)*

T5: I do a *criteria* sheet for each task and I give that to the kids from the word go. The first criterion might be about the aim and then underneath might be two or three points that I want the kids to pick up on in their *aim* and what kind of *solution* they are looking for ... So I tend to give them the criteria sheet of (relating to) the sort of things I want them to do, and then they know if they have done it then they might get a *High, Medium* or *Low* depending on how well they've done it. *(School 4)*

T6: In marking reports of problem solving in Year 9 and 10, we are essentially using and showing students the sheet (*criteria sheet*) that is used in Year 12 ... not all the categories but most ... like the *presentation of the report*, the *justification*, their *conclusions*. ... Problem solving and project work are direct consequences of the VCE. Had it not been for the VCE and the *assessment techniques therein*, I doubt that we would be doing it. *(School 5)*

T7: In Year 10, they (students) are actually making statements about, first of all, their *interpretation* of the problem, then they need to state quite clearly what their *assumptions* are..., then the method by which they have solved the problem, stating the sorts of mathematics that they've used, coming up with some sort of *conclusion*... By the time they get to Year 10 they are getting the idea of what problem solving really is and what we would expect of them at the VCE level. *(School 6)*

T8:   We modified the *criteria sheet* and they (students) get little ticks there *High, Medium,* or *Low*, and they get an overall summation of the piece of work that they did. *(School 7)*

T9:   Another maths teacher put forward one of the problem solving questions ... that came from VCE material, and it is surprising how it could be used with Years 8 and 9. *(School 8)*

Similar collections of interview excerpts could be made with regard to other aspects of VCE adoption and adaptation. Differences of meaning emerged in two situations:

1.   Where the term or practice was not part of VCE mathematics.
      • In the case of "journals", for instance, at least one teacher was prepared to consider the conventional student notebook a form of journal.

2.   Where the term or practice was peripheral to the key structural elements, or simply not prescribed in any detail within the VCE Study Design, even though its use might be implicit and even inevitable.
      • Teachers clearly differed on what constituted "substantial written comment" on students' work.
      • Teachers were not unanimous on what constituted an "open-ended activity".

Adopting non-VCE practice

Student self-assessment and student journals were instances of practices generally endorsed by the mathematics education community which were not enshrined in the VCE and so therefore could be taken as a useful test of whether documented change was best explained through the creation of a culture of change, or as the deliberate and selective mimicry of the practices of high stakes assessment. The following exchange might not have occurred had the use of student journals been seen as an integral part of mandated assessment at Year 12.

      I: Do you make use of student journals?
      T: Some of the kids as soon as you start introducing some writing component to it, if their writing skills aren't that good it's almost going to put them off what I'm trying to achieve in mathematics.

The use of investigative projects and problem solving tasks could be seen to impose similar linguistic demands on students (with respect to both reading and writing). Since no specific practices were mandatory for Years 7 to 10, it is noteworthy that the above argument did not carry sufficient weight to prevent the widespread introduction of investigative projects and problem solving into Years 7 to 10 mathematics.

The phenomenon of adopting the structural elements while asserting professional discretion on the fine details of implementation was variously evident. For instance, written reports by students of mathematical investigations or problem solving activities were not uniformly required, although use of the activities themselves was universal.

Common purpose

The use that teachers made of activities such as open-ended tasks and problem solving activities varied in ways which reflected their individual conceptions of professional responsibility and mathematical activity.

I: How important is it that a problem activity relates specifically to the topic being taught?

T1:   It's not. It's nice if it does but it doesn't matter if it doesn't.

T2:   I would select problems that are relevant to the work, if I'm doing expansion and factorising in algebra for instance, I'd try and get a problem that involves expansion and effective use of expansion and solving equations on top so you've got a bit of a mix. A good example of that would be the one with the equilateral banner with 30 metre and 40 metre sides. It involves quite extensive expansion, yet you can do it off a scale diagram if you so desire.

At this preliminary stage, it is our perception that VCE practices, adopted and adapted for Years 7 to 10, are endorsed and implemented by teachers in a way consistent with the teacher's personal beliefs.

Valuing the VCE

All interviewees were given the specific question:

I: In your opinion, has the introduction of the VCE mathematics had a beneficial effect on the teaching of mathematics at Years 7 to 10?

T1:   Yes, I would say an immense benefit because ... rather than confining ourselves to teaching Skills, which on reflection it seems that's what I was doing up until a few years ago ... Without the VCE, I might have moved just as far in that direction, but the VCE was an initial thing to enlighten me considerably how to go about it.

T2:   Any introduction of a new course has a beneficial effect because you stop and think about what you are doing. This one has certainly improved teaching in [that] we stop and really consider whether kids understand what they are doing rather than just do it and regurgitate.

It appeared that there was general endorsement of the VCE as a beneficial input into the secondary mathematics curriculum.

Attributing changes in practice to the VCE

The issue of whether the VCE was the engine of change or simply one of the outward manifestations of a large-scale reconceptualisation of mathematics instruction and assessment is summarised very nicely in the following interview excerpt.

I: What do you now do in class in Years 7 to 10 mathematics that you consider to be a consequence of the introduction of VCE mathematics?

T: I think the main thing is probably the variety of tasks that we give them and I think that has been encouraged by the VCE . . . I don't know which came first, whether we were doing it down below or not and it's been confirmed by the VCE or whether VCE came first and then we started doing it down.

DISCUSSION

Taken together, the three phases of this study substantiate the hypothesised Ripple Effect in Years 7 to 10 of changed assessment practices at Years 11 and 12. In addition to their confirmatory value, the second and third phases of the study have provided a more detailed characterisation of this Ripple Effect and of the mechanisms by which it occurs. In particular, specific terminology and practices associated with the VCE could be found consistently in mathematics instruction at every level of the secondary school. Other practices, such as student self assessment and the use of student journals, while endorsed by the informed community, did not have the explicit sanction of inclusion in high stakes assessment. As a consequence, the uneven occurrence (and widely different interpretations and implementation) of these non-VCE practices in the sample schools is taken as significant confirmation of our research hypothesis. It is a specific finding of this study that teachers are reluctant to embrace new assessment and instructional practices unless these are policy driven, that is, have the endorsement of inclusion in high stakes assessment.

Schools have adopted VCE structural and instructional correlates at Years 7 to 10. Most teachers are employing VCE-like terminology, work requirements, and assessment and reporting procedures. Different teachers may be doing this with very different motivations and value systems. These value system differences are evident at the level of actual classroom practice, in the choice of specific activities, and in the justifications teachers provide to students for classroom activities.

Teaching experience and current involvement in the VCE were both associated with significant variance in the valuing and use of certain teaching practices, particularly with respect to the perceived value of problem solving activities. However, with respect to teachers' actual experience in teaching VCE mathematics, there was a general lack of variance in the reported practices and beliefs among teachers of Years 7 to 10 mathematics. This suggests that the extent of change documented in stage one is less attributable to the actual experience of teaching VCE mathematics than it is to the creation of a climate of change associated with the introduction of the new assessment practices.

At the commencement of this chapter, six motivations were suggested as possible sources for the Ripple Effect:
- preparation for new assessment
- curricular uniformity
- a reconceived notion of mathematical activity
- a reconceived notion of mathematical assessment
- a general "climate of change"
- a paradigm shift within the mathematics education community

While evidence was found for the presence of each of these within the study sample, and teachers displayed some awareness of changing values within mathematics education, it appeared that the principal motivations leading to change in a school's mathematics instruction and assessment were the pragmatic ones of preparing students for the demands of the new senior assessments and a consequent need for curricular uniformity to anticipate these demands. While this had the effect of creating a "climate of change", the close correspondence between instructional and assessment practices employed at Years 7 to 10 and those required by the VCE suggests that the primary mechanism for change was a school-level requirement to effectively prepare students for senior study. At the level of the school, the observed climate of change should be seen as a consequence of the Ripple Effect rather than as part of its operation.

CONCLUSIONS

The teaching and assessment of mathematics in Years 7 to 10 in Victorian schools has taken on new and important dimensions. It was an hypothesis of this study that the major engine of change was the introduction of a coherent set of work requirements and associated assessment practices in VCE mathematics. It seems reasonable to infer from the substantial body of diverse data accumulated in this research study, that the existence of the postulated Ripple Effect has been substantiated, and that significant progress has been made towards identifying its character and the mechanisms by which such change processes are effected.

To describe the VCE as an engine of change is not to ignore other influences. Rather, the VCE is the enactment of the newly emerging set of directions and purposes which has its origins in an international movement for change in mathematics education. Those directions and purposes which are endorsed by high stakes assessment take on a consistency of practice, which is not evident for those advocated practices not so endorsed. The significance of the Ripple Effect lies in the transformation of the mathematics curriculum in year levels where assessment was not mandated. Characteristic of the Victorian school context was the high status of VCE assessment in Year 12, not only as certification of high school graduation, but also as the key determinant of university access. Changes introduced through the VCE therefore had inevitable significance for school communities. Through the VCE Mathematics Study Design, school communities were offered a new model of school mathematical activity. The changes modelled within the VCE were also consistent with developments advocated by the informed mathematics education community. The inclusion of practices such as problem solving and project work within the VCE provided a high degree of shared meaning and a consistency of implementation to these advocated practices. Other practices, similarly advocated by the informed community, but lacking inclusion in the VCE structure, were left open to local interpretation and were implemented unevenly and in a more fragmented fashion in the schools participant in this study. This study has demonstrated the effectiveness of curricular change through this approach.

ACKNOWLEDGMENTS

This research received significant financial support from the National Center for Research in Mathematical Sciences Education, University of Wisconsin-Madison. The assistance of Margarita Pavlou in all three stages of the project is gratefully acknowledged. Use of the facilities of the Mathematics Teaching and Learning Centre, Australian Catholic University, is also acknowledged.

REFERENCES

Amit, M., & Hillman, S. (1994, October). *Confronting teachers' conceptions through mathematical models elicited in performance assessment activities.* Paper presented at a colloquium, Faculty of Education, University of Melbourne.

Australian Education Council (AEC) (1991). *A national statement on mathematics for Australian schools.* Carlton, Victoria: Curriculum Corporation.

Clarke, D.J. (1992). The role of assessment in determining mathematics performance. In G. Leder (Ed.), *Assessment and learning of mathematics*, Chapter 7 (pp. 145-168). Hawthorn: Australian Council for Educational Research.

Madaus, G.F., & West, M.M. (1992). *The influence of testing on teaching math and science in grades 4 - 12.* Chestnut Hill: Boston College.

National Council of Teachers of Mathematics (NCTM) (1989). *Curriculum and evaluation standards for school mathematics.* Reston, VA: NCTM.

Niss, M. (1993). Assessment in mathematics education and its effects: An introduction. In M. Niss (Ed.), *Investigations into assessment in mathematics education: An ICMI study.* Dordrecht: Kluwer.

Northfield, J., Brown, J., Corrigan, D., Gill, M., Lewis, L., Loughran, J., Redley, L., Shannon, C., & Slattery, M. (1992). *Understanding the challenge: An evaluation of the VCE implementation after three years.* Clayton, Victoria: Monash University.

Northfield, J., Brown, J., Corrigan, D., Gill, M., Loughran, J., Shannon, C., Slattery, M., & Winter, R. (1993). *The challenge continues: An evaluation of the VCE implementation after four years.* Clayton, Victoria: Monash University.

Romberg, T.A., & Price, G. (1983). Curriculum implementation and staff development as cultural change. In Gary A. Griffin (Ed.), *Staff development.* Eighty-second Yearbook of the National Society for the Study of Education. Chicago, IL: NSSE.

Stephens, M. (1992). Foreword. In M. Stephens, & J. Izard (Eds.), *Reshaping assessment practices: Assessment in the mathematical sciences under challenge.* Melbourne: Australian Council for Educational Research.

Streefland, L. (Ed.). (1991). *Realistic mathematics education in primary school.* Utrecht: Freudenthal Institute, University of Utrecht.

Swan, M. (1993). Improving the design and balance of mathematical assessment. In M. Niss (Ed.), *Investigations into assessment in mathematics education: An ICMI study.* Dordrecht: Kluwer.

Van Reeuwijk, M. (1993). *Assessment tasks designed to improve learning of mathematics.* Paper presented at the 1993 Annual Meeting of the American Education Research Association.

Victorian Curriculum and Assessment Board (VCAB) (1990). *Mathematics study design.* Carlton, Victoria: VCAB.

Science Assessment

Pinchas Tamir

INTRODUCTION

This introduction presents the major goals of science teaching and highlights the recent movement for improving student assessment. The selection of topics and issues for discussion is based on the assumption that there is no need to repeat what has recently been published in other sources, such as the comprehensive review by Doran, Lawrenz, and Helgeson (1993b). Many lists of goals/aims/objectives for science education have been published, featuring a variety of levels of detail and emphases. Perhaps the most useful is the list proposed by Bybee and DeBoer (1993), who identified three basic goals for the science curriculum and showed how these goals differ in emphasis and scope in different periods. These goals are:

> Affecting personal and social development of the individuals and the influence it has on the wellbeing and improvement of society.... Personal development includes such things as intellectual growth, personal satisfaction, career awareness and building moral character. Social development includes maintenance of public health, a productive economy, a stable and orderly society, a physically safe environment... Learning science facts and principles...is simply considered a basic element of science education that needs no justification.... Another extremely important focus of science teaching has been the development of both *understanding* of the methods of science and *abilities* in applying those methods (pp. 358-359).

Our chapter describes the variety of approaches, strategies and means used to assess the extent to which these goals are attained.

The 1960s are known for the concerted efforts to reform science education by centrally produced programs emphasizing the structure of the discipline and the processes used in conducting scientific investigations. In the 1970s the pendulum moved back to school-based curriculum that built on the local environment and stressed relevance to the lives of people and the use of science to meet their needs. The 1980s may be characterized as the decade of Science-Technology-Society (STS), emphasizing concepts and processes that highlight the interrelationships and the interactions between science, its applications, and the social forces that shape science and technology. It appears that the 1990s will be remembered as the decade of reform in student assessment. In this chapter, I shall try to identify the factors which lead to this recent development in education in general and in science education in particular.

Student assessment may be defined as a systematic collection of information about student learning and other variables that are associated with particular learning experiences. It involves description of knowledge at, at least, two points of time, namely, prior to the learning experience and upon completion of the learning task. Additional points of time may be considered during the period in which learning is taking place and others at various periods after the completion of the task, the latter intending to measure retention. Student assessment has traditionally relied on measures, instruments and methodologies developed by measurement experts and based on measurement theories which yield quantitative data that serve to rank-order individuals within given groups such as a classroom, a school or a particular age cohort. The results of assessment have been typically used for selection and classification, for example, serving as criterion for admitting candidates to prestigious schools of medicine, law or business. Although additional potential functions of assessment, such as providing feedback to the learners and the teachers, are cited in books, in reality these functions have often been played down.

Because results of student assessment have been used in making important decisions concerning the present and future of many students, assessment has typically driven the curriculum. Yet for many decades curriculum reformers have failed to consider the inadequacy of currently used assessment procedures to the innovations that were designed to improve learning, and hence, tests, especially standardized tests that were administered at national or state levels, have acted as barriers to many innovations. There are, at least, two major reasons why testing acts as a barrier. First, teachers teach and students study toward success in the tests. *Innovations that compete with tests are bound to fail.* Second, tests that do not match the innovation fail to reveal the impact of the innovation. The commonly heard criticism that the 'new' curricula of the 1960s have failed to achieve their goals has been based on results of paper and pencil multiple choice questions that favor rote learning and memorization and, consequently, cannot reveal gain in higher-order thinking. Ideally, an assessment program should reflect the goals and experiences of the curriculum to such an extent that when students study toward the tests they will be doing what they are intended to do in their school studies.

The increased interest in new directions for assessment has occurred especially in the USA, featuring terms such as 'alternative,' 'authentic,' 'curriculum driven,' and 'socially relevant.'

In their comprehensive *Review of Research on Assessment in Science* (Doran et al., 1993b), the authors define assessment as the 'collection of information, both quantitative and qualitative, obtained through various tests, observations, and many other techniques (e.g., checklists, inventories) used to determine individual, group or program performance' (p. 388). Seventeen techniques and types of assessment are mentioned, of which four (True-false, Multiple choice, Completion and Short answer) items are designated as *traditional*, whereas thirteen (e.g., Practical laboratory, Self-rating and Portfolios) are designated as *alternative*.

LEARNING THEORIES: IMPLICATIONS FOR ASSESSMENT

Two learning theories have dominated science education over the second half of the twentieth century: The equilibration theory of Piaget and the theory of meaningful verbal learning of Ausubel.

As for Piaget's theory, we adopt the view of Lawson (1993, pp. 139-140):

> The key point is that external knowledge can become internalised if the teacher accepts the notion that the equilibration process is the route to that internalisation. This means that students (1) must be prompted to engage their previous ways of thinking about the situation to discover how they are inadequate to assimilate the new situation and (2) must then be given ample opportunity to think through the situation to allow appropriate mental reorganisation (accommodation) which in turn allows successful assimilation of the new situation. The teacher becomes an asker of questions, a provider of materials, a laboratory participant, a class chairperson and secretary.... Most important, the teacher is not a teller.

Turning to Ausubel, we present his famous claim which underlies the theory, namely:

> If I had to reduce all of educational psychology to just one principle, I would say this: The most important single factor influencing is what the learner already knows. Ascertain this and teach him accordingly ... the principal effect of cognitive structure is on learning and retention of newly presented material...[it] influences new cognitive functioning irrespective of whether it is in regard to reception learning or problem solving (Ausubel, 1968, p. 130).

Although debates and arguments in favor of either one of the theories over the other abound, the major principle, namely the centrality of prior knowledge and the view of learning as a knowledge-constructing process on the part of the learner, is shared by both. Obviously, the implications for teaching as well as for assessment reflects this similarity. A brief discussion of some selected implications follows.

Meaningful vs. Rote Learning

Clearly this is a most important distinction. Many educators have noted the wide use of rote learning in schools. Teachers in many classrooms are so anxious to cover the syllabus that they tend to spend a great deal of class time pouring information into the heads of their students. Often both teachers and students are unaware of the futility of such rote learning since 'long experience in taking examinations makes students adept at memorizing not only key propositions and formulas, but also causes, examples, reasons, explanations and ways of recognizing and solving "type problems" (Ausubel, 1968, p. 111).

The *clinical* interview developed by Piaget is an excellent tool for assessing genuine understanding. It is usually based on manipulation of concrete materials which counteracts sole reliance on verbal ability. It also helps in ascertaining standardized context. The wording of questions is carefully chosen and maintained so that administration is standardized and results may be safely attributed to the measured skill. Moreover, towards the end of the task, an attempt is made to 'shake' the confidence of the child by saying '...but yesterday the interviewee disagreed and said that...[for example] "there is more water in the taller container," what would you have told him?'

Whereas Piaget and his followers used the clinical interview to find out the stage of children's cognitive development, other researchers adapted the interview to the study of alternative conceptions (e.g., Nussbaum & Novak 1986).

One may attribute the fast increasing qualitative research in science education to the adoption of Piaget's methodology to the study of alternative conceptions. Since individual interviews are costly and time-consuming, they cannot be used as a regular assessment tool in classrooms. However, the need for assessment to ascertain that meaningful learning takes place is widely recognized. A variety of techniques and tests have been developed and successfully employed in schools. These tests and techniques constitute the *alternative assessment* that is the focus of this chapter.

SCIENCE COGNITIVE ACHIEVEMENT OUTCOMES

Improved Multiple Choice Questions

Multiple choice questions have often been blamed for a variety of negative educational outcomes such as rote/ superficial learning, under-development of communication skills, deficient ability to develop and present an argument, and more. The major justifications offered for their widespread use, especially in the United States, are:

1) They permit coverage of a wide range of topics in a relatively short time.

2) They are objective in terms of scoring and therefore more reliable.

3) They are easily and quickly scored and lend themselves to machine scoring.

4) They avoid unjustified penalties to students who know their subject matter but are poor writers.

In this chapter we show how multiple choice items can be designed and used as an effective diagnostic tool by avoiding their pitfalls and by taking advantage of their potential benefits.

Correct vs. best answers

It is relatively easy to design multiple choice items in which one option is correct and the rest (the distractors) are incorrect. Items of this kind tend to be of a lower cognitive level, requiring most often no more than memorization of particular facts. Since most teacher-made tests comprise such items, they indeed deserve the harsh criticism put forward against them. However, as shown by many authors (e.g., Schwab, 1963), when the focus shifts from correct/incorrect to the *best* answer, the picture changes dramatically. Now the student is faced with the task of carefully analyzing the various options, each of which may present factually correct information, and select the answer that best fits the context and the data given in the item's stem. Multiple choice items of this kind cater for a wide range of cognitive abilities. When compared with open-ended questions, they admittedly do not require the student to formulate an answer, but, at the same time, they do impose the additional requirement of weighing the evidence provided by the different options.

In a way the distractors in a multiple choice item function much like one of the standard procedures in a Piagetian classical interview in which the interviewer is not fully satisfied even when the child gives the correct answer. Thus, as observed by Tamir (1991b), in the famous interview regarding area conservation, when the child indicates that cows have the same grazing area, regardless of the manner in which the houses are scattered in the field, the interviewer keeps pressing: 'Yesterday another child told me that here [where the houses are scattered all over] the cows have more food than here [where the houses are close together] -- what do you say?' Children who do not really understand that the two areas are equal may fall into the trap. The distractors in a good multiple choice item serve as such traps. It may be concluded that wisely designed multiple choice items have a high diagnostic potential.

Construction of diagnostic multiple choice items

There are two ways to go about constructing diagnostic multiple choice items: (a) using known misconceptions as distractors and (b) using students' answers to open-ended questions as a basis for constructing distractors.

The research literature in science education is full of studies which identify students' misconceptions in relation to a variety of topics. These misconceptions may serve as excellent distractors. When such items are used the results quickly indicate not only how many choose the best answer, but also how many students hold particular misconceptions.

In spite of extensive research there are, and will continue to exist, many topics and concepts for which there is no a priori information regarding misconceptions. In such cases the alternative approach suggested more than 20 years ago is still viable. According to this approach, teachers who administer open questions to their students collect, while assessing the papers, typical student answers, correct and incorrect. These answers, which represent the ways the students think on given questions, actually reveal certain conceptions, including misconceptions which are excellent sources for item options (Tamir 1971).

Confidence in chosen response

Students are asked to provide two responses for each item: first, to choose the best answer, and second, to indicate if they are sure or not sure of their choice. The following marking procedure is used:

correct sure	2 points
correct not sure	1 point
incorrect not sure	0.5 point
incorrect sure	0 points

This marking procedure has been found to be very useful in two ways. First, its reward hierarchy is regarded as fair, thereby facilitating honest reporting by students; and second, it provides very important feedback to the teacher as well as to the students. If, for example, most students in the class are not sure about a particular item, the teacher may conclude that there is a need to revisit the relevant subject matter in class. As for the students, they learn how to self-evaluate their knowledge. If many mismatches occur, the student may attempt to find the reasons and adjust his/her learning strategies. Finally, this procedure lends itself easily to machine scoring.

The use of justifications

In the context of this chapter, the term justification is assigned to reasons and arguments given by a respondent to a multiple choice item for the choice she/he has made. Very little is reported in the literature about the use of justifications, mainly because very little use has been made of this approach. The main reason for avoiding the use of justifications is, most probably, that all the advantages associated with objective items, namely, high reliability, machine scoring, and economical coverage of a wide range of topics in a relatively short time, are lost. On the other hand, however, there are at least two important reasons for using justifications with multiple choice rather than using short essay questions. First, as already explained, the distractors serve as traps. When students are required to justify their choice, they have to consider the data in all the options and explain why a certain option is better than others. By including wise options, both as the best answer and as distractors, we 'force' the students to consider specific matters and to express their position in writing.

The second reason for requiring justifications for multiple choice items is the 'back-wash' effect. Students who know that they may be asked to justify their choices will attempt to learn their subject matter in a more meaningful way and in more depth, so that they are prepared to write the justification adequately.

The results of the Israeli matriculation examination in biology reveal substantial gaps between the scores on the multiple choice responses and those on the justifications. For example, in four items included in the 1985 biology matriculation examination, the percentages of students correctly choosing the best answers were 78, 65, 81, 38 and that of students providing satisfactory justifications were 59, 40, 61, 29, respectively. On the average the gap between choice and justification scores reached a whole standard deviation.

This gap indicates that a considerable number of students who correctly choose the best answer do not really understand the relevant subject matter. This itself is worth noting. However, the most important contribution of the justifications is that they provide information about students' conceptions and reasoning patterns beyond that which can be obtained by the various procedures outlined above (for more details, see Tamir, 1991b).

Self-assessment

Current use of self-assessment

Self-evaluation is not new. However, based on review of the rapidly accumulating papers and book chapters featuring various approaches to assessment, it appears that self-assessment, a strategy which can be readily integrated with instruction and which has, as we shall show, a very high educational potential, has so far not received the attention it deserves. In fact, self-assessment of cognitive achievement has been very rare in science education. In over more than 700 pages in the second edition of *Educational Measurement* (Thorndike, 1971) self-assessment is mentioned briefly in two places: (a) in relation to personality traits where the author states: 'The major concern of authors of these kind of tests has been the ease with which applicants can deliberately distort their answer' (Schwartz, 1971, p. 325) and (b) in relation to learning and instruction where the author states that 'in the light of present educational innovation it is highly likely that the job of the teacher will be influenced by procedures which allow assessment decisions to be made increasingly by the student himself.' The author further observes that 'the design of tests for use by the student in self-assessment has been seriously neglected in the past by educational test constructors' (Glaser & Nitko, 1971, p. 627). An extensive review of books dealing with student evaluation and assessment, has failed to come up with even one that presents an instrument to be used for self-assessment of achievement. Several authors recommend informal self-evaluation (e.g., Ahman & Glock, 1967, pp. 238-239; Mehrens, 1973, pp. 607-608; Renners, 1960, 188-191). Usually the only suggestion is to seek students' agreement that test results truly reflect their knowledge. Stader, Colyar and Berlinger (1990) found that 'children who possess well developed meta-cognitive strategies might be expected to provide clear non-verbal clues that accurately reflect their comprehension' (p. 4). These authors used confidence marking as a measure of self- assessment ability. Other authors also advocate the use of a confidence scale to increase test reliability (e.g., Lechlerg, 1982). In the university, especially in medical schools, students are sometimes asked to assign grades to themselves. The results of one study cast some doubts about the validity and reliability of self-reports (Falchikov & Boud 1989). It may be observed that self-reports are quite common in the evaluation of attitude and personality but practically absent from the assessment of achievement. It is worth noting that a main reason for the reluctance to use self-reports of attitudes, namely intentional faking guided by social desirability, may play only a minor role, if any, in self-evaluation of knowledge. This is especially true when a self-report knowledge inventory is used as a prior knowledge test (see below) in which students are *not* expected to possess the knowledge which they are about to study. As to the possibility of obtaining inaccurate and unreliable data due to lack of expertise in assessment on the part of students -- this should be watched carefully, but our experience shows that this does not happen in most cases and that students quickly gain the capacity to estimate their level of knowledge.

Certain characteristics belonging to the affective domain can be expected to be related to self-assessment. These include self-concept, fate control, locus of control and social values such as self-reliance, self-sufficiency and self-control (see Simpson, Koballa, Oliver, & Crawley, 1993, pp. 213-215). Similarly, the notion of self-efficacy (see Tobin, Tippins, & Aljandro, 1993, p. 63) can be expected to be related to self assessment. However, research on self-efficacy has focussed on teachers, not on students. Generally speaking, the nature of the relationships between self-assessment and the various characteristics mentioned above have yet to be established.

The instrument

A Self-Report Knowledge Inventory (SRKI) is designed by compiling a list of concepts and/or skills that students are expected to master in a particular course. The students are asked to indicate for each item their perceived mastery on a five-point scale (see Table 1). This five-point scale was found to provide valid and reliable results with college students (Tamir & Amir, 1981) and with secondary school students (Tamir, 1991a).

Table 1
Levels of Self-Assessment

Level	Knowledge	Skill
1.	Don't know, don't understand	Cannot do
2.	Not sure if I know/understand	Not sure if I can do
3.	I believe I know what it's about	I think I can do to some extent
4.	I know/understand *well*	I can do *well*
5.	I can explain to friends	I can teach others how to to do it

Establishing validity and reliability

In a study of the effect of high school biology on learning and achievement in college biology, SRKI was used along with multiple choice tests and an attitude scale measuring perceptions of difficulty of and interest in various parts of the college biology course (Tamir & Amir, 1981). A number of findings of that study can be regarded as evidence of the validity of the self-assessment inventories: The instructors of the general biology college course prepared a list of 86 concepts and 15 skills which covered what they expected their students to learn. Based on content analysis of high school curricula, the concepts and skills were subdivided by independent experts into two groups: those that students might have been expected to acquire in high school (to be referred to as 'high school') and those which have not been taught in high school (to be referred to as 'college'). Examples of concepts included in the high school list (N=57) are: basic structure of carbohydrates, fats, and proteins, pH, enzymes, mitosis, membrane, centriole, electron transport chain negative feedback, aerobic, dendrite. Examples of college level concepts (N=29) are: polysomes, microfilaments, ions pump, procaryotic, enzymatic induction, structural gene, operon, hemostat, post-synoptic membrane, action potential, syncytium. Examples of high school level skills (N=10) are: preparing a microscopic slide, using a microscope, using a burette. Examples of college level skills (N=5) are: measuring pH with a pH meter, using a calorimeter, using a centrifuge. The inventories were administered at a special orientation session two weeks before the first class meeting by the course instructors as part of the orientation requirements of the course. The results that support the validity and reliability are presented in Tables 2 and 3 and in the text below.

Findings support the validity of the self-assessment instruments. First, the differences between high school and college level items are very conspicuous regarding both prior knowledge and prior study. It is not surprising to find that 90% of the subjects indicated that they did not know and did not understand the concepts classified at college level. Somewhat smaller differences were found between high school and college level skills, but still twice as many students felt that they mastered high school level skills. The fact that 45% reported that they knew the high school concepts but only 22% were willing to rate themselves as 4 or 5 (see Table 1) may be explained by the length of time (two to four years) that elapsed between high school graduation and entrance to the university, due to military service. Table 3 shows relatively high correlations between prior knowledge and prior learning. While a priori one may question the validity of self-report assessments, the results offer support to the validity of these self-reports, since both the differences between high school and college level items and the positive correlations between prior learning and prior knowledge are in the expected directions.

Table 2
Distribution of Responses Regarding Prior Knowledge and Prior Study (N=116)*

Concept or skill	No. of items	Knowledge Distribution %				Prior study %		
		1 + 2	4 + 5	M	SD	2	M	SD
Concepts: High school	57	35	22	2.92	0.71	72	1.72	0.23
College	29	90	2	1.77	0.58	36	1.36	0.23
Skills: High school	10	28	38	3.10	0.92	76	1.76	0.24
College	5	49	16	2.54	0.88	54	1.54	0.30

*   Internal consistency coefficients (Cronbach's α) were above 0.9 for concepts and above 0.8 for skills. Knowledge response scale: 1 = don't know; 3 = not sure; 5 = can explain to others. Prior study scale: 1 = did not study; 2 = studied.

Table 3
Intercorrelations* Between Levels of Prior Study and Knowledge (N=114)

Prior Study		High School		College	
		Concepts	Skills	Concepts	Skills
High school	Concepts	0.63	0.45	0.39	0.45
	Skills	0.65	0.59	0.24	0.50
College	Concepts	0.44	0.35	0.55	0.40
	Skills	0.72	0.42	0.30	0.61

*Pearson correlations. All values are significant beyond 0.01.

Second, high school students in Israel elect to specialize in certain subjects in grades 11 and 12. Those who specialize in biology study six periods of biology a week in each of the two grades. Obviously these students would be expected to score higher on both SRKI and prior study than students who had not specialized in biology. Indeed, the biology specialists (N=70) had higher scores than the remaining students (N=36). The effect sizes (in standard deviation units) were as follows: Knowledge of Concepts --1.44; of Skills -- 0.90; Prior Study of Concepts -- 1.00; of Skills -- 0.80. These differences are very substantial. The *reliability* of the self-assessment inventories has been established by the most widely used index of internal consistency, namely Cronbach's alpha. The Cronbach's alpha indices of SRKI were higher than 0.9 and of prior study higher than 0.8. These levels of reliability are considered highly satisfactory for group comparisons.

The use of SRKI

In spite of the recommendation included in most assessment courses and textbooks for teachers to use prior knowledge tests in their courses, very few teachers actually administer such tests. Prior knowledge tests can fulfill two important functions: a) their results can be used to plan effective teaching by allocating resources and time according to the needs, and b) the results of prior knowledge tests are necessary for estimating the actual gain which has occurred as a result of studying a particular lesson/unit/ course.

Through discussions with teachers I have found that the time needed to construct additional test and evaluate its results is not the main reason for avoiding prior knowledge tests. The major reason for not administering prior knowledge tests is the wish of teachers to save their students from an unpleasant experience which might result in negative attitudes toward the course. Table 4 compares the advantages and disadvantages of regular paper and pencil tests with those of the SRKI. The data in Table 4 are based on informal discussions of the author with teachers of all grade levels.

Table 4
Comparing Paper and Pencil Test and SRKI as Prior Knowledge Test*

Attribute	Paper and pencil test	Self-report knowledge inventory
Number of concepts included	a sample	all
Number of skills included	a sample	all
Time to develop prior knowledge test	much	relatively little
Time to repond to test	much	relatively little
Time to score and analyze results	much	relatively little
Effect on students' attaitudes toward test	negative	positive
Effect on students' attitudes toward course	negative	not affected
Validity for concepts included	higher	lower
Reliability for concepts included	higher	lower
Validity as a functin of content coverage	lower	higher
Reliability as a fnction of content coverage	lower	higher
Effectiveness of feedback	deeper	broader
Probability of use by teachers	low	high
Effect as advance organizer	weak	strong

*Based on conversations with teachers and on author's analysis.

The information in Table 4 explains why most teachers are reluctant to administer prior knowledge tests in their courses. At the same time, it reveals the potential benefits of using SRKI as a substitute for paper and pencil tests. SRKI has a unique advantage as a research tool. It is well known that many students who are asked to respond to questions for research purposes do not perform the tasks as well as they can because they do not see why they should invest efforts where no compensation may be expected. Since responding to SRKI is much quicker and does not require so much time and effort, chances for obtaining representative responses are higher.

Concept Mapping

The use of concept maps in science education has been promoted by Novak (1980, 1981). Concept maps can be used in many ways for purposes such as learning new material, planning, summarizing, and overviewing. Here we focus on the use of concept maps as tests.

Concept maps resemble objective tests such as multiple choice in that they can present minimum demands on students for writing and they can be scored relatively easily and objectively: 'On those occasions where you do wish to have students express in their own words what they read, a concept map constructed prior to writing may lead to surprisingly good essays' (Novak 1981, p. 19). Concept maps can be employed as tests in various ways. Listed below are instructions given to examinees in four different tasks.

Analysis of a prepared map

The following map (Figure 1) shows the relationships among concepts related to genetic continuity. The concepts are arranged hierarchically and linked to each other. Please examine the map and supply, in the space provided, a word or two for labeling each link such that the association between concepts is made clear. (For the purpose of illustration, the connecting labels have been filled in the appropriate spaces.)

Constructing a concept map based on a list of concepts

Following is a list of concepts related to genetic continuity. Please construct a hierarchical concept map including all the listed concepts. Each link should be accompanied by an appropriate descriptor. The concepts are *not* listed in the right order.

Genetic continuity
Fertilization
Mitosis
Meiosis
Male
Female
Sperm
Egg
New generation

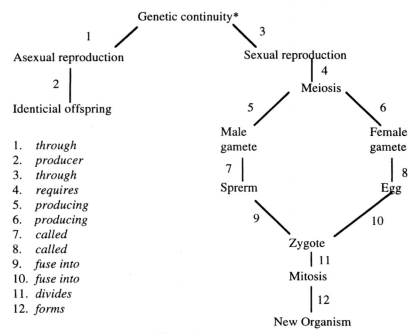

Figure 1
Linking Concepts in a Concept Map

Constructing a concept map based on a textbook paragraph

Read the following paragraph and construct a map which presents the main concepts and their interrelationships.

Mutagens are physical or chemical agents known to cause mutations. Mutations are changes in single genes or in chromosome structure. The first strongly mutagenic chemical identified was mustard gas. Tests on fruit flies showed that mustard gas was highly mutagenic. In 1927 an American geneticist, Herman Muller showed that X-rays could cause mutations in fruit flies. Carcinogens are physical or chemical agents known to cause cancer. All carcinogens have been found to be mutagens, also. Can we tell in advance which chemicals are mutagenic? This is more difficult than we may think. First, it is difficult to predict how a chemical will be metabolized. A chemical might be mutagenic for some people but not for others. Second, chemicals that seem perfectly harmless alone can be mutagenic in combination with other substances.

The serious threat posed by radiation to the reproductive cells was demonstrated in 1927. Following the explosion of the atomic bomb during World War II, extensive research was begun to study the effects of radiation on living things.

It is generally believed that point mutations and chromosome breaks are caused by highly energized subatomic particles striking an electron in an atom of DNA and bouncing it out of orbit. The ionized atom then reacts chemically to form a different DNA base. Mutations may also be induced by the reaction of DNA with ionized chemicals in close proximity to DNA.

Variation on the previous section

In the map you construct, please include the following concepts: mutagens, mutations, chromosome, carcinogen, chemical, radiation, DNA, electron, atom, atomic bomb.

Assessment of Concept Maps

Novak (1981, p. 20) describes a comprehensive form for assessing concept maps. According to this form five criteria are employed and scored separately: relationships, hierarchy, branching, general to specific, and cross links. Following is a detailed description and scoring procedure for each criterion.

Relationship: One point is given for each relationship between two concepts, provided that the relationship is content correct and explicitly stated.

Hierarchy: The number of points given depends on the number of levels in the constructed map. One point is given for each level up until two levels beyond the last branching.

Branching: One point is given for the first branching where two or more concepts are connected to the concept above. Three points are given for any subsequent branching.

General to specific:
If less than 10% of the relationships are general to specific--	0 points
If 10 to 29% are general to specific	-- 1 point
If 30 to 49% are general to specific	-- 2 points
If 50 to 69% are general to specific	-- 3 points
If 70 to 89% are general to specific	-- 4 points
If 90 to 100% are general to specific	-- 5 points

Cross links: Cross links show relationship between concept in one branch and concept in another branch. A rating of one point is given for each cross link.

As an example we score the map presented in Figure 1:
Relationships	-- 12 points
Hierarchy	-- 6 points
Branching	-- 7 points
General to specific	-- 5 points
Cross links	-- 0 points

Concept Linking Propositions

As we have seen in the previous section, concept maps are used to assess understanding of concepts through the construction of a network of relationships among concepts. There are two major limitations to concept mapping. First, introducing students to concept mapping requires preparation and training (Novak & Gowin 1984, Tables 2-3, pp. 32-34), thereby restricting their use to students who have experienced concept mapping. A second limitation is that the links in concept maps consist of one or two words and consequently cannot indicate how well the student understands the relationship between the two given concepts. Stewart (1979) observed that

> there are numerous valid propositions that could be generated to link two nodes.... Which of the many possible relationships did the students have in mind?.... If one is interested in the nature of meaning in cognitive structure one must ensure that assessment devices assess the nature of that meaning. (p. 400)

One way to deal with this problem is to ask students to consider just two concepts at a time (compared with many concepts required to construct a concept map) and build a full sentence to explain the nature of the link between these concepts. This would uncover more of the students' knowledge and understanding pertaining to these two concepts. This kind of task was called a Concept Linking Proposition (CLP). CLP is offered as an efficient and effective alternative to concept maps.

CLP is presented to the students as in the following example: 'Write a sentence which captures as well as you can the nature of the relationship between photosynthesis and respiration. The sentence should consist of more than 3-4 words; avoid sentences such as "photosynthesis and respiration are important..."'

To continue, in this example, CLP was administered as part of a prior knowledge test, before instruction, and as a post-test immediately after completion of a unit on photosynthesis (Amir & Tamir 1994). Table 5 presents the results in terms of categories generated on the basis of students' answers. Revealing substantial differences between prior knowledge test and post-test may be considered as evidence of the capability of CLP to detect various levels of achievement. This capability is an indication of validity. Moreover, in addition to the CLP, both prior knowledge and post-tests included items in a variety of test formats including multiple choice, multiple choice and justification, and open-ended questions. The results of these tests were similar to those obtained with CLP.

Table 5

Distribution of Propositions Linking Photosynthesis and Respiration Prior to and After Studying a Unit on Photosynthesis (In Percentages, N=516)

Category	Prior knowledge test	Post-test
No proposition	17	0
Photosynthesis = respiration	31	4
Photosynthesis is the opposite of respiration	18	26
Photosynthesis and resirtion have common attributes	5	11
Photsynthesis and respiration complement each other	18	54
Other	11	5

To sum up, concept linking propositions have the following advantages:
1)   The task is 'user friendly'.

2) There is no need for prior experience or for special preparation.
3) CLP is a valid and reliable measure of achievement.
4) The linking proposition provides detailed information about students' conceptions.
5) Both the task and the scoring consume little time.
6) The simplicity of the task provides a clear account of students' knowledge.
7) Feedback is simple and accurate.

Problem Situations

By problem situations we refer to a wide range of questions in which a particular situation is presented through data. The testee is essentially required (a) to describe the situation in words, and (b) to offer explanations based on prior knowledge. These questions call for application and sometimes for analysis, synthesis, and evaluation as well.

A situation taken from the history of science (Klinckman 1970, pp. 424-426)

Questions 1-8 refer to van Helmont's account of an experiment he performed in the seventeenth century:

> That all vegetable matter immediately and materially arises from the element water alone I learned from this experiment. I took an earthenware pot and planted in it a willow shoot weighing 5 lb. After 5 years had passed the tree weight 169 lb. The earthenware pot was constantly wet only with rain or (when necessary) distilled water; and it was ample in size and imbedded in the ground; and, to prevent dust flying around from mixing with the earth, the rim of the pot was kept covered with an iron plate coated with tin and pierced with many holes. I did not compute the weight of the leaves of the four autumns. Finally, I again dried the earth of the pot, and it was found to be the same 200 lb. minus about 2 oz. Therefore 164 lb. of wood, bark, and root has arisen from the water alone.

In van Helmont's day it was thought that there were only four 'elements', earth, water, air and fire. It was further thought that air and fire had no weight.

1. Van Helmont thought the 164 lb. of matter in the plant came
    (a) entirely from the earth in the pot;
    (b) entirely from water provided to the plant;
    (c) from both the earth in the pot and the water provided;
    (d) from matter in the air which entered the plant;
    (e) from matter dissolved in the water provided to the plant.

2. Van Helmont probably assumed all the following EXCEPT:
    (a) air in the atmosphere contains a considerable amount of dust;
    (b) matter is neither created nor destroyed;
    (c) gases in the atmosphere are a source of matter for the plant;
    (d) rain water contains no dissolved matter;
    (e) the leaves produced had appreciable weight.

3. Van Helmont would probably have realised that his conclusion was wrong, if he had
   (a) measured the weight of water given off by the plant;
   (b) determined the weight of the pot used in the experiment;
   (c) more accurately weighed the tree at the beginning and end of the experiment;
   (d) not provided water to the tree in addition to rain water;
   (e) weighed the leaves produced in the four autumns.

4. If van Helmont had found that the earth in the pot weighed considerably less at the end of the experiment than at the beginning, he would probably have concluded that
   (a) the matter in the tree came entirely from the 'element earth';
   (b) the matter in the tree came entirely from the 'element water';
   (c) earth is soluble in water;
   (d) the matter in the tree came from both water and earth;
   (e) water can enter a plant only through its roots embedded in earth.

5. On the basis of the assumptions of his day regarding the four 'elements,' van Helmont
   (a) should have grown the tree in an air-tight container;
   (b) reached an incorrect conclusion because he failed to weigh the leaves produced;
   (c) made an error in failing to weigh the water used by the tree in the experiment;
   (d) should have burned the tree which grew and found the weight of the ashes produced;
   (e) was correct in the plan and performance of the experiment.

6. Van Helmont distilled the water he provided the tree because
   (a) he probably though that undistilled water would kill the tree;
   (b) distilled water is less dense than undistilled water;
   (c) he did not wish to introduce an unknown weight of the 'element earth' to the pot;
   (d) this was the easiest procedure to follow under the circumstances;
   (e) he did not realize that the pot already contained water-soluble minerals.

   It is now known that there are over a hundred chemical elements, all of which possess weight and that earth, water, and air are each composed of two or more of these elements.

7. It could be hypothesised that elements originally present in the air became part of the weight of the willow tree. This hypothesis
   (a) is not in agreement with the information;
   (b) has already been ruled out by the results of von Helmont's experiment;
   (c) was tested by van Helmont in his experiment with inconclusive results;
   (d) is in agreement with van Helmont's original idea about the source of matter in the plant;
   (e) could be tested by growing plants in a sealed container with provision for weighing all matter that enters and leaves the container.

8. Van Helmont's incorrect conclusion resulted mainly from
   (a) wrong ideas about the composition of air;
   (b) inaccurate weighing of the 'element earth';
   (c) faulty reasoning from correct assumptions;

(d) failure to weigh the leaves produced;
(e) using a tree rather than a flowering plant in the experiment.

Interpretation of data presented in a table

Examine the presented table and then answer the questions.

Table 6
The Relationship Between the Light Intensity and the Rate of Photosynthesis

Light intensity (foot candle) x	CO_2 used average micro-liters y	Ratio y/x
100	16	0.160
200	36	0.180
300	50	0.166
400	68	0.170
500	86	0.172
600	101	0.168
700	123	0.176
800	135	0.168

1. Describe in words what the data in the table show.
2. Can you predict what amount of CO_2 will be used in light intensity of 150 foot candles? Explain your prediction.
3. The manager of a greenhouse asked the scientist to give him an estimate of the rate of photosynthesis at 1200 foot candles. The scientist pointed out that his data (which was presented in the table) did not permit such predictions. Do you agree with the response of the scientist? Explain.

COGNITIVE PSYCHOMOTOR OUTCOMES

Practical Laboratory Tests

The practical mode (See Tamir, 1972c)

With the advent of the inquiry oriented science curricula which stress the processes of science and emphasize the development of higher cognitive skills, the laboratory has acquired a central role, not just as a means for demonstration and confirmation, but rather as the core of the science learning process. What is so special about laboratory experiences? Olson (1973) asserts that through learning experiences we acquire two types of information: the first, reflecting the features of the objects and events more or less invariant across different experiences, may be called 'knowledge'. The second, reflecting the features of the experience across different objects and events, may be called 'skills'. Gilbert Ryle's famous distinction between propositional knowledge (knowing that) and procedural knowledge (knowing how) corresponds to the distinction between 'knowledge' and 'skill'. Olson has further observed that our schools are reasonably successful in serving the goals pertaining to the acquisition of knowledge but they serve poorly the educational goals pertaining to the development of skills, mainly because instruction relies heavily on symbolically coded information (speech, print, pictures, films), which happens to be a convenient and efficient way for transmitting bodies of knowledge to large groups of students. The science laboratory is certainly an exception in this regard. The most important role that the laboratory can play is to provide opportunities for direct experiences, which are so rare in our schools (Woolnough & Allsop ,1985) The unique role of the laboratory at the university level has been described by Hegarty-Hazel (1990) and by Kirschner (1991). Laboratory experience at all levels is conducive to the development of motor as well as intellectual skills. At the same time these experiences also help in the acquisition of knowledge as well as in the development of attitudes. Hence, assessment of outcomes of laboratory instruction needs to include all three domains, namely cognitive, psychomotor and affective.

Assessment of science laboratory outcomes

No learning experience can be classified exclusively in any one of the three domains. Nevertheless, since we plan to deal with practical examinations which focus on the cognitive and psychomotor domains, we shall not discuss specifically affective outcomes such as curiosity, perseverance, interest and enjoyment.

Although practical examinations can be used to assess such affective outcomes, to our knowledge so far they have not been used for this purpose. We do have evidence, however, which indicates that many students enjoy practical tests and prefer them over regular paper and pencil tests (e.g., Tamir, 1973). Table 7 presents a laboratory outcomes inventory based on Jeffrey (1967), Tamir and Lunetta (1978), Lunetta and Tamir (1979), and Tamir, Nussinowitz, & Friedler (1982).

Table 7
Laboratory Outcomes Inventory

1.0 Planning and Design
    1.1 Formulates a question or defines a problem to be investigated
        1.2 Predicts experimental results
    1.3 Formulates hypothesis to be tested in this investigation
    1.4 Designs observation or measurement procedures
    1.5 Designs experiment
        1.5.1 Identifies dependent variable
        1.5.2 Identifies independent variable
        1.5.3 Designs control
        1.5.4 Fits the experimental design to the tested hypothesis
        1.5.5 Provides a complete design (including replications, for example)
    1.6 Prepares the necessary apparatus
2.0 Performance
    2.1 Carries out observations and measurements
        2.1.1 Carries out qualitative observations
        2.1.2 Carries out quantitative observations/measurements
    2.2 Manipulates apparatus; develops techniques
    2.3 Records results, describes observation (including drawings)
    2.4 Performs numeric calculations
    2.5 Explains or makes a decision about experimental technique
    2.6 Works according to own design
    2.7 Overcomes obstacles and difficulties by himself
    2.8 Cooperates with others when required
    2.9 Maintains orderly laboratory and observes safety procedures

Table 7/ (cont.)

3.0 Analysis and interpretation
   3.1 Transforms results to standard forms
      3.1.1 Arranges data in tables or in diagrams
      3.1.2 Graphs data
   3.2 Determines relationships, interprets data, draws conclusions
      3.2.1 Determines qualitative relationships
      3.2.2 Determines quantitative relationships
   3.3 Determines accuracy of experimental data
   3.4 Defines or discusses limitations and/or assumptions that underlie the experiment
   3.5 Formulates or proposes a generalization or model
   3.6 Explains research findings and relationships
   3.7 Formulates new questions or defines problem based upon results of investigation.
4.0 Application
   4.1 Predicts, based upon results of this investigation
   4.2 Formulates hypothesis based on results of this investigation
   4.3 Applies experimental technique to new problem or variable
   4.4 Suggests ideas and ways to continue this investigation

---

The general tendency in the USA and elsewhere has been to test for most of the objectives listed in Table 7 by paper and pencil tests (e.g., Korth, 1968; Ruda, 1979). In the few cases where practical tests were used, they tended to focus on performance categories, mainly on categories 2.2 and 2.3 (e.g., Yager, Engen, & Snider, 1969).

In the UK there has been a long tradition of practical work followed by practical examinations. Even there the general tendency has been to test for processes included in Table 7 under categories 1.0, 3.0 and 4.0 in paper and pencil tests and restrict the practical examinations to some of the subcategories of category 2.0.

The Assessment of Performance Unit (APU) in the UK identified the following six process skills to be included in their assessment scheme: using symbolic representations (graphs, chemical symbols, formulae, diagrams); using apparatus and measuring instruments; observation; interpretation and application; design of investigations and performing investigations. Only three of the six processes, namely manipulation of apparatus, making observations and performing investigations were assessed by the actual performance of students, while the other three were tested by paper and pencil (Assessment of Performance Unit, 1978).

More recently a new wave of interest in performance testing stimulated interesting developments. Wiggins (1989) suggested several ways to improve assessment of achievement in science. In a special issues of the journal, *Educational Leadership,* Shavelson and Baxter (1992) described their work in assessing hands-on elementary science learning. New York State has required all fourth grade students to take a manipulative skills test as part of their elementary science evolution program (Doran, Lawrenz, & Helgeson, 1993b). Using practical laboratory tests at the high school and university levels were described by several authors, e.g. Kirschner (1991), Doran et al. (1993b), and Lazarowitz and Tamir (1993).

Types of practical tests

We define a practical examination as a task which requires some manipulation of apparatus or some action on materials and which involves direct experiences of the examinee with the materials or events at hand. Practical examinations may be administered individually or to groups.

(i) Individually administered test. This involves a student who performs the required tasks and an examiner who observes and/or guides the performance and assigns marks. Three different procedures will be described.

Observations. In the *first*, the examiner observes the performance and assigns marks following a prepared checklist. Usually s/he neither asks questions nor gives directions, but rather allows the examinee to follow written directions and hence assessment is confined to the observed behaviors. Here is an example based on Tyler's (1942) microscope checklist.

The teacher's goal is to see whether the student is able to operate a microscope so that a specimen present in a culture is located. The raw score is obtained by counting the number of YES responses.

a.	Does the student wipe the slide with lens paper?	YES NO
b.	Does the student place a drop or two of culture on slide?	YES NO
c.	Does the student wipe cover glass properly?	YES NO
d.	Does the student adjust cover glass adequately?	YES NO
e.	Does the student wipe off surplus fluid?	YES NO
f.	Does the student place slide on stage adequately?	YES NO
g.	Does the student look through eye piece and hold one eye closed?	YES NO
h.	Does the student turn to objective of lowest power?	YES NO
i.	Does the student adjust light and concave mirror?	YES NO
j.	Does the student adjust diaphragm?	YES NO
k.	Does the student use properly coarse adjustment?	YES NO
l.	Does the student break cover glass?	YES NO
m.	Does the student locate specimen?	YES NO

Interviews. The *second* kind of individually administered practical examination is essentially an interview quite similar to that developed by Piaget. Piaget did not limit himself to asking children the same set of questions. Rather, after beginning an interview with a standard question or two, he felt free to create spontaneous additional queries designed to probe the thought process that produced the child's initial answer. This approach was used, for example, by Nussbaum (1979) in assessing children's understanding of the concept Earth. Using a globe, a small figure of a person that could be attached to the globe, a styrofoam ball with a long straight hole in it to demonstrate holes in three dimensions, and a set of drawings, he was able to identify a number of alternative notions of Earth held by different children. These alternatives then became categories to be used in the assessment of other students' understanding of Earth. Here is an example of a result of one interview:

> Ruth (11 years old) told in detail how astronauts go on a space voyage and how they see from their spaceship that the Earth is round. Only after probing with the aid of the concrete props was it found that she had believed that we live on a flat Earth. The round Earth is up in the sky and when

astronauts go high enough they can photograph it and thus see that the Earth is round.

The Assessment of Performance Unit (APU 1978) has employed a combination strategy in their category designated as 'performing investigations.' They wrote:

> The problems lie in finding a way to take advantage of the richness of information the answers provide and to interpret the performance as correctly as possible. In some cases it is possible to assess the performance by observation using a checklist or sets of categories; in a few cases, what the pupils write gives a fair account of what they have done; in other cases, it may be necessary to use a combination of these two kinds of information plus additional data from interviewing pupils when they have finished. (p. 15)

Oral examinations. The *third* kind of individual practical is an oral examination based on concrete phenomena or materials. Examples are identification of parts in a prepared dissection or the kind of oral included in the matriculation of high school biology students in Israel who carry out an ecological project for several months and then bring a selection of organisms that they had studied to serve as objects for their oral examination. Here is an example (see Tamir 1972a):

> On the table lie a few pine tree branches with flowers and cones of different ages. The examinee is asked to suggest as many ways as he can to determine the age of a particular branch. He has to examine the branch to identify and point at the clues that may be used, such as the stage of development of the ovulate cones, the bare patches created by the falling of the staminate flowers -- one patch per year -- and the pattern of new growth. During the discussion the student talks and demonstrates and reveals his general familiarity with the structures and their functions.

> Although the examination started with one specific question, it continued in accordance with the student's responses and the questions they led the examiner to ask.

(ii) Group administered practical tests. Unlike the one-to-one examination, where assessment is based on direct observation and oral probing, group examinations are based on written responses. Three types of group administered practical examinations are described below. The first type involves the use of a dichotomous key to identify the name of an unrecognized object such as a rock or an organism. Tamir (1972b) describes this type of examination as follows:

> The ability to identify an unknown plant with the aid of a key is considered an important skill in biology. While developing this skill some corollary objectives may be achieved, such as developing observational skills, getting acquainted with principles of taxonomy, getting to meet and observe plants, experiencing the diversity of type and the unity of patterns: one of the major themes of biology.

The following procedures may be used: A group of students, usually no more than thirty, is seated one student per desk. A key, magnifying glass, needles, razor blade, pencil and paper, and a plant bearing flowers, fruit and roots are provided. On some occasions students are asked to make a full description of the plant, referring to the unique characteristics of roots, stem, arrangement of leaves, shape of leaves and their edges, arrangement of flowers, structure of flower, type of fruit. Following this description they proceed to the actual process of identification. In order to save time it is possible to skip the advance description and to proceed directly to the identification with the aid of the key. However, in order to keep track of the sequence used by the examinee and her/his ability to identify correctly the different features of the organism, the student is required to record the numbers of items which s/he followed, as well as the descriptions in the text which fit the organism under examination. A detailed scoring key is used according to which the student loses a pre-agreed mark for each mistake. Fifty percent of the marks are assigned to correct identification of the family, genus and species, while the other 50% are assigned to the correct recording of sequence and features. The examination lasts 30 to 45 minutes and inter-rater reliability averages 85% of agreement.

The second type of examination which is used often in the UK and in college science courses elsewhere is often designated as a 'circus' or 'stations.' Each table in the laboratory room constitutes a station. Each station provides equipment, materials and instructions for a particular task. The student gets between 5 and 25 minutes to perform, depending on the nature of the task. It is essential that the tasks require more or less the same length of time so that students can be conveniently moved from one station to another. One examiner can control six sets of three students each, altogether 18 students. Examinees perform such tasks which ask for written reports so that marking is, by and large, based on the written report. In certain tasks the examiner is asked to make occasional checks. For example, in a task which requires the use of a microscope, the student is instructed to call the examiner when s/he has completed mounting a slide for observation. The examiner checks the preparation, lighting and adjustment and assigns a mark which will constitute part of the overall mark of this particular task. Here is an example of a station task for 13 year-old students taken from the Assessment of Performance Unit (1978, p. 8):

Materials: Three dropping bottles labelled P (distilled water), Q (acetone in water), R (citric acid in water). Dry cobalt chloride paper in desiccator; blue litmus paper; six clean test tubes; safety spectacles.

To the student: You are given three clear liquids labelled P, Q and R, one of which is just water on its own. Follow the instructions below to find out which is just water.

a.   When cobalt chloride paper is put in a liquid which contains water it changes colour from blue to pale pink.

b.   When blue litmus paper is put in a liquid which is acid, it changes colour from blue to red.

1.   Test each liquid, one after the other, using a clean test tube and a fresh piece of indicator paper each time, first by the cobalt chloride paper and then by the blue litmus paper. Record your results in the table below.

Test	Liquid P	Liquid Q	Liquid R
Cobalt chloride paper			
Litmus paper			
Smell			

2.   Smell each liquid and tick in the table below which of the liquids has a smell.

3. Which liquid is just water? Give your reasons.

(Assessment of Perfomance Unit, 1978, p. 8)

A third type of examination was developed within the framework of the Israeli matriculation examination and is used each year with thousands of twelfth grade students. It was designated as inquiry-oriented practical examination; its test problems were designed and selected with the following considerations in mind (Tamir, 1974):

1. They should pose some real and intrinsically valuable problems before the students.
2. It should be possible to perform the task and conclude the investigation within a reasonable time limit (i.e., two hours).
3. The problems should be novel to the examinee, but the level of difficulty and the required skills should be compatible with the objectives of and experience provided by the curriculum.
4. Since every student will be able to perform just one full investigation, several different problems must be used simultaneously to ensure independent work within a group setting. However, for the sake of comparability, the different tests should be convergent on a number of skills with specific weights given to each skill (for example: manipulation -- 10 points; self-reliance -- 10; observation -- 10; experimental design -- 25; communication and reporting -- 15; reasoning -- 30). It may also be necessary to control for differences in the levels of difficulty by employing appropriate statistical procedures for the purpose of assigning grades.
5. The student performing a complete investigation may encounter certain difficulties at various steps of her/his work. It is inconceivable that s/he should fail the whole examination just because, for instance, s/he made some incorrect observations. Therefore, a procedure is needed for prompting -- or providing certain leads during the examinations without damaging the standards of assessment.
6. Since the tests are based on open-ended problems, measures of divergence are needed, but accepted limits of this divergence must still be set.
7. When tests of this kind are used as external examinations, special logistic problems are to be solved. For example, while certain materials can be prepared by the schools, some materials and organisms must be brought by the examiners in order to prevent examinees from obtaining clues regarding the tasks to be assigned during the examination. Also, careful preparation is needed for test administration as well as for assessment in order to provide standardized criteria. Moreover, since novelty is an important feature, new problems must be designed every year.

An example follows:

Problem 1

Materials: yeast, buffered carbonate solution, 0.2% neutral red unlabelled; NaOH, NH_4OH_1HCL (all 0.1 N); test tubes, flasks, etc.

When the student enters the laboratory s/he finds the materials and the examination paper. S/he is requested at several points during the examination to call the examiner who will circle specific answers with red ink and hand over cue notes that direct the continuation of the investi-gation. These notes are used to avoid or reduce the need for discussion between the examiner and the examinee.

Examination paper:

1. On the table you will find a red liquid. Using the materials on your table, find out the colour of this liquid in various pH concentrations. Write down the procedure and the results.
2. Prepare a yeast suspension (detailed instructions are given).
3. Mix 25 ml of the yeast suspension with an equal amount of the red liquid. Observe for five minutes. Record your observations.
4. Design a control to the test performed in No. 3 and show it to the examiner. (Examiner circles the answer and hands over a cue note.)
5. Perform the controlled test and record the results.
6. Explain your observation.
7. Suggest a way to test whether your explanation is correct. Show your design to the examiner. (Examiner circles the answer and hands over a cue note with instructions.)
8. Perform the test and write down your results and conclusions.
9. Do the results support your suggested explanation? If not, suggest another explanation.
10. In any case, suggest an additional way to test your explanation.
11. Carry out the test and record the results and conclusions.
12. Do you think that the yeast you worked with was alive?
13. Design an experiment to test your answer in No. 12. (Examiner will hand over a cue note.)
14. Perform the experiment and record the results.
15. Briefly sum up the findings and conclusions of your investigation.

The examiner gets a sheet with detailed instructions regarding her/his behavior during the examination as well as sample answers. For instance, sample answer 15 reads:

> Yeast cell membrane permits absorption and accumulation of neutral red. Since the pH in the yeast is acid, the colour of the cell is red. The buffer solution is basic and therefore has a yellow colour. When the yeast cells are dead, they lose their selective permeability, their content mixes with the buffer solution and hence the yellow colour dominates.

In order to standardize the assessment and increase its reliability, a special instrument designated as a Process Tests Assessment Inventory (PTAI) was developed (Tamir et al., 1982).

PTAI was designed on the basis of an analysis of answers of hundreds of students who had taken the laboratory biology matriculation tests in the years 1976-1979. The PTAI was validated by three science educators who read 100 papers and classified the questions and answers into categories. They reached 93-100% agreement. Inter-rater reliability was checked by three raters who assessed independently the same 40 tests, assigning marks to each response. They reached 81% agreement. Following that, the items in which there was disagreement were identified and certain revisions were made. The same 40 tests were assessed again by three raters and the level of inter-rater agreement reached 90%.

PTAI consist of 21 categories of which six are described below. However, when the need arises it is possible to add or modify categories. Following are the six categories, accompanied by brief descriptions.   A description of selected rubrics are then presented in Figure 2.

1.   Formulating problems

This category includes any item which requires the students to formulate a problem to be investigated. For example, a certain experimental system is presented and the examinee is asked: 'Formulate a problem which you can investigate with this system'. Another example: Having performed a particular experiment, the student is asked: 'What was the problem that you have tried to investigate?'

2   Formulating hypotheses

This category includes any item which requires the student to formulate an hypothesis. For example, a certain experimental system is presented and the examinee is asked: 'What hypothesis can be tested with this system?' Another example: Having performed a particular experiment, the student is asked: 'What was the hypothesis tested by this experiment?'

3.   Identifying dependent variable

The dependent variable is that variable whose behavior is determined by the treatment in the experiment. For example, an experiment is designed to investigate the effect of temperature on the respiration rate. In this case the dependent variable is the respiration rate. The treatments are the different temperatures. The respiration rate will be measured for each of these temperature.

4.   Making tables

This category is used when the examinee is specifically required to make a table of his/her results. When a table outline is included in the test paper, this category should not be used, but rather category 9.

5.   Interpreting observed data

This category includes interpretation of direct observations. For example: 'Observe the difference in colour between the solution in the two test tubes. How would you explain this difference?'

6.   Drawing conclusions

This category includes any item which requires the examinee explicitly to draw a conclusion or which implies the drawing of a conclusion. For example: 'Based on your results, what was the effect of temperature on the carrot cells? Explain.'

PTAI categories can be helpful not only in the evaluation but also in the design of process skills tests. As for evaluation, once the student 's answer has been matched with its category, a predetermined scale is used. Figure 2 presents the scales (rubrics) for selected categories. Since the scales are hierarchical -- namely the higher the level the better the answer -- answers classified to levels can easily be translated into scores. More details can be found in Tamir et al. (1982).

Formulating problems
   6 Relevant problem formulated as a question
   5 Relevant problem not formulated as a question
   4 Relevant problem supplemented by hypothesis
   3 Hypothesis instead of a problem
   2 Non-relevant problem, ambiguous formulation
   1 Problem not formulated
Formulating hypotheses
Hypothesis fits the problem or the situation
   7 (a) Formulated as 'if...then...'
   7 (b) Well formulated, but not using 'if...then...'
   6 Cumbersome or ambiguous formulation
   5 Formulation contains logical or factual fallacy
   4 Hypothesis does not fit the problem or the situation
   3 Problem instead of hypothesis
   2 Assumption instead of hypothesis
   1 Hypothesis not formulated
Identifying dependent variable
   5 Dependent variable fits the problem or the hypothesis
   4 Dependent variable formulated in terms of measuring techniques
   3 Independent instead of dependent variable
   2 Dependent variable does not fit the hypothesis
   1 Dependent variable not identified

Figure 2

Selected Rubrics of PTAI (The numbers preceding every topic are raw scores)

In summary, PTAI may be used in the following ways:
It helps in obtaining standardized and more objective assessment.
It facilitates marking and increases its reliability.
It provides description of skills measured by a particular test (content analysis).
It provides easy-to-interpret feedback to teachers.
It may provide useful feedback to students.
It may provide useful data for the purpose of curriculum evaluation.
It may help in exercises designed to provide experiences in the identification and analysis of inquiry and intellectual skills.
It may help in the design of inquiry-oriented laboratory examinations.
It may help in the assessment of written inquiry examinations.
It may serve for research purposes.

Other Individually Administered Performance Examinations

These are common in vocational and professional subjects such as typing, driving, medicine and agriculture. Here, however, we confine ourselves to practical examinations in science.

GENERAL OUTCOMES (ADDITIONAL TOOLS)

The tests described so far focus on the outcomes which are usually associated with science learning in school. The major emphasis has been on objectives related to the cognitive domain with some attention given to the psychomotor domain.

In the present section we describe briefly some procedures which are not used commonly in schools and which may be used to assess outcomes which go beyond those which are regularly included in the assessment of students' achievement. Some of these relate to the cognitive domain, others to the affective domain and still others have both cognitive and affective ingredients.

Cognitive Outcomes

Understanding the nature of science

Understanding the nature of science is considered one of the most important goals of science education. The two most widely used instruments for this purpose are the Test of Understanding Science (TOUS) and the Science Process Inventory (SPI). TOUS (Cooley & Klopfer, 1961) includes 60 multiple choice items which cover three scales: (1) understanding about the scientific enterprise; (2) understanding about scientists and (3) understanding about the aims and methods of science. SPI (Welch & Pella, 1967-68) consists of 150 true-false items covering assumptions, activities, products, and ethics of science.

Cognitive development

Testing for cognitive development is usually based on the theory of Piaget. There are two main reasons to employ such tests in the context of science: First, the stage of cognitive development may impose restrictions on the concepts that can be learned meaningfully, and second, science learning may facilitate cognitive development. In both cases there is a need to measure cognitive development. The individual clinical interview as used by Piaget is not feasible for teachers to use in their classrooms. However, a number of group tests were developed and successfully used (e.g., Lawson, 1978; Tisher & Dale, 1975; Tobin & Capie, 1980). These tests focus on skills such as conservation of weight, proportional reasoning, controlling variables, probabilistic reasoning, correlational reasoning, and combinational reasoning. The relevance of such skills to science learning is quite obvious.

Creativity

Although the potential of science learning as a means for developing creativity has often been mentioned (e.g., Getzels, 1964; Romey, 1970), practically no standard measures are available to assess creativity in the context of science. The instrument most widely used has been the Torrance Test of Creative Thinking (Torrance, 1974). Lehman (1972) measured creativity in science in the following way: Students who observed a scientific experiment were asked to write down questions concerning the experiment. Questions classified as creative were open-ended and required responses that propose new or different applications of principles learned. The number of such creative questions served as a measure of creativity.

Critical thinking and logical reasoning

Critical thinking is also considered to be a major goal of science education. The most widely used instruments are the Watson Glazer Critical Thinking Appraisal (Ramsey & Howe, 1969) and the Cornell Critical Thinking Test (Ennis & Millman, 1967). Neither test focuses specifically on science. Recently Jungwirth (1987) has developed and used a test of logical reasoning in the context of science. This test examines the ability of students to avoid the following fallacies:

1. Assuming that events which follow others are caused by them.
2. Drawing conclusions on the basis of an insufficient number of instances (samples too small).
3. Drawing conclusions on the basis of nonrepresentative instances.
4. Assuming that something which is true in specific circumstances is true in general.
5. Imputing causal significance to correlations.
6. Drawing inferences about individual cases from the mean of the population.
7. Drawing conclusions on the basis of very small and fortuitous differences.
8. Explaining by use of tautologies (circular reasoning).

A sample item, relating to the first logical fallacy, follows:

Some pupils grew tomatoes in the laboratory. One day the plants were watered with soapy water by mistake. They continued to grow, but purple spots appeared on the leaves. What is your opinion? (Choose the appropriate answer.)
(a)   No conclusion can be drawn, since we are not told what kind of soap was used.
(b)   The soap caused the appearance of the purple spots since none had been there before.
(c)   I often water my garden with soapy water and never saw purple spots on the leaves, so that cannot be the reason.
(d)   I don't agree with any of these choices.

AFFECTIVE OUTCOMES

Interests

According to Klopfer (1971) interest in science may be viewed under two dimensions, namely, interest in science-related activities and interest in pursuing science or science-related careers. Interest in science activities is further divided as follows:

1. Voluntary out-of-school science activities, such as doing chemical experiments, collecting insects, visiting science museums, building radios, flying model airplanes, growing plants.
2. Formalized science learning activities in school, such as reading science textbooks, doing laboratory experiments, watching science films.

Two widely used interest masuring instruments are the Science Activity Inventory (Cooley & Reed, 1961) and Meyer's Test of Interests (Meyer, 1970). Interest in a science career has been measured by inventories presenting lists of careers and asking students to indicate their level of interest in each career (e.g., Butcher & Pont, 1968).

Relatively little research on interests and science learning has been published. In the Second International Science Study (SISS), positive but low correlations are reported between interest and achievement in science. An international conference to which participants were personally invited and only invited persons could participate was held in 1985 in IPN and a full report was published (see Lehrke, Hoffmann, & Gardner, 1985).

A major study of the structure of interest in biology was conducted by Tamir and Gardner (1989). The main findings of this study were summarized by the authors as follows:

1.   In Israel 56% of high school students are science oriented with two-thirds of this group electing to specialize in biology. The specializing students have a distinctly more positive interest profile than other students.
2.   Interest in biology is multidimensional. The highest levels of interest for each dimension were: *Topics* -- Human biology; *Activities* -- Problem solving; *Learning mode* -- Experiential, taking place in the laboratory or outdoors; *Motive* -- Instrumental, e.g., success in the matriculation examination and preparing for future career.
3.   Attitudes toward the study of biology are strongly related to interest.
4.   Boys are more interested in the applications of science and in science-based careers, whereas girls are more interested in certain topics such as reproduction and human physiology.

Curiosity

Curiosity has been acknowledged as 'a human resource which facilitates learning, intellectual development and the pursuit of scientific discovery' (Peterson, 1979, p. 185). Curiosity has been defined as 'a kind of intrinsic motivation...an intention to seek information about an object, an event or idea through exploratory behavior' (Klausmeier, 1975, p. 221).

Two measures of curiosity are described below:

1. Campbell Curiosity Inventory (CCI) consists of 54 Yes/No items which sample the first three levels of the taxonomy in the affective domain (Krathwohl, Bloom, & Masia, 1964), namely Receiving, Responding and Valuing. Following is a typical CCI item (Campbell, 1972):
*   Have you ever wondered what chemicals are in aspirin?   (receiving)
*   I would enjoy doing research on the chemical properties of aspirin (responding)
*   I would go to a meeting where questions of this kind will be discussed (valuing)

2. Cognitive preference tests
Studies of cognitive preferences (see following section) have identified a dimension which was designated as intellectual curiosity. The level of intellectual curiosity is obtained by measuring the preferences of an individual or a group for recall of facts (designated as R) and critical questioning (designated as Q). The derived score Q minus R represents intellectual curiosity within a given science discipline (Kempa & Dube, 1973).

Cognitive Preferences

Cognitive preferences constitute a kind of cognitive style strongly related to subject matter and school learning. Essentially, cognitive preferences is a measure of what students *are likely to do* with scientific information presented to them and not of whether they can identify correct or incorrect information. Four preference modes were identified by Heath (1964) in relation to scientific information, as follows:

1. *Recall (R)*: Acceptance of information without consideration of its implications, applications or limitations.
2. *Principles (P)*: Acceptance of information because it exemplifies or illuminates a fundamental principle, concept or relationship.
3. *Questioning (Q)*: Critical questioning of information regarding its completeness, generalizability or limitations.
4. *Application (A)*: Emphasis on the usefulness and applicability of information in a general, social, or scientific context.

Every item in a cognitive preference test presents an introductory statement followed by four options, each of which corresponds to one of the four modes just defined. The examinee is told that all four options are correct and is asked to rank the options by assigning 4 to the most appealing, 3 to the next, 2 to the next and 1 to the least appealing. Four scores are obtained, one for each of the modes.

Following are two sample items, the first in the physical and the second in the biological sciences:

1. The pressure of a gas is directly proportional to its absolute temperature.
   a. The above statement fails to consider the effects of volume changes.
   b. Charles' or Gay-Lussac's Law.
   c. The statement implies a lower limit to temperature.
   d. The principle is related to the fact that overheated car tires may 'blow out'.
2. Sugars are provided to the body by various foods.
   a. The concentration of glucose in the blood of healthy humans is constant.
   b. Food rich in carbohydrates is a good source of energy for farm animals.
   c. Since proteins can also supply energy, can the body survive without a supply of carbohydrates?
   d. The general formula of carbohydrates is $C_3(H_2O)_3$.

In these items R is represented by options b and d; P by c and a; Q by a and c; and A by d and b respectively.

Research has shown that cognitive preferences may be modified by curriculum and instruction and that achievement is negatively correlated with preference for R and positively correlated with preference for P and Q (Tamir, 1985).

The value of intellectual curiosity and application of knowledge has already been mentioned. Hence, an important goal of science education is to promote a preference for P, Q and A and to decrease a preference for R. Whether and to what extent this goal has been achieved may be measured by appropriate cognitive preference tests, namely tests whose content relates directly to the content of the curriculum studied.

ADDITIONAL MEASURES

The tools in this section are, as yet, not widely used. They may be employed to assess any learning outcomes.

Portfolios

A portfolio may be defined as 'a container of documents that provide evidence of someone's knowledge, skill and disposition' (Collins, 1993, p. 1106). Portfolios have been in operation in several professional areas including the arts, medicine, law and the military. Portfolios have been adopted by the Teacher Assessment Project (TAP) at Stanford University to provide authentic assessment of teachers. An excellent review of the work of TAP is available (Collins, 1993). Eventually it was realized that portfolios may be used to assess student performance as well and the approach was indeed implemented for obtaining alternative assessment of student achievements (Hamm & Adams, 1991). In the USA, the state of Vermont uses student portfolios for accountability (Brewer, 1989) and the state of Michigan has instituted a requirement that all high school students develop employability portfolios (Doran, Borman, Chen, & Hegarty, 1993a).

Although good teachers have been using students' products for assessment purposes for ages, the formalization of portfolio-based assessment has occurred only recently. The actual use, benefits and limitations of portfolios for assessing students' achievement has yet to be empirically examined.

Computer Based Tests

The microcomputer has an enormous potential for testing. Any problem solving task can serve as a test, since the computer can accurately monitor and record the steps that the student employs in the process of solving the problem. Moreover, the computer can provide immediate feedback and actually interact with the examinee. The computer can also provide unique contexts which simulate real life situations, thereby enabling students to demonstrate their decision making skills.

One limitation of practical laboratory tests is the need to identify experiments that can be completed in a relatively short time (no more than two hours). This excludes important areas such as genetics and microbiology. However, the computer can easily change that by its time lapse capability. Thus a student can actually cross-breed various phenotypes, obtain immediate results and proceed from one generation to another. In microbiology it is possible to combine actual laboratory performance with computer-based performance. For example, a student may actually seed certain cultures of bacteria in petri dishes, but instead of waiting long hours for the results, simulated data may be provided by the computer and the student may proceed by interacting with these data.

Cooperative Tests

Although cooperative learning does not necessarily imply cooperative testing, the latter may also be used. Certainly individual accountability for mastering the assigned materials is essential and requires individual testing (Johnson & Johnson, 1987, p.

85). However if our interest is to assess the ability of students to function as group members, or if we are interested in promoting group work through competition among groups, then cooperative tests may be employed. These tests comprise certain tasks assigned to the groups and the grade assigned to the group is counted as that of each member of that group. When desired, it is possible to assign individual marks as well.

Open-book Tests

In every-day life people do not take regular classroom tests. Often, however, we need to solve problems -- a task for which we need more information. Developing the ability to locate relevant information and use it to solve problems is an important goal of education in general and of science and technology education in particular. A good way to facilitate the development of this ability is to use open book tests which also encourage students to collect and organize the various resources available in the course.

Take Home Tests

These are usually open book tests which involve complex tasks which may require the use of a library or other out-of-class resources. Often the product is an integrated document such as a plan for action.

Long Term Transfer Tasks

Ausubel (1968) argues that commonly used tests are inadequate measures of meaningful learning because students are capable of memorizing large bodies of knowledge for successful performance in these examinations even though they have not really understood the relevant concepts (see also our discussion in the 'Learning Theories' section). The best evidence of meaningful learning, according to Ausubel, is the ability of the student to learn and understand new concepts which are substantively related to and based on the previously learned material. This kind of relationship is designated as the 'long term transfer paradigm.' Accordingly a test for understanding mitosis and meiosis, for example, may be an unseen paragraph describing the life cycle of a fern accompanied by pertinent questions which assume knowledge and understanding of the differences between mitosis and meiosis.

Cloze Tests

Cloze procedure is often used for the purpose of assessing reading comprehension. When applied to scientific paragraphs this procedure can serve as a measure of long term transfer as described under Long Term Transfer Tasks. Instead of questions, however, every fifth word in the paragraph is deleted and the student is required to fill the blanks so that the completed paragraph makes sense, thereby providing evidence for the student's knowledge and understanding.

Modified Cloze Tests

In order to make the test more interesting, somewhat playful and entertaining, it is possible to present a paragraph in which certain key concepts have been replaced by nonsense words. The student has to identify the right words according to the content and meaning of the sentences.

Game-like Tests

The modified cloze test was one example of a game-like test. There are endless possibilities of game-like tests. Any word game can be adapted to serve as a test. Crosswords is a good example.

FUTURE TRENDS

Two conflicting trends appear in the educational arena. On the one hand, an increasing interest in school and teacher autonomy may be observed. School-based curriculum is being discussed and implemented as yet in a few schools only. Regarding assessment, this trend implies a larger share of teachers in assessment which will probably become less formal and decrease the use of tests. At the same time, there is a growing interest in alternative assessment which will be more authentic and will better serve the needs of students and teachers as a diagnostic tool and a guide for teaching and learning.

In this chapter we presented a broad variety of ideas, strategies and tools which have the potential of supporting and enriching teaching and learning, regardless of which trend is being followed. In order to ascertain that assessment in schools will indeed live up to our expectations, more time and attention should be given to assessment in preservice and in-service education. Finally, many of the ideas and suggestions in this chapter are tentative and may need to be modified to fit different contexts. There is a great need for research in assessment to obtain guidelines on how to adapt assessment to local needs.

REFERENCES

Ahman, S.S., & Glock, M.D. (1967). *Evaluating pupil growth*, Boston: Allyn & Bacon.

Amir, R., & Tamir, P. (1994). Detailed analysis of misconceptions as a basis for developing remedial instruction: The case of photosynthesis. *The American Biology Teacher, 56*, 94--99.

Assessment of Performance Unit. (1978). *Science progress report 1977-78.* London: Elizabeth House.

Ausubel, D.P. (1968). *Educational psychology - A cognitive View.* New York: Holt, Rinehart & Winston.

Brewer, R. (1989), *State assessment of student performance.* Paper presented at the Education Commission of the States Annual Assessment Conference, Boulder CO.

Butcher, H.S., & Pont, H.B. (1968). Options about careers among Scottish secondary school Children of high ability, *British Journal of Educational Psychology, 38*, 272--279.

Bybee, R.W., & DeBoer, G. (1993). Research on goals for the science curriculum. In D.L. Gabel (Ed.), *Handbook of research in science teaching and learning* (pp. 357-387). New York: Macmillan.

Campbell, J.R. (1972). Is scientific curiosity a viable outcome in today's secondary school science program? *School Science and Mathematics, 72*, 139-146.

Collins, A. (1993). Performance based assessment of biology teachers: Promises and pitfalls. *Journal of Research in Science Teaching, 30*, 1103-1120.

Cooley, W.W., & Klopfer, L.W. (1961). *Test of understanding science.* Princeton NJ: Educational Testing Service.

Cooley, W.W., & Reed, W. (1961). *Science activities inventory.* Princeton NJ: Educational Testing Service.

Doran, R.L., Borman, J., Chen, F., & Hegarty, N. (1993a). Alternative assessment of high school laboratory skills. *Journal of Research in Science Teaching, 30*, 1121-1132.

Doran, R.L., Lawrenz, B., & Helgeson, S. (1993b). Research on assessment in science. In D. Gabel (Ed.), *Handbook of research in science teaching and learning,* (pp. 388-432). New York: Macmillan.

Ennis, R.H., & Millman, J. (1967). *Cornell critical thinking test form Z.* Ithaca: Cornell University .

Falchikov, N., & Boud, D. (1989). Student self-assessment in higher education: A meta-analysis. *Review of Educational Research, 59*, 395-430.

Getzels, J.W. (1964). Creative thinking, problem solving and instruction. In E.R. Hilgard (Ed.), *Theories of Learning and Instruction,* (pp. 240-267). Chicago: University of Chicago Press.

Glaser, R., & Nitko, A.I. (1971). Measurement in learning and instruction. In R.L. Thorndike (Ed.), *Educational Measurement.* Washington, DC: American Council of Education.

Hamm, M., & Adams, D. (1991). Portfolio Assessment. *The Science Teacher 58*(5), 18-21.

Heath, R.W. (1964). Curriculum cognition and educational measurement. *Educational and Psychological Measurement, 24,* 230-253.

Hegarty-Hazel, E. (1990). Life science laboratory classroom at tertiary level. In E. Hegarty-Hazel (Ed.), *The student laboratory and the science curriculum,* (pp. 357-382). London: Rutledge.

Jeffrey, J.C. (1967). Evaluation of science laboratory instruction. *Science Education, 51*, 186-194.

Johnson, R.T., & Johnson, D.W. (1987). Cooperative learning and the achievement and socialization crises in science and mathematics classrooms. In A.B. Champagne, & L.E. Hornig (Eds.), *Students and science learning,* (pp. 67-94). Washington DC: American Association for the Advancement of Science.

Jungwirth, E. (1987). Avoidance of logical fallacies: A neglected aspect of science education and science teacher education. *Research in Science and Technological Education, 5*, 43-58.

Kempa, R.F., & Dube, G.E. (1973). Cognitive preference orientations in students of chemistry. *British Journal of Educational Psychology, 43*, 279-288.

Kirschner, P.A. (1991), *Practicals in higher science education.* Lamma Centre for Educational Technology and Innovations. Amsterdam, The Netherlands: Open University of The Netherlands.

Klausmeier, H.J. (1975). *Learning and human abilities: Educational psychology.* New York: Harper & Row.

Klinckman, E. (1970). *The biology teachers' handbook* (2nd ed.). New York: Wiley.

Klopfer, L.E. (1971). Evaluation of learning science. In B.S. Bloom, T.Y. Hastings, & G.E. Madaus (Eds.). *Handbook of formative and summative evaluation of student learning.* New York: McGraw Hill.

Korth, W.W. (1968). *Life science process test: Form B.* Cleveland OH: Educational Research Council of America.

Krathwohl, D.R., Bloom, B.S., & Masia, B.B. (1964). *Taxonomy of educational objectives. Handbook II: Affective domain.* New York: McKay.

Lawson, A.E. (1978). The development and validation of a classroom test of formal reasoning. *Journal of Research in Science Teaching, 15,* 11-24.

Lawson, A.E. (1993). Research on acquisition of science knowledge: Epistemological foundations of cognition. In D. Gabel (Ed.), *Handbook of Research in Science Teaching and Learning,* (pp. 131-176). New York: Macmillan.

Lazarowitz, R., & Tamir, P. (1993). Research in using laboratory instruction in science. In D.L. Gabel (Ed.), *Handbook of research in science teaching and learning* (pp. 94-130). New York: Macmillan.

Lechlerg, D. (1982). Confidence marking: Its use in testing,' *Evaluation in Education, 6,* 163-287.

Lehman, R.A. (1972). The effects of creativity and intelligence on pupils' questions in science. *Science Education, 56,* 103-121.

Lehrke, M., Hoffmann, L., & Gardner, P.L. (Eds.). (1985). *Interests in science and technology education.* Kiel: University of Kiel, IPN.

Lunetta V.N., & Tamir, P. (1979). Matching lab activities with teaching goals. *The Science Teacher, 45,* 494-502.

Mehrens, W.A. (1973). *Measurement and evaluation in educational psychology.* New York: Holt, Rinehart & Winston.

Meyer, G.R. (1970). Reaction of students to Nuffield Science Teaching Trial materials at O level of the GCE. *Journal of Research in Science Teaching , 7,* 283-297.

Novak, J.D. (1980). Learning theory applied to the biology classroom. *The American Biology Teacher, 42,* 280-286.

Novak, J.D. (1981). Applying learning psychology and philosophy of science to biology teaching. *The American Biology Teacher , 43,* 12-20.

Novak, J.D., & Gowin, D.B. (1984). *Learning how to learn.* London: Cambridge University Press.

Nussbaum, J. (1979). Israeli children's conceptions of earth as a cosmic body: A cross age study. *Science Education, 63,* 83-93.

Nussbaum, J., & Novak, J.D. (1986). An assessment of conceptions of the earth utilizing structured interviews. *Science Education, 60,* 535-550.

Olson, D.R. (1973). What is worth knowing and what can be taught. *School Review, 82,* 27-43.

Peterson, R.W. (1979). Changes in curiosity from childhood to adolescence. *Journal of Research in Science Teaching, 16,* 185-192.

Ramsey, G.A., & Howe, R.W. (1969). An analysis of research on instructional procedures in secondary school science, Part I: Outcomes of instruction. *The Science Teacher, 36*(3), 62-70.

Renners, H.H. (1960). *A practical introduction to measurement and evaluation,* New York: Harper.

Romey, W.D. (1970). What is your creativity quotient?. *School Science and Mathematics, 70,* 3-8.

Ruda, P. (1979). *Unpublished chemistry laboratory practical examination,* Checktowaga NY: Cleveland Hill High School.

Schwab, J.J. (1963). *The biology teacher handbook.* New York: Wiley.

Schwartz, P.A. (1971). Prediction instruments for educational outcomes. In R.L. Thorndike (Ed.), *Educational Measurement.* Washington, DC: American Council of Education.

Shavelson, R., & Baxter, G. (1992). What we have learned about assessing hands-on science. *Educational Leadership, 48*(8), 20-25.

Simpson, R.D., Koballa Jr., T.R., Oliver, J., & Crawley, F.E. II (1993). Research on the affective dimension of science learning. In D.L. Gabel (Ed.), *Handbook of research in science teaching and learning* (pp. 211-236). New York: Macmillan.

Stader, E., Colyar, T., & Berlinger, D. (1990). *Expert and novice teachers' ability to judge student understanding.* Paper presented at the Annual Meeting of the American Educational Research Association, Boston.

Stewart, J. (1979). Content and cognitive structure: Critique of assessment and representation techniques used by science education researchers. *Science Education, 63,* 395-405.

Tamir, P. (1971). An alternative Aapproach to the construction of multiple choice test items, *Journal of Biological Education, 5,* 305-307.

Tamir, P. (1972a). The role of the oral examination in biology. *School Science Review, 54,* 162-165.

Tamir, P. (1972b). Plant identification -- A worthwhile aspect of achievement in biology, *Australian Science Teacher Journal, 18,* 62-66.

Tamir, P. (1972c). The practical model: A distinct model of performance in biology. *Journal of Biological Education, 6,* 175-182.

Tamir, P. (1973). Attitudes of students and teachers towards the practical examinations in biology. *BSCS Newsletter, 53,* 2-5.

Tamir, P. (1974). An inquiry oriented laboratory examination. *Journal of Educational Measurement, 11,* 25-33.

Tamir, P. (1985). A meta-analysis of cognitive preferences. *Journal of Research in Science Teaching, 22,* 1-17.

Tamir, P. (1991a). Factors associated with the acquisition of functional knowledge and understanding of science, *Research in Science and Technological Education, 9,* 17-38.

Tamir, P. (1991b). Some issues related to the use of justifications to multiple choice items, *Journal of Biological Evaluation, 24,* 285-292.

Tamir, P., & Amir, R. (1981). Retrospective curriculum evaluation: An approach to the evaluation of long term effects. *Curriculum Inquiry, 11,* 259-278.

Tamir, P., & Gardner, P. (1989). The structure of interest in high school biology. *Research in Science and Technological Education, 7,* 113-140.

Tamir, P., & Lunetta, V.N. (1978). An analysis of laboratory activities in the BSCS Yellow version. *American Biology Teacher, 40,* 426-428.

Tamir, P., Nussinovitz, R., & Friedler, Y.(1982). A practical tests assessment inventory. *Journal of Biological Education, 16,* 42-50.

Thorndike, R.L. (Ed.). (1971). *Educational measurement.* Washington DC: American Council on Education.

Tisher, R.P., & Dale, L.G. (1975). *Understanding in science test.* Victoria: Australian Council for Educational Research.

Tobin, K.G., & Capie, W. (1980). *The test of logical thinking, development and application.* Paper presented at the Annual Meeting of the National Association of Research in Science Teaching, Boston.

Tobin, K.G., Tippins, D.J., & Aljandro, J.G. (1993). Research in instructional strategies for teaching science. In D.L. Gabel (Ed.), *Handbook of research in science teaching and learning* (pp. 45-93). New York: Macmillan.

Torrance, E.P. (1974). *Norms technical manual: Torrance tests of creative thinking.* Lexington , MA: Personal Press.

Tyler, R.W. (1942). A test of skill in using a microscope. *Educational Research Bulletin, 9,* 493-496.

Welch, W.W., & Pella, M.O. (1967-68). The development of an instrument for inventorying knowledge of the processes of science. *Journal of Research in Science Teaching, 5,* 64-68.

Wiggins, G. (1989). A true test: Toward more authentic and equitable assessment. *Phi Delta Kappan, 7,* 703-713.

Woolnough, B.E., & Allsop, T. (1985). *Practical work in science.* Cambridge: Cambridge University Press.

Yager, R.E., Engen, H.B., & Snider, B.C.F. (1969). Effects of the laboratory and demonstration methods upon outcomes in secondary biology. *Journal of Research in Science Teaching, 6,* 76-86.

On the Content Validity
of Performance Assessments:
Centrality of Domain Specification

Richard J. Shavelson
Xiaohong Gao
Gail P. Baxter

Performance assessments--such as writing prompts in language arts, hands-on experiments in science, or portfolios in mathematics--are being heralded as "authentic" assessments (e.g., Wiggins, 1989). They play a central role in the rhetoric, if not the reality, of proposed state and national testing programs (e.g., Bush, 1991; see Shavelson, Baxter & Pine, 1992). Unfortunately, in the headlong pursuit of testing reform, technical considerations may be pushed aside (e.g., Linn, Baker, & Dunbar, 1991; Shavelson & Baxter, 1992). Technical considerations include reliability and validity of performance assessments, and the interchangeability of alternative methods of measuring performance (e.g., hands-on investigations, computer simulations, short-answer questions). Empirical research has, to date, focused primarily on interrater and intertask reliability (e.g., Dunbar, Koretz, & Hoover, 1991; Shavelson, Baxter, Pine, & Yuré, 1991; Shavelson, Baxter, Pine, Yuré, Goldman, & Smith, 1991). The findings are consistent. Interrater reliability is not a problem. Raters can be trained to score performance reliably in real time or from surrogates such as notebooks (e.g., Baxter, Shavelson, Goldman, & Pine, 1992; Shavelson, et al., in press). Task-sampling variability, however, is large, substantially reducing the reliability of the measurements (e.g., Dunbar et al., 1991; Linn et al., 1991; Shavelson, Baxter, & Gao, in press). If performance assessments are to prove useful in practice, task-sampling variability must be addressed.

Task-sampling variability arises, in part, from the complexity of the domain from which assessment tasks are drawn. The larger and more complex the domain, the greater the potential reduction in reliability due to task heterogeneity. This variability may also arise from individual differences among students' performances on particular tasks (e.g., person x task interaction). The magnitude of task sampling variability and the reliability of performance assessments, then, rest importantly on content validity--the extent to which a sample of tasks and performances on them represent the set of tasks and corresponding behavior in the domain of interest.

Content validity addresses four closely related but distinct questions (Cronbach, 1971; Messick 1989): (a) How accurately is the subject-matter domain specified? (b) How well does the test content represent the domain? (c) Do the behaviors exhibited on the test constitute a representative sample of behaviors in the domain? and (d) Are the cognitive processes used by examinees in responding to an assessment representative of the processes underlying the domain of responses? This paper focuses on domain and test specification.

In job-performance assessment, the centrality of domain and test specification is well recognized (e.g., Wigdor & Green, 1991). The domain, finite and countable, can be specified on the basis of either a job analysis or information in personnel documents. In creating a job performance test, a sample of tasks can be drawn from the domain and inferences can be made to performance on the job as a whole (cf. Guion, 1977). In addition, with this sampling framework, errors of inference can be evaluated formally (Wigdor & Green, 1991, especially Chapter 4).

In educational performance assessments the role of content validity is as important as in job-performance measurement, but is more difficult to tie down because domain specifications for education are, of necessity, somewhat vaguer (cf. Cronbach, 1971). Nevertheless, Baxter, Shavelson, Herman, Brown, & Valadez (in press) provided one example of how a subject-matter domain might be defined and tasks specified for performance assessments. In their work, they used California's Mathematics Framework (California State Department of Education, 1985) to define the fifth-grade mathematics domain. The Framework stratified the domain to major areas (e.g., place value, measurement, probability) and Baxter et al. searched for representative activities or tasks for a sample of the major areas. They found these tasks in books with hands-on teaching exercises, and through consultation with teachers in the California Mathematics Project, mathematics educators, and a UCSB mathematician. They then characterized each major area by a large set of representative teaching tasks. A sample of these tasks was then translated into hands-on performance assessments (see Baxter et al., in press, for details).

In our research on elementary science assessments (e.g., Shavelson et al., 1991), we began with the domain of "living things" from the California Science Framework (1990). A typical set of classroom activities within this domain dealt with choice behavior of meal worms. Students set up experiments to determine which of two to four substances (e.g., sugar, cornflakes) meal worms choose to eat. In creating performance assessments we used sow bug experiments to parallel the meal worm experiments. Fifth- and sixth-grade students conducted three experiments to determine sow bugs' choices of various environments. The first experiment was to determine whether sow bugs would choose light or dark environments. The second asked whether the bugs would choose damp or dry environments. Having somewhat exhausted the major environmental conditions, the next obvious step was to combine them in a factorial experiment. The third experiment, then, asked students to investigate choice behavior in a factorial combination of the first two experiments: which combination of environments do sow bugs prefer--dark and dry? dark and damp? light and dry? or light and damp?

Students performing the experiments were observed by scientists and science educators; their performance was scored in real time, as well as from notebooks in which they recorded their experimental setups and procedures. Observations and subsequent data analyses (e.g., Shavelson et al., 1991) showed convincingly that the third experiment was qualitatively different and more difficult than the first two.

This finding led us to take a close look at elementary classroom experiments with meal worms. What became clear was that none of the experiments included factorial designs. Classroom teaching tasks systematically manipulated a single variable. If we had done our homework instead of simply combining the variables in the first two experiments, we would have found that factorials fell outside the domain of 5th or 6th grade science. Instead, we would have included a third experiment such as asking whether sow bugs choose dry, damp, or wet environments. We had unintentionally misspecified the domain. This unintentional misspecification error, however, provided a glimpse at the link between content validity, task-sampling variability and reliability--issues central to the technical evaluation of performance assessments.

Our purpose, then, is to empirically demonstrate this link. In our particular example, we show that domain misspecification in science assessment may give rise to overestimates of task-sampling variability and, consequently, to overestimates of the number of tasks needed to achieve some minimal level of reliability. The consequence of misspecification affects decisions about individual students or about aggregates of students--in this study, class mean performance.

The magnitude of task-sampling variability and the number of tasks needed to reach minimum generalizability (cf. reliability), however, can be underestimated as well, depending on the choice of boundaries for the domain. For example, suppose the domain of 11th grade science was misspecified by restricting it to single independent variable experiments when the curriculum actually includes factorials. In this case, the tasks included in an assessment might be "easy," so easy that almost all students perform well. This misspecification would lead to an underestimate of task- sampling variability.

METHOD

Subjects

We drew 143 fifth- and sixth-grade students from schools varying in science curricula from traditional textbook to hands-on science. Specifically, a random sample of 11 students was drawn from each of 13 classrooms (see Shavelson et al., 1991, for details).

Procedures

Students carried out the three sow bugs experiments described above without a predetermined time limit. Each student's performance was observed and scored in real time by a trained observer. The decision to use a single observer was based on prior research (Shavelson, et al., in press), and on a reliability check after rater training in this study (interrater reliability = .95). Upon completing each experiment students recorded their setups and procedures in a notebook. For a random sample of 48 of the 143 students, notebooks were scored by two raters (see Design and Analysis below).

Scoring

A procedure-based scoring system was developed for the bugs investigation (cf. Baxter, et al., 1992). For each of the three experiments, students were scored on the following: (a) the design of the investigation (e.g., dark and light incorporated into a single trial); (b) the variables controlled (e.g., equal area for each condition), and (c) the method for determining results (count the number of bugs in each location). Students' scores could range from 1 to 14 points (F to A+).

Design and Analysis

The impact of domain misspecification on task-sampling variability and generalizability (reliability) can be examined with generalizability (G) theory (Cronbach, Gleser, Nanda, & Rajaratnam, 1972; see also Brennan, 1992; Shavelson & Webb, 1991). Three sets of analyses were carried out. The first analysis examined the task-sampling variability and generalizability (reliability) of the observer scores for measuring individual performance. A person x task G-study was used. The second analysis examined domain misspecification at the classroom level. We used a person:class x task G-study to evaluate the task-sampling variability and reliability in measuring class-level performance (cf. Cardinet, Tourneur, & Allal, 1981). Because in the previous two G studies the person x task interaction was confounded with other unidentified sources of measurement error, the role played by task-sampling variability--i.e., the magnitude of the variance component (σ^2_{pt})--is somewhat ambiguous. For this reason (and because statewide assessments use notebooks, not observers), the third analysis used a person x rater x task (p x r x t) G study with notebook scores. This design disentangles the p x t interaction from undifferentiated error (e). This analysis, nevertheless, is closely related to the previous ones with observer scores. Past research has shown that notebook scores are reasonable surrogates for observer scores (Baxter, et al., 1992). In this study, the correlation between observer and notebook scores for the 48 students was .78.

Person x Task G Study

For the observer scores, we assume that the sample of 143 students was drawn randomly from a fifth and sixth grade population[1], and that the tasks (experiments) were drawn randomly from a universe of all tasks (see Shavelson & Webb, 1981, for a discussion of this assumption). Using a random-effects model analysis of variance, we decomposed a score into three sources of variation: person (p), task (t), and a residual (pt, e). The impact of each source of variation on assessment scores can be estimated with variance components from the ANOVA. For example, the variance component for person indexes systematic variability among students' performances (cf. true score variance in classical test theory). The variance component for tasks indexes the variation in difficulty from one task to another in the task domain. The variance component for the person x task interaction indexes the difficulty particular students have with particular tasks. In this case, the p x t interaction falls in a residual term (pt,e) and is confounded with other unidentified sources of error (e).

These variance components involving tasks are of special interest in our examination of domain misspecification. The variance components can also be used to form a generalizability (G) coefficient, a coefficient analogous to classical test theory's reliability coefficient. The G coefficient is pertinent to norm-referenced interpretations and the accuracy with which person's scores are rank ordered. The coefficient for the p x t design is:

(1)
$$\hat{\rho}^2 = \frac{\hat{\sigma}_p^2}{\hat{\sigma}_p^2 + \dfrac{\hat{\sigma}_{pt,e}^2}{n'_t}}$$

The *n* refers to number and the prime (') indicates that n can be varied to equal the number of tasks actually sampled, or that n can be determined so as to reach a generalizability coefficient of (say) .80, much as the Spearman-Brown formula is used in classical reliability theory. The number of tasks needed to achieve adequate generalizability can be translated into dollar and human resource costs.

In addition to the G coefficient, G theory also provides a dependability coefficient. This coefficient indexes not just the rank ordering of students' (persons') scores, but also the *level* of the scores. The dependability coefficient is pertinent to domain referenced or criteria-referenced interpretations of scores. The dependability coefficient for the p x t design is:

(2)
$$\hat{\phi} = \frac{\hat{\sigma}_p^2}{\hat{\sigma}_p^2 + \dfrac{\hat{\sigma}_t^2}{n'_t} + \dfrac{\hat{\sigma}_{pt,e}^2}{n'_t}}$$

This coefficient depends on how difficult the tasks are, as well as on the sources of variation that influence rank order (students and the residual). For our purposes, ϕ differs from ρ^2 in that it is sensitive to both σ_t^2 and $\sigma_{pt,e}^2$, two major sources of task-sampling variability. Nevertheless, both ρ^2 and ϕ may reflect the impact of domain misspecification.

Person: Class x Task G Study

Eleven students were randomly selected from each of 13 classrooms (11 x 13 = 143) to participate in this study. At the classroom level, we can identify five sources of variation in assessment scores: (1) classroom (c), (2) persons (students) nested within classrooms (p:c), (3) task (t), (4) the interaction of classrooms with tasks (ct), and (5) the residual [pt, (p:c)t,e]. Variation from one classroom to another reflects systematic differences in the mean performance across classrooms. Variation among students within a classroom creates uncertainty with respect to the classroom mean and so becomes a source of measurement error. Task variance reflects the difficulty across tasks while the residual reflects the interaction of tasks with other sources of variation. Generalizability and dependability coefficients for the classroom-level design are, respectively:

$$(3) \qquad \hat{\rho}^2 = \frac{\hat{\sigma}_c^2}{\hat{\sigma}_c^2 + \dfrac{\hat{\sigma}_{p:c}^2}{n'_p} + \dfrac{\hat{\sigma}_{ct}^2}{n'_t} + \dfrac{\hat{\sigma}_{pt,\,(p:c)t,e}^2}{n'_p n'_t}}$$

$$(4) \qquad \hat{\phi} = \frac{\hat{\sigma}_c^2}{\hat{\sigma}_c^2 + \dfrac{\hat{\sigma}_{p:c}^2}{n'_p} + \dfrac{\hat{\sigma}_t^2}{n'_t} + \dfrac{\hat{\sigma}_{ct}^2}{n'_t} + \dfrac{\hat{\sigma}_{pt,\,(p:c)t,e}^2}{n'_p n'_t}}$$

Person x Rater x Task G Study

For the notebook scores, we assume that the sample of 48 students was drawn randomly from a fifth- and sixth-grade population, and that two raters and three tasks were drawn randomly from a universe of all raters and tasks. Using analysis of variance, we can decompose a student's score into seven sources of variation: (1) person (p), (2) rater (r), (3) task (t), (4) person x rater (pr), (5) person x task (pt), (6) rater x task (rt), and (7) a residual (prt,e). The generalizability and dependability coefficients corresponding to this design are, respectively:

$$(5) \qquad \hat{\rho}^2 = \frac{\hat{\sigma}_p^2}{\hat{\sigma}_p^2 + \dfrac{\hat{\sigma}_{pr}^2}{n'_r} + \dfrac{\hat{\sigma}_{pt}^2}{n'_t} + \dfrac{\hat{\sigma}_{pt,e}^2}{n'_r n'_t}}$$

$$(6) \qquad \hat{\phi} = \frac{\hat{\sigma}_p^2}{\hat{\sigma}_p^2 + \dfrac{\hat{\sigma}_r^2}{n'_r} + \dfrac{\hat{\sigma}_t^2}{n'_t} + \dfrac{\hat{\sigma}_{pr}^2}{n'_r} + \dfrac{\hat{\sigma}_{pt}^2}{n'_t} + \dfrac{\hat{\sigma}_{rt}^2}{n'_r n'_t} + \dfrac{\hat{\sigma}_{pt,e}^2}{n'_r n'_t}}$$

RESULTS AND DISCUSSION

Person x Task G Study

The p x t G study estimates three sources of score variation: persons, tasks, and residual (pt,e). Task-sampling variation accounted for less than 1% of the total variability when experiments 1 and 2 were considered but, increased to 12.32% when all three tasks were included (Table 1). Moreover, systematic differences among students (universe-score variance; cf. true-score variance) decreased from about 63% of the total variance with two tasks to 51% with three tasks. Apparently by introducing the factorial experiment, one not properly belonging to the elementary life science domain, measurement error was increased and systematic differences among students were masked. Correspondingly, the domain-referenced generalizability coefficient decreased from 0.62 to 0.51 (for a single experiment).

Table 1

Estimated Variance Components for the p x t Design Under Conditions of Accurate (n_t = 2) and Inaccurate (n_t = 3) Domain Specification: Observer Scores

| | Domain Specification | | | |
| | Accurate | | Inaccurate | |
Source	Estimated Variance Component	Percent Total Variability	Estimated Variance Component	Percent Total Variability
Person (p)	11.94	63.17	10.35	50.58
Task (t)	0.03	0.13	2.52	12.32
pt,e	6.94	36.70	7.59	37.10

Person:Class x Task G Study

In large-scale (e.g., state-wide) assessments, scores may be produced at an aggregated level such as the class or school. Accordingly, we conducted a G study using the class as the object of measurement to see if the conclusions reached at the student-level held at the class level (Table 2). At the class level, variance due to students is considered measurement error and the magnitude of this variance component overshadows all other sources of error. As with the student-level analysis, sampling variability due to tasks increased with misspecification from less than 1% of the total variability to 12% while systematic differences among students within classrooms decreased from 54 to 42%.

The increase in task-sampling variability dramatically affected the dependability coefficient. For the accurately specified domain, six tasks would be needed to achieve generalizability .80 (assuming 25 students per class). For the inaccurately specified domain, a total of 25 tasks would be needed (!). The estimated number of tasks based on inaccurate domain specification may be totally impractical and may discourage the use of performance tests in large-scale assessment.

Table 2
Estimated Variance Components for the p;c x t Design Under Conditions of
Accurate (n_t = 2) and Inaccurate (n_t =3) Domain Specification: Observer Scores

	Domain Specification			
	Accurate		Inaccurate	
Source	Estimated Variance Component	Percent Total Variability	Estimated Variance Component	Percent Total Variability
Class (c)	1.85	9.70	1.76	8.60
Person:				
Class (p:c)	10.22	53.70	8.71	42.30
Task (t)	0.01	0.10	2.52	12.20
ct	0.22	1.10	0.08	0.40
pt, (p:c)t,e	6.74	35.40	7.51	36.50

Task-sampling variability increased with domain misspecification (from .1 to 12% of total variability) at the expense of person variance (54% for accurate and 42% for inaccurate). This trade-off had a peculiar effect on the generalizability coefficient--this coefficient is higher for the misspecified (.53 with 11 students and 1 task) than the accurately specified domain (.51). A comparison of equations 3 and 4 reveals why this happens. At the class level, person variance is one component of error. Hence, this error component is smaller for the misspecified than the accurately specified domain. Furthermore, the task-sampling variance (σ^2_t)--much larger for the inaccurately than accurately specified domain--does not change the ranking of classrooms and so does not enter into the generalizability coefficient. Here is a case, then, where the G coefficient masks the effects of task-sampling and universe-score variability. It points to the need to carefully examine variance components and the choice of coefficient.

Finally, another striking finding was that systematic variability among classroom (mean) performances was quite small, even though classes varied in curricular experience (from very traditional to hands-on) and grade-level (fifth and sixth grades). As a consequence, the dependability coefficient for 11 students performing one experiment (task) is low, 0.51 and 0.30 for accurately and inaccurately specified domains, respectively[2].

Person x Rater x Task G Study

Of particular concern in examining the impact of domain misspecification are variance components corresponding to tasks (t) and the person x task interaction (pxt). Because the p x t interaction was confounded with other unidentified sources of variation in the previous analyses, we isolated this interaction in the p x r x t G study using notebook scores. The findings, reported in Table 3, dramatically illustrate our concern. By misspecifying the domain we increased the estimate of task sampling variation (σ^2_t) from 2% to 27%. Moreover, the misspecification reduced the proportion of total variation due to systematic differences in students' performances (universe-score variance) from 51 to 28%. Apparently universe score variance was traded off for an increase in task-sampling error variance.

Table 3

Estimated Variance Components for the p x r x t Design Under Conditions of Accurate (n_t = 2) and Inaccurate (n_t = 3) Domain Specification: Notebook Scores

| | Domain Specification | | | |
| | Accurate | | Inaccurate | |
Source	Estimated Variance Component	Percent Total Variability	Estimated Variance Component	Percent Total Variability
Person (p)	7.40	51.15	6.94	27.81
Rater (r)	0.00	0.00	0.00	0.00
Task (t)	0.25	1.74	6.69	26.81
pr	0.00	0.00	0.00	0.00
pt	6.04	41.75	10.61	42.55
rt	0.00	0.00	0.00	0.00
prt,e	0.78	5.36	0.71	2.84

In this particular example, misspecification did not affect the estimate of the person x task variance component. The "bounce" in the level of students' performances from one task to another was estimated to be about the same whether based on two or three task samples. Rather, the impact of domain misspecification in this example was to overestimate the task variance component. The impact of domain misspecification is also reflected in generalizability estimates. For the correctly specified domain, assuming an assessment with 3 experiments and 1 rater, generalizability (ρ^2) would be .81 and dependability (ϕ) would also be .81. But with the misspecified domain, ρ^2 dropped to .65 and ϕ dropped even further to .53. The practical implications of this misspecification are telling. To obtain a coefficient of .80, one rater and three experiments would be needed for both relative (ρ^2) and absolute (ϕ) decisions, when the domain is correctly specified. When misspecified, one rater and no less than seven experiments would be needed for relative decisions, and one rater and eleven experiments for absolute decisions.

Cost implications of domain misspecification can be inferred from the projected number of tasks to reach dependability (ϕ) of .80. Based on our field experience, we estimate that the three bugs experiments used in this assessment took, on average, 30 minutes for students to perform, or about 10 minutes per experiment (even though experiment 3 took a bit longer than experiments 1 and 2). For a correctly specified domain, then, a total of 40 minutes would be needed to obtain a dependable score. But, for a misspecified domain, a total of 110 minutes, or almost 2 hours, would be needed (!).

IMPLICATIONS

Task-sampling variability in performance assessments is a critical concern both because of accuracy of inferences about the level of student achievement in a subject-matter domain, and because of increased time, personnel, and dollar costs required to administer and score a large number of tasks. Our findings show that the accuracy with which the domain is specified--content validity--may influence task sampling variability. By misspecifying a domain, measurement error due to task-sampling variability may be overestimated and systematic differences in students' performances may be underestimated. Of course, the degree of generalizability can be overstated as well as understated if the domain is underspecified. Incidentally, including factorial design in the elementary science curriculum might not change our findings because this topic might be developmentally inappropriate, as suggested by the topic's absence from the elementary science framework. The clear implication is that we need to pay close attention to content validity--the justification of the domain boundaries--of performance assessments.

NOTES

This research was supported by grants from the National Science Foundation (No. SPA-8751511 and TPE-9055443) and the U.S. Department of Education through the Center for Research on Evaluation, Standards, and Student Testing (No. R117G10027). We wish to acknowledge the helpful comments of Mark Reckase, JEM editor, and Noreen Webb and Bob Linn on earlier drafts of this paper. The findings and interpretations reported herein are those of the authors and are not necessarily endorsed by the funding agencies (or our colleagues).

[1] These students were drawn from 13 classrooms. To simplify the presentation at this point, we ignore this nesting of students in classrooms. However, we do treat the nesting when we examine the impact of misspecification at the classroom level. Nevertheless, the findings and conclusions are the same regardless of whether or not the nesting is modeled at the individual level.

[2] These reliabilities are based on 11 students. Assuming an elementary class size of 25 students, the reliabilities for a single experiment would be 0.67 and 0.35 for accurate and inaccurate domain specification, respectively.

REFERENCES

Baxter, G. P., Shavelson, R. J., Goldman, S. R., & Pine, J. (1992). Evaluation of procedure-based scoring for hands-on science assessment. *Journal of Educational Measurement, 29* (1), 1-17.

Baxter, G. P., Shavelson, R. J., Herman, S. J., Brown, K. A., & Valadez, J. (in press). Mathematics performance assessment: Technical quality and diverse student impact. *Journal of Research in Mathematics Education.*

Brennan, R. L. (1992). *Elements of generalizability theory* (rev. ed.). Iowa City, IA: American College Testing.

Bush, G. W. (1991). *America 2000: An educational strategy.* Washington, DC: U. S. Department of Education.

Cardinet, J., Tourneur, Y., & Allal, L. (1981). Extension of generalizability theory and its applications in educational measurement. *Journal of Educational Measurement, 18* (4), 183-204.

California State Department of Education. (1985). *Mathematics framework for California public schools: Kindergarten through grade twelve.* Sacramento, CA: The Curriculum Framework and Textbook Department Unit, California State Department of Education.

California State Department of Education. (1990). *Science framework for California public schools: Kindergarten through grade twelve.* Sacramento, CA: The Curriculum Framework and Textbook Department Unit, California State Department of Education.

Cronbach, L. J. (1971). Test validation. In R. L. Thorndike (Ed.), *Educational Measurement* (2nd ed.), pp. 443-507. Washington, DC: American Council on Education.

Cronbach, L. J., Gleser, G. C., Nanda, H., & Rajaratnam, N. (1972). *The dependability of behavioral measurements.* New York: John Wiley.

Dunbar, S. B., Koretz, D. M., & Hoover, H.D., (1991). Quality control in the development and use of performance assessments. *Applied Measurement in Education 4* (4), 289-303.

Guion, R. (1977). Content validity--the source of my discontent. *Applied Psychological Measurement, 1,* 1-10.

Linn, R. L., Baker, E. L., & Dunbar, S. B. (1991). Complex, performance-based assessment: Expectations and validation criteria. *Educational Researcher, 20* (8), 15-21.

Messick, S. (1989). Meaning and values in test validation: The science and ethics of assessment. *Educational Researcher, 18* (2), 5-11.

Shavelson, R. J., & Baxter, G. P. (1992). Performance assessments in science: A symmetry of teaching and testing. *Educational Leadership, 49* (8), 20-25.

Shavelson, R. J., Baxter, G. P., & Gao, X. (in press). Sampling variability of performance assessments. *Journal of Educational Measurement.*

Shavelson, R. J., Baxter, G. P., & Pine, J. (1992). Performance assessments: Political rhetoric and measurement reality. *Educational Researcher, 21* (4), 22-27.

Shavelson, R. J., Baxter, G. P., Pine, J., & Yuré, J. (1991, April). *Alternative technologies for assessing science understanding.* Paper presented at the annual meeting of the American Educational Research Association, Chicago.

Shavelson, R. J., Baxter, G. P., Pine, J., Yuré, J., Goldman, S. R., & Smith, B. (1991). Alternative technologies for large-scale science assessment: Instruments of educational reform. *School Effectiveness and School Improvement, 2*(2), 97-114.

Shavelson, R. J., & Webb, N. M. (1981). Generalizability theory: 1973-1980. *British Journal of Mathematical and Statistical Psychology, 34,* 133-166,

Shavelson, R. J., & Webb, N. M. (1991). *Generalizability theory: A primer.* Newbury Park, CA: Sage Publications.

Wigdor, A. K., & Green, B. F. (1991). *Performance assessment for the workplace.* Washington D.C.: National Academy Press.

Wiggins, G. (1989). A true test: Toward more authentic and equitable assessment. *Phi Delta Kappan, 70* (9), 703-713.

Language Testing:
Matching Assessment Procedures
with Language Knowledge

Elana Shohamy

INTRODUCTION

Language testing is concerned with the measurement of language knowledge. Language knowledge is the trait and how we go about measuring it is the method. Trait involves the 'what', i.e., the domain of language knowledge, and method involves the 'how', the appropriate procedures for measuring language knowledge. It is the complexity of the language trait that creates a need for a special discipline called language testing, for there is still no full understanding of what is involved in knowing a language. In constructing language tests, it is essential therefore to have a defined curriculum or set body of knowledge from which testers determine what to test. At the same time it is important to apply appropriate psychometric criteria to assure that tests constructed from such definitions are test-proof, that is, reliable and valid. Most of the work in language testing theory focuses on these two areas - the definitions of what it means to know a language and the appropriate procedures for measuring it. Thus, language testers have devoted much time and effort to defining the construct of language knowledge, as according to Spolsky (1968) "Fundamental to the preparation of valid tests of language proficiency is the theoretical question of what does it mean to know a language" (p. 79). A clear definition and identification of the structure of language enable language testers to design testing procedures that will match such descriptions as these will have direct consequences on the construct validity of language tests.

By matching the 'how' with the 'what' one can identify a number of phases and periods in the development of language testing, each reflecting the different definitions of language knowledge of the time and the specific measurement procedures that went along with it. Thus, *discrete point* testing is typical of the period when language tests consisted of isolated and discrete point items utilizing primarily objective testing procedures and reflecting the view that language consisted of lexical and structural items; an *integrative* era in which language tests tapped the integrated nature of language; a *communicative* period where tests were expected to replicate actual interaction in the language among real language users, utilizing authentic oral and written texts and tasks; a *performance* testing era when language was viewed in a contextualized manner, employing tasks that the language user is expected to perform often in real life, in well defined contexts, often on the job, and the present *alternative* era with the types of tests that are beginning to be used today, where language knowledge is viewed in varied ways - exemplified in a variety of contexts and resulting in a variety of different assessment procedures each capturing a different aspect of language knowledge. This chapter will describe those different periods by focusing on the close link between the definitions of language knowledge and the procedures used to measure it. The chapter will end with a description of an assessment battery where alternative procedures are used for assessing the second language acquisition by immigrant children in a school context.

DISCRETE POINT TESTING

In the discrete point era language tests focused primarily on the assessment of isolated and discrete point items, mostly grammatical and lexical, and following structural linguistic principles of the time. Thus, tests in that era included multiple choice, true-false, and other types of objective items which focused on single and independent items like conjugation of verbs and identification of lexical elements in a decontextualized manner. These tests were applied to all language skills - reading, writing, listening and speaking, and assessed discrete and isolated aspects of language. Even a productive skill such as writing was tested in a way that required test takers to identify distractors which contained errors through multiple choice testing, rather than asking test takers to produce actual written language samples.

TESTING INTEGRATIVE LANGUAGE

In the integrative era language tests were viewed in a holistic and more contextualized manner focusing on the testing of global language samples - complete paragraphs and full texts. Testing tasks included writing letters and comprehension of whole texts with minimal reference to isolated elements in the text. In this period special attention was given to a specific type of tests, the cloze, in which words were deleted from longer texts and the test taker was expected to fill in the missing slots. Oller (1975, 1979) who promoted the cloze, claimed that it tapped integrative language and reflected a unitary notion of language which underlies the language knowledge based on the learner's pragmatic *grammar of expectancy*. He contended that this knowledge represented a psychological representation of the language user's ability to map utterances onto contexts. Oller argued that the grammar of expectancy was the chief mechanism underlying the skills of thinking, understanding, speaking, reading and writing, and it was to be activated in circumstances which required the processing of language under normal contextual constraints. This ability was to be operationalized through integrative tests such as the cloze (and dictation) since in these tests learners had to mobilize their linguistic and extra-linguistic knowledge to reconstitute the meaning of a text. While integrative tests such as the cloze were widely used and accepted by many language testers, there was strong criticism among language testers as to the lack of evidence of construct validity of these tests and doubt as to the extent to which they actually tapped the integrative nature of language. The fact that all evidence was based on correlations and that test takers were not required to actually produce real language (just to fill in blanks) made this type of test untrustworthy to language testers and users. Yet, the main contribution of these tests was that it became apparent that language tests need to include comprehension or production of discourse and not just of isolated sentences, words and structures.

TESTING COMMUNICATIVE LANGUAGE

Communicative testing arose from developments in the field of linguistics and language teaching. In linguistics it related to the introduction of communicative competence and communicative performance by Hymes (1972) and in language teaching it was associated with the shift from the teaching of isolated language elements to those of communicative language. Chomsky (1965) distinguished between competence and performance; Hymes (1972) expanded the notions of competence and performance and added a communicative component, thus referring to linguistic and communicative competence, and linguistic and communicative performance pointing to the relationship and interaction between grammatical and sociolinguistic competence and performance. Canale and Swain (1980) refined the terms introduced by Hymes and listed the components of communicative competence to be linguistic competence, sociolinguistic competence, discourse competence and strategic competence. The changes in language teaching were to a large extent a reflection of those new definitions emphasizing the communicative component of language knowledge. In this period there had also been a growing emphasis on the notion of *language proficiency*, defined as the language knowledge needed for a specific future situation. The notion of proficiency was to be differentiated from *achievement* which was related to the language knowledge learned in a given course, usually in the past. Thus, the communicative era can be characterized also as the period in which a strong emphasis was put on learning outcomes, i.e., those related to the ability of language learners to actually use language in 'real life' communicative situations.

The new definitions in linguistics, the new approaches to teaching and the emphasis on proficiency in language, resulted in a wave of criticism of traditional non-communicative language tests, as it was claimed that these tests were limited in their concepts and were producing artificial language. There was a demand, therefore, for tests which would require test takers to produce 'real' language, the kind of language that is used among real people. Clark (1975) differentiated between direct and indirect language tests. Direct tests were those in which the testing format and procedure attempted to duplicate, as closely as possible, the setting and operation of the real-life situation in which the proficiency is normally demonstrated. The high correlations obtained between direct and indirect tests did not provide sufficient evidence that indirect tests could substitute for direct tests (Shohamy, 1982). It was claimed that indirect tests may have a negative impact on language teaching as tasks such as identifying errors or supplying single words are used instead of direct tasks which required students to produce actual writing and speaking language samples. The direct tests had higher face validity and were therefore believed to have a positive effect on learning and teaching.

Thus, testers called for the use of communicative tests. Jones (1977) proposed performance tests in which test takers would provide information on functional language ability. Canale and Swain (1980) called for communicative tests which would require test takers to display their knowledge by actually using the language in real situations in which test takers would have to consider criteria such as saying the right thing at the right time to the right person. Morrow (1977) recommended offering test takers the opportunity for spontaneous operation of the language in authentic settings, in activities which the candidate would recognize as relevant to the use s/he would be likely to make of the target language. He defined the conditions of such tests as those which would need to take the participants in unforeseen directions; to be situated in a context which is linguistic, discoursal and sociocultural; to have a purpose in that participants will strive to achieve something with their use of language; to use authentic stimulus materials; to be based on real psychological conditions such as time pressure, and to be evaluated by their final outcome in terms of whether the communicative purposes had been achieved.

Thus, the trend in subsequent years proceeded in the direction of the development and use of communicative language tests which contained features of real language use and required test takers to perform language that is authentic, direct and communicative. It was expected that tests containing such features would assess a more valid construct of what knowing a language really means and thus provide evidence of actual language proficiency.

An example that illustrates the communicative trend is the testing of oral language. The earlier tests of oral proficiency were administered in the language laboratory, i.e., a small booth equipped with a tape recorder with which individual test takers were expected to 'converse'. The oral tasks usually included mechanical repetition of words and sentences and supplying pattern answers to pattern questions. It was important for the test taker to talk at a pace fast enough to beat the 'beep' sound of the tape and slow enough so as not to have too many silent moments before the beep sounded. However, with the advent of the communicative and direct era, these tests seemed very artificial as the language produced when test takers talked to machines rather than to other human beings, was very different from their normally used language. Intonation and sentence length were found to differ from real spoken discourse. Thus, with the introduction of communicative tests, test takers were expected to produce direct and authentic oral language which involved a test setting where the examinee and one or more human interlocutors do, in fact, engage in a communicative dialogue and perform in actual communicative situations.

The Foreign Service Institute (FSI) Oral Interview (OI) test was one example of such a direct and communicative test (Clark, 1975; Jones, 1977, 1978; Wilds, 1975). It consisted of a face-to-face oral interaction between a tester (the interviewer) and a test taker (the interviewee); the tester asked questions on a variety of topics, and the responses provided the oral language sample, which was then evaluated by the tester with the aid of a rating scale. Shohamy, Reves, and Bejerano (1986) introduced an oral test in which test takers were required to use four interactions - an oral interview, a role play, a reporting task, and a group discussion. Raffaldini (1988) describes an oral test which included a role play and a number of situational tasks. Tests such as the TEEP (Test for English for Educational Purposes) and the Royal Society of Arts test are also examples of instruments which attempted to be communicative and authentic. Even the more traditional standardized tests, such as the TOEFL, was revised so as to include some direct and communicative texts and tasks (Stansfield, 1986).

Semi-direct tests represented another version of communicative tests used to assess oral proficiency (Stansfield & Kenyon, 1988). The tests required test takers to respond orally to L-1 oral stimuli which were situated in a communicative context; the test takers heard the stimuli and responded with an extended speech by speaking to the audio recorder.

Rating scales were the instruments which were developed as criteria for assessing the quality of the language samples obtained from the different types of communicative tests. They were based on hierarchical and functional descriptions of different levels, usually ranging from zero to five. Different types of rating scales were developed according to the purpose of the assessment. Thus, holistic scales were used for assessing global language based on the raters' impression of the entire oral or written samples produced; these scales were used mainly for summative evaluation purposes such as for placement and proficiency testing. Analytic scales related to specific features within the language such as grammar, lexicon, fluency, or pragmatics, and were more suited for classroom situations as they allowed the provision of feedback to students and teachers about specific language aspects. Primary trait scoring referred to ascertaining whether a language sample exhibits certain characteristics crucial to the specific rhetorical task the written or oral language samples was trying to perform. Global, holistic rating scales were also developed as yardsticks in Australia and in the US and served as standards of hierarchical functional proficiency of performance in the four language skills (ACTFL, 1986), and are widely used today in secondary schools, colleges and for adult immigrants.

PERFORMANCE TESTING

The term performance testing which is nowadays widely used in the general educational literature, was used in a variety of contexts in language testing already in the 70's. It was used mostly in the communicative testing era as one of the features of communicative tests, along with a number of other terms such as *direct, functional* and *authentic* testing. The unique aspect of the *performance* feature was that the test takers were expected to replicate, as much as possible, the type of language used in non-testing situations (Bachman, 1990; Bailey, 1985; Jones, 1978). Thus, performance testing referred to tests where a test taker is tested on what s/he can do in the second language in situations similar to 'real life'. Jones (1985) specified the term performance more clearly by stating that such tests would require the application of learning in actual or simulated settings where either the test stimulus, or the desired response, or both were intended to lend a high degree of realism to the test situation. Thus, language testing required the integration of linguistic, situational, cultural and affective constraints which interact in the process of communication.

In the other contexts, the term *performance* became associated with specific tasks and contexts of professional preparation and certification, mostly in the work place (Wesche, 1992). In this context performance testing borrowed from the field of vocational testing where a test taker is expected to carry out realistic tasks which call for the application of language skills in actual or simulated settings (Carroll & Hall, 1985). In such tests a learner is presented with tasks requiring language use in specific, often work-related situations that simulate 'real life' purposes for which s/he will need the language in the future. The criterion used to evaluate the performance was an approximation of the way performance would be judged in the specific and actual target circumstances, including adequate fulfillment of tasks. Wesche (1992) notes that these tests tap both second language ability and the ability to fulfill nonlinguistic requirements of the given tasks. With these types of tests the main psychometric features are those of predictive validity so the test can predict how well a test taker will perform under real conditions in a well-defined and specific context (Jones, 1985). The underlying assumption with these performance tests is that nonlinguistic factors are present in any language performance and that it is important to understand their role and to channel their influence on language performance.

It is important to note that the term performance testing is used differently in language testing than in general educational testing. In educational testing, performance testing is associated mostly with testing procedures which do not employ paper-and- pencil multiple choice items but rather procedures such as open ended, constructed responses, problem solving, essays and some hands-on problems. In language testing, on the other hand, as was noted, performance testing is associated mostly with proficiency testing and/or with actual hands-on tasks taken from the real world, often associated with proficiency in the work place, or some other well-defined future context. One reason why performance tests penetrated into language testing is decision makers on-going need to select candidates for jobs and programs that require language skills.

McNamara (in prep.) proposed a distinction between strong and weak hypotheses of performance testing. In the strong sense, knowledge of the second language is a necessary but not sufficient condition for success on the performance test; rather, success is measured in terms of performance on the task. In the weak sense, knowledge of second language is the most important and main factor relevant for success on the performance test.

Jones (1985) distinguished among three types of performance tests according to the degrees to which the tasks require actual performances. In a *direct* assessment type the examinee is placed in the actual target context and the second language performance is assessed in response to the naturally evolving situation. In the *work sample* type there are realistic tasks, generally set in the target context, and they enable control of the elicitation task and a comparison of the performance of different examinees, while simultaneously retaining contextual realism. In the *simulation* type simulation settings and tasks are contrived in such a way that they represent what are thought to be pertinent aspects of the real life context. *Role play* is frequently used as a simulation technique where both the examiner and the examinee play roles.

While most performance tests are viewed as proficiency tests attempting to predict future behaviors in the work place, Wesche (1992) differentiated between performance testing in the work place and in the instructional context. In the work place type, performance tests are used for job certification and for prediction of post-training behaviors, and are thus considered as *proficiency* tests. In the instructional context, on the other hand, tests are used for increasing students' motivation, washback and diagnostic feedback. Thus, performance tests can actually be introduced in the pre-instruction phase for placement, formative diagnosis and achievement, during the program itself for achievement, and for summative testing at the end of a program, often for certification purposes. Wesche (1992) claims that early introduction of performance tests can help communicate to learners the importance of language objectives, instructors' expectations and criteria for judging performances. Thus, text and tasks which are used in performance testing make very good instructional tasks, and rating obtained from performance tests can be translated to diagnostic feedback in the form of profiles scores.

The specific contexts in which performance tests are needed are wherever there is a clientele with certain shared second language needs that can be identified and described and can subsequently be translated into test tasks and overall test design. In constructing a performance test, a needs analysis is conducted in order to provide a detailed description of the specific context and tasks which learners will need to perform, the specific conditions under which the task will be performed, how well learners can do it, and the criteria against which the performance can be judged. Then, the learners' performances are judged over a range of tasks that need to be sampled, using a variety of instruments and procedures. Thus, the first phase is to conduct a needs analysis, so as to specify the context of the second language use, the type of interactions foreseen, the role, discourse types, language functions to be performed, and the basis on which successful fulfillment of the second language tasks is to be judged. It is with respect to these needs that the performance test is designed, texts and tasks are selected, and evaluation criteria are determined. These are then translated into appropriate test objectives and tasks, and later into an actual test design and scoring. Performance tests are generally assessed with the aid of rating scales which specifically describe what a person can do in the language in the specific situation.

There are many examples of performance-based language tests. The English for Special Purpose (ESP) test (Caroll, 1978) includes specific performances needed for students to use in academic situations. It is based on a needs analysis proposing test specifications for assessing whether prospective students at British universities are capable of coping with the language demands of their studies. The Oral Interview (Lowe & Stansfield, 1988) is also considered a performance test since test takers are required to perform their language in a face to face oral interaction, often in government, work-related context. Later versions include role plays as well. Cole and Neufeld (1991) report on a test used by the Canadian Public Service to certify second language skills of employees in bilingual positions. It includes performance tasks that form a vast bank of work-related role plays reflecting a range of situations that might occur in each of the major public service job classifications. Contextualized interviews are introduced into each interview, according to the situations in which employees might need to use the second language. These tasks are based upon a detailed analysis of second language needs in bilingual government positions. The writing tasks include filling out forms and writing short work-related messages; on a higher level the tasks include also correspondence and executive summaries. Milanovic (1988) reports on a listening test in which the tasks are taking down telephone messages, completing weather forecast charts, reading and writing based on authentic materials such as brochures, official forms and letters asking for information. Wesche (1992) reports on a multiple approach to a specific problem that incorporates both individualized performance tasks and a more general proficiency measure. This testing has been used with candidates in different fields and provides comparable general proficiency information as well as a profile of strong and weak areas of candidates' performances. The latter information is often used diagnostically by the individual or by a tutor to tailor further language instruction that may have washback effects in letting candidates know that the bilingual requirements are relevant to their work situation. The test is used for evaluating the second language skills of professionals who must perform professional tasks requiring relatively high level of receptive ability in their second language and more limited production skills.

Sajavaara (1992) describes the Finnish Foreign Language Diploma for Professional Purposes which offers necessary information for employers to be able to screen new professionals in terms of foreign language skills. The test provides certificates for various workplace situations and it serves business sectors that require ability to communicate in foreign languages in different professions - business administration, engineering management, public administrations, etc. McNanamara (1990) reports on a performance test used for health professionals in Australia, the Occupational English Test, which is used for immigrants and refugees who are medical practitioners - nurses, psychotherapists, occupational therapists, dentists, etc. It assesses various skills of performance in the work place. The listening component requires test takers to answer questions on a talk about a professionally relevant subject and on a consultation between a general practitioner and a patient. The reading part is based on articles from professional journals or magazines. The speaking test is a profession-specific content in a common form that consists of role plays and short interviews. The assessment contains six categories of overall communicative effectiveness, intelligibility, fluency, comprehension appropriateness and resources of grammar and expression. The writing test is also profession-specific and requires writing a referral based on case notes or extracts from medical record. Wesche (1992) reports on a performance test which is part of the instructional process and also includes a self assessment instrument based on performance description for initial placement. Students rate themselves on a series of descriptions of everyday situations requiring listening or reading comprehension and thus indicating skill levels on a five-point scale ranging from *I cannot do this at all* to *I can do this all the time*. A work-related semi-direct performance test was developed by the Center of Applied Linguistics (Stansfield & Kenyon, 1988) for prospective teachers, where candidates are required to use the second language in school/teaching related tasks. The language is assessed on the basis of the ACTFL rating scale.

Since performance testing consists of the interaction of linguistic skills and a specific domain it is no longer a *pure* language test, but rather depends heavily on the knowledge of the domain in which the language is exercised. This is a strong requirement for a linguistic theoretical model as theory needs to incorporate language mastery as domain knowledge. Yet, no such theoretical model is currently available that could guide the development of performance tests. Even the more advanced model of communicative ability (Bachman, 1990), does not account for the domain knowledge in performance testing. Thus, the performance testing described above are test driven and the testing tasks have become the *de facto* theory of performance tests. Thus, the process of development of such tests is: a specific context in which the language is used, is defined; a specific sample of the behaviors that occur in that context is described; a task that elicits the performance is determined; the task is performed by a test-taker in a simulated situation; a language sample is obtained; the language sample is assessed on a rating scale which hierarchically describes what it means to know a language. For example, if a person can order a meal, s/he may receive a score of '1', if s/he can conduct a casual conversation on a familiar topic with a boss s/he may receive a score of '2', and if s/he can read a menu or a brochure in a certain business office s/he may receive a score of 2+ or a 3.

However, serious questions arise with regards to such a task-oriented approach which is not driven by a theory of language knowledge. Performance tests do look authentic, do have high face validity, are taken from real life and require test takers to perform. Yet, many questions arise, for example, regarding the relative weighting that should be given to the different criteria; the way the scoring information should be interpreted and presented to test-takers; the criterion for considering successful performance, and the proportions of 'language' vs. 'domain knowledge'. Also, who should the judge of the performance be - a native speaker, a domain specialist or a teacher, and what should the criteria for successful performance be -- native speakers or advanced language learners? (Although most performance tests do use the native speaker as the top level of the scale (ACTFL, 1986) this issue has been a topic of debate in the language testing literature for many years (Alderson, 1980, Bachman, 1990). Hamilton, Lopes, McNamara and Sheridan (1993), for example, claim that performance on the test involves factors other than straight second language proficiency, and since these factors are included in the assessment, it is expected that there will be an overlap in the performance of native and non-native speakers; therefore the reference to native speaker performance may be unwarranted.

Other questions arise regarding the validity of *task-oriented* approaches in general. Messick (1994) draws a sharp distinction between constructs and tasks. Constructs refer to theories such as competencies, knowledge, and skill underlying performance. Tasks refer to behavioral performances. The main point that Messick makes is that although competence must be inferred from observations of performance or behaviors, this inference is not often straightforward, particularly inferences about lack of competence from poor performance. Indeed, he states that this is the core problem of construct validity, i.e., establishing via a theoretical integration of empirical evidence, that an observed behavioral consistency can be accounted for by a particular construct interpretation rather than by plausible rival interpretation. In education, he states, we are rarely concerned just with the particular performance per se, but rather with the knowledge, skill, and other attributes that enable not only the given performance but also a range of other performances engaging in the knowledge and skill. This suggests that construct-like relevant knowledge and skill, rather than domain-relevant tasks and performance, ought to drive the development, scoring, and interpretation of performance assessment. According to Messick a construct-centered approach begins by asking what complex of knowledge skills or other attributes should be assessed, presumably because they are tied to explicit or implicit objectives of instruction, or are otherwise valued by society. Only next we ask which behaviors or performances should reveal those constructs, and what tasks or situations should elicit those behaviors. Thus, the nature of the construct guides the selection of the construction of the relevant tasks as well as the rational development of construct-based scoring criteria and rubrics. Focusing on constructs also alerts one to the possibility of construct-irrelevant variables which might distort either the task performance or its scoring, or both. With respect to scoring as well, construct irrelevant variables can distort subjective judgment of performance, as when scores on essay tasks focusing on the persuasiveness of arguments, say or knowledge of biology concepts, are influenced by handwriting. Thus, task-centered scores could lead to a proliferation of task-dependent constructs in much the same way that operational definitions led to a proliferation of constructs tied to specific measurement operations.

A construct-driven approach to language assessment rather than a task-driven approach needs to be adopted in language performance testing because the meaning of the construct guides the selection or construction of relevant tasks as well as the rational development of scoring criteria and rubrics. Clearly, focusing on constructs will address the issues of construct under-representation and construct-irrelevant variables which are the two main threats to validity. Yet, in order to develop such constructs there is a need to understand better what is meant by performance or which variables are to be included in it.

McNamara (in prep.) notes that there is a need for a broader concept of communicative competence which should include variables that relate language to other cognitive and affective areas, such as subject matter knowledge, integration of language knowledge with other performance, communication skills, personalities and gender of the communicator and the communicatee, attitudes and beliefs, as well as a whole set of variables occurring in the communication process. There is, therefore, a serious question regarding the validity of the performance-based, task-driven tests presently used, as they are based on a narrow view which does not include such components. There is moreover a need for a sound theoretical model of performance testing based on a more comprehensive understanding of the factors that are relevant to consider as underlying ability for use.

In addition, there are questions regarding the psychometric properties of performance tests. Performance, as was noted, is a most involved and complex construct consisting of a large number of linguistic and extra-linguistic variables which interact and cause variance. Some studies indicate high reliability, mostly inter-rater. Yet, in the past few years a variety of studies used IRT analyses in order to examine reliability of raters on different types of performance tests (McNamara, 1991). Validity also poses a problem as sociolinguists have claimed that the interaction of linguistic and extra-linguistic variables would affect the language produced and cause it to vary from one context to another (Hymes, 1967, 1971, 1972). Thus, a variety of variables such as location, time, content, setting, type of interaction, etc., may affect test scores (Shohamy, 1982; Shohamy & Inbar, 1991). Whether this interaction is part of variance in the trait or in the method still needs to be examined, as it will help sort out whether differences which are obtained as a result of contextual variables are part of the construct of language performance or of the procedures used to assess it.

Yet, strong emphasis on testing language performance meant that only limited effort had been invested in achievement testing. In other subject matter areas, on the other hand, tests were more geared towards achievement, mostly in school contexts, yet authentic or 'real life' tests were overlooked as the belief had always been that what is learned in school will be transferred to real life.

ALTERNATIVE ASSESSMENT

In the past few years there has been a call by language testers to emphasize the *achievement* component of language knowledge (Hancock, 1994; Liskin-Gasparro, 1995; Lynch & Davidson, 1994; Shohamy, 1992). Collins and Brown (1988) note that in the real world tasks are not necessarily the same as problems in school, since problems in school are structured typically to teach a particular skill, more or less in isolation from other skills. In the real world problems tend not to be structured predictably and are strongly dependent on the situation itself. Thus, in foreign language learning, the tasks in school are organized systematically to teach language skills more or less in isolation. This means that procedures that learners need to master in order to strive for proficiency such as reading strategies, vocabulary, grammar, and sociolinguistic rules, are usually taught in separate units. On the other hand, in real life, language is unpredictable and strongly dependent on the contexts in which it arises. While proficiency is ideally the end goal of foreign language learning, one must realize that it is not possible to reach proficiency without a series of carefully structured steps which precede it, i.e., the achievement component of knowing a language. Thus, both achievement and proficiency are essential components for knowing a language. While proficiency is clearly the ultimate goal, school learning is important as the means to that end.

Alternative assessment is one approach for incorporating the two types of language knowledge as it promotes the use of a variety of instruments, each capturing different aspects and domains of language knowledge, as exemplified in different situations, in and out of the classroom. In alternative assessment it is also realized that there are different types of language knowledge and mastering one type is no guarantee for mastering another, as different instruments are capable of 'seeing' different things. Consequently, no one procedure can capture the complex phenomena of language knowledge and there is a need for multiple assessment procedures. Thus, alternative procedures are needed, for assessing the different types of language knowledge, which are exemplified in different situations and for different purposes. One should therefore interpret alternative assessment as complementary assessment, as each procedure adds new and unique information which the other instruments did not provide. Thus, procedures such as portfolios, observations, peer assessment, interviews, simulations and self-assessment are beginning to be used in language testing as well. Some of these procedures have been used for some time; in language testing specifically, the procedure of self assessment (Oscarson, 1989).

Below is a description of one example of an assessment battery which employed a variety of such alternative procedures in assessing the learning of Hebrew as a second language (HSL) by immigrant children. The rationale for using alternative procedures in this context was that language proficiency of immigrants children is exemplified in a variety of contexts and that meaningful insight into language needs to be sampled in these varied contexts. Thus, variety of instruments which tap different aspects of the language is used, each contributing unique and new information to the understanding of the language knowledge of the test takers. It is through the use of multiple instruments that a comprehensive picture of the achievement and proficiency of the immigrant children is obtained. The information from the varied sources is then contextualized and interpreted through a dialogue among different assessment participants - the student, the HSL teacher, the subject matter teacher, and often a parent.

The basic principles of the assessment are: a. There is a need for precise definition of what it means to know how to read and write in L-2 for immigrant children in the different age levels; b. different procedures need to be employed in order to tap language knowledge in the variety of situations where it is used; c. the information obtained from the different sources must be interpreted and contextualized, and d. the information leads to pedagogical and instructional strategies.

The assessment model developed based on the above principles, displayed in Figure 1, includes the following components of the knowledge of reading and writing in that context: a. basic *threshold* language (mastering elementary features of the language), b. *academic* (the language needed for each school subject), c. *life* (the language needed for use in out of school contexts), and d. *learning aids* (ability to use learning resources such as dictionary, library, etc.). These components were arrived at through discussions with educational experts such as subject-matter teachers, HSL teachers, and curriculum planners. These components were then converted into tables of specifications for each of the four age levels (elementary low, grades 2-4; elementary high, grades 5-6; junior-high, grades 6-9; and senior high, grades 10-12).

As can be seen in Figure 1, four procedures were selected for the assessment - a test, self assessment, observations by two teachers (one a humanities teacher, the other a science teacher), and a portfolio (in which students select language samples of reading and writing from a set list). An assessment conference in which the HSL teacher, the home teacher, and often a parent, meet with the student to discuss and interpret the results from the four instruments, follows the administration of the other instruments. The assessment conference leads to conclusions, recommendations and pedagogical strategies.

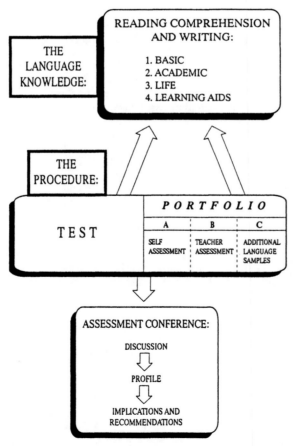

Figure 1: The Components of the Evaluation

In the process of validating the alternative (complementary) assessment battery a number of questions are being asked:
- what are the correlations among the different assessment procedures?
- what is the inter-rater reliability of the instruments?
- are there differences between the performances of males and females on each of the procedures?
- what is the process by which the HSL teachers arrive at the individual profiles and recommendations? (e.g., documenting the role of the assessment conference).

In addition, questions are asked regarding the order of administration of the four assessment procedures, i.e., is there a difference in the scores obtained when the self assessment is administered before or after the test? how is the information utilized by the HSL teachers and by the students? to what extent do the profiles and recommendations affect the HSL teaching strategies? what are the attitudes of students, teachers and administrators towards the assessment battery and what is the nature of the assessment conference.

Results of some of these questions are still being analyzed, yet answers to the first set of questions, based on a sample of 57 students, are currently available. The results show the following: Correlations among the different procedures, as displayed in Table 1, show that they range from .38 between the teacher assessment and the self assessment to .66 between the portfolio and the test. Yet, the correlations between the different procedures and the general profile (arrived at as a sum of all the four procedures) indicate that the highest correlation is between the test and the general profile. This indicates that the test correlates the highest with all the other instruments (.64 with the self assessment, .66 with the portfolio, and .52 with the teacher assessment.) Clearly, the test is still considered by the teacher as the most important assessment procedure, to which they pay most of their attention in assigning the final score.

Table 1
Correlations Among the Assessment Procedures

Procedure	1	2	3	4
Test	--			
Self assessment	.64*	–		
Portfolio	.66*	.43*	–	
Teacher assessment	.52*	.38*	.57*	–
General	.90*	.74*	.66*	.59*

* p <.01

In the examination of the inter-rater reliability between the two teachers, one a science teacher and one a humanities teacher, we found that the correlation was as low as .24, thus indicating that there is very low agreement between the two teachers. This can be due to error variance, but it can also be that an immigrant student behaves differently in two different classes as these two classes differ in terms of the reliance on knowledge of the Hebrew language. Typically, a science class requires less reliance on language than a humanities class does. Thus, it may very well be that children behave differently in these two classes, an observation that was also confirmed in the self assessment as students rated their knowledge of the two subjects differently and consistently claimed that they had more difficulties in a humanity class (i.e. Hebrew literature, Bible, history) vs. science subjects (i.e., math and biology). The implication of these results is that the observation of the student by each of his/her teachers can be considered as a separate assessment instrument.

In terms of the differences between males and females, the results indicated significant differences only in teacher assessment (see Table 2), where females outperformed males and obtained higher scores.

Table 2
Means, Standard Deviations and t-Values for Scores of Male and Female Students

Assessment Procedure	Males		Females		
	Mean	SD	Mean	SD	t-Value
Test	3.05	.37	3.48	1.15	-1.60
Self assessment	3.36	.69	3.54	.82	-.87
Teacher assessment	2.62	.81	3.37	.95	-3.16*
Portfolio	3.31	.97	3.77	1.17	-1.55
Profiles	2.91	.98	3.36	1.17	-1.54

* $p < .01$

The final analysis was performed on the recommendations assigned by the teachers at the completion of the assessment conference. The recommendations were sorted into three categories - *description, context* and *recommendation type* (see Table 3). *Description* referred to whether the HSL teacher considered the results obtained from the different assessment procedures; *context* referred to whether the results were contextualized in terms of the new information obtained from the assessment conference (e.g., how long the student had been in Israel, whether s/he had help at home, whether s/he was better in oral vs. written skills) and *recommendation-type* referred to how specific the recommendations were, i.e., whether the type of recommendation could be used for planning HSL teaching strategies and methods. The analysis of the recommendations showed that in many of the cases the HSL teachers focused mainly on the tests and overlooked the other 'non-testing' instruments. The recommendations often ignored important data that resulted from the assessment conference and did not relate it to the information obtained from the test. For example, the teacher reached the same conclusions in the case of a student who had been in Israel for 6 months as the one who had been in Israel for 18 months, while clearly, the equivalent results must be interpreted entirely differently. There were also a number of cases in which the HSL teacher relied exclusively on the assessment conference and ignored all the information obtained from the various assessment procedures. In terms of the type of recommendations, all the recommendations were too general and too simplistic and therefore could not be used by teachers to plan specific teaching strategies. It seems that teachers found it very difficult to describe, synthesize, contextualize and interpret the information leading to specific recommendations for action. The implications of these findings are that when introducing alternative assessment there is a special need to train teachers in their use, especially in relating to the results obtained from *all* the different instruments, and more importantly to train the users in procedures of synthesizing, summarizing and contextualizing information leading to meaningful recommendations that can be used by language teachers for making pedagogical decisions. If this is not done, the whole advantage of using multiple assessment procedures is defeated. Thus, a shift towards alternative assessment, requires asking different questions about the quality of the instruments, and attending to different components of the assessment process, otherwise the strong benefit of using such complex systems gets lost.

Table 3
Types of Recommendations

| | | Category | | |
Types	Description	Context	Recommendation General	Specific
A	+	-	-	-
B	-	+	-	-
C	+	+	-	-
D	-	-	+	-
E	+	-	+	-
F	-	+	+	-
G	+	+	+	-

+ = existed in the recommendation
- = did not exist in the recommendation

CONCLUSIONS

Language testing has been a very productive discipline in terms of theory, research and test development and various approaches to language testing have been developed depending on the definitions of language knowledge of the time. Language testing was probably the first discipline to be concerned with the measurement of a specific domain, in this case, language knowledge. The fact that language testing is an outgrowth of applied linguistics, a field that has varied theories of language acquisition and learning, enabled language testing to proceed in varied directions, usually driven by language theory. Thus, it is unique to language testing that it attempted to relate testing procedures to language knowledge as well as to incorporate developments in general education measurement into its own domain. While it is clear how language testing can benefit from general educational testing, it is hoped that this chapter will also demonstrate the benefits that general educational testing can obtain from the broad areas of research and development of language testing, especially those of performance and communicative testing.

REFERENCES

Alderson, J. (1980). Native and non-native speaker performance on cloze tests. *Language Learning, 30,* 59-76.

American Council on the Teaching of Foreign Languages. (1986). *ACTFL proficiency guidelines.* Hastings-on-Hudson, NY: American Council on the Teaching of Foreign Languages.

Bachman, L. (1990). *Fundamental considerations in language testing.* Oxford: Oxford University Press.

Bailey, K. (1985). If I had known then what I know now: Performance testing of foreign teaching assistants. In P. Haumptman, R. LeBlanc, & M. Wesche (Eds.), *Second language performance Testing.* Ottawa: University of Ottawa Press.

Brown, J., Collins, A., & Duguid, P. (1989). Situated cognition and the culture of learning. *Educational Researcher, 18,* 32-42.

Canale, M., & Swain, M. (1980). Theoretical bases of communicative approaches to second language teaching and testing. *Applied Linguistics,1,* 1-47.

Carroll, B., & P. Hall. (1985). *Make your own language tests.* Oxford: Pergamon.

Chomsky, N. (1965). *Aspects of the theory of syntax.* Cambridge, Mass: MIT Press.

Cole, G., & D. Neufeld (1991). Les tests d'evaluation de langue seconde de la fonction publique du Canada. *Actes du Colloque Bulletin: Association quebequoise des enseignants du francais langue seconde* (AQEFLS) *12* (3,4), 47-63.

Collins, A., & Brown, J. (1988). Cognitive apprenticeship: Teaching students the craft of reading, writing, and mathematics. In L. Resnick (Ed.), Cognition and instruction: Issues and agenda. Hillside, NJ: Erlbaum.

Clark, J.L.D. (1975). Direct testing of speaking proficiency: Theory and practice. Princeton, NJ: Educational Testing Service.

Hancock, C. (1994). *Teaching, testing, and assessing: Making the connection.* Northeast Conference on the Teaching of Languages. Chicago: National Textbook Company.

Hamilton, J., Lopes, M., McNamara, T., & Sheridan, E. (1993). Rating scales and native speaker performance on a communicatively oriented EAP test. *Melbourne Papers in Applied Linguistics, 2,* 1-24.

Hymes, D. (1967). Models of interaction of language and social setting. *Journal of Social Issues, 23,* 8-28.

Hymes, D. (1971). On linguistic theory, communicative competence and the education of disadvantaged children. In M. Wax, S. Diamond, & F. O. Gearing (Eds.), *Anthropological perspectives on education,* (pp. 51-66). New York: Basic Books.

Hymes, D. (1972). On communicative competence. In J.B. Pride and J. Holmes (Eds.), *Sociolinguistics: Selected readings,* (pp. 269-293). Harmondsworth, England: Penguin.

Jones, R. (1977). Testing: A vital connection. In J. Phillips (Ed.), *The language connection: From the classroom to the world.* (pp.237-265). Skokie, Illinois: National Textbooks Company.

Jones, R. (1978). Interview techniques and scoring criteria at higher proficiency levels. In J.L.D. Clark (Ed.), *Direct testing of speaking proficiency: Theory and application* (pp. 899-102). Princeton, NJ: Educational Testing Service.

Jones, R. (1985). Second language performance testing: An overview. In H.P. Hauptman, R. LeBlanc, and M. Wesche (Eds.), *Second language performance testing.* Ottawa: University of Ottawa Press.

Liskin-Gasparro, J. (1995). Practical approaches to outcomes assessment: The undergraduate major in foreign languages and literature. *ADFL Bulletin, 26,* 21-27.

Lowe, P., & Stansfield C. (1988). *Second language proficiency assessment.* Englewood Cliffs, NJ: Prentice Hall Regents.

Lynch, B., & Davidson, F. (1994). Criterion-referenced language test development: Linking curricula, teacheres and tests. *TESOL Quarterly, 28* (4), 727-743.

McNamara, T. (in preparation) *Second language performance assessment: Theory and research.* London: Longman.

McNamara, T. (1990). Item response theory and the validation of an ESP test for health professionals. *Language Testing, 7,* 52-75.

Messick, S. (1994). The interplay of evidence and consequences in the validation of performance assessment. *Educational Researcher, 23,* 13-23.

Milanovic, M. (1988). *The construction and validation of a performance-based battery of English langauge progress tests.* Unpublished doctoral dissertation, Institute of Education, University of London.

Morrow, K. (1977). *Techniques of evaluation for national syllabus.* London: Royal Society of Arts.

Oller, J. (1976). Evidence for a general language proficiency factor: An expectancy grammar. *Die Neueren Sprachen, 2,* 165-74.

Oller, J. (1979). *Language tests in school.* London: Longman.

Oscarson, M. (1989). Self assessment of language proficiency: Rationale and applications. *Language Testing, 6,* 1-13.

Raffaldini, T. (1988). The use of situation tests as measures of communicative ability. *Studies in Second Language Acquisition, 10,* 197-216.

Sajavaara, K. (1992). Designing tests to match the needs of the workplace. In E. Shohamy and R. Walton (Eds.), *Language assessment for feedback: Testing and other strategies* (pp. 123-144). Dubuque, IA: Kendall-Hunt.

Shohamy, E. (1983). The stability of the oral proficiency trait on the oral interview speaking test. *Language Learning, 33*(4), 527-539.

Shohamy, E. (1984). Does the testing method make a difference? The case of reading comprehension. *Language Testing, 1*(2), 147-170.

Shohamy, E. (1992). New modes of assessment: The connection between testing and learning. In E. Shohamy, & R. Walton, R. (Eds.), Language assessment for feedback: Testing and other strategies (pp. 7-28). Dubuque, IA: Kendall-Hunt.

Shohamy, E. (1994). The validity of direct versus semi-direct oral tests. *Language Testing, 11*(2), 99-124.

Shohamy, E., Donitsa - Schmidt, S., & Waizer, R. (1993, August). *The effect of the elicitation mode on the language samples obtained on oral tests.* Paper presented at the Language Testing Research Colloquium, Cambridge, England.

Shohamy, E., & Inbar, O. (1991). Validation of listening comprehension tests: The effect of text and question. *Language Testing, 6* (1), 23-40.

Shohamy, E., Gordon, C., Kenyon, D., & Stansfield, C. (1989). The development and validation of a semi-direct test for assessing oral proficiency in Hebrew. *Bulletin of Higher Hebrew Education, 4.*

Shohamy, E., Reves, T., & Bejarano, Y. (1986). Introducing a new comprehensive test of oral proficiency. *English Language Teaching Journal, 40(3),* 212-220.

Stansfield, C. (1986). A history of the test of written English: The evelopment year. Language Testing, *3* (2), 224-234.

Stansfield, C. W., & Kenyon, D.M. (1988). *Development of the Portuguese speaking test: Year One Project Report on Development of Semi Direct Tests of Oral Proficiency in Hausa, Hebrew, Indonesian and Portuguese.* Alexandria, VA: ERIC Document Reproduction Service. ED 296 586.

Spolsky, B. (1968). Preliminary studies in the development of techniques for testing overall second langauge proficiency. Problems in foreign language testing. *language learning*, Special Issue No. *3*, 79-101.

Swain, M. (1993). Second language testing and second language acquisition: Is there a conflict with traditional psychometrics? *Language Testing, 10*(3), 193-207.

Wesche, M. (1992). Performance testing for work-related second language assessment. In E. Shohamy & R. Walton (Eds.), Language assessment for feedback: Testing and other strategies (pp.103-122). Dubuque, IA: Kendall-Hunt .

Wilds, C. (1975). The oral interview test. In R. Jones, & B. Splosky (Eds.), Testing language proficiency (pp. 29-44). Arlington, VA: Center for Applied Linguistics.

Academic Literacy as Ways of Getting-to-Know: What Can be Assessed?

Gissi Sarig

INTRODUCTION

Building a case for alternative ways of assessing academic literacy appears to entail two sets of questions. The first concerns our thinking of literacy as such: What is literacy? What is academic literacy? Whose literacy, or literacies, are we aiming to assess? What is it about literacy that we specifically wish to assess? The second set of questions concerns the possible assessing instruments compatible with our alternative view of literacy, and is more specific in nature: What assessment instruments can we use to operationalize our conceptualization of literacy? In what ways is the implementation of the suggested alternative problematic? These and other ensuing questions underlie my plan for this chapter.

Following this overview, I will outline a theoretical rationale for assessing literacy from a semiotic-epistemic perspective. To begin with, I will propose a broad, relativistic framework for defining literacy, and suggest two of its implications to literacy assessment in general. I will then offer three dimensions for defining and assessing literacy within this relative-neutral approach. In the final part of the rationale I will turn to a discussion of one specific type of literacy -- academic literacy -- and offer one of its specific current conceptualizations, one within which learning is viewed as thoughtful knowledge manipulation.

In the second part of the chapter I will present a Model of Academically Literate Learning Goals, based on this semiotic-epistemic view of academic literacy. This model will be later used as a framework for an alternative approach to assessing academic literacy. The model I will present comprises learning goals, which, so I will suggest, can be subjected to direct performance-based assessment.

In the third part of the chapter I will present a semiotic-epistemic approach to assessing academic literacy. I will discuss one specific instrument for assessing academic literacy: the reflective knowledge journal and the rubrics for assessment accompanying it, based on five dimensions of knowledge quality. Finally, I will discuss the complexities involved in assessing knowledge journals.

THEORETICAL BACKGROUND

Defining Literacy: A Relative-Neutral Perspective

A Social, Context-Specific View of Literacy

In an opening chapter of his book **Toward Defining Literacy**, Venezky refers wryly to the task of defining literacy:

> Unlike such lexical entries as **oxide, birch** and **tibia,** this word has no neutral, precise definition. It is one of that class of autopositive terms, like **liberty, justice,** and **happiness,** that we assume contain simple, primal qualities -- necessary and desirable attributes of our culture - but that under scrutiny become vastly more complex and often elusive, yielding to no simple characterization or definition. (1990, p. 2)

Venezky's enlightening words capture the gist of a currently accepted approach to understanding literacy: the relative-neutral approach, as opposed to the deterministic-ideological one (Gee, 1986). Researchers working within the neutral-relative approach to literacy share an understanding of literacy as a social, context-specific phenomenon.

Two important implications result from this understanding, with regard to both the conceptualization of literacy and its assessment. The first concerns the **pluralistic** nature of the various literacies characterizing one complex discourse community, on one hand, and the **particularistic** nature of each of these distinct literacies, on the other. The second implication has to do with a crucial aspect of literacy: its **normativistic** nature. It concerns the discourse practices that each member of the discourse community must exercise to legitimately belong to it. From this perspective literacy can be viewed as a set of norms, determined by community leaders and followed by other actors, members of the community.

Perspectives for Defining and Assessing Literacy from a Social, Context-Specific Perspective

Literacy can be defined and assessed from three perspectives once it is viewed as a social, context-specific phenomenon. The first perspective is the **contextual function.** This perspective highlights the practical goals, which a particular literacy is meant to fulfill within a given social context. From this perspective, literacy is defined and assessed in terms of its context-specific social goals.

The second perspective from which literacy can be defined and assessed, is the **performances** involved in fulfilling the contextual goals. From this point of view, literacy can be studied, defined and assessed in terms of the various tasks a literate person is expected to perform successfully within a given social situation. These tasks can be viewed as an operationalization of the norm-dependent goals underlying the functions.

The third perspective from which literacy can be defined and assessed is the semiotic-epistemic perspective. From this view, researchers look into the nature, sources and limitations of knowledge. Here, literacy can be defined and assessed once we understand how community-specific **ways of knowing** are displayed in the particular discourse practices characterizing that community. This means that literacy can be defined as the relation between a given meaning or interpretation, which a specific community constructs for a given piece of reality, on one hand, and its various discourse practices, on the other. This dimension of literacy highlights the cultural characteristics of a given literacy and hence various inter-cultural differences in literate practices among different discourse communities.

Different theorists attempt to conceptualize this semiotic-epistemic aspect of literacy. Polany (1972; cf. Harrington, 1985) views literacy education as a channel through which ways of thinking, that a given community practices in order to interpret the world get internalized by its members. Following Polany, Harrington (1985) labels this process intellectual socialization. Street (1984) defines it as a socially acceptable way of constructing meaning, while Gee (1986), following Scollon and Scollon (1981), goes even further in defining literacy as an essential component of a person's identity.

The three perspectives of a social, context-specific view of literacy -- contextual function, performances, and the semiotic-epistemic perspective -- can help construct a model of the literacy we may wish to describe and then assess. If we are to gain an inside understanding of the discourse practices that define the literacy of the discourse community under assessment, we need a deep understanding of its semiotic-epistemic foundations. This will enable us to recognize and understand the functions and goals underlying the practices, and the tasks and performances that fulfill them.

A Case in Point: Academic Literacy as Thoughtful Knowledge Manipulation

Academic Literacy as a Dynamic Social Practice:

If from a general social perspective literacy can be viewed as *a* set of norms, then from a narrower, context-specific perspective, academic literacy can be defined as **a set of norms for the manipulation of knowledge, which is currently prevalent in a given academic institution**. From a semiotic-epistemic perspective, academic literacy concerns ways of knowing and ways-of-getting-to-know, which characterize academic discourse communities at a given point in time. Thus, different conceptualizations of academic literacy, which are prevalent in different academic discourse communities, can be viewed as different ideologies of knowledge and education.

Ideologies of knowledge and education evolve and transform over time, due to social, political and intellectual change (Berkenkotter & Huckin, 1993; Freedman, 1993; Sarig, 1994). Thus, to portray any ideology of academic literacy, one must provide answers to the following questions: What can be considered as significant, socially valued knowledge? What does it mean to know? What is the preferred way of communicating our knowledge to others? What type of thinking should we engage in, in order to know? What ways of learning can promote this view of knowledge and knowing?

The particular ideology of academic literacy to be presented here is a view of knowing and learning as **creative, mindful, reflective and thoughtful manipulation of knowledge**. This view of academic literacy feeds from novel as well as classical concepts in various disciplines, such as semiotics, psychology of learning, philosophy of language and communication, as well as educational philosophy. These concepts represent prevalent ideas about the nature of knowledge, language and communication, as well as thinking and learning. What I will be presenting later in this section is a synthesis of these concepts, as I see them relate to reading- and writing-to learn. To present this understanding of academic literacy I will first lay out its theoretical foundations. Next, I will present a Model of Academically Literate Learning Goals which I constructed on their basis.

Academic Literacy as Thoughtful Knowledge Manipulation: Theoretical Foundations

Insights from Peirce's Notion of Reflection as Semiosis. The first body of knowledge I drew from in devising the Model of Academically Literate Learning Goals came from the disciples of Charles Saunders Peirce. Peirce, the turn-of-the-century American philosopher, created the seminal concept of **semiosis** as a quest for meaning, and of reflection as specific case of semiosis (Cornbleth, 1985; Dewey, 1933; Eco, 1979; Siegel & Carey, 1989; Snyder, 1986). Three major principles underlie Peirce's semiotic view of reflection. The first one is the view of reflective reasoning as a quest for meaning rather than the discovery of "truth", a quest motivated by informed skepticism. The second principle concerns the cyclical nature of the meaning-making process, and hence the transient nature of meaning. The third principle is the focus on processes of reflection and reasoning rather than their products. These three principles are inter-related and work together in the process of reflection.

Semiosis starts once reflecting persons use knowledge they own to create informed skepticism. The awareness of skepticism, in its turn, starts one of several cycles of semiosis: signs are considered in the multiple contexts of their **interpretants** and are assigned a hypothetical meaning. Once a certain meaning is assigned, a series of reasoning moves starts. Their purpose is to ascertain the validity of the assignation, or the relevance of the mediating interpretants, which gave way for the particular meaning hypothesis under reflection. These tests may include the comparative consideration of new or different contexts, which can lend a different, more valid meaning to the sign. Another important validity test is the degree of compatibility between the reflecting persons' hypotheses and their outcomes (see also Dewey, 1933; Schon, 1987, in Ho & Richards, 1994). Thus, any given product of these tests might now act as new knowledge in its own right. As it "enters" the semiotic system, it can undermine the validity of the former meaning product, produce informed doubt, and start a new cycle of meaning-making yet again. A contemporary correlate of this critical aspect of semiosis comes from philosophy of education: from Paulo Freire's notion of the critical dialogue, which should underlie any educational process and learning event (Freire, 1972, 1976; Shor & Freire, 1990/1987).

A major characteristic of this quest for meaning is, thus, its cyclicality. Each new meaning assignation starts, in its turn, a new cycle of reflective reasoning. This cyclical process is an expression of the semiotic approach to both meaning itself and the process of its making. The reflecting person is thus interested in the process of reflective meaning-making, no less than she or he is interested in its final (yet always tentative) product. As to meaning itself, the meaning constructor knows that unlike "truth", meaning is always transient and is constantly fluid. Thus, he or she is "out there" to look for new, different **interpretations** of reality, rather than for one absolute truth. This aspect of Peirce's knowledge of semiosis was corroborated by extensive research on one particular process of meaning-making: writing (Flower & Hayes, 1984; Fitzgerald, 1986; Flower, Hayes, Carey, Schriver & Stratman, 1986; Sarig, 1993b).

From the vantage point of the reader of our time, Peirce's idea of reflection as semiosis can be viewed as an auspicious, prescientific conception of thinking. It anticipated a combination of three major contemporary concepts: first, a Marxist approach to meaning-making (Schmidt, 1978), second, process-oriented, metacognitively-inclined models of text processing, and third, Freire's notion of the critical dialogue (Freire, 1972, 1976; Shor & Freire, 1990/1987). Thus, combining insights from Peirce's heritage with more current ones seemed promising and fruitful.

Insights from Current Knowledge on Learning, Thinking and Writing. Current models of learning put complex understanding performances at the focus of learning, and therefore of testing. An understanding performance view of learning and teaching rejects the **localism** and **presentism** (Gardner, 1991), which characterize the learning products of students at all ages, even at university level. Developed by Gardner (1991) and Perkins (1992, 1993), an understanding performance view of learning is geared to "being able to perform in a variety of thought-demanding ways with the topic..." (Perkins 1993, p. 7). This view of learning strives for **thoughtfulness**, or higher-order thinking, which, to cite Newman (1990), involves interpreting, manipulating or evaluating "information in new, or non-algorithmic ways" (p. 254). In short, this approach encourages creative manipulation of incoming knowledge.

Two important concepts related to learning thoughtfully are the concepts of mindfulness (Langer, 1989, 1994; Salomon, 1983) and that of disposition (Perkins, Jay & Tishman, 1993). Langer (1993) defines mindfulness as

> a state of mind that results from drawing novel distinctions, examining information from new perspectives and being sensitive to context. It is an open, creative probabilistic state of mind, in which the individual might be led to finding differences among things thought similar and similarities among things thought different...it is the capacity to see any situation or environment from several perspectives. (p. 44)

Mindfulness, which appears to be a pre-requisite condition for thoughtful learning, can be viewed as an intellectual disposition, because "it has to do with how disposed people are to process information in an open, alert, flexible way" (Perkins, Jay & Tishman, 1993, p.76). In an educational context, successful learners are those, who are disposed to invest mental effort in any particular activity they are engaged in (Salomon, 1983, in Perkins, Jay & Tishman, 1993).

Insights from Notions of the Writing Process. The third body of knowledge underlying a knowledge manipulation view of academic literacy is research on the writing process and its contribution to creative, thoughtful learning. From this literature I drew on insights coming from two major approaches to writing: the social-dialogic and expressivist-cognitive views of writing. The expressivist-cognitive view of writing is the earlier of the two approaches and focuses on the impact that verbalizing in general, and writing in particular, have on the writer (Belsey, 1980, in Faigley, 1989; Flower & Hayes, 1984; Meichenbaum & Arsanow, 1979; Moffett, 1988 in Lunsford, 1990; Kelly, 1972 and McPherson, 1977, in Fulkerson, 1990; Sarig, 1989, 1993a; Scardamalia & Bereiter, 1987; Vygotsky, 1962). The social-dialogic approach is more complex, and views written communication as both an inter-subjective, public, audience-directed rhetorical activity, and as a self-directed, private activity (Bakhtin, 1981, in Lunsford, 1990 and in Dyson, 1992; Vygotsky, 1978; Nystrand, Greene & Wiemelt,1993). Freire's dialogic pedagogy appears to be an educational correlate of this approach.

The Writing-Learning Connection. The expressivist, individual approach to writing views it as a "magical", private event, in the course of which writers "construct", "compose" or "reveal" themselves and their knowledge (Belsey, 1980, in Faigley, 1989; Moffett, 1988, in Lunsford, 1990; Kelly, 1972; McPherson, 1977 in Fulkerson, 1990). This Platonian view of writing emphasizes the power of the writing situation itself to enable writers invent new knowledge while writing.

Indirect evidence for writing as an activity that enhances thinking comes from several research domains. The first of these is the research into the relation between induced verbalization of thought and metacognitive awareness. From this body of research we learn about the contribution of verbalization to the metacognitive regulation of complex cognitive endeavors in general (Vygotsky, 1962; Meichenbaum & Arsanow, 1979), and writing-to-learn tasks, in particular (Sarig & Folman, 1990). I found this body of research relevant to the model I was seeking to develop for two reasons. First, writing is an important form of thought verbalization. Second, metacognitive monitoring of thought is a kernel reflective behavior.

More indirect evidence for the relation between writing and the enhancement of thinking comes from pedagogical research on thoughtfulness. Newman (1990) studied characteristics of thoughtful learning and teaching in the social studies domain and found that handling open-ended, complex reading-writing tasks was related with thoughtfulness in learning social studies. Newman's study corroborates Penrose's (1989) earlier finding that though writing is not helpful in gathering information, high-level writing tasks seem to provide learners with "an opportunity for critical reflection and elaboration" (p. 15), and aid them in "achieving higher level learning goals" (ibid.). Similar claims to the contribution of writing pedagogy to thinking in general, and to reflective thinking in particular, come from studies on journal writing as a means of reflection on thought and action in teacher education (Ho & Richards, 1994). Though claims as to the contribution of writing to thinking and learning do not appear to have yet been consistently substantiated (Ackerman, 1993; Penrose, 1989, Tierney, Soter, O'Flahavan & McGinley, 1989; Ho & Richards, 1994), some inherent characteristics of journal writing do seem to be intuitively promising. The most relevant of these concerns the privacy that the journal writing context affords its authors: these writing journals are generally directed to the writers themselves.

Another important aspect of the writing situation is the objectivization of knowledge that it may afford, and the **mentality of detachment** (Elbow, 1985) that can ensue from it. The claim is, that once our thoughts become a physical reality in the form of print, they get emotionally and cognitively severed from the writer, their creator. Now, that knower and knowledge are apart, the knower can treat his or her thoughts as an independent entity, an object more open to critical, reflective thought. Thus, the journals have the promise of encouraging writers to take thoughtful risks and use the writing experience for intellectual exploration.

Another insight from the cognitively-rhetorically oriented research in writing, which I found most relevant to a knowledge manipulation view of academic literacy comes from studies concerned with writing as **knowledge transforming** (Flower & Hayes, 1984; Sarig, 1993b; Scardamalia & Bereiter, 1987, Spivey & King, 1989; Spivey, 1990). These studies traced the evolvement of thoughtful, cognitively efficient, reader-friendly prose out of raw writer-based material. They showed that systematic reconceptualization of formerly crude, associative thought units is a major rhetorical goal for mature, expert writer-learners. However, the studies also show that knowledge transforming is often absent from the writing processes and products of young, or immature learners; or else that it is too cognitively demanding to fulfill, even when writers do set it as their goal. Thus, knowledge transforming is a major goal for instruction and assessment. This goal is ideologically linked with dialogic philosophies of language and learning.

Dialogic Views of Language, Thinking and Learning. The first notion of dialogism I will present comes from the Russian intellectual Mikhail Bakhtin. In conceptualizing language as a concrete, living, socio-ideological entity, Bakhtin places language on the borderline between the self and the other (Bakhtin, 1981, in Lunsford, 1990 and in Dyson, 1992). Bakhtin further claims that half of the words we are exposed to belong to "Others". If we want to possess them completely, we need to "populate" them with our own meaning, intentions and emphasis, to "appropriate" them and mold them to accommodate our own expressive, semantic meaning. Prior to this "appropriation", he claims, words exist only in other peoples' minds, to serve other peoples' meanings and intentions. Bakhtin goes on to suggest that this is where we need to take "words" from, and make them our own.

Conceptually paraphrasing Bakhtin, making his words mine, I would like to extend their validity and enlarge their meaning to the literacy acts, that learners perform as they encounter other peoples' spoken and written texts. These should undergo a series of mental manipulations and transformations on the part of the learners, so that they become truly their own. Thus, Bakhtin's dialogic concept of language adds socio-communicative depth to individualistic models of thoughtful knowledge manipulation. Combining the individualistic, cognitive approaches to writing, thinking and learning with the inter-subjective, social ones enables us to envision learners, who are engaged in two dialogues. The first, private one, would take place "in" the subjective, private "space", created when the writer can converse rationally and reflectively with herself or himself. The second, public dialogue, would take place "in" the inter-subjective rhetorical "space" where writers and readers meet. The products of these two dialogues would recursively and mutually feed each other, in a social, yet Peircean manner. Thus, the Bakhtinian notion of the dialogue between the "words" of the self and the "words" of Others, characterizing language in general, can be applied to knowledge processing in particular.

A powerful and influential pedagogical correlate of Bakhtin's notion of dialogism comes from the ideology of Paulo Freire (Freire, 1970, 1976; Shor & Freire, 1990/1987). A crucial aspect of this ideology is Freire's emphasis on critical knowledge personalization. Not unlike Bakhtin's image of "invasion", Freire uses militant imagery to describe his idea: he claims that learners should "wrestle" with knowledge they encounter. They should not allow themselves to get "captivated" by it; they should bring themselves to a creative "confrontation" with it and fight it -- even when they find themselves liking it. One strategy suitable for this battle that Freire (1990/1987) suggests is mental re-writing of texts learners read. This creative and critical knowledge creating process is socially and individually empowering and liberating, and is a product of a social and intellectual dialogue. This dialogue is the core of what Freire (1976) calls the **Gnosiological Cycle** -- the knowledge cycle, where Others' knowledge gets critically transformed and personalized to create new, informal, free knowledge.

A Semiotic-Epistemic View of Academic Literacy. Looking at the foregoing insights as a basis for an educational ideology of academic literacy, a coherent picture of a mindful, creative learner emerges. The picture is coherent, because though the notions presented so far come from different theories in various disciplines, they are mutually corroborative. Let me point out three conceptual relations I see among these ideas.

The first conceptual relation concerns the cyclicality characterizing the meaning-making process. Peirce's classical notion of the cyclicality of semiosis is corroborated by modern models of the reading-writing process (e.g., Flower & Hayes, 1984; Sarig, 1993b). It is also echoed in Langer's (1993) description of mindfulness as a probabilistic state of mind. Another related link between Peirce and Langer is their emphasis on the importance of context in meaning construction: Peirce, in his notion of context dependent interpretants and their role in semiosis, and Langer, in characterizing mindfulness as sensitivity to context. A related conceptual link concerns the skeptical side of Peirce's semiotic cycle: the skeptical disposition motivating Peirce's semiotic cyclicality is close to the critical disposition underlying Freire's pedagogy of freedom. The second conceptual link concerns the relation between private and internal dialogues on one hand, and public, external dialogues, on the other. Bakhtin's communicative, dialogic approach to discourse is in line with Vygotsky's (1962) idea of the contribution of verbalization of thought to both internal and external communication. Both complement the Platonic, expressionistic view of writing as self-revelation. The third conceptual connection relates to the individualistic, creative side of knowledge manipulation. Peirce's concept of the role of individualistic interpretants in semiosis is echoed both in Bakhtin's emphasis on the personalized input of the language user and by its educational correlates: Freire's critical, empowering dialogic pedagogy (Freire, 1972; 1976; Shor & Freire, 1990/1987), Newman's (1990) notion of the creativity underlying thoughtfulness and Perkins' (1993) and Gardner's (1991) concept of individual understanding performances.

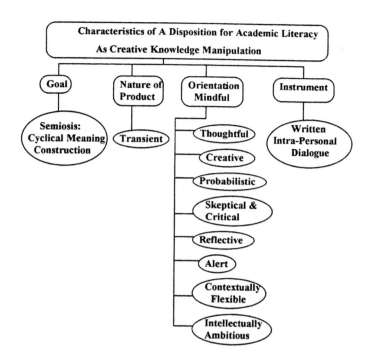

Figure 1: Characteristics of the Learner with a Disposition for Academic Literacy

Langer's (1993) concept of mindfulness and Salomon's (1983) emphasis on the mental effort it involves in educational contexts seem to be related to all the insights, as they are pre-requisite for all the processes involved. It is only learners disposed (Perkins, Jay, & Tishman, 1993) to learn mindfully (Langer, 1994; Salomon, 1983), who can adopt the learning goals emerging from these insights. Figure 1 presents a synthesis of the various traits characterizing the intellectual disposition of these learners, or, in other words, the academic literacy to which they are committed. Their goal is to be engaged in semiosis: the cyclical construction of transient meaning from knowledge they are in contact with. Their orientation to learning acts is mindful: they manipulate knowledge creatively, critically, thoughtfully, probabilistically and tentatively. They are alert, contextually flexible, and intellectually ambitious. They are competent in using a powerful thinking instrument: reflective writing. They verbalize their thoughts in writing, turning them into a detached object for thoughtful consideration, and create new thoughts as they write along. Doing so, they know they make their own audience, but they can use writing to conduct inner dialogues with internalized external audiences in mental times and places.

The profile just presented describes characteristics of learners who have adopted a semiotic-epistemic view of literacy. Following are the operative learning goals that can be construed from of this profile.

A PROPOSED MODEL OF ACADEMIC LEARNING GOALS

Learning Goals As Goals of Academic Literacy

In this section of the chapter I will present a Model of Academically Literate Learning Goals, which attempts to operationalize a view of academic literacy as creative manipulation of knowledge. It is important to understand the nature of this model and of the products it is meant to generate, because these products serve as a data-base to which the rubrics for assessing knowledge quality (to be presented later in the chapter) are applied. To explain how this instructional model became part of an assessment instrument, let me give a short account of how the model was developed.

The Model of Academically Literate Learning Goals was originally developed with an instructional, rather than evaluative purpose. The purpose was to create a learning environment, which would generate thoughtfulness in handling course material by means of reflective writing (Sarig, 1993c, 1993e). The working hypothesis was that if learners adopted the various categories in the model as writing-to-think goals, and regularly reflected on course material in writing, they would eventually internalize the learning behavior which these categories entailed. The model was first developed for use with students in a teachers college (Sarig, 1993d), and later refined for use with school children (Sarig, 1993e). Once it became clear that keeping the writing-to-reflect knowledge journal was both a feasible and beneficial endeavor, it became necessary to develop a set of relevant criteria for its assessment. The rationale for turning the writing-to-learn journal into a knowledge portfolio, to be used as a data base for a course score, was that an extensive mental and time investment went into it. Thus, it was only fair to let the learners get credit for it. Moreover, institutionalizing the journal as a data base for assessment gave it social prestige and pragmatic value, thus effecting a positive backwash effect.

In what way do the learning goals in the model reflect the view of academic literacy discussed earlier in the chapter? Academic literacy has been defined here from a semiotic-epistemic perspective as **the ability to manipulate knowledge creatively and reflectively**. In assessing the learners' academic literacy within the framework of this definition, we are interested in two aspects of this ability. The first concerns the process of getting-to-know, i.e., the literacy acts learners engage in while acquiring and creating knowledge. The second aspect concerns the learning product: the academic nature of the learners' final (or best) pieces of knowledge. Thus, in assessing the learners' learning goals and the quality of the products ensuing from them, we look into the nature and quality of the particular academic literacy underlying them. In sum: the learning goals in the suggested model can be perceived as goals that an academically literate learner should strive to achieve. The nature and quality of these goals, as well as those of the knowledge products that ensue from them, constitute in concert the learners' ways of knowing and ways of getting-to-know: their academic literacy.

A Model of Academically Literate Learning Goals

In this section of the chapter I will present the Model of Academically Literate Learning Goals and explain how it works. I will first offer a bird's eye view of the model. Next, I will give authentic examples for most of the categories in the model. The model appears in Figure 2.

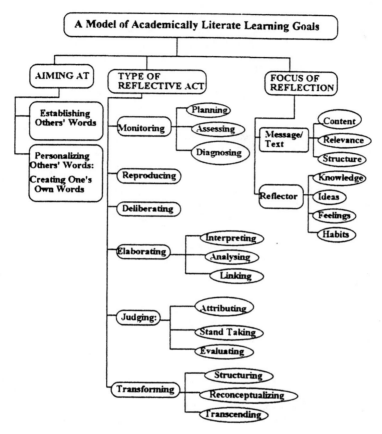

Figure 2: A Model of Academically Literate Learning Goals

An Overview of the Model

The Model of Academically Literate Learning Goals allows a view of a given learning event from three perspectives: the learning **Aims** toward which learners work, the **Types** of Reflective Acts they engage in during the learning event and the **Focus** of these acts. The major learning aim underlying the model is **Personalizing Others' Knowledge**. However, **Personalizing** does not take place in a vacuum: it must be based on a valid version of the "words of Others". The other major aim of the reflective process is thus **Establishing Others' Words**.

Before elaborating on the various categories of the model, it is important to grasp its dynamic nature. The major characteristic of the model is its cyclicality: reflecting on course material is cyclical, synergetic and interactive in nature. Any reflection product, created at any stage of learning, can at any moment change its status and become the object of various other reflective acts. In this way, for example, learners can **Link** a given piece of new knowledge to their prior knowledge, an act, which will consequently lead them to **Diagnosing** a serious flaw in their current meaning-making. Thus, the two reflective acts, **Linking and Diagnosing**, bring learners back to **Reproducing Content** elements in the **Message**, or **Text** that they were dealing with. This tentative, transient product of reflection serves as a data base on which the reflection process revolves and evolves. The reflection base gets larger and richer as the process of reflection per a given unit of contents proceeds. Numerous interactions among the various reflective acts, focusing on the various aspects of the task, the text, the learner and the learning situation characterize the development of personal knowledge, based on a valid reproduction of "Others'" knowledge.

Examples for Entries in Knowledge Journals Based on the Model of Academically Literate Learning Goals

To look more closely at the model, I will now present samples from the knowledge journals of five learners, different in age, education and background, who were writing-to-reflect in different contexts, on different topics and in different formats. As the journals were written in Hebrew, the samples to be presented were translated into English. Otherwise, the texts appear here as in the original. Following the spirit of the interactive and synergetic nature of the process of writing-to-reflect, I have opted to present the categories in the model in the order of their spontaneous occurrence in the learners' entries. This will afford us a dynamic, coherent and contextualized view of the model.

The first entry is taken from Sue's journal. Sue is an experienced humanities junior-high teacher in her early thirties, who kept a knowledge journal as part of her duties in an in-service training course entitled "Academic literacy education in junior high schools". The students in this course were asked to accompany the course with weekly entries of reflective writing. The purpose was to bring about thoughtful understanding performances of course material (lectures, readings and discussions) throughout the duration of the course. The students were guided in using a simple version of the Model of Academically Literate Learning Goals as a framework for their free reflective writing. Thus, Sue kept a knowledge journal for a whole college schoolyear, writing one entry following each weekly class. In her knowledge journal, Sue **Assesses** her understanding of a concept brought up in class: the relation between mental effort and learning. First, she **Reproduces** the **Content** units in the **Message** on which she is focusing:

> *What is meaningful learning? What takes place in the course of a meaningful learning event? Meaningful learning is when I exit my prior knowledge on a certain topic and set myself challenges/ challenges involving mental effort. - if there is no mental effort then meaningful learning will not take place.*

She goes on to **Elaborate** on this idea, teaching it to herself, by **Interpreting** and **Analyzing** it:

> *The difficulty is part of the learning - if I don't feel I'm having a hard time, and didn't invest extensive mental effort - it means a meaningful learning process has not taken place. Namely, no*

significant change has taken place in the level of my knowledge, understanding, insight -

Sue then turns to **Assessing** her learning product, focusing on the **Content** and **Complexity** of the **Message** she is wrestling with, but -- no less -- on herself as a **Reflector**, her **Knowledge, Ideas** and **Feelings**:

Have I understood the issue? - I am not sure. I am trying to write out what I have understood and I have a feeling that actually I did not understand it right through to the core. I have a feeling of lack of clarity.

Having Assessed her understanding product as flawed, Sue now turns to Diagnosing what the nature of the flaw is. She does so by **Elaborating** on the **Message**, bringing forth **Prior Knowledge** of her own learning **Habits as a Reflector**:

Maybe my sense of lack of clarity results from the simplicity of the message. [Maybe] It is not complicated, and I am looking for the complicated and incomprehensible?

A few lines later, wrestling in similar fashion with another **Content** unit in the **Message**, she returns to **Assessing** both the reflective process done so far and its ensuing products, and proceeds to **Diagnosing** what is wrong with it, if at all:

Now that I am writing I feel it is hard for me. Very hard for me. Because I am up against a mental difficulty - I find it hard to get to the bottom of things. Or maybe not? Maybe I did understand?

This insightful turning point in the assessment process brings her back to **Monitoring** her reflection process, as she **Plans** a **Diagnosing**-oriented learning goal for herself: "*I will read [my notes] all over again!*" After doing so, she reassesses her understanding and writes: "- *Yes! - After rereading I think I did understand.*" It is reflection on the **Message**, as well as on herself as a **Reflector**, that inspired Sue to give an already processed unit of contents another "once over", in the true spirit of Peircean semiosis.

Sue's entry displays the two learning **Aims** in the model: **Establishing Others' Words'** (her teachers'), as well as **Personalizing Others' Words: Creating One's Own Words.** It displays a rich array of reflective acts in the model: **Planning, Assessing and Diagnosing** in the **Monitoring** group, **Reproducing**, and **Interpreting, Analyzing** and Linking moves in the **Elaborating** category. These reflective moves focused on the **Content** and **Complexity** of the **Message**, and on the **Knowledge, Ideas, Feelings** and **Habits** of the learner herself, as the **Reflector**. However, Sue's reflective process falls short of the most sophisticated type of reflective act: **Transforming.**

To demonstrate what **Transforming** is, let us take a look at a transforming act in the knowledge journal of Gilla. Gilla is a 24 year old third-year student in a teachers College. As part of her training in a special education program, she took a pre-service course in Literacy Education, similar in aims and syllabus to the in-service course Sue took. While Sue was an experienced teacher, Gilla still has no real experience in teaching. As part of their duties in the course, the students had to write weekly in a knowledge journal. The students were guided to use another simple version of the Model of Academically Literate Learning Goals as a framework for their free reflective writing. As a final task, they were asked to reflect retrospectively on the on-line, concurrent reflections they wrote throughout the year.

In the transforming act presented in Figure 3, Gilla reconceptualizes an idea discussed in class -- Whole Language Approach as a possible extension of Chomsky's concept of the Language Acquisition Device. Gilla's **Structuring Transformation** shows her own personal way of integrating various pieces of information into a single coherent concept map.

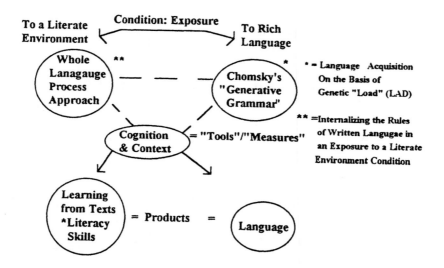

Figure 3: Gilla's Transforming Map: The Whole Language Approach as an Extension of Chomsky's LAD Concept

Children's knowledge journals display reflective acts similar to the ones presented so far, though, naturally, less elegantly put together. Following is an analysis of one entry from Dori's journal. Dori, a ten year old fifth grader, writes-to-reflect on a short poem entitled "A Sad Song" (Kalo, 1982). The entry was written as the first task in a treatment meant to coach the children to keep a knowledge journal. They wrote their entry as a response to general, open, written prompts. The poem Dori reflects about tells about a bird mourning its affluent life in a cage. Dori starts with her response to the **Knowledge Base** prompt. She Reproduces the **Content** to the Text she is reflecting about:

> *-A bird is locked up which wants to fly to the sky.*
> *-wishes for freedom*
> *-has all the best*
> *-Nothing will make the bird happy but freedom*

This list of **Content** units is immediately followed with an unprompted **Link** act, as Dori spontaneously enters a series of **Personalizing** acts. Focusing on the Message of the Text she has read, she links the knowledge she established from the poem with prior **Knowledge** she acquired in class. This is a spontaneous, unprompted act of transfer:

> -*I think this story fits the folk tale*
> *["]The Advice of the Bird["].*
> *-A bird wishes to fulfill a dream.*
> *-The bird sings a sad song.*

This linking act continues, this time upon cue, when Dori responds to the Prior Knowledge prompt. This time, she does so more formally. First, she repeats the first **Linking** act, referring to the same linked piece of knowledge, a folk tale she studied. Immediately following this, she **Links** the poem to two additional pieces of knowledge, the revolt in the Warsaw ghetto during the holocaust and her own dogs' escapades:

> *My new knowledge related to my old knowledge in this way: We*
> *learned about the story ["]The Advice of the Bird["]. And in*
> *["]The Advice of the Bird["] too the bird is locked up and asks*
> *for freedom.*
> *-It reminds me of the war and of the people in the ghetto that they*
> *did everything only to be free.*
> *-My dog receives all the best and always runs away from me but*
> *returns.*

Dori goes on reflecting by responding to the **Judging** prompt. She starts a spontaneous series of **Evaluating, Stand Taking and Attributing** acts regarding the **Message** in the **Text** she has read. First, she expresses her approval of the way the bird is characterized in the poem. She then **Takes Stand** against the situation depicted in the poem, i.e., protesting against the bird's being locked up in a cage and deprived of its rights. She then reflects on the situation yet again by re-Linking it to **Prior Knowledge** she has already instantiated earlier in the journal. She rounds off the **Judging** act by shifting her focus from the **Message** in the **Text** to focusing on herself, the **Reflector**. She now expresses the Feelings that the situation depicted in the poem aroused in her:

> *In the poem I like it that the bird too has wishes and emotions*
> *and I do not agree with it that they don't give the bird freedom*
> *and don't let her express itself/*
> *It's like being locked in jail forever.*
> *Like the people in the ghettos during the wars.*
> *The people are piteous and animals are piteous and it touches*
> *my heart because it is sad.*

Next, Dori embarks on a deeper cycle of reflection on the Message in the Text, as she responds to the **Monitoring** prompt. She Assesses her understanding of the poem by **Diagnosing** what it is, exactly, that deters her understanding. She starts with **Diagnosing** two **Interpreting** problems. The first she solves easily, but the other remains unsolved:

I don't understand the word "strives" [for freedom] - I think that the meaning of the word is wants, wishes.
- I do not understand why the poem is called "A Sad Song". We can see for ourselves that it is a poem [Note that in Hebrew, the word "song" also means "poem"].

She then **Diagnoses** a difficulty when she **Links** prior knowledge about the relation between sadness on one hand, and the singing of the bird, on the other. As a result, she **Deliberates** the dissonance which the text creates for her, revealing an emerging **Evaluative** act of **Judging** the feasibility of the **Content**:

There are contrasts in the title of the poem, because one sings when one is happy and when we are sad in our hearts we are sad. -How does the poet know that the bird is sad?

She then goes on to a similar **Deliberating** act, when she again **Links** prior **Knowledge** about the yet inexplicit dissonance she **Diagnosed**, arising from the conflict between security and freedom:

-Why does the bird sing a sad song if it has all the best. If it goes free it will have many dangers and lack of food.

Toward the end of the entry, Dori responds to the **Transforming** prompt. She does so by attempting a Structuring act. She tries to conceptualize the meaning she constructed during the reflective process she underwent by wrapping up her insights within an economic, but revealing schematic structure, a semantic map. The map appears in Figure 4.

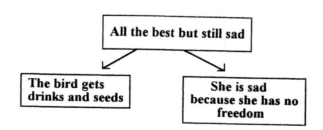

Figure 4: Dori's Map: A Reconceptualization of the Poem

The third entry I will analyze comes from a knowledge journal written by Ron, a 9 year-old fourth grader. Keeping the journal was part of the routine activities in a Bible studies class Ron participated in. Unlike Dori's entry, which still shows heavy dependence on the prompts, Ron's entry is free and spontaneous. It seems that he has previously internalized the aspects of reflective thinking involved in the knowledge acquisition process typical of the Bible studies class. Ron is writing following a discussion of the first part of chapter 7 in the Book of Judges. This part of the chapter tells the story of Gideon's preparations for the battle against Midian. Following God's commands, Gideon narrows down the number of his soldiers from 32,000 down to 10,000 and then down to 300, so that the future victory will be perceived as an act of Providence rather than as a military achievement of Gideon and his soldiers. Ron starts his entry with a **Reproduction** of the main points of the plot:

> *In chapter 7 in the book of Judges, God asks Gideon to take from the people of Israel men who want to fight in Midian and then he says that he who laps the water like a dog will fight Midian. I understood that God wanted few warriors, so that he could make miracles and not send many and then they will say that God did not help the people of Israel but it was they who won the battle with Midian.*

Ron's next reflective act is an attempt at **Elaborating** on the story he has **Reproduced**, by trying to **Link** it with prior **Knowledge**. The attempt fails, and Ron reports: *"The chapter does not remind me of anything."* Having come up with no prior knowledge, Ron starts a **Monitoring** act by **Diagnosing** a source of incomprehension. Ron has already stated clearly -- and correctly -- the purpose of God's command:

> *I understood that God wanted few warriors, so that he could make miracles and not send many and then they will say that God did not help the people of Israel but it was they who won the battle with Midian.*

However, in **Diagnosing**, he pinpoints an information gap in the **Text,** concerning the particular strategy that God chose for Gideon to implement so as to select the 300 warriors. (One traditional inferential Interpretation which Ron apparently could not produce on his own is that lapping the water, rather than drinking it in other manners, involved inconvenience. This inconvenience was presumed to lure the less devoted soldiers to disarm themselves, so as to drink more comfortably. Thus, soldiers who did not disarm themselves to drink more comfortably, and were therefore qualified as devoted soldiers, would be selected for the battle):

> *I did not understand why it was important for God to have the People of Israel lap the water like dogs.*

This **Assessment** of comprehension, and the following **Diagnosis** of what it is exactly that the learner had difficulty to comprehend, is a sophisticated and useful reflective act. Sophisticated, as it involves pinpointing information gaps, and useful, as no measures to complete comprehension can be taken without it. Perhaps due to this unfilled information gap, Ron reports a temporary "blank spot" in his mind. In doing so, he focuses on himself as a **Reflector**, and on the knowledge **Acquisition** process: *"I am not deliberating anything and not reflecting on anything."* Still troubled by the difficulty he diagnosed earlier, Ron proceeds with a **Judging** act, **Evaluating** the **Relevance,** or **Importance** of God's action. In this he capitalizes on his prior understanding of God's purpose: *"I think God will make miracles for the People of Israel and then they will keep on believing in him."* Next, **Monitoring** his thinking products, Ron **Diagnoses** another information gap he would like to see filled. This Reflector-based information ensues from the Text-based information gap Ron has pinpointed earlier: *"I would like to know why God did not select a thousand men, but purposefully 300 men."*

Ron concludes the entry with a **Judging** act, **Evaluating** his impressions of the chapter, thus shifting the focus of his reflection from the **Content** of the **Message/Text** to himself as **Reflector**, its reader: *"I like this chapter."*

To sum up the presentation of the model, following is an entire, uninterrupted entry from another knowledge journal. The entry is taken from the journal of Yael, who took the same in-service course Sue took. Yael's characteristics as a learner are similar to those of Sue, and she wrote the journal under the same conditions. Yael's entry follows an introductory lesson on the cognitive and communicative aspects of a literacy event. Yael's entry appears in Figure 5.

I'm re-reading the lesson's summary and can't seem to "connect" with it. While reading, things seem to me very trivial and self-evident, but when I try to transform them, reorganize them in my thoughts, or on paper, I run into difficulty - difficulty on the level of putting my thoughts into words, not to mention recontextualizing, or evaluating them critically. Stage by stage. Conversing with anybody or writing out my ideas, that is, externalizing and distancing myself from them enables me to evaluate and assess them critically. And through this to internalize them, too. That is, the external aspect of criticism gets linked to the internal aspect. You also claimed that good inner communication does not come easily, it comes only as a result of an investment of mental effort. That is why we don't reach this all the time, and not everyone can reach this, only those who are committed to an audience, like a teacher. This is acceptable to me. I think that everyone does that some time or other. That is, every person has a need to create good communication with those he's close to. And if he is tongue-tied, cryptic and lame in his thought, he will have to wreck his brains again and again to have his interlocutor understand him (I'm not saying write it up, because usually people who are tongue-tied won't put their thoughts into writing) and thus, he will crystallize his ideas for himself and will reach good inner communication. Children can also express themselves so that they get to be understood - that is, reach good internal and external communication. They do so by drawing, glueing, pantomime. (Physically abused children draw a little body full of blood, which a big man crushes - I saw such a drawing of a 7 year old child. In his way they concretize the pain and humiliation for themselves).

Cognitive Aspects	Communicative Aspects
↓	↓
Focus on knowledge and knowledge manipulation	*Focus on considerateness towards audience*

on internalization → inner communication and monitoring

    In writing a text the motive is communicative, that is in writing I notice (a) Knowledge gaps between me and my reader - and then I try to bridge them, and also to (b) The reader's norms - textual, rhetorical, cultural norms. All this in order for external communication to be good - to have him understand me adequately. But the action itself is cognitive - I'm "using" old and new knowledge. Good! I understand. During writing things become so simple and clear. It's a wonderful feeling. So what have I done here? Comprehension, transformation and evaluation. O.K.

Figure 5: Yael's Entry from December 12, 1993

Training Students to Keep the Knowledge Journal

(1) Operative Versions of the Model of Academically Literate Learning Goals

The reflective acts presented above do not represent spontaneous learning behavior. They were produced under the constraints of the Model of Academically Literate Learning Goals. How can we train the learners to adopt it as a regular learning habit? In this section of the chapter I address this question.

Mediating the model to the learners, so that they use it regularly, involves decisions related to the following variables: (a) The specific operative version of the model to be used; (b) the timing and frequency of writing reflectively in the journal and (c) learners' freedom in responding to the various tasks in the model. In this section of the chapter I will discuss these variables.

The Model of Academically Literate Learning Goals can be presented to the learners in different versions, varying in degrees of simplification. Following are three simplified versions of the model which I used in the three learning contexts mentioned in the former section of the chapter.

Learning Goals as Questions. The simplest version of the Model of Academically Literate Learning Goals consists of five learning tasks put as questions. This version of the model suits young learners, who are used to this type of learning cue. This version of the model was used in Dori and Ron's classes. Figure 6 presents the questions that the fourth and fifth graders in Dori and Ron's class had to address. Some of the questions were presented to the learners in writing; others were presented as clarifications, and then added to the written version.

The Model of Academically Literate Learning Goals Presented as Questions

1. a. What are the main ideas, or claims, in the lesson/ text/discussion?
2. a. What are the main difficulties in the lesson/ texts/discussion?
   b. What is it exactly that you do not understand?
      What do you plan to do about it?
   c. Are there any contradictions in the lesson/text/discussion?
      What do you plan to do about it?
3. a. What do the ideas in the lesson/text/discussion remind you of?
   b. Do you know/Have you already learnt anything that is similar or related to an idea, or some ideas in the lesson/text/discussion?
4. a. What is your opinion about the ideas in the lesson/text/discussion?
   b. What feelings do the ideas in the lesson/text/discussion arouse in you?
   c. Do you approve/disapprove of what you read/ heard/saw/ witnessed?
   d. How would you describe the ideas in the lesson/text/discussion? (e.g., "interesting", "stupid"...etc.)
      Why do you think so?
      Do you approve of them?
      Why?
5. a. Can you present the ideas in the lesson/ text/discussion in a new, different way, all your very own?
   b. Can you invent a new idea of your very own, based on the lesson/text/discussion?
      You can invent a map, a story, a play, an ad, or any other new invention you can think of.

Figure 6: The Model of Academically Literate Learning Goals Presented as Questions

Learning Objectives Stated as Simple Learning Tasks. In this version of the model, the main categories were translated into simple learning tasks, representing different kinds of knowledge manipulation. This simplified version of the model was used in Gilla's class. It appears in Figure 7.

Knowledge Manipulating Acts	
1. <u>Extracting Knowledge</u>:	Reproduce the main points/ ideas/ claims/ messages in the incoming knowledge.
2. <u>Anchoring Knowledge</u>:	Link the new knowledge with your own prior knowledge.
3. <u>Clarifying Knowledge</u>:	Locate unclear/difficult/problematic spots in the material. Find out exactly what the problem is. Plan what to do about the problems. Seek and consider more than one solution.
4. <u>Transforming Knowledge</u>:	Find an original, creative way of your own to represent the meaning you made of the knowledge.
5. <u>Judging Knowledge</u>:	Evaluate the knowledge critically. Take your own stand. Express your own views.
6. <u>Using Knowledge</u>:	Show how you can use the new knowledge in the future.
7. <u>Expanding Knowledge</u>:	Create your own new knowledge, based on all six knowledge manipulating acts done so far.

Figure 7: Learning Goals as Simple Learning Tasks

Learning Goals as A Semantic Map with Clarifying Questions. This version of the model presents the various reflective tasks in a structured semantic map. Like in the other version, the map is also accompanied with clarifying questions. This map, one of the earlier versions of the model, was used in Sue and Yael's class. Figure 8 presents the map.

(2) Time and Frequency of Writing in the Journal

Writing Introspectively-Concurrently. Teachers can encourage learners to write after each session with them, as preparation for the next one. In this case, reflection on the new knowledge takes place in a concurrent, introspective manner -- almost "on-line" -- on a regular basis. In this case, the learners are encouraged to write in the journal as often as they can. The optimal frequency would be writing during, or after each session in the course: a lecture, a workshop, or any other type of meaningful course activity. The advantage of using the knowledge journal in this way lies in the generative nature of the type of writing it involves: as the learners "wrestle" with the new knowledge, they get to know it. The disadvantage is that this type of writing lacks the time perspective, which can afford a riper, more coherent, after-the-fact reflection on the new knowledge. Sue and Yael's journals were written in this concurrent, introspective format, and, indeed, the entries taken from their journal show how comprehension is being created in their minds, as they write.

Writing Retrospectively. Teachers can also opt to encourage retrospective versions of the knowledge journal. They can encourage the learners to write in the journal following the completion of a whole cycle of new knowledge (i.e., a topic, a concept, a book, etc.). In this case, the frequency of writing is lower, and the reflection is more retrospective in nature. Reflecting on course material retrospectively may enable the learners to upgrade their thoughts in two respects. First, the passage of time can create new perspectives, from which to reflect on the knowledge base. Second, as knowledge increases acumulatively, it grows in depth and coherence. Thus, periodical retrospective reflection may afford the learners fresher perspectives for new cycles of reflective semiosis, and therefore a deeper, more meaningful conceptualization of the material.

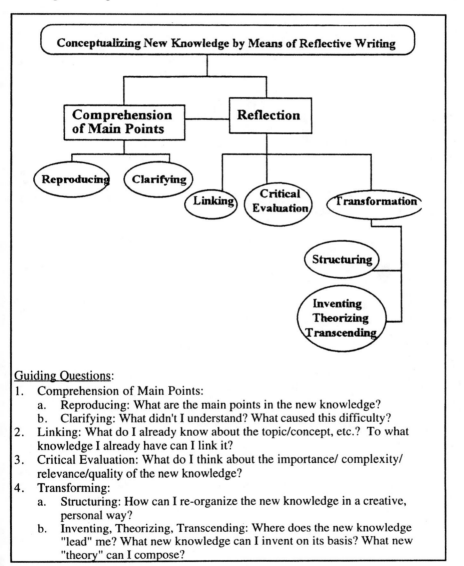

Guiding Questions:
1. Comprehension of Main Points:
    a.   Reproducing: What are the main points in the new knowledge?
    b.   Clarifying: What didn't I understand? What caused this difficulty?
2. Linking: What do I already know about the topic/concept, etc.? To what knowledge I already have can I link it?
3. Critical Evaluation: What do I think about the importance/ complexity/ relevance/quality of the new knowledge?
4. Transforming:
    a.   Structuring: How can I re-organize the new knowledge in a creative, personal way?
    b.   Inventing, Theorizing, Transcending: Where does the new knowledge "lead" me? What new knowledge can I invent on its basis? What new "theory" can I compose?

Figure 8: Learning Objectives Presented as a Semantic Map, Followed by a Set of Accompanying Questions

Writing Both Concurrently-Introspectively and Retrospectively. An ideal possibility is, naturally, to combine concurrent-introspective with retrospective reflective-writing. A learner, who writes in the journal frequently and uses it to reflect on course material both concurrently and retrospectively, stands a good chance of implementing his or her intellectual potential to the full. Gilla's journal is an example for a journal written in this format.

In spite of the differences among the various formats presented above, all of them involve documentation of both learning processes and products. Note, however, that the terms process and product used here are both relative and dynamic in the context of the knowledge journal. As each entry in the knowledge journal is completed -- regardless of the format in which it is written -- it represents the learners' current final knowledge product. However, once additional entries get written on the same topic, the former ones can be considered as interim, process entries -- the precursors of more mature knowledge to come. Thus, at times, only a thin line differentiates getting-to-know from knowing.

(3) Using the Categories of the Model Freely or Systematically

Another important variable to consider in planning the use of the journal is the degree of obedience to the various categories in it. The question related to this variable is: should the learners write on the basis of each category each time they write-to-reflect, or should they be given the freedom to respond only to those categories which seem relevant to them at a given point in the learning process? It seems to me that only at the initial stage, when learners are in the process of learning how to use the model, they may be encouraged to respond to all the categories, as practice. Later, once the various learning goals have been understood and internalized, they should feel free to use any category that seems relevant to a particular learning context at hand. Thus, although the learners work within a fixed framework of literate expectations (i.e., the model) they are free to engage in any of the learning acts in it, as they see fit at a given reflective situation.

I would recommend the same freedom regarding the order in which the learners may respond to the various categories in the model. As we have seen, the reflective acts in the model work interactively and synergetically. Thus, as long as the learners monitor their reflection process appropriately, there is no real sense in dictating the order in which they should respond to the categories in the model. Dori's entry represents the initial stage, where the learners follow the various reflecting tasks systematically, one by one. All the other entries presented in the former section of the chapter were written in the free format.

In sum, the knowledge journal can be used flexibly to accommodate various learning contexts. It can be mediated to the learner in various levels and forms. It can be used both introspectively and retrospectively, freely or systematically -- as the need may arise.

A SEMIOTIC-EPISTEMIC APPROACH TO ASSESSING ACADEMIC LITERACY

The Reflective Knowledge Journal As An Instrument for the Assessment of Creative Knowledge Manipulation

In the forgoing sections of the chapter I justified and presented a semiotic-epistemic Model of Academically Literate Learning Goals. In the last part of the chapter I would like to suggest using the knowledge journal, which is produced on the basis of this model, as one component of an instrument for performance-based assessment of academic literacy. First, I will comment on the relation between the Model of Academically Literate Learning Goals and the instrument. Next, I will present the instrument and demonstrate its use. Following this, I will discuss different uses of the proposed instrument for various assessing purposes, and comment on who is qualified to use it. Finally, I will discuss the complexities of the proposed approach.

Assessing the Quality of the Reflective Knowledge Journal

(1) The relation between the Model of Academically Literate Learning Goals and the Rubrics for Assessing Knowledge Journals

The instrument for assessing the quality of knowledge manipulation to be proposed here comprises two independent components: a data base -- the knowledge journal -- and rubrics for the assessment of its quality. The rubrics are an assessment device, based on five dimensions of knowledge quality. These do not ensue directly from the categories in the Model of Academically Literate Learning Goals presented above. In what way, then, are the two components related? Both the Model of Academically Literate Learning Goals and the rubrics accompanying it derive from the same view of academic literacy as creative and reflective manipulation of knowledge. However, each of these components has a different purpose. The model is basically an instructional instrument. It is meant to generate learning processes and products commensurate with the semiotic-epistemic view of academic literacy. The rubrics for assessment -- also firmly established in this view -- represent aspects of the quality of these learning processes and products. They are therefore meant to assess their quality. In sum, the two components comprising the assessment approach proposed here are theoretically interrelated, but pragmatically independent.

(2) Dimensions of Knowledge Quality and Rubrics for Assessment

What are the aspects of knowledge quality that derive from a view of academic literacy as creative and reflective manipulation of knowledge? In this section of the chapter I will suggest five dimensions of knowledge quality and the rubrics for assessment deriving from them.

The first dimension is **Veritability**. This dimension represents a pre-requisite aspect of the quality of knowledge the learners reproduce and manipulate in the course of their reflective acts: its credibility and trustworthiness. This is an essential dimension from which to begin the process of assessing learners' knowledge journals, as even the most sophisticated act of reflection will be useless, unless it is based on valid, veritable information. This dimension relates to the **accuracy**, the **spirit** and the **integrity** of the learners' reproductions and reflections.

The second dimension I propose is **Relevance**. This dimension refers to the learners' ability to show that they have been able to select for reproduction and reflection all the pieces of information that are indeed meaningful and pertinent to the phenomenon under study -- and only those. Thus, this dimension relates to the degree of **comprehensiveness** of the learners' choices, as well as to the **pertinence** of these choices to the issue at hand.

The third dimension is **Complexity**. This dimension represents the level of the intellectual challenges the learners have opted to cope with in manipulating knowledge in their journals. This criterion is an interactive combination of the cognitive investment the learners put in their reflective acts, and the goals they aim at. It relates to the degree of **coherence, inherent logical structure** and **sophistication** of the learners' reflections.

The fourth dimension is **Creativity**. This dimension refers to the learners' ability to sound their own voices in manipulating knowledge and, consequently, to contribute to the domain, to which their reflections apply. It relates to the degree of **originality** and **inventiveness** in the learners' reflections, as well as to the **contribution** of their reflections to the domain.

The fifth and last dimension is **Communicativity**. This dimension refers to the learners' ability to conduct a clear, interactive dialogue both with themselves and with non-present, internalized partners in an audience-sensitive manner. It relates to the degree of *clarity* and *explicitness* of the learners' reflections.

Following is a set of rubrics for assessing the quality of the knowledge journals on the basis of these five dimensions.

Rubrics for Assessing the Knowledge Journals

Veritability:
5   The knowledge presented is highly veritable:
   a.   **Accuracy:** The knowledge the learner monitored, reproduced, deliberated, elaborated on, judged and transformed in his or her reflections is accurate, and therefore convincing.
   b.   **Spirit:** The reproductions represent the spirit in which the claims/concepts/ideas in the source materials were presented.
   c.   **Integrity:** The claims/ideas/attitudes sound sincere, and represent what transpires as a deep conviction.
3   The knowledge presented is reasonably veritable:
   a.   **Accuracy:** The knowledge the learner monitored, reproduced, deliberated, elaborated on, judged and transformed contains some inaccuracies. However, on the whole, these inaccuracies do not damage the overall reasonability of the reflections based on them.
   b.   **Spirit:** On the whole, the reproductions represent the spirit in which the claims/concepts/ideas in the source materials were presented. However, a slight invalid variation is noticeable.

c. **Integrity:** On the whole, the claims/ideas/attitudes sound sincere. At times, the writer seems to have been carried away, and some of the claims /ideas /positions sound slightly contrived.

1 **The knowledge presented is on the whole distorted and partial:**
a. **Accuracy:** The knowledge the learner monitored, reproduced, deliberated, elaborated on, judged and transformed in his or her reflections contains a considerable number of inaccurate claims/concepts/ideas/positions. These inaccuracies invalidate the reasonableness of these reflections.
b. **Spirit:** The reproductions distort, or leave out altogether, the spirit, in which the claims/ concepts/ideas in the source materials were presented. This distortion undermines the validity of the reflections based on them.
c. **Integrity:** Most of the claims/ideas/attitudes sound insincere and contrived. On the whole, the writer seems to have been carried away and captivated on an invalid, self-made concept set.

Relevance:
5 **The knowledge presented is highly relevant:**
a. **Comprehensiveness of relevant reproductions:** The reproductions provide a fully comprehensive representation of all crucial points in the source materials to be reflected upon.
b. **Comprehensiveness of relevant reflections:** The learner manipulated (i.e., monitored, deliberated, elaborated on, judged and transformed) all idea units in the source materials which merited manipulation.
c. **Pertinence of reproductions:** The reproductions selected by the learner to reflect upon are all cardinally relevant to the issue under reflection. They are all related to inherent, core aspects of the issue under discussion.
d. **Pertinence of reflections:** All pieces of knowledge (i.e., aspects of the message, of his/her own knowledge, ideas, feelings, habits and of learning, teaching and thinking), which the learner manipulated as he or she monitored, reproduced, deliberated, elaborated on, judged and transformed, pertain directly to the issue at hand and are related to core aspects of the issue under discussion.

3 **The knowledge presented is partly relevant:**
a. **Comprehensiveness of relevant reproductions:** The reproductions provide a representation of major crucial points in the source materials to be reflected upon. However, not all crucial points are represented and reflected upon.
b. **Comprehensiveness of relevant reflections:** The learner manipulated important ideas which merited manipulation in the source materials, but did not cover all.
c. **Pertinence of reproductions:** Some of the reproductions selected by the learner to reflect upon are relevant to the issue under reflection. Others are trivial and insignificant.
d. **Pertinence of reflections:** Some pieces of knowledge, (i.e., some aspects of the message, of the learner's own knowledge, ideas, feelings and habits and of learning, teaching and thinking), which the learner manipulated as he or she monitored, reproduced, deliberated, elaborated on, judged and transformed, pertain directly to the issue at hand, and are related to core aspects of the issue under discussion. However, others are trivial and immaterial.

1   The knowledge presented   is trivial:
  a.   **Comprehensiveness of relevant reproductions:** The reproductions lack representation of a considerable number of crucial points to be reflected upon.
  b.   **Comprehensiveness of relevant reflections:** The learner did not manipulate (i.e., monitor, reproduce, deliberate, elaborate on, judge and transform) important idea units in the source materials, which did merit manipulation.
  c.   **Pertinence of reproductions:** Most of the reproductions selected by the learner to reflect upon are irrelevant to the issue under reflection and do not pertain to core elements of the issue at hand.
  d.   **Pertinence of the reflections:** Most pieces of knowledge, (i.e., most aspects of the message, of the learner's own knowledge, ideas, feelings and habits and of learning, teaching and thinking), which the learner focused on in his/her reflections as he or she monitored, reproduced, deliberated, elaborated on, judged and transformed, do not pertain directly to the issue at hand, and are not related to core aspects of the issue under discussion. Rather, they are trivial and immaterial.

Complexity:
5   The knowledge presented   is complex:
  a.   **Coherence:** Many pieces of knowledge, which the learner manipulated as he or she monitored, reproduced, deliberated, elaborated on, judged and transformed, are intertwined logically and intricately, creating one coherent whole.
  b .   **Inherent   logical   structure:** The logical structure of the reconceptualized ideas/ notions/ messages, etc. is intrinsic, and is not created by means of an artificial, super-imposed logical structure.
  c.   *Sophistication:*
     (1)   Major content units are treated profoundly and from a few perspectives.
     (2)   Important pieces of knowledge, which the learner manipulated are inter-related in more than one way, creating elegant, multi-dimensional meaning units.
     (3)   The conceptual structure the learner used, or created, as he or she transformed source materials allows for a variety of possible meanings.

3   The knowledge presented is simple and elementary:
  a.   **Coherence:** Ideas within groups of reflections, which the learner created as he or she monitored, reproduced, deliberated, elaborated on, judged and transformed, are inter-connected logically, but the groups themselves do not cohere. Groups of reflections thus constitute discrete units of thought.
  b.   **Inherent logical structure:** The structure of the reconceptualized ideas/notions/messages etc. is logical, but it is not intrinsic to the content; it is artificially super-imposed on it.
  c.   **Sophistication:**
     (1)   Important content units are treated superficially and uni-dimensionally.
     (2)   Many reflections are inter-related in only one way, creating uni-dimensional meaning units.
     (3)   The conceptual structure limits the potential variety of possible meanings of the reflections.

1   The knowledge presented   is simplistic and naive:

   a. **Coherence:** Most of the pieces of knowledge, which the learner created as he or she monitored, reproduced, deliberated, elaborated on, judged and transformed, are discrete units of thought, which do not cohere as one whole.

   b. **Inherent logical structure:** Discrete pieces of knowledge are connected in a contrived manner, by means of an external, formulaic conceptual structure. Thus, they do not cohere.

   c. **Sophistication:**

     (1)   Most content units are treated superficially and from one perspective only.

     (2)   Most of the pieces of knowledge, which the learner manipulated as he or she monitored, reproduced, deliberated, elaborated on, judged and transformed, are straightforward, uni-dimensional renderings of the issue at hand.

     (2)   Most of the reflections constitute naive, crude idealizations of a possibly complex notion/phenomenon/situation.

Creativity:

5   The knowledge presented is highly creative:

   a. **Originality of reproductions:** Major elements of the source materials were reproduced in an original, unexpected, brilliant manner.

   b. **Originality of reflections:** The learners' reflections showed unique elaborations, reached unpredictable applications and carried out far-reaching recontextualizations.

   c. **Inventiveness:**

     (1)   The learner shed a new light, created a new "reading" of the source materials.

     (2)   The learner discussed, viewed or judged the issues at hand from a hitherto unheard of perspective.

     (3)   The learner invented new theories based on the source material.

     (4)   The learner invented a new conceptual structure with which to transform the meaning of the source materials.

   d. **Contribution:** The learner's inventiveness constitutes a substantial contribution of knowledge to the domain.

3   The   knowledge   presented   is   somewhat   predictable   and unoriginal:

   a. **Originality of   reproductions:** Major elements of the source materials are reproduced in a traditional, expected manner.

   b. **Originality of reflections:** The reflections do reflect elaborations, applications and recontextualizations of the source materials, but, on the whole, they are predictable and relate to near domains.

   c. **Inventiveness:**

     (1)   The reflections make a traditional "reading" of the source materials.

     (2)   The learner discussed, viewed or judged the issues at hand from a traditional perspective.

     (3)   The reflections do not present new theories based on the source material.

     (4)   The transformations of source materials are based on a conventional conceptual, or rhetorical structure.

   d. **Contribution:** The reflections do not add new knowledge to the domain.

1   **The knowledge presented is highly predictable and at times, mundane:**
    a.   **Originality of reproductions:** Most elements of the source materials are reproduced in a conventional, even trite manner.
    b.   **Originality of reflections:** There are very few applications and recontextualizations, and these are predictable and relate to near domains.
    c.   **Inventiveness:**
       (1)   The reproductions are no more than replicas of pieces of the source materials.
       (2)   The views and opinions, which the learner voiced are echoes of views and opinions voiced in the source materials.
       (3)   The reflections do not represent new theories based on the source material.
       (4)   There is no transformation of the source materials.
    d.   **Contribution:** The reflections do not add new knowledge to the domain.

Communicativity:
5   **The knowledge presented is highly communicative:**
    a.   **Clarity:** The learner's text is clear, reader-friendly and easy to comprehend. The text is quickly read and does not demand high mental effort on the part of the reader.
    b.   **Explicitness:** The learner's text is explicit, autonomous and self-contained: it requires no extra-textual clarifications. It can be fully comprehended without the learner's oral comments.
3   **The knowledge presented is partly communicative:**
    a.   **Clarity:** Parts of the learner's text are clear, reader-friendly and easy to comprehend. Other parts are not. Some parts of the learner's text need a few reading cycles, and demand some mental effort on the part of the reader.
    b.   **Explicitness:** Parts of the learner's text are explicit, autonomous and self-contained. These parts require no extra-textual clarifications. Other parts are inexplicit, and cannot be understood without oral clarifications on the part of the writer.
1   **The knowledge presented is highly uncommunicative:**
    a.   **Clarity:** Large parts of the learner's text are vague and hard to comprehend. Most of the text requires quite a few reading cycles, and demand high mental effort on the part of the reader so as to comprehend them.
    b.   **Explicitness:** Large parts of the learners' text constitute an implicit, writer-dependent piece of discourse, and require extensive oral clarifications and elaborations on the part of the writer.

To demonstrate how this set of rubrics is applied to entries in the knowledge journal, let me first apply it to Ron's entry. Figure 9 presents Ron's entry as a whole. Line numbers are added to his text to facilitate the discussion. I will assess Ron's entry by considering each quality dimension separately.

```
4.6.93
```

Chapter 7 1-6

```
1     In chapter 7 in the book of Judges God
2     asks Gideon to take from the people of Israel
3     men who want to fight in Midian and then he
4     says that he who laps the water
5     like a dog will fight Midian.
6     I understood that God wanted few
7     warriors, so that he could make miracles
8     and not send many and then they will say
9     that God did not help the people of Israel but it was they
10    who won the battle with Midian.
11    The chapter does not remind me of anything.
12    I did not understand why it was important for God
13    to have the People of Israel lap the water like dogs.
14    I am not deliberating anything and not reflecting on anything.
15    I think God will make miracles
16    for the People of Israel and then they will keep on believing in him.
19    I would like to know why God did not select a thousand men,
20    but purposefully 300 men.
21    I like this chapter.
```

Figure 9: Ron's Entry

Veritability: If Ron could have filled the information gap he successfully pinpointed (lines 12-14), then I think his entry would have qualified for the 5 mark on all counts: the knowledge which he manipulated is accurate, true to the spirit of the source text and characterizes him as an learner with intellectual integrity. However, Ron did miss a core element in the source material (the reason why God wants the People of Israel to lap the water like dogs). This distorts an important element of the source text. Thus, he cannot qualify for the full 5 mark. I would give him 4 points on this scale, as he does not qualify for a full 5 mark, but is closer to it than to the 3 mark.

Relevance: I would place the relevance of Ron's reflections on the 5 mark. All his reflections -- both reproductions and manipulations -- are cardinally relevant to the text he is reflecting on. In addition, Ron reflected on all relevant aspects of the text he was manipulating. His monitoring comments (lines 12-13; 14; 19-20) also pertain to a relevant aspect of his reflection process.

Complexity: Ron's entry is not highly complex. I would place it between the 3 and 1 mark, and would give it 2 points. The ideas in the entry are interconnected only unidimensionally, and they do not cohere to create one whole (e.g., his comment in line 11 does not cohere well with the rest of his entry). In addition, Ron makes no attempt at transforming the source material. From this aspect, he does not even reach the threshold level for complexity.

Creativity: I think Ron's entry does not merit more than the 2 mark on this scale. His reproductions are traditional. No applications or recontextualizations appear. No new knowledge is created. However, Ron does make a spontaneous prediction (lines 15-16) as to the continuation of the story, and does ask one original question (lines 19-20).

Communicativity: I would place Ron's entry on the 5 mark. His reproductions, as well as his reflections, are clear and reader-friendly. They are quickly read, and do not demand high mental investment on the part of the reader. Ron's text is an explicit, autonomous text. There is no need for any clarifications or elaborations on his part. On the whole, Ron's entry scores 18 out of a maximum of 25 points. Note, that this assessment process did not take Ron's age or cognitive development into consideration. Thus, the rubrics afford a criterion-referenced assessment, diagnostic in nature.

Let us now look at an entry equivalent to that of Ron's. The entry I will assess is Ariel's, Ron's peer. Ariel reflects on the same chapter Ron did. Figure 10 presents the entry.

4.6.93   Today is Friday (Hebrew date deleted)
1   Chapter 7
2   Why do they need to lick the water
3   It was a nice story The people of Israel were afraid to go to war so
4   [anyone who] is scared goes home
5   They also went into the pool and
6   had to lick the water
7   like a dog and it is
8   terribly funny.

Figure 10: Ariel's Entry

Accuracy: I would place Ariel's entry on the 1 mark. The entry contains a few inaccuracies. First, not all the soldiers were afraid of fighting, as can be inferred from Ariel's version of the events (line 3). Second, the men did not go into a pool (line 5). Third, although Ariel's humorous interpretation of the scene (lines 7-8) does read as an honest reaction to the text, it is definitely not true to the spirit of the text. Had Ariel understood the meaning of the scene, it would not have assumed its funny character. Thus, Ariel's reproductions and reflections distort the source text.

Relevance: As a whole, Ariel's reproductions are at best partial. They leave out a considerable number of crucial points to be reflected upon. Most of the reproductions that Ariel did select to reflect upon do not pertain to core elements of the issue at hand: the fact that prior to the battle discussed in the chapter, some of the soldiers were afraid to fight and were exempted from it (lines 3-4) does not pertain to the "lapping test" in the way that Ariel presents it. Thus, a large part of the knowledge in the specific context Ariel chose to present it in this entry lacks relevance. However, like Ron, Ariel also discovers a crucial information gap in the source text (line 2). I would give this entry 2 on the relevance dimension, rather than 1, thanks to the important question raised in line 2 regarding this information gap.

Complexity: Ariel's entry is simplistic and naive. It is less complex than Ron's. Whereas some of Ron's reflections were inter-connected, all of Ariel's were discrete units of thought. The interpretation of the chapter is straightforward and uni-dimensional. Ariel's mark on this dimension is, therefore, 1.

Creativity: Ariel's comment about how terribly funny the lapping scene (lines 7-8) is, is definitely unpredictable. However, the entry presents no applications or recontextualizations, and there are no expansions or transformations of the source material. Though the entry does present an unusual reading of the chapter, it can not merit creativity, because no interpretation or "theory" is presented in any form. Ariel's mark for creativity is therefore 1.

Communicativity: I would place Ariel's entry between the 3 and 1 mark. On one hand, most of the sentences in Ariel's entry are clear, and therefore placing the entry on the 1 mark for Communicativity would be too harsh. However, it seems as though some of Ariel's significant thoughts did not get written down in the entry, and are missing from the text. It is therefore difficult to make sense of the entry, even after reading it a few times. The entry is a classical example of a text requiring oral clarifications and elaborations on the part of the writer, and thus, constitutes an nonautonomous piece of discourse. I would therefore describe Ariel's entry as considerably uncommunicative. Ariel's score on this dimension is therefore 2.

On the whole, Ariel score is rather low -- only 7 points out of 25. Hopefully, the diagnostic information that ensues from the assessment process may serve as a basis for individual corrective work with this young learner.

(3) Unit of Assessment

The rubrics based on the dimensions of **Veritability, Relevance, Complexity, Creativity and Communicativity** are meant to guide the assessor in conducting a rational and purposeful interpretive evaluation of the knowledge journal. This assessing instrument can be put to use with varying degrees of systematicity and thoroughness, depending on the pragmatic objectives and potential consequences of the expected score. The degree of systematicity and thoroughness desired will affect the assessor's decision as to the scope and nature of the **unit of assessment,** to which the assessor will apply the rubrics. Let us consider, for instance, the case where the assessment is only meant to give a general idea of the learners' competence, or potential for academic literacy, and is not an act of assessment carrying far-reaching pragmatic outcomes. In this case, an impressionistic assessment of the journal as a whole will do, and the unit of assessment will be the journal in its entirety. Thus, the rubrics will be applied to the journal as a whole. The richness of the information resulting from this type of assessment depends, of course, on the number and the scope of the entries in the journal. The entries may be larger or smaller, as the case may be, depending on the point of time in the schoolyear when the assessment takes place, as well as on the frequency in which the learners opted to write in the journal. The more numerous and larger in scope they are, the richer the data base, on which to apply the rubrics. If, on the other hand, the assessment is meant to diagnose, or carries far reaching consequences for the learners' future, then a more thorough analysis is called for. Moreover, I would suggest to define each entry in the journal as a separate unit of analysis. In this case, I would suggest to apply the rubrics to the data base twice: first, to apply them to each entry independently, and then, once again -- to all the entries in the journal as one whole. An in-between possibility is to divide the journal into chunks of entries, each dealing with one coherent topic of study. The journal may very well break down "naturally" into coherent units, as course topics do. This possibility is recommended in three respects. First, it merits a larger number of assessment units on which to base the assessment. Second, it enables the assessor to trace the intellectual development of the learner, as it affords an on-line, process-oriented, formative appreciation, as well as a post-hoc, product-oriented, summative appraisal of the learner's evolving knowledge. Third, it can be more fair to the learner, who may not have found all the topics of the course equally interesting and worth-investing mental effort in. In sum: the rubrics can be applied flexibly to different units of assessment, varying in number and scope, to accommodate various assessment constraints. This flexibility enables both a quick and impressionistic, as well as a more accurate and systematic assessment of the journal, as the need may arise.

Using the Knowledge Journal and the Assessment Instrument Together and Separately

As pointed out above, the two components of the assessment instrument I proposed here -- the knowledge journal and the rubrics -- are theoretically interrelated but independent. Following is a discussion of various uses of these two components, together and separately.

In the last section I have demonstrated how the two components are applied together; namely how the rubrics are applied to the knowledge journal. In applying the rubrics to the journal in this way, assessors can get a good grasp of the learners' intellectual ability to manipulate knowledge in a manner commensurate with the view of academic literacy as creative and reflective manipulation of knowledge. In other contexts, assessors may not be interested in the learners' ways-of-getting-to-know, but rather in the learner's current nature and level of knowledge, as it is displayed in final and conventional knowledge products. Indeed, as a text in its own right, the journal lacks the formal generic traits of a classical academic essay, or research paper. If assessors are interested in applying the rubrics to traditional, open-ended academic tasks, such as an analytic report, an essay, or a research paper, they can indeed do so. This choice would allow the instructors a semiotic-epistemic assessment of the learners' final knowledge products, regardless of the "getting to know" data in the journal.

Another possibility is to use the knowledge journal for learning purposes alone (see, for example Sarig, 1993d). In this case, instructors can use the model of learning goals to encourage thoughtful and mindful learning, and refrain from assessing it altogether. In this case, too, if they are interested in assessing the learner's knowledge from a semiotic-epistemic perspective, they can apply the dimensions of the assessment model to traditional writing products outside the journal. In sum: the assessment approach I propose here includes two components: the knowledge journal, based on thoughtful learning goals, and an accompanying assessment model. Instructors can opt to use them flexibly for various purposes.

Assessing Getting-To-Know Ability in Context

In the former section I made a distinction between two important aspects of academic literacy: academic literacy displayed in knowledge-in-the-making and that, which is displayed in final knowledge products. In this section, I would like to emphasize the importance of assessing these aspects of academic literacy in the context of the specific domain content, in which they are activated. Let me justify the importance of this emphasis. Research on thinking over the past 30 years has shown that "sophisticated thinking virtually always reflects a rich knowledge base in the domain in question..." (Perkins, Jay, & Tishman, 1993, p. 71). If we take thinking and knowing to be interrelated concepts, it follows that the thinking involved both in getting-to-know abilities and in final specific ways of knowing is accessible for authentic assessment only when fused with content. It is quite clear, thus, that it would take expertise in the specific knowledge under assessment to make a sound judgment of various aspects of the quality of that knowledge.

This constraint has a bearing to the question of who is qualified to assess academic literacy in various domains. True: the demands for creative and reflective manipulation of knowledge may cut across disciplines and domains that adopt them as a set of norms. In this sense they may be considered universal. However, only assessors with expertise in the specific domain in which the learner writes can assess the nature of the knowledge-making and the quality of knowledge products exhibited in his or her written products. Thus, while I do recommend using the instrument proposed here for generating and assessing products across various domains and disciplines, I would leave their assessment to assessors with expertise in the domain within which the learner has to display his or her academic literacy.

Assessing Knowledge Journals: The Complexities

In this section of the paper I will point out some of the complexities of assessing knowledge journals. I say "complexity", rather than "problematicity", because the complex aspects of open and interpretive assessment can be conceived of as both problems and advantages. A reasonable way of treating them is perhaps considering them as advantages with a price tag attached to them.

Inter-Individual Differences and the Fairness Challenge

Assessing a knowledge journal is an interpretive act, and as such it is problematic (Delandshere & Petrosky, 1994). One specific problem arising from this process of interpretation is a possible conflict of cognitive preferences between different learners and the instructors, who assess their ways of getting to know via the journal. A gap may exist between what the assessor may consider to be high-level reflection acts, and the cognitive preferences or style of his or her students. In technical terms, this gap concerns the distribution and frequency of evidence for any of the knowledge quality dimensions, and the relative weight certain dimensions ought to receive in comparison to others. For example, how can we tell who can be considered more academically literate: a learner high on **Relevance, Creativity** and **Communicativity,** but low on **Veritability** and **Complexity** -- or a learner high on **Veritability, Complexity** and **Relevance,** but low on **Communicativity** and **Creativity**? Should we allocate a greater weight for **Creativity** than to **Veritability**? To **Relevance** than to **Communicativity**? Is it advisable to allocate equal weight to all? My concern in this regard is ethical: Is it justifiable to regard certain acts of reflection on the part of the student as inferior in relation to others, judged more sophisticated by the teacher-assessor? Different assessors will have to come up with their own justifications as rationale for their answers to these problems. When they do, I believe they should make their policy known to their students, or better yet, have the learners take active part in shaping it (Birenbaum, personal communication). Another possibility is to view the series of scores for each dimension in the model as a learning profile (Birenbaum, personal communication).

The problem of cognitive preferences is related to yet another problem: overcoming the teacher-assessors' inclination to actually engage in norm-referenced evaluation. In a Husserlian sense, it is extremely hard *to bracket* impressions of journals, which the assessor has already read and judged up to a certain point in time, as he or she sets out to read and assess a new one. The journals really bring out in relief just how far each student can go on his or her own, in relation to all other students. It is difficult to ignore this, especially if a certain journal displays intellectual tendencies different from those of the assessor; or worse: from those of other students, whose preferences are in line with those of the assessor.

Instrument's "Ecology": Invading the Privacy of the Learners

As mentioned earlier, the duty of keeping a knowledge journal has the potential of contributing to the quality of the students' learning experiences. Writing the journal hopefully encourages the learners to take intellectual risks and allows them the mental and social privacy essential for engagement in otherwise hazardous mental experimentation. The journal is also meant to set the environment appropriate for inner dialogue, free of inhibitions. In this respect, the knowledge journal is an ecologically valid assessment instrument: from a pedagogical point of view, it is potentially a beneficial instrument. However, a problem may arise when the learners know that their knowledge journal will be eventually assessed. In this situation, while writing the journal, the students might feel that the teacher is forever looking over their shoulder, not in order to participate in the intellectual dialogue, but rather to judge and evaluate it. In certain social educational settings, the students might feel that there is nowhere "to hide". When the privacy condition of the reflective event is breached, and tentative knowledge products become subjects to public scrutiny by a powerful teacher, the learner's intellectual disposition to experiment and take risks might be jeopardized. Thus, using the journal for the purposes of fair and valid assessment of the learner's academic literacy may contradict and undermine the pedagogical purpose that the journal now serves: thoughtful learning.

However, in an atmosphere of mutual trust and respect between teacher and learners, the learners may benefit from this public aspect of their private learning experience. First, they have a tangible audience to internalize and think of when writing (note, for example, how Yael "converses" with her instructor in Figure 5). Second, they know they may receive real feedback, which may at a later stage help them advance their knowledge, and eventually, their score. Thus, in an atmosphere of true partnership between learners and their teacher, the fact that the journal will serve as a pool of data for assessment may not undermine its educational benefits.

CONCLUSION

In this chapter I presented a semiotic-epistemic view of academic literacy. In the first part of the chapter I presented a relative-neutral view of what literacy is. In doing so, I proposed a broad, relativistic framework for defining literacy, and suggested two of its implications -- pluralistic particularism and normativism -- to literacy assessment in general. I then offered three perspectives from which to define and assess literacy within this relative-neutral approach: contextual function, performances and the semiotic-epistemic perspective. In the framework of this approach, I next focused on one particular type of literacy: academic literacy. First, I pointed out the dynamic, social nature of this specific literacy. Following this, I offered a specific conceptualization of academic literacy as thoughtful knowledge manipulation, and presented the theoretical rationale underlying it. The rationale included insights from Peirce's process of semiosis (Siegel & Carey, 1989), Perkins' concept of understanding performances (1993), Bakhtin's (1981) dialogic view of language and Freire's (1972; 1976; Shor & Freire 1990/1987) dialogic pedagogy. The rationale was also based on a view of learning as a high-level intellectual enterprise, and more specifically on the notion of the need for a disposition (Perkins, Jay, & Tishman, 1993) for thoughtfulness (e.g., Newman, 1990) and mindfulness (Langer, 1993; Salomon, 1983). Various notions of the writing process, especially regarding writing as an instrument of getting-to-know, were also part of the rationale.

Next, I offered a Model of Academically Literate Learning Goals, based on a view of academic literacy as thoughtful manipulation of knowledge. The general learning objectives in this model were **Establishing a Reflection Base** from "words" of Others, and then **Personalizing** them. The major reflective acts in this model were **Monitoring, Reproducing, Deliberating, Elaborating, Judging Transforming.** Within this model, these reflective acts focused on the **Message,** the **Reflector** and the **Acquiring Process.**

The presentation of the model was based on authentic samples from the knowledge journals of five different learners, who wrote them in different learning contexts. This was followed by a presentation of differential ways to mediate the model and adapt it to learners in a variety of learning situations.

In the third part of the chapter I presented a semiotic-epistemic approach to assessing academic literacy. I discussed ways of using the knowledge journal as a data base on which to perform an assessment of the learner's academic literacy. For that purpose I presented a set of rubrics for the assessment of the knowledge journal, derived from five dimensions of knowledge quality: **Veritability, Relevance, Complexity, Creativity,** and **Communicativity**. Following a demonstration of the use of the rubrics, I discussed several possible units of assessment to work with when applying the rubrics to the knowledge journal. I pointed out how the journal and the rubrics can be used to assess both -- or either -- the process of getting-to-know and the knowledge products. I also emphasized the importance of assessing knowledge products and processes in authentic domain-specific contexts.

Finally, I discussed some complexities involved in assessing the knowledge journals: inter-individual cognitive preferences and their effect on the act of interpreting the journal for assessment purposes, the possible conflict between the cognitive preferences of different learners, as well as between the learners and their assessors, and finally, the problem of invading the privacy of the learners in using their learning journals as data for assessment.

The assessment approach I proposed in this chapter represents one particular favored view of the what it means to learn and to know in a modern, liberal and humanistic academic discourse community. As such, I believe it merits both experimenting with and reflecting on.

ACKNOWLEDGMENTS

I would like to thank my students and the teachers I worked with for the opportunity they gave me to put my ideas to the test in their classes. I would also like to thank the editors for their enlightening remarks on earlier drafts of this chapter.

REFERENCES

Ackerman, J. M. (1993). The promise of writing to learn. *Written Communication, 10* (3), 334-370.

Bakhtin. M. (1981). Discourse in the novel. In M. Holquist (Ed.), C. Emerson & M. Holquist (Trans.) *The dialogic imagination: Four essays by M.M. Bakhtin*, (pp. 259-422). Austin: University of Texas Press. (Original work published in 1934-1935)

Belsey, C. (1980). *Critical practice.* London: Methuen.

Berkenkotter, C., & Huckin, T. (1993). Rethinking genre from a sociocognitive perspective. *Written Communication, 10,* (4), 475-510.

Cornbleth, C.T. (1985). Critical thinking and cognitive processes. In W. B. Stanley et al. (Eds). *Review of Research in Social Studies in Education (1976-1983),* (pp. 11-64), Washington, D.C.: National Council for the Social Studies.

Delandshere, G., & Petrosky, A.R. (1994). Capturing teachers knowledge: Performance assessment. *Educational Researcher, 13,* 11-18.

Dewey, John. (1933). *How we think.* Boston: D.C. Heath.

Dyson Hass, A. (in press). A whistle for Willie, lost puppies and cartoon dogs: The sociocultural dimensions of young children's composing, or toward unmelting pedagogical pots. *Journal of Literacy.*

Eco, Umberto. (1979). The role of the reader's place in American thought. *Semiotica, 1* (2), 21-37.

Elbow, P. (1985). The shifting relationship between speech and writing. *College Composition & Communication, 36,* 281-308.

Emig, J. (1983). Literacy and Freedom. In D. Goswami & M. Butler (Eds.), *The web of meaning* (pp. 171-178). Portmouth, NH: Boynton/Cook, Inc.

Faigley, L. (1989). Judging writing: Judging selves. *College Composition & Communication, 40,* 395-414.

Fitzgerald, J. (1986). Research on revision in writing. *Review of Educational Research, 57* (4), 481-507.

Flower, L. & Hayes, J. (1984). Images, plans and prose: The representation of meaning in writing. *Written Communication, 1,* 120-160.

Flower, L., Hayes, J., Carey, L., Schriver, K., & Stratman, J. (1986). Detection, diagnosis, and the strategies of revision. *College Composition & Communication, 37,* 16-55.

Freedman, A. (1993). Show and Tell? The role of explicit teaching in the learning of genres. *Research in the Teaching of English, 27* (3), 222-251.

Freire, P. (1972). *The pedagogy of the oppressed.* Harmonsworth, UK: Penguin.

Freire, P. (1976). *Education: The practice of freedom.* London: Writers and Readers Co-operative.

Fulkerson, R. (1990). Composition theory in the eighties: Axiological consensus and paradigmatic diversity. *College Composition & Communication, 41,* 409-430.

Gardner, H. (1991). *The unschooled mind: How children think and how schools should teach.* New York: Basic Books.

Gee, P.J. (1986). Orality and literacy: From the savage mind to ways with words. *Tesol Quarterly, 20* (4), 719-747.

Harrington, A.J. (1985). Classrooms as forums for reasoning and writing. *College Composition & Communication, 36 (4),* 404-413.

Heath, S. B. (1983). *Ways with words.* Cambridge: Cambridge University Press.

Ho, B., & Richards, J. (1994, March). *Reflective thinking through journal writing: Myths and realities.* Paper presented at the annual TESOL meeting, Baltimore.

Kalo, M. (1982). "A sad song." In *Tomorrow I Will Go to School,* Jerusalem: Dvir (In Hebrew).

Kelly, L. (1972). *From dialogue to discourse: An open approach to competence and creativity.* Glenview: Scott.

Langer, E. (1989). *Mindfulness.* Reading: MA: Addison-Wesley.

Langer, E. (1993). A mindful education. *Educational Psychological, 28* (1), 43-50.

Lunsford, A.A. (1990). Composing ourselves: Politics, commitment, and the teaching of writing. *College Composition & Communication, 41,* 71-83.

McPeck, J.(1981). Critical thinking and education. (1981). New York: St. Martin's Press.

McPherson, E. (1977). "Composition". In J.R. Squire, (Ed.), *The teaching of English.* Vol. 76, Part 1, Chicago, National Society for the Study of Education, (pp. 178-188). The University of Chicago Press.

Meichenbaum, D., & Arsanow, J. (1979). Cognitive-behavioral modification and metacognitive development: Implications for the classroom. In P. Kendall & S. Hollon (Eds.), *Cognitive behavioral interventions: Research and procedures.* New York: Academic Press.

Moffett, J. (1988). *Storm in the mountains.* Carbondale and Edwardsville: Southern Illinois UP.

Newman, F. M.(1990). Qualities of thoughtful social studies classes: An empirical profile. *Curriculum Studies, 22-23,* 253-275.

Nystrand, M., Greene, S., & Wiemelt, J. (1993). Where did composition studies come from? An intellectual history. *Written Communication, 10* (3), 267-333.

Penrose, A.M. (1989). *Strategic differences in composing: Consequences for learning through writing* (Technical Report No. 31). Center for the Study of Writing. Pittsburgh, PA: Carnegie-Mellon University.

Perkins, D.N. (1992). *Smart schools: From training memories to educating minds.* New York: The Free Press.

Perkins, D. N. (1993). *An apple for education: Teaching and learning for understanding.* A paper prepared for the ELAM (Educational Press Association of America Annual Conference) lecture, Philadelphia.

Perkins, D.N., Jay, E., & Tishman, Sh. (1993). New conceptions of thinking: From ontology to education. *Educational Psychologist, 28* (1), 67-85.

Salomon, G. (1983). The differential investment of mental effort in learning from different sources. *Educational Psychologist, 18*, 42-50.

Sarig, G. (1989). The use of mentalistic measures in the acquisition of high-level reading skills. *Education and Its Context, 11*, 61-47. (In Hebrew).

Sarig, G. (1993a). T*he wisdom of learning: Acquiring knowledge from and through texts.* Tel Aviv: Massada. (In Hebrew).

Sarig, G. (1993b). Composing a study-summary: A reading-writing encounter. In J. Carson, & I. Leki (Eds.), *Reading in the composition classroom: Second language perspectives.* (pp. 161-183). Boston: Heinle & Heinle.

Sarig, G. (1993c, May). *Assessing teachers' documentary learning goals.* Paper presented at the annual meeting of The Academic Committee for Research on Language Testing (ACROLT), Kiriyat Anavim, Israel.

Sarig, G. (1993d, July). *Conceptualizing new knowledge through initiated reflective writing in teacher education.* Paper presented at the MOFET. International Congress on Teacher Education: From theory To practice. Tel Aviv.

Sarig, G. (1993e). *Writing-to-reflect in children's initiated "think-aloud" journals.* Paper presented at EARLI's Fifth Conference on Learning and Instruction, Aix-en-Provence, France.

Sarig, G. (1994, July). *A neutral-relative view of literacy: Whose literacy is it anyway?* Paper presented at the annual meeting of the Special Committee for Research in Text Processing (SCRIPT). Maale Hachammisha.

Sarig, G., & Folman, Sh. (1990). Metacognitive awareness and coherence production. In M. Spoelders (Ed.), *Literacy Acquisition.* (pp. 195-208). Lier, Belgium: Van In - C&C.

Sarig, G. (In preparation). What is Literacy? In *Literacy Cycles, Knowledge cycles: The foundations of academic literacy.*

Scardamalia, M., & Bereiter, K. (1987). *The psychology of composition.* Hillsdale, NJ: Erlbaum.

Schmidt, S.J. (1978). Some problems in communicative text theories. In W.V. Dressler (Ed.), *Current trends in textlinguistics.* Berlin: Walter de Gruyer.

Schon, D.A. (1987). *Educating the reflective practitioner.* New York: Basic books.

Scollon, R., & Scollon, S.B.K. (1981). *Narrative, literacy and face in interethnic communication.* Norwood, NJ: Ablex.

Shor, I., & Freire, P. (1990/1987). *A pedagogy of liberation.* Tel Aviv: Mifras. (Translated into Hebrew by N. Goober).

Scribner, S., & Cole, M. (1981). *The psychology of literacy.* Cambridge. MA: Harvard University Press.

Siegel, M., & Carey, R. F. (1989). *Critical thinking: A semiotic perspective.* Monographs on Teaching Critical Thinking No. 1 (ERIC: ED 30 3802).

Snyder. S. (1986). *The literacy-logic debate: Towards a clarification from a Peircean perspective on logic.* Unpublished Doctoral dissertation. Bloomington, IN: Indiana University.

Spivey, N. (1990). Transforming texts: Constructive processes in reading and writing. *Written Communication, 7,* 256-287.

Spivey, N., & King, J. R. (1989). Readers as writers composing from texts. *Reading Research Quarterly, 24,* 7-26.

Street, B.V. (1984). *Literacy in theory and practice.* Cambridge: Cambridge University Press.

Tierney, R., Soter, A., O'Flahavan, J., & McGinley, W. (1989). The effects of reading and writing upon thinking critically. *Reading Research Quarterly, XXIV/2,* 134-173.

Venezky, R.L. (1990). Definitions of literacy. In R.L. Venezky, D.A. Wagner, & B.S. Ciliberty (Eds.), *Toward defining literacy.* Newark, Del: IRA. 2-9.

Vygotsky, L. (1962). *Language and thought.* Cambridge, MA: MIT Press.

Vygotsky, L. (1978). *Mind in society.* Cambridge, MA: Harvard University Press.

Assessment in a Problem-Based Economics Curriculum

Mien S.R. Segers

INTRODUCTION

The statement 'the degree of validity is the single most important aspect of a test' represents probably one of the most widely accepted requirements for assessment instruments (Ebel & Frisbie, 1991; Mehrens & Lehmann, 1984). The situation where the test is intended to measure higher-order thinking skills but most items require only recall of facts, terms and principles, illustrates a well-known validity concern. The validity question is also relevant on a higher level of aggregation. Together with Gronlund (1971), Van der Vleuten & Wijnen (1990) state that "the key problem in designing any assessment system is to make the assessment procedures congruent with the educational and instructional principles" (p. 27).

The basis for the educational program of the Maastricht School of Economics and Business Administration is problem-based learning. Problem-based learning (PBL) is an instructional method which can be described by a set of characteristics: student-centered, self-directed learning, the acquisition of interdisciplinary and recurrent knowledge, the application of knowledge to solve economic problems, and small tutorial groups. These instructional key features are translated into a number of specific requirements for the assessment system: assessment based on problems, the assessment of the acquisition and the application of knowledge and the assessment of integrative knowledge. This chapter starts with an elaboration of these issues. The second section will deal with the results of the experimental as well as the empirical research. The experimental research was intended to contribute to the improvement of the quality of the OverAll Test. The results of the empirical study indicated the effect of three educational variables on students' scores on the OverAll Test.

A PROBLEM BASED EDUCATIONAL SYSTEM: FIVE CHARACTERISTICS

The faculty of Economics and Business Administration at the University of Maastricht, established in 1984, is a relatively young faculty. Together with its sister faculties, it developed a problem-based curriculum with an interdisciplinary character, whose main characteristics will be described below.

1. Learning is More Important Than Teaching

De Block (1960) formulated a number of 'essential changes' in the practice of education, based on the ideas of pioneers of educational science such as Dewey (1929), Selz (1913, 1922), Kerschensteiner (1926), Langeveld (1934, 1959) and Willmann (1934). One concrete change is the shift from teacher to tutor, from instruction to support (Wijnen, 1990; Dochy & Wijnen, 1987). Wijnen (1990) and Kaufman et al. (1989) stress the idea that learning is the aim of education whereas the teacher's role is "to guide, probe and support the student's initiatives" (p. 286). Teaching is at most a means: it stimulates learning. This is referred to as student-centered and self-directed learning (Wijnen, 1990; Blumberg & Michael, 1992).

The PBL-approach requires students to be actively involved in the discussion, the analysis and solving of economic problems. They are encouraged to study for meaning. They are expected to be oriented less toward memorization and more toward studying by reflection and by conceptualization (Albanese & Mitchell, 1993). In this way, the PBL-approach implements the results of recent research in instructional psychology that stress learning as an active and constructive process (de Corte, 1990). PBL can be characterized by a balance between discovery learning and personal exploration on the one hand and systematic instruction and guidance on the other. De Corte (1990) defines this approach as designing a powerful learning environment.

2. The Use of Problems as a Focus for Learning Economics

According to Barrows (1986), Wilkerson and Feletti (1989), Neufeld, Woodward, and MacLeod, (1989) PBL can be described, at its most fundamental level, as an instructional method characterized by the use of problems, compelling the acquisition of 'new' knowledge and the learning of problem-solving skills. In contradiction with other problem-centered methods such as the case method, the problem is presented before students have learned basic science, not after (Albadene & Mitchell, 1993). The analysis of problems is the main method of acquiring and applying knowledge. The method of the "Seven-Jump" (Schmidt & Bouhuijs, 1980) is used to guide the process of 'learning on the basis of problems'. It defines seven steps for the learning process:

(1) clarify terms and concepts
(2) define the problem
(3) analyze the problem
(4) make a systematic inventory of the various explanations found in step 3
(5) formulate learning objectives
(6) collect additional information outside the group
(7) synthesize and test acquired information. (Bouhuijs and Gijselaers, 1993)

Empirical studies in the field of cognitive psychology support the PBL approach (Dochy, 1992; Chi, Feltovich, & Glaser, 1981; Schoenfeld & Herrmann, 1982; Voss, Blais, Means, Green & Ahwesh, 1983; Voss, Greene, Post, & Penner, 1989). Bedard (1989) compared a number of studies on the development of expertise in the domain of business administration. He concludes that experts in this domain possess an organized knowledge base which is, in comparison with that of novices, more complete and detailed. According to these findings, Schmidt (1993) formulates five principles of cognitive learning. They are the rationale for the learning process as schematized by the Seven-Jump method:

(1) The activation of prior knowledge through the discussion of a problem within small tutorial groups (step 1 and step 2).

(2) Elaboration on prior knowledge through small-group discussions (step 3, 4, 5, 6). New information is actively related to prior knowledge through elaboration processes (Stein et al., 1982).

(3) Restructuring of knowledge in order to fit the problem presented (step 7). Barrows (1986) contends that in traditional basic science, knowledge is structured around theoretical hierarchies and models, not realistic situations such as symptoms, course of illness, etc. Restructuring of knowledge in order to fit the problem presented will enable students to retrieve it when they need it in real life.

(4) Learning in context. Because real cognitive activities and learning occur in context (de Corte, 1990; Resnick, 1987) and concrete and practical situations seem to be better learning environments than highly abstract ones (Shuell, 1986; Tuma & Reif, 1980), the learning processes are embedded "in contexts that are representative of the kinds of tasks and problems to which the learners will have to apply their knowledge and skill in the future" (de Corte, 1990, p. 3). Schmidt (1993) describes it as follows: "The problem serves as a scaffold for storing cues that may support retrieval of relevant knowledge when needed for similar problems" (p. 428).

(5) Since students will tend to see the problems presented as relevant and since they engage in an open-ended discussion, epistemic curiosity can be expected to emerge.

3. Recurrent and Interdisciplinary Knowledge

There is a vast amount of research which indicates that, in order to solve problems in a productive way, the retrieval of well-organized domain-specific knowledge is determinant (Chi et al., 1981,; Voss et al., 1983). For an instruction method to be effective in attaining the goal of problem-solving, it must enable students' retention and retrieval of knowledge. The studies of Son and Van Sickle (1993), Adams, Kasserman, Yearwood, Perfetto, Bransford, and Franks (1988) and Sherwood, Kinzer, Bramford, and Franks (1986) demonstrate that problem-solving experience before exposure to new information results in better reproduction of the new information. The findings suggest a positive influence of PBL on the acquisition of recurrent knowledge.

Since problems in real life are seldom unidimensional in a sense that knowledge from different domains is necessary in order to analyze and solve the problem, the acquired knowledge needs to be recurrent as well as integrative. Therefore, the integration of disciplines is an essential requirement for any curriculum which stresses the importance of problem-solving.

4.   The Application of Knowledge

The ultimate goal of a problem-based curriculum is not the acquisition of knowledge but the use of this knowledge base to analyze authentic problems and to contribute to their solution. The Seven-Jump method stresses the importance of the application of knowledge: Testing the relevance of the collected information for the solution of the problem discussed is an essential step in the students' learning process.

5.   The Small Tutorial Group

Probably one of the first characteristics often mentioned when comparing conventional curricula with a PBL-approach, is the small tutorial group. Instead of lectures with large groups of students, students in a PBL-curriculum learn by self-study and by discussing their ideas in small groups of students, guided by a tutor. Lectures, labs and other instructional methods can be introduced as a supplement to these core activities in order to have some extra training for skills (e.g., computer sciences) or in order to summarize or introduce some new findings in the field of study.   To what extent do these five principles of PBL apply to the assessment system? We will deal with this question in the next section.

A PROBLEM-BASED ASSESSMENT SYSTEM: SOME CHARACTERISTICS

It is often stressed that evaluation and assessment shape students' learning (Balla & Boyle, 1994; Ebel & Frisbie, 1991; Hounsell, 1990). This implies that if the faculty wants students to become competent problem-solvers, the assessment of students' level of competence in problem-solving is a determinant stimulus for the focusing of students' learning activities on problem-solving. "If an assessment programme is not congruent with educational goals, the assessment can drive student learning in antithetical directions." (Swanson, Case, van der Vleuten, 1991, p. 78).

A number of articles have been published on the issue of assessment in PBL (van Berkel, Sprooten, de Graaff, 1993; Hand, 1993; Hassan, Ezzat, Faris, & Fam, 1993; Marchais, Onmais, Jean, & Nu Viet Vu, 1993; van der Vleuten & Verwijnen, 1990). They all refer to curricula of medicine or health sciences. This chapter focuses on the assessment system of a problem-based economics curriculum, as implemented in the School of Economics and Business Administration at Maastricht. Three characteristics of the assessment system indicate the relationship between the principles of PBL and the rationale of the assessment system.

1. The assessment system is based on authentic problems: contextualized assessment. In PBL it is essential that students learn by the analysis and solving of problems which are representative of the problems to which students will have to apply their knowledge in future. Consequently, a valid assessment system should evaluate students' competencies with an instrument based on real life problems.

2. The acquisition and application of knowledge is assessed. The acquisition and application of knowledge are complementary elements in a PBL-curriculum. Consequently, they should be equally presented in the assessment system. In many educational systems, there is an exclusive reliance on instruments measuring knowledge. Because of the educational rationale, the assessment of problem-solving skills seems to be a logical choice. Test items should require examinees to apply their knowledge to commonly occurring and important problem-solving situations (Swanson, Case, & van der Vleuten, 1991). Because a sufficient level of domain-specific knowledge is a determinant for productive problem-solving, the assessment instruments focusing on the acquisition of knowledge should not only serve a certification function but also a feedback function. For the instrument(s) assessing knowledge this implies that it has to indicate the weak points in students' knowledge base. This information enhances students' future learning in the direction of the knowledge base necessary to tackle problems.

3. Integrative knowledge is assessed. Since real life problems are mostly multidimensional, this means they integrate different disciplines within one field of study; the assessment system should be based on integrated problems.

These three characteristics of the Maastricht assessment system are operationalized in the development of two assessment instruments which differ in format as well as in learning goals measured: the Knowledge Test and the OverAll Test. In the next section I will elaborate on both instruments.

THE MAASTRICHT ECONOMICS CURRICULUM AND ASSESSMENT SYSTEM

The Economics Curriculum

The faculty offers a four-year program. During the first year, all students take the same courses. At the beginning of the second year, all students start with their graduation option for each of which there is a special program consisting of compulsory and elective courses. In this chapter we will only focus on the first year because the assessment system described is currently being implemented and evaluated only in the first year. On the basis of evaluation results, it will be gradually implemented in the entire curriculum. This first year comprises four modules or blocks of eight weeks each (see Figure 1). The central theme is The Market as a mechanism of Coordination and Allocation. Within this central theme, four sub-themes are formulated: Firms and Markets (principles of organizational behavior and marketing; central case Macintosh, a large Dutch company), Micro-economic policy and Market (centering on the Dutch anti-trust law), Growth, Fluctuations and Stabilization policy (centering on the annual policy report of the Dutch Central Planning Office), Financial Markets (corporate financing and accounting; focusing on the Dutch ceramics firm Sphinx). At the end of the first year, the economy game is played by the students. The economy game is a computer simulation game. The students have to formulate the management of a firm, making use of different kinds of data and information systems. The game makes use of what they learned about business administration, micro- and macro-economics.

FIRST YEAR
THE MARKET, COORDINATION AND ALLOCATION

BLOCK 1: FIRMS AND MARKETS
  Knowledge Test 1
BLOCK 2: MICROECONOMIC POLICY AND THE MARKET
  Knowledge Test 2
  OverAll Test 1
BLOCK 3: GROWTH, FLUCTUATIONS AND
        STABILIZATION POLICY
  Knowledge Test 3
BLOCK 4: FINANCIAL MARKETS
  Knowledge Test 4
ECONOMY GAME
  OverAll Test 2

Figure 1: The Structure of the First Year Curriculum at the Faculty of Economics

During every block of eight weeks, students meet in small groups (10-12 students) where the learning process follows the Seven-Jump method. For the duration of the block, the students meet in two-hour sessions twice a week. They are guided by a tutor. As the Seven-Jump method indicates, the problems, formulated with respect to the block theme, play a steering role in the learning process. During the same eight weeks, skills-training sessions are organized to develop essential skills in mathematics, statistics, financial information systems, computers and written communication.

The Assessment System

After each block (i.e., eight study weeks) the acquired knowledge and insights are assessed by the so-called Knowledge Test. After two blocks, the OverAll-Test is administered. The main difference between the two assessment methods is the kind of competency measured. The Knowledge Test focuses on the assessment of the ability to reproduce knowledge, to understand or have insight in the theories/ models/principles studied. The OverAll Test measures objectives on the level of application, analysis and synthesis. Both tests are summative. Passing them is a prerequisite for entering the second year.

The Knowledge Test

The Knowledge Test primarily measures declarative knowledge. Dochy and Alexander (1995) define this kind of knowledge as the knowledge of facts, the meaning of symbols, and the concepts and principles of a particular field of study. It requires students to appreciate, to recognize and to reproduce the information. The Knowledge Test measures subject-oriented knowledge, a formal part of a certain domain specific knowledge which contains a specialized field of study, covered by a subdomain.

The first Knowledge Test concerns business administration (principles of organization and marketing), the second micro-economics, the third macro-economics and the fourth financing and accounting. The Knowledge Test consists of 100 to 150 true-false items with the question mark possibility. Through the question mark option, students can indicate they did not master the learning goal assessed. To correct for guessing the scoring rule is the number of correct answers reduced by the number of incorrect answers, while the question mark answers are scored neutral.

The OverAll Test

The OverAll Test measures to what extent students are able to analyze problems and to contribute to their solution by applying the instruments acquired, such as economic concepts, models and theories. Therefore, we can describe the OverAll Test-items as measuring procedural knowledge as defined by de Corte (1990) and Dochy and Alexander (1995). Additionally, the OverAll Test-items measure if students are able to select and retrieve the most relevant instruments for solving the problem presented, if they know "when and where". Dochy and Alexander (1995) identify this type of knowledge as conditional knowledge. The OverAll Test is planned within the first year curriculum as follows (see also Figure 1). After two blocks, the students get two weeks free of courses for self-study. During these weeks, they study on the basis of the study manual they received at the beginning of this period. This manual involves information about the main goals of the OverAll Test, the parts of the curriculum which are relevant for the study of the material presented in the manual, an example of an elaborated case with test items, some practical (organizational) information and finally a set of articles of different types. Some describe a case relating to innovations in or problems of a national or international firm (as published in a newspaper or a journal). Other articles express theoretical considerations of a scientist, the report of a research, comments on a theory or model. During the self-study period the students are expected to apply the knowledge they acquired over the past week in view of being capable to explain the new, complex problem situations which are presented in the set of articles. They are asked, by reading the articles, to try to explain spontaneously to themselves (i.e., without being explicitly prompted by a tutor) the ideas/theories described in these articles by relating them to previously acquired knowledge. This behavior is often called 'self-explanation' (Chi et al., 1992). In short, the self-study period can be described as an opportunity for students to exercise the Seven-Jump method they used in the tutorial groups for analyzing problems. This is why the study manual offers them a set of new problems as presented in a set of articles.

After the two weeks of self-study, the OverAll Test is administered. The OverAll Test questions refer to the articles: they assess if the students are able to interpret and analyze the problems as presented in the articles by applying the concepts, models and instruments they acquired during the tutorials. Since the curriculum consists of four blocks, students go through two OverAll Tests: the first after block 1 and block 2, the second after block 3, block 4 and the economy game. The first OverAll Test (OAT 1) assesses the application of knowledge as acquired during the first two block periods. This knowledge base (declarative, subject-oriented knowledge) is measured by the Knowledge Test 1 and Knowledge Test 2. The second OverAll Test (OAT 2) refers to the same subject matter as assessed in Knowledge Test 3 and Knowledge Test 4. The OverAll Test combines two item formats: true-false questions with the question mark option and essay- or open-ended questions. The true-false items are mainly intended to measure if students can apply the acquired knowledge in a new situation, if they can use an abstract concept in a specific, quite complex situation which is relevant for the 'real life of economists'. The essay-questions assess, for example, students' ability to determine the common elements in three different plans for reducing inflation, or if the student can detect the similarities and differences between an economic model explained by the author of an article and the model as described by the authors studied in the small-groups. These items measure students' analytic ability. Other essay-questions ask students to formulate solutions for a problem described in an article, or to develop a strategy for reducing inflation described in the article, taking account of the micro- and macro-elements mentioned by the author or by the test-constructor. Such items measure students' capability to synthesize and evaluate.

Some specific examples of types of questions are the following:
- the student has to indicate on which principle or theory the ideas of the author are based;
- the student has to explain arguments for and against the innovations a firm proposes in an article/case;
- the student has to indicate the correct concept for a description of the author or a decision made by an organization;
- the student has to draw a polygon and give a short comment to explain the expected evolution of a given set of data, on the basis of an example in the article;
- the student has to formulate new hypotheses on the basis of a research report, where the test constructor proposes some changes of data.

The OverAll Test is a paper-and-pencil test. The questions are based on the articles studied at home and the case handed out during the test. The essay subtest and the true-false subtest have the same weight since the maximum subtest scores are equal. The OverAll Test takes three hours and consists of seven to twelve cases or articles, describing one or several different related economic problems. The OverAll Test, moreover, is an open-book test. This means that students are allowed to bring with them the study material they think they will need. Consequently, the test constructor is forced to pose questions with answers that cannot be detected directly in the articles. Students have the possibility to check the relevance of a thought, but, because of time constraints, they cannot study the literature in depth during the test administration.

THE MAASTRICHT STUDIES

Since the implementation of the Maastricht assessment system, a number of studies have been conducted. First, experimental research was conducted to improve the quality of the OverAll Test. The main research goal was to search for the effect of the number of cases on the generalizability of the test scores. Secondly, empirical research was conducted to evaluate the effect of three educational variables on the scores on the OverAll Test: prior knowledge, study strategies and time of study. The results of these studies will be presented in this section.

Experimental Research

The use of written simulations which require students to analyze and solve authentic problems is not new. In medicine as well as in the field of economics, many instruments have been developed. Especially for economics and business administration, the supply of simulation games on the market is abundant. Up till now, for several reasons, they are seldom used for selective purposes. Van der Vleuten & Verwijnen (1990) refer to the critical appraisal of the empirical achievements of instruments measuring medical problem-solving in studies of reliability and validity. Secondly, research information points to the problem of content specificity of problem-solving. Achievement on one problem is, only to a small extent, predictive for solving another problem within the same context. Taking account of these warnings, the faculty of Economics and Business Administration carried out an experiment with the OverAll Test before implementing it as a selective instrument within the first year curriculum.

Research questions

The experiment was intended to consider such issues as: the feasibility of the OverAll Test, its acceptability for students and tutors, validity and generalizabilty. I will confine myself to the results of the generalizability study which focuses on the impact of the number of cases on the students' scores on the experimental OverAll Test and the effect of the raters on the open-ended questions.

Four research questions will be dealt with:
* What is the effect of the number of cases on the scores of students?
* What is the number of cases required for achieving an acceptable level of generalizability?
* What is the effect of the rater on students' scores?
* Which correction procedure is the most appropriate with respect to the test reliability?

Subjects

From the population of 570 first year students of the Maastricht School of Economics and Business Administration, a random sample of 57 students was selected for the experiment with the OverAll Test. Forty students finally took the experimental OverAll Test.

Instrument

The OverAll Test was constructed by a team of tutors who were actively involved in the first year curriculum and experts in the specific subject domains measured. They constructed the test on the basis of the inventory of the learning goals of the first year curriculum. The test included six cases, with a total of six open-ended questions and 54 true/?/false questions.

Results

First, a one-facet design (SxC) random effects analysis of variance (ANOVA) was performed on students' scores for the two subtests of the OverAll Test separately: the true/false questions subtest and the open-ended subtest. Variance components were estimated using the GENOVA package. The sources of variance included were: students (S) and cases (C). Table 1 provides the pooled results of generalizability analyzes for the true/?/false subtest. The 'students S' row provides information about the magnitude of true differences between students. The 'cases C' row indicates the variance in OverAll Test-scores as explained by the content-specificity of cases. The 'PxC' row provides information about the extent to which students are differently ranged by the cases. It indicates the extent to which achievement on one case has a predictive value for the achievement on another case. It must be indicated that it is not possible to isolate this effect from other sources of error. Table 1 also displays the results of the Decision study which indicate the number of cases and the number of testing hours required to achieve a certain level of test reliability.

Table 1

Results of the Generalizability Study and Decision Study for the True / False Questions subtest of the OverAll Test

Effect	Variance Component	Standard Error	Percentage of Total Variance
Students S	74.48	29.87	13.99
Cases C	109.35	5.26	20.53
S x C	348.73	2.93	65.48

Testing Time	No. of Cases	Generalizability Coefficient
1 hr	6	.56169
2 hr	12	.71934
3 hr	18	.79358
4 hr	24	.83676

For the open-ended subtest, the effect of the variance component 'rater R' was also included. The results of the generalizability analysis for this subtest are displayed in Table 2. In addition, Table 2 shows the results of the Decision study. They indicate the number of cases required for the open-ended questions subtest and the most appropriate correction procedure.

For the true-false questions subtest as well as for the open-ended questions subtest, the component "cases" explains approximately 20% of the variance in scores. Content-specificity seems to be an important source of error. The figures confirm the idea that achievement on one case will have a low predictive value for achievement on another case. The results of the Decision study indicate that, in the case of true-false questions, 12 cases have to be included in order to obtain a test reliability of .71. For the open-ended questions, 12 cases still result in a low test reliability. The correction of each case for all students by two raters are the most appropriate. Secondly, the variance components for the OverAll Test, including both subtests, were estimated. Table 3 displays the results. The effect "item format I" refers to the impact of the different item formats, i.e., open-ended and true/?/false questions on the variance in OverAll Test-scores. Because the mean scores for both subtests differed to a large extent, the effect of the item-format (36.55%) was expected to be relatively large. This is confirmed by the figures in Table 3. Additionally, the results of the analysis of the OverAll Test stresses the content-specificity of the cases (interaction effect SxC, value 14.91%). The SxTxC variance component is analogous to error variance in classical test theory. The Decision study indicates that for the OverAll Test including true-false questions as well as open-ended questions, 12 cases are required to obtain a generalizability coefficient of .68.

Table 2
Results of the Generalizability Study and Decision Study for the Open-ended Subtest of the OverAll Test

Effect	Variance Component	Standard Error	Percentage of Explained Variance
Students S	25.79	21.64	3.46
Cases C	149.77	102.99	20.12
Raters R	5.38	14.79	0.72
S x C	236.55	40.26	35.41
S x R	2.69	10.10	0.36
C x R	60.89	35.71	8.18
S x C x R	236.24	23.80	31.74

		Different raters for each case		Different raters for each student	
Testing Time	No. Cases	One Rater	Two Raters	One Rater	Two Raters
1 hr	3	.13342	.16804	.11682	.15424
2 hr	6	.23543	.28773	.20257	.26178
3 hr	9	.31595	.37731	.26819	.34105
4 hr	12	.38113	.44688	.32002	.40189

Table 3
The Results of the Generalizability Study and the Decision Study for the OverAll Test, including the True/?/false Questions and Open-ended Questions

Effect	Variance Component	Standard Error	Percentage of Total Variance
Students S	36.36	16.00	2.63
Item-format I	505.80	30.87	36.55
Cases C	30.21	18.91	2.18
S x I	58.18	27.19	4.20
S x C	206.30	20.79	14.91
I x C	177.23	99.68	12.80
S x I x C	369.89	37.27	26.73

Table 3 (cont.)

No. of Cases	Generalizability Coefficient
3	.34584
6	.51394
9	.61330
12	.67894

EMPIRICAL RESEARCH

The empirical research reported addresses several main questions. They are not only valid with regard to the Maastricht assessment system. Because of the ecological validity of the research, they generate empirical evidence for some main questions addressed in recent educational and psychological research. The studies presented are based on the model of Decruyenaere and Janssen (1990), which schematizes the different educational variables that influence academic performance. Decruyenaere and Janssen tested a causal model for differences in academic performance in higher education. They distinguished cognitive and motivational factors. The major cognitive components are prior knowledge, procedural knowledge and learning strategies. The motivational variables are achievement motivation, interest in the subject matter, self-confidence and persistence. In addition, the students' perceptions of the examination requirements are taken into account. I will focus on the influence of three variables on students' competence in problem-solving, as measured by the OverAll Test: students' knowledge base, time spent on studying, and study strategy. The first important issue can be formulated as follows: If students acquire a sufficient knowledge base, can we expect them to be better able to solve authentic problems? Secondly, if students spend more time working on problems and if they do so in a structured way as described by the Seven-Jump method, can we expect them to achieve better? This leads to the following three hypotheses:

1.   Prior knowledge is an important determinant of students' capability to solve real life economic problems.

As described, research findings on problem-solving suggest that an organized knowledge base plays a crucial role. Decruyenaere and Janssen (1990) indicate that prior knowledge, i.e., knowledge available before a certain learning task, has the greatest influence on academic achievement. This is in line with the findings of Dochy (1992). As Glaser and De Corte point out

> Indeed, new learning is exceedingly difficult when prior informal as well as formal knowledge is not used as a springboard for future learning. It has also become more and more obvious, that in contrast to the traditional measures of aptitude, the assessment of prior knowledge and skill is not only a much more precise predictor of learning, but provides in addition a more useful basis for instruction and guidance. (in: Dochy, 1992, p. 1).

It was expected that the mean scores on the Knowledge Tests would correlate highly with the OverAll Test scores. Furthermore, it was expected that the scores on the

Knowledge Test would explain the variance in the OverAll Test scores to a great extent.

2. There is a weak relation between study time and achievement.

The real value of the time students spend on studying is the underlying notion of this hypothesis. The faculty expects them to study 80 hours in two weeks, but how many hours do they really spend on studying? Are there time effects on test achievement? Based on previous research a weak correlation was expected between the time devoted to studying and test results (Dempster, 1987; Frederick & Walberg, 1980; Heyns, 1986; Karweit, 1983; Leinhardt & Bickle, 1987). More time available for study doesn't necessarily result in better achievements. Karweit and Slavin (1981) revealed that adding enough minutes of engaged time to produce noticeable effects on achievement, is not always possible in practice. Additionally, the findings indicate that engaged time explained only 1% to 10% of the individual variance in achievement.

3. There is a weak correlation between study strategies and achievement.

An intriguing question is whether, no matter how many hours they study, the way students study makes any difference in achievement. There is a vast amount of research focusing on the association between study strategies and study results. They suggest a moderate association between both variables (see Dochy, 1992). The investigations of Decruyenaere and Janssen (1990) which test the relative influence of the variable learning strategies within their casual model, demonstrate that learning strategies have no explanatory value. Lonka, Lindblom-Ylanne, & Maury (1994) show that certain study strategies are related to success in tasks, albeit weakly. However, these studies were conducted in a traditional curriculum. It is interesting whether these findings can be replicated in a PBL-curriculum. Since students learn to analyze and solve problems in the tutorial groups, it could be argued that in PBL students study the cases in a more effective way. This is done by following the essential steps of the Seven-Jump method:
- searching for the main concepts, main ideas in the cases/articles, writing them down for themselves,
- structuring the article (elaboration and restructuring),
- trying to apply their knowledge to analyze and evaluate the case.

According to the findings of comparable research, it can be expected that students with higher OverAll Test-scores study in a more effective way, although there will be no significant differences with low scorers.

Subjects

The four Knowledge Tests and the two OverAll Tests were administered to the 575 first-year students during the academic year 1991-1992. Because of drop-outs during the first year, 257 students took all tests. For the descriptive statistics per test, the whole population of participating students are included in the statistical analysis. For the analysis of the effect of prior knowledge on students' capability to analyze and solve problems, the 257 students who took all tests are included. The number of students completing the questionnaire was 287 for the first Overall Test (56%) and 235 for the second Overall test (69%).

Instruments

Evaluation of the assessment system of the School of Economics and Business Administration is based on different sources of information. First, students' test scores on the main assessment instruments, the Knowledge Tests and the OverAll Test are analyzed. Second, a survey among students is conducted to evaluate the OverAll Test as an assessment instrument and to reflect on their study strategy during the two weeks of self-study. The three hypotheses described are tested on the basis of these two sources of information.

Achievement was measured by two different assessment instruments: the Knowledge Tests and the OverAll Test. In order to find evidence for the difference in learning goals assessed by the two instruments, a factor analysis was conducted (Tempelaar, 1992). The results support the idea that both instruments assess a different kind of competence. The Knowledge Test measures the extent to which students acquired domain-specific knowledge by 100-150 true-false items (with the question mark option). This means 141 items for the first Knowledge Test, 100 items for the second Knowledge Test, 126 items for the third Knowledge Test and 119 items for the fourth Knowledge Test. Test reliability averaged 0.70 (Cronbach's alpha coefficient), with small test-to-test variation. The OverAll Test measures the extent to which students are able to apply the acquired knowledge (concepts, models, theories) to analyze problems and to contribute to their solution. This is measured by true/?/false items and short essay-questions. The raw test scores are transformed to percentages. The OverAll Test reliability averaged 0.60 (coefficient alpha). The descriptive statistics for the four Knowledge Tests and the two Overall Tests for the academic year 1991-1992 were calculated and an ANOVA was conducted.

Students were asked to estimate how many hours of self-directed study, on average, they had spent during the two weeks planned. Additionally, they completed a questionnaire about the study strategy they had used while studying the problems presented in the articles. They were asked to score on a six-item Likert-type rating scale. The items are statements to which students agreed or disagreed on a scale of five choices ranging from strongly disagree (1) to strongly agree (5). These items dealt with the various steps expected to be taken when analyzing a problem, according to the Seven-Jump method. Some examples of items are:
- I schematized the content of the articles.
- I marked the main concepts in the article.
- I looked for the main ideas of the articles in the blockbook and in the requested literature of the block.

In order to understand the effect of students' insight on the main goals of the self-study period and the OverAll Test, a nine-item Likert-type rating scale was added to the rating scale on study strategy. Some examples of items are:
- The study guidelines sufficiently indicated how to read for the test.
- I knew what the OverAll Test intended to assess (the objectives).
- I knew which kind of questions I could expect.

A preliminary form of the OverAll Test and the questionnaire were administered to fifty first year students from another cohort (Segers, Tempelaar, Keizer, Schijns, Vaessen & van Mourik 1991, 1992a, 1992b).

Results and Discussion

The results with respect to the three main hypotheses are reported in the following section.

1.   Prior knowledge is an important determinant for the solving of real life economic problems.

The first hypothesis includes two issues. The first issue refers to the quality of students' prior knowledge state and the extent to which the students are able to solve real life economic problems. The second issue deals with the influence of the students' prior knowledge on their capability to solve real life economic problems.

The first issue can be operationalized as follows: to what extent do students possess domain-specific knowledge as measured by the Knowledge tests and to what extent are they able to apply this knowledge to analyze and solve problems as assessed by the Overall-Tests? As displayed in Table 4, the descriptive statistics indicate that students acquired 50% to 64% of the subject matters assessed by the four Knowledge Tests (according to the percentage of items correctly answered). They also misunderstood or partly understood 18% to 25% of the subject matters assessed (according to the percentage incorrect answers). As indicated by the mean score of the Overall Tests, students master approximately 30% of the learning goals assessed by the OverAll Tests.

Table 4
Means and Standard Deviations of the Knowledge Test and the OverAll Test

Test	M			SD
	% C	% I	% C-I	
KT 1	64%	18%	46%	11.46
KT 2	51%	24%	27%	12.90
KT 3	50%	25%	25%	11.74
KT 4	50%	22%	28%	15.44
	M(%)			SD
OAT 1	31.03			11.89
OAT 2	29.22			11.77

Note:
   %C: the average percentage correct answers
   %I: the average percentage incorrect answers
   %C-I: the average percentage correct answers reduced by the incorrect numbers.
   This percentage is the mean score of the test

Interpretation of the OverAll Test-scores is more complex than the interpretation of the Knowledge Test scores because they are the sum (equal weight) of the scores for true-false questions (with the scoring rule for guessing) and the scores for open-ended questions. Additionally, the scores are based on the achievement of students on various articles.

Analysis of the test scores with a breakdown for item-format (Table 5) indicates that higher scores are obtained on the essay-questions. These higher scores are partly an effect of the scoring rule for essay questions. As opposed to true/?/false questions, incorrect elements in the answer or partly correct insights are not punished by reducing the number of correct answers by the number of incorrect ones. The descriptive statistics indicate that, for the true-false questions, students answer 48% to 55% of the items correct. On the other hand, they partly master approximately 24 % of the learning goals assessed. For the true/?/false questions, this implies that approximately 50% students are able to relate a concept, theory or model to a authentic problem. On the other hand, as indicated by the mean scores for the subtest with the essay-questions, students are able for 25% to 31% of these questions to analyze, synthesize and evaluate a problem. The descriptive statistics for the two subtests (true-false questions and essay-questions) are displayed in Table 5.

Table 5
Means and Standard Deviations of the Two Subtests of the OverAll Tests

| | Overall Test 1 | | |
	M	SD	N (items)
Essay Form	31.24%	11.67	7
True-False Form	30.97% C-I	14.62	60
	Overall Test 2		
	M	SD	N(items)
Essay Form	25.19%	12.53	12
True-False Form	32.24% C-I	14.62	55

Analysis of the OverAll Test scores with a breakdown for cases indicates differences in performance on cases with items which require different kinds of competence. Students obtain lower scores for articles which present data requiring them to analyze and evaluate the data by applying an economic model. Students have less difficulties with more descriptive articles assessed by items which require the interpretation and evaluation of a problem presented by using the relevant principle or theory. By way of an example, Table 6 displays the mean scores and standard deviations for the different cases of OverAll Test 2. Case 3 reports a research and students are asked to formulate and explain new hypotheses by adding new data.

Table 6
Means and Standard Deviations for the Different Cases of OverAll Test 2

Case	M(%)	SD
1	34.17	16.08
2	39.96	21.28
3	23.99	19.54
4	40.54	22.61
5	35.71	18.08
6	20.32	20.63

Case 6 is the report of an experiment. The result of two phases of the experiment are shown and discussed. The results of phase 3 are vaguely described. Students are asked to draw the missing curves for phase 3. In comparison with the other cases, they assess on a more analytic level: It is not sufficient to understand the problem presented and to interpret it by applying the relevant concepts, principles or theories. Students are asked to actively analyze the data presented (e.g., by drawing the relevant curves on the basis of the relevant economic model). Subsequently, they are required to formulate conclusions and evaluate different options in order to contribute to the solution of the problem presented in the article.

The descriptive statistics presented above refer to the first issue: The quality of the students' prior knowledge and the extent to which they are able to solve real economic problems.

The second question is: To what extent do the scores on the Knowledge Tests explain the variance in the results for the relevant OverAll Tests? Does the knowledge base (as measured by the Knowledge Tests) have an effect on students' capability to solve authentic problems (as measured by the OverAll Test)? The scores on the Knowledge Tests are defined as the independent variable. The dependent variable is the score on the OverAll Tests. Multiple regression analyzes (by a stepwise method) were applied to the data, with the scores on the Overall Tests as dependent variables. Tables 7 and 8 display the results of these analyzes. The multiple regression coefficient (R^2) is given together with the final beta with all variables entered in the equation. The adjusted R^2 is given in brackets.

First, the influence of the first and the second Knowledge Tests on the variance of the scores on the first Overall Test was measured.

Table 7

*Results of the Multiple Regression Analyses with the Scores on OverAll Test 1
as the Dependent Variable, and the Scores on the first and the second Knowledge
Test as the Independent Variables*

Independent variable	Knowledge Test1 R^2	Knowledge Test2 R^2
Scores OverAll Test 1	.07** (.07)	.08** (.08)
Dependent	OverAll Test 1 Final Beta	
Knowledge Test 2	.23**	
Knowledge Test 1	.08*	

** $p<.01$;   * $p<.05$

The results in Table 7 indicate that prior knowledge or the knowledge base- as measured by the two Knowledge Tests- helps to explain 7% of the variance of the OverAll Test results. This indicates that both Knowledge Tests, with Knowledge

Test 2 having the greatest weight, have a small but significant influence on the variance in results for the first OverAll Test.

Students were administered the four Knowledge Tests before OverAll Test 2. Therefore, a second multiple regression analysis was applied to the data, explaining the second OverAll Test as a function of all four Knowledge Tests.

Table 8

Results of the Multiple Regression Analyses with the Scores on OverAll Test 2 as the Dependent Variable, and the Scores on the Four Knowledge Tests as the Independent Variables

Dependent variable	OverAll Test 2 R^2
Knowledge Test 4	.26** (.25)
Knowledge Test 3	.28** (.28)
Knowledge Test 1	.29** (.28)
Dependent Variable	OverAll Test 2 Final Beta
Knowledge Test 4	.38**
Knowledge Test 3	.17**
Knowledge Test 1	.09**

** $p<.01$; * $p<.05$

The results of the multiple regression analysis (Table 8) show that Knowledge Test 4, Knowledge Test 3 and Knowledge Test 1 account for a significant amount of the variance in scores on the second OverAll Test. The results further show that, according to the final beta, Knowledge Test 4 and Knowledge Test 3 have the most important regression weight. The second Knowledge Test is not included in the equation because of its minor importance. Based on this result, the hypothesis cannot be rejected. The findings confirm comparable research results. In ecologically valid settings, such as real educational practice, a percentage of explained variance in scores which ranges between 20 and 45 is considered high (Dochy, 1992, Tobias, 1994). Experimental research finds higher percentages of up to 90%.

It is interesting why the scores on Knowledge Test 1 and Knowledge Test 2 only have a minor, although significant, effect on the first OverAll Test. It is possible that other variables play an important role and therefore reduce the effect of prior knowledge. When students are administered the first OverAll Test, they can still be considered inexperienced with the educational and examination system. Problem-based learning which stresses self-directed learning and assessment instruments which require   skills other than memory reproduction, is new for students entering university. Factors such as a lack of self-confidence, and lack of motivation due to insecurity about what to do with two weeks self-study may have an effect on their scores on the first OverAll Test.

2.   There is a weak relation between study time and achievement.

Students were asked to write down how many hours they spent on studying. The results are shown in Table 9. On the average, students spend 35 to 32 hours on studying the cases, although they are supposed to study 80 hours (two weeks, 40 hours per week). But, there are important differences between students (standard deviation between parenthesis).

An interesting question is whether students who spend more time on studying obtain higher test scores. The figures in Table 9 suggest that the correlation between time devoted to studies and OverAll Test results is very weak. This implies that study time makes no contribution to explain variances in OverAll Test results. This result confirms the results of previous studies (e.g., Dochy, 1992).

Table 9
Average Hours of Study and their Correlation with the OverAll-Test Results

Test	Time of Study	Correlation
OverAll Test 1	35.0 (20.1)	.098
OverAll Test 2	31.87 (20.18)	.054

3.   There is a weak relation between study strategies and achievement.

Students were asked how they studied, their approach to studying:
-   did they search for the main concepts, main ideas in the article?
-   did they write them down for themselves?
-   did they structure the articles?
-   did they relate the cases to previous acquired knowledge?

The results show that most students do search for the main concept and ideas, and structure the article but do not relate them to previously acquired knowledge (OverAll Test 1 and OverAll Test 2: average rate of 2.8 on a five-point Likert scale, SD=1.1). This means that elaboration and restructuring of knowledge is missing. Observations during the test administration showed that quite a lot of students still need some time to read the articles. It is clear students didn't study in an effective way. They read the articles in order to understand the content, but they didn't relate the ideas or principles explained in the articles to what they learned during the 16 weeks. Because these previous learning activities are essential elements of working in small tutorial groups, it is surprising students are not able to handle the cases in an effective way. The answers to other items in the questionnaire indicate some of the reasons for this finding. The students remark that the study-advice was not sufficiently clear (OverAll Test1: M=2.5 SD=1.0; OverAll Test2: M=2.8 SD=1.0). The study-advice didn't motivate them to study (OverAll Test1: M=2.4 SD=0.9; OverAll Test2: M=2.6 SD=0.9) and the information about the design and the main goals of the OverAll Test were not sufficiently clear (OverAll Test1: M=2.5 SD=0.9; OverAll Test2: M=2.9 SD=0.9).

Although the guidance of the self study period can be improved, it is still a question why students, used to working on the basis of problem solving, can't transfer the way they work in the tutorial groups (Seven-Jump) to the self study period. Probably further analysis of the practice within the tutorial groups and of the resemblance between the type of cases/problems of the blockbooks and the test can give some indications. Finally, it is interesting to examine whether there is a relation between students' study strategies and their test scores. The findings conform to the results of comparable research (Lonka, Lindblom-Ylanne, & Maury, 1994; Vermunt, 1992; van Berkel, Sprooten, & de Graaff, 1994). The correlation between the students' study approaches as measured by the questionnaire and the test score is weak ($r = .15$).

CONCLUSIONS

The assessment system of the Maastricht School of Economics and Business Administration is based on the core characteristics of the learning environments implemented in a problem based curriculum. It stresses learning as an active and constructive process. Learning is anchored in real life situations: Authentic problems are the starting point of learning. Learning is not only directed towards the acquisition of knowledge. The core goal of students' learning is the application of integrative knowledge: Being able to solve authentic multidisciplinary problems by the use of the relevant concepts, models and theories. The small tutorial group guided by an expert intends to realize a favorable social context for learning. These insights in the core characteristics of learning have not only resulted in a problem-based curriculum but also in the development of an assessment system which reflects these main ideas. The two main assessment instruments are the Knowledge Test, measuring declarative knowledge, and the OverAll Test, assessing procedural and conditional knowledge.

Experimental research was carried out to improve the quality of the OverAll Test as a selective assessment instruments. The results indicate the problem of content-specificity. Achievement on one problem is only to a small extent predictive for solving another problem. An acceptable test reliability can be obtained when using 12 cases in the OverAll Test, including true/?/false questions as well as open-ended questions. Empirical research intended to investigate the effect of three educational variables on students' capability to solve authentic problems, as measured by the OverAll Test. The findings can be summarized as follows:

1. Students acquired 50% of the subject matter assessed by the Knowledge Tests. For 50%, they are capable of relating the relevant concepts, models and theories to a problem presented. For 25-31% they are able to analyze, synthesize and evaluate a problem. The knowledge base acquired has an important effect on students' capability to analyze problems and to contribute to their solution. The better students acquired declarative knowledge, the better they are able to use this knowledge to analyze problems and to contribute to their solution.

2. There are no time effects on achievement. The results of the students' survey indicate students don't study as many hours as the staff expects them to (and as stipulated by the curriculum).

3. Study strategies have no explanatory value for the students' scores on the OverAll Test. The survey results indicate students study neither in a way the staff expects them to nor in a way we would describe as effective. There seems to be no transfer of study strategies (Seven-Jump method) to the self-study period. The last two findings refer to the effectiveness of the self-study period. The problems indicated may be partly due to the organization of the self study period (information, study advice). Probably, questions can be raised about the practice within the tutorial groups. More attention should be paid to a mindful use of the Seven-Jump method for analyzing problems and for contributing to their solution. Secondly, the application of the core concepts, theories and models should be exercised in a wider variety of problem situations.

REFERENCES

Adams, L.T., Kasserman, J.E., Yearwood, A.A., Perfetto, G.A., Bransford, J.D., & Franks, J.J. (1988). Memory access: The effects of fact-oriented versus problem-oriented acquisition. *Memory and Cognition, 16,* 167-175.

Albanese, M.A., & Mitchell, S.M.A. (1993). Problem-based learning: A Review of literature on its outcomes and implementation issues. *Academic Medicine, 68* (1), 52-81.

Balla J., & Boyle, P. (1994). Assessment of student performance: A framework for improving practice. *Assessment and Evaluation in Higher Education, 19,* 17-28.

Barrows, H.S. (1986). A taxonomy of problem-based learning methods. *Medical Education, 20,* 481-486.

Bédard, J. (1989). Expertise in auditing: Myth or reality. *Accounting Organizations and Society, 14,* 113-131.

Berkel, H.J.M., Nuy J.P., & Geerligs, T. (1994). *Progress Testing and Study-behaviour* (memo). Maastricht: University of Limburg.

Berkel, H.J.M. van, Sprooten, J., & Graaff, E. de (1993). An individualized assessment test consisting of 600 items. The development of a progress test for a multi-master program health sciences' curriculum. In: P.A.J. Bouhuijs, H.G. Schmidt, & H.J.M. van Berkel. *Problem-based learning as an educational strategy.* Maastricht: Network Publications.

Block, A. de (1960). *Algemene didactiek.* [General didactics] Antwerpen-Amsterdam: Standaard Wetenschappelijke Uitgeverij.

Blumberg, P., & Michael, J.A. (1992). Development of self-directed learning behaviours in a partially teacher-directed problem-based learning curriculum. *Teaching and Learning in Medicine 4* (1), 3-8.

Chi, M.T.H., Feltovich, P., & Glaser, R. (1981). Categorization and representation of physics problems by experts and novices. *Cognitive Science, 5,* 121-152.

Corte, E. de (1990, April). *A state-of-the-art of research on learning and teaching.* Keynote lecture presented at the first European Conference on the First Year Experience in Higher Education, Aalborg University, Denmark.

Decruyenaere, M., & Janssen, P.J. (1990). A structural model for individual differences in academic performance of freshmen. In: H. Mandl, E. de Corte, S.N. Bennett, & H.F. Friedrich, (Eds.), *Learning and instruction.* Oxford: Pergamon Press.

Dempster, F.N. (1987). Time and the production of classroom learning: Discerning implications from basic research. *Educational Psychologist, 22,* 1-21.

Dewey, J. (1929). *Comment nous pensons.* Paris: Flammarion.

Dochy, F.J.R.C. (1992). *Assessment of prior knowledge as a determinant for future learning.* Utrecht/London: Lemma/Jessica Kingsley.

Dochy, F.J.R.C., &, Alexander, P.A. (1995). Mapping prior knowledge: A framework for discussion among researchers. *European Journal for Psychology of Education, X* (2), 123-145.

Dochy, F.J.R.C., & Wijnen, W.H.F.W. (1987). Nieuwe onderwijskundige inzichten aan de basis van een moderne onderwijsopvatting en het vaardigheid-sonderwijs. [New educational insights based on a contemporary study approach] In: F.J.R.C. Dochy, & S.J. van Luyk (Eds.), *Handboek vaardigheidsonderwijs.* Lisse: Swets & Zeitlinger.

Ebel, R.L., & Frisbie D.A. (1991). *Essentials of educational measurement.* New Jersey: Prentice Hall.

Frederick, W.C., Walberg, H.J. (1980). Learning as a function of time. *Journal of Educational Research, 73,* 183-193.

Gronlund, N.E. (1971). *Measurement and evaluation in teaching.* New York: MacMillan.

Hand, J.D. (1993). Problem-based paper cases for evaluating students in "Issues in Contemporary Medicine". In P.A.J. Bouhuijs, H.G. Schmidt, & H.J.M. van Berkel. *Problem-based learning as an educational strategy.* Maastricht: Network.

Hassan, F., Ezzat, E., Faris, R., & Fam, R. (1993). The development of a valid student assessment system in community-based medical schools. In P.A.J. Bouhuijs, H.G. Schmidt, & H.J.M. van Berkel (Eds.), *Problem-based learning as an educational strategy.* Maastricht: Network Publications.

Heyns, B. (1986). Educational effects: Issues in conceptualization and measurement. In J.G. Richardson (Ed.), *Handbook of theory and research for the sociology of education.* Westport, CN.: Greenwood.

Hounsell, D. (1990). Assessing the quality of learning climates. In *Proceedings of the 2nd International Conference on Assessing Quality in Higher education* (pp. 267-269).University of Saint Andrews, Scotland.

Karweit, N.I. (1983). *Time on task: A research review.* Baltimore, MD: The Johns Hopkins University Center for Social Organization of Schools.

Karweit, N.I., & Slavin, R.E. (1981). Measurement and modelling choices in studies of time and learning. *American Educational Research Journal, 8,* 157-171.

Kaufman, R., Mennin, S., Waterman, S., Duban, S., Hansbarger, C., Silverblatt, H., Obenshain, S., Kantrowitz, M., Becker, T., Samet, J., & Wiese, W. (1989). The New Mexico experiment: Educational innovation and institutional change. *Academic Medicine, 64,* Supplement 6, 285-294.

Kerschensteiner, G. (1926). *Theorie der bildung.* Leipzig: Teubner.

Langeveld, M.J. (1934). *Taal en denken.* [Language and thought] Groningen: Wolters.

Langeveld, M.J. (1959). *Beknopte theoretische pedagogiek.* [Theoretical pedagogy] Groningen: Wolters.

Leinhardt, G., & Bickle, W. (1987). Instruction's the thing wherein to catch the mind that falls behind. *Educational Psychologist, 22,* 177-207.

Lonka, K., Lindblom-Ylanne, S., Maury, S. (1994). The effect of study strategies on learning from text. *Learning and Instruction, 4* (3), 253-271.

Marchais, J.E. Des, Dumais, B., Jean, P., & Nu Viet Vu (1993). An attempt at measuring student ability to analyze problems in the Sherbrook problem-based curriculum: A preliminary study. In P.A.J. Bouhuijs, H.G. Schmidt, & H.J.M. van Berkel. *Problem-based learning as an educational strategy.* Maastricht: Network Publications.

Mehrens, W.A., & Lehman, I.V. (1984). *Measurement and evaluation in education and psychology.* New York: The Dryden Press.

Neufeld, V.R., Woodward, C.A., & MacLeod, S.M. (1989). The McMaster M.D. program: A case study of renewal in medical education. *Academic Medicine, 64*, 423-432.

Resnick, L.B. (1987). Learning in school and out. *Educational Researcher, 16* (9), 13-20.

Schmidt, H.G., & Bouhuijs, P.A.J. (1980). *Onderwijs in taakgerichte groepen.* [Education in task-oriented groups] Utrecht: Spectrum.

Schmidt, H.G. (1993). Foundations of problem-based learning: Some explanatory notes. *Medical Education, 27*, 422-432.

Schoenfeld, A.H., & Herrmann, D.J. (1982). Problem perception and knowledge structure in expert and novice mathematical problem solvers. *Journal of Experimental Psychology: Learning, Memory, and Cognition, 8*, 484-494.

Segers, M.S.R., Tempelaar, D., Keizer, P., Schijns, J., Vaessen, E., & Mourik van, A. (1991). De overall-toets: een eerste experiment met een nieuwe toetsvorm. [The overall test: A first experiment] Maastricht: University of Limburg.

Segers, M.S.R., Tempelaar, D., Keizer, P., Schijns, J., Vaessen, E., & Mourik van, A. (1992a). Overall-toets 1: analyze op toets- en itemniveau. [Overall test 1: Analysis on test and item level] Maastricht: University of Limburg.

Segers, M.S.R., Tempelaar, D., Keizer, P., Schijns, J., Vaessen, E., & Mourik van, A. (1992b). De overall-toets: een tweede experiment met een nieuwe toetsvorm. [The overall test: Second experiment with a new type of test] Maastricht: University of Limburg.

Selz, O. (1913). *Uber die Gesetze des geordneten Denkverlaufs.* Stuttgart: Sjemann.

Selz, O. (1922). *Zur psychology des produktivem Denkens und des Irrtums.* Bonn: F. Cohen.

Sherwood, R.D., Kinzer, C.K., Bransford, J.D., & Franks, J.J. (1986). *Macro-contexts in science teaching* (Technical report No. 86.1.5). Nashville, TN: Vanderbilt University, Learning Technology Centre.

Shuell, T.J. (1986). Cognitive conceptions of learning. *Review of Educational Research, 56*, 411-436.

Son, B., & Van Sickle R.L. (1993, April). *Problem-solving instruction and students' acquisition, retention and restructuring of economics knowledge.* Paper presented at the annual meeting of the AERA, Atlanta.

Stein, B.S., Bransford, J.D., Franks, J.J. Owings, R.A., Vye, N.J., McGraw, W. (1982). Differences in the precision of self-regulated elaborations. *Journal of Experimental Psychology, 11*, 399-405.

Swanson, D.B., Case, S.N., & Vleuten, C.P.M. van der (1991). Strategies for student assessment. In D. Boud, & G. Feletti, *The challenge of problem-based learning.* London: Kogan Page.

Tempelaar, D. (1992). Handleiding toetsconstructie. [Manual for test instruction] Maastricht: University of Limburg.

Tobias, S. (1994). Interest, prior knowledge and learning. *Review of Educational Research, 64*, 1, 37-54.

Tuma, D.T., & Reif, F. (1980). Problem solving and education: Issues in teaching and research. Hillsdale, NJ: Erlbaum.

Vermunt, J. D.H.M. (1992). *Leerstijlen en sturen van leerprocessen in het hoger onderwijs. Naar procesgerichte instructie in zelfstandig denken.* [Study styles and directing study processes in higher education] Amsterdam-Lisse: Swets & Zeitlinger.

Vleuten, C.P.M. van der & Verwijnen, M. (1990). A system for student assessment. In C.P.M. van Vleuten, & W.H.F.W. Wijnen, *Problem-based learning: Perspectives from the Maastricht experience.* Amsterdam: Thesis.

Voss, J.F., Blais, J., Means. M.L., Greene, T.R., & Ahwesh, E. (1989). Informal reasoning and subject matter knowledge in the solving of economics problems by naive and novice individuals. In L.B. Resnick, (Ed.), *Knowing, learning, and instruction.* Hillsdale-New Jersey: Erlbaum.

Voss, J.F., Greene, T.R., Post, T.A., & Penner, B.C. (1983). Problem solving skill in the social sciences. In G. Bower, G. (Ed.), *The psychology of learning and motivation.* New York: Academic Press.

Wijnen, W.H.F.W. (1990). The importance of learning in relation to teaching. In C.P.M. van Vleuten, & W.H.F.W. Wijnen, (Eds.), *Problem-based learning: Perspectives from the Maastricht experience.* Amsterdam: Thesis.

Wilkerson, L., & Feletti, G. (1989). Problem-based learning: One approach to increasing student participation. In A.F. Lucas (Ed.), *The department chairperson's role in enhancing college teaching, New Directions for Teaching and Learning* (pp. 51-60). San Francisco CA: Jossey-Bass.

Willmann, O. (1934). *Didactiek. Deel III: Vormingsdoelen en vormingsinhoud.* [Didactics, III: Formative aims and contents]. Antwerpen: Standaard.

II

ASSESSMENT OF PRIOR KNOWLEDGE AND LEARNING PROCESSES

Assessment of Domain-Specific and Domain-Transcending Prior Knowledge: Entry Assessment and the Use of Profile Analysis

Filip J.R.C. Dochy

INTRODUCTION

Recent investigations into human cognition (Alexander, Pate, Kulikowich, Farrell, & Wright ,1989; Alexander, Kulikowich & Schulze, 1992; Dochy, 1992, 1994) have shown that prior knowledge is an important student variable in learning. Indeed, "a well-organized and coherent knowledge base initiates inference, conceptualization and the acquisition of principled understanding", as Glaser and De Corte state (in Dochy, 1992, p. 1).

The central finding of investigations of the past fifteen years is that a key to developing such an integrated and generative knowledge base is to build upon the learners prior knowledge. According to Glaser and De Corte: "Indeed, new learning is exceedingly difficult when prior informal as well as formal knowledge is not used as a springboard for future learning. It has also become more and more obvious, that in contrast to the traditional measures of aptitude, the assessment of prior knowledge and skill is not only a much more precise predictor of learning, but provides in addition a more useful basis for instruction and guidance" (Dochy, 1992, p.1). In recent work (Dochy, Valcke & Wagemans, 1991; Dochy, 1994;1995), the analysis of the quality and impact of the students' prior knowledge states has been a major focus. Several instruments have been developed to measure the prior knowledge state, especially within the domain of economics. In analyzing the prior knowledge state, we especially focused on its structure.

In this chapter, we report on a study which supports the development of knowledge profiles. In educational practice, a major problem is that study materials and guidance are usually not completely adapted to the individuals' needs (De Corte,

Lodewijks, Parmentier, & Span, 1987). It is assumed that the information gained from knowledge profiles will reveal the students strengths and weaknesses and that this will provide a more objective basis for diagnosis and guidance after entry assessment during the learning process.

In the first part of this chapter, we will give a short overview of principal terms related to the study of prior knowledge. First, an answer will be given to the need for a generally recognized map of prior knowledge. The model of a conceptual map is presented on which European and American researchers (De Corte, Dochy, Alexander, Judy, Kulikowich, Patton, Jetton) agree and taken as a starting point. Second, the model distinguishes between content and metacognitive prior knowledge and puts such terms as declarative, procedural, strategic, domain-specific and domain-transcending knowledge into this framework.

After this, we will discuss a new and distinct approach which is based on analysis of theories, models and practice-based strategies about the *structure of knowledge* found in the literature. In earlier research on domain-specific prior knowledge, we focused on the structure of prior knowledge along the content dimension. A series of investigations was conducted within the field of economics (Dochy, 1992, 1994). In this chapter we investigate the structure of prior knowledge along a variety of dimensions. Our discussion of the structure of prior knowledge introduces a new approach towards the structure-of-knowledge problem. A set of *dimensions* is defined which is helpful in constructing *knowledge profiles*. The concept of profile is derived from the practice, common in educational research, of plotting (in the form of a graph or profile) a person's scores as raw scores or as standardized scores (Keeves, 1988). Four types of dimensions are designated : cognitive-psychological dimensions, educational-psychological dimensions, psychometric dimensions, and content-based dimensions.

In the second, empirical part of this chapter, data that support the relevance and validity of the knowledge profile dimensions are collected by means of administering a domain-specific knowledge state test in the field of economics. The data, gathered during an investigation involving a sample of 627 university students, are analyzed by means of profile analysis (parallelism tests, discriminant analysis and flatness tests). Data are provided that support the relevance and validity of the knowledge profile dimensions. Two approaches will be adopted, based on data gathered during a research project involving a sample of university students. First, an analysis of the extent to which the variables along the dimensions give information about different components of prior knowledge. Second, an analysis of the discriminatory power of the knowledge profile dimensions to make apparent prior knowledge differences between student sub-populations.

PRIOR KNOWLEDGE TERMINOLOGY

Based on our prior reviews of the literature (e.g., Alexander et al., 1991; Dochy, 1992), we identified a number of problems associated with the usage of knowledge terminology in the educational research literature. For the purpose of this discussion, we will highlight three of these pervasive problems:
1.   Most knowledge concepts used were undefined or vaguely defined.
2.   Nominal definitions prevailed over real definitions.

3. Different aspects of knowledge were referred to by the same terms, or the same aspects of knowledge were referenced by different terms.

However, as we stated, our prior reviews of the literature have shown that even the most basic prior knowledge terms are not consistently defined (Alexander et al., 1991; Dochy, 1988, 1992). Before proceeding further with this review, we offer the definition of prior knowledge that guides our thinking. Specifically, we will define prior knowledge as the whole of a persons knowledge. As such, prior knowledge:

*   is dynamic in nature;
*   is available before a certain learning task;
*   is structured;
*   can exist in multiple states (i.e., declarative, procedural, and conditional knowledge);
*   is both explicit and tacit in nature and
*   contains conceptual and metacognitive knowledge components.

In the research on cognition and learning and artificial intelligence, the broad term *prior knowledge* has been broken down into an array of subsidiary and interrelated concepts. Several of these concepts play a central role in this discussion of prior knowledge terminology. They are what we refer to here as key dimensions of prior knowledge.

Domain-Specific Knowledge and Domain-Transcending Knowledge

Recent research has pointed to the fact that both domain-specific knowledge and domain-transcending knowledge exist in the knowledge base (Glaser, 1984). Further, there is evidence that learning may be more domain-specific than earlier theorists of learning believed; that is, concrete and practical situations seem to be better learning environments than highly abstract ones (Shuell, 1986; Tuma & Reif, 1980). Carey (1985) suggests that the acquisition of knowledge during the total period of development (i.e., throughout ones life) is based on increasing knowledge within various domains. This domain-specific restructuring view of development has received a great deal of support in research on novice-expert differences within various domains, such as physics (Chi, Glaser, & Rees, 1982), chess (Chase & Simon, 1973), radiology (Lesgold, Feltovich, Glaser, & Wang, 1981) and the social sciences (Voss, Greene, Post, & Penner, 1983).

Nevertheless it is unlikely that all learning is domain-specific (Alexander & Judy, 1988). If this were the case, it would be difficult to explain how individuals deal with new situations or how they handle entirely new information. Viewed objectively, learning, according to Shuell (1986), comprises domain-specific and domain-independent processes. How these processes interact with one another is as yet unclear. Alexander and Judy's (1988) contention is that undue emphasis on either domain-specific or domain-transcending knowledge is ineffective in learning and instruction. Both forms of knowledge are essential in human learning and development. Emphasis must vary appropriately as a function of the interplay of characteristics of the learner, the domain, the task, and the context (Alexander, 1992; Alexander & Kulikowich, 1992). Therefore, we consider the total of domain-specific prior knowledge (all domains) and the domain-transcendent knowledge as a person's prior knowledge or knowledge base.

Research over the last two decades has directed increasing attention toward domain-specific knowledge. The vagueness of concepts like domain and subject matter is a problem when they serve as a basis for prediction (Ennis, 1990). Therefore, it is highly advisable to clearly state the meaning of domain-specificity beforehand. Domain-specificity is the empirically-based view that learning or thinking: (a) requires prior knowledge, (b) is unlikely to transfer from one domain to another without explicit transfer-inducing instruction, and (c) is unlikely to be learned from general learning or thinking instruction (Dochy, 1992). According to Ennis (1990) there is complete agreement about the first principle and a majority of educational psychologists agree with the second principle. However, psychologists and researchers do not agree upon the third principle (Ennis, 1989).

In the remainder of this section, we will present our attempt at understanding the basic knowledge constructs by showing how these terms are related to one another within a conceptual framework. It should be stated that the current mapping we offer in Figure 1 is, in reality, a reconciliation of earlier presented investigations into this subject (Alexander et al., 1991; Dochy, 1988, 1992,1994). In the present mapping, therefore, we will stress those dimensions of prior knowledge that we hold to be most basic.

This resulting conceptual map, although illustrating the relations between key prior knowledge terms, may be somewhat misleading since it displays prior knowledge as something inert. That is, this mapping may be mistakenly seen to represent a static, non-interactive view of knowledge. To avoid this misconception, it is necessary to state some of our basic assumptions about our view of knowledge; assumptions that do not receive direct representation in our visual display.

- The conceptual framework focuses on a system that represents an individual learners prior knowledge. As indicated by the surrounding sociocultural context, we recognize that individual knowledge is continually and significantly impacted by the context in which it is situated.
- The framework is meant to be a conceptual map of prior knowledge terminology and not a processing model of knowledge use. Therefore, we do not intend to suggest how knowledge is acquired or how it comes to be explicated or interfaced.
- The forms of knowledge represented in the model are fluid and dynamic. Not only do these forms vary between individuals but they vary within individuals as well. That is, the state of knowledge is changing from moment to moment within the individual and cannot be adequately captured in any one-dimensional or even multidimensional display.
- The relative shapes, size, and positions of the knowledge terms are largely arbitrary in that they are not intended to approximate the quality or quantity of each knowledge type. Thus, the fact that we depict the conceptual knowledge or metacognitive knowledge planes as rectangles, for example, has no significance other than convention.
- All forms of knowledge are interactive. That is, the presence or activation of one form of knowledge can directly or indirectly influence any other. This interactivity of knowledge has been well illustrated by the work of Voss, Blais, Means, Greene, and Ahwesh (1986), Alexander, Pate, Kulikowich, Farrell, & Wright (1989) and others (Walker, 1987). Therefore, even when various forms of knowledge are displayed separately, they should be understood as overlapping or interacting.

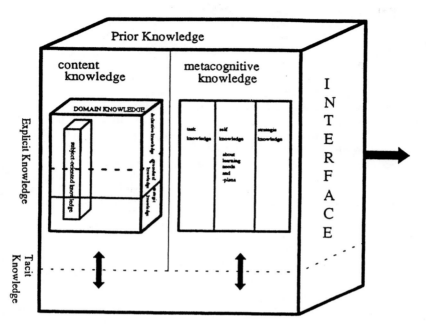

Figure 1. A Conceptual Map of Prior Knowledge

THE DETERMINING INFLUENCE OF PRIOR KNOWLEDGE ON LEARNING

In psychological models of educational performance, prior knowledge plays a major role (for an overview, see Haertel, Walberg,, & Weinstein., 1983). The effect of prior knowledge on learning outcomes has been shown in studies that try to explain the variance in test scores as well as in research that focuses on the construction of causal models.

The Contribution of Prior Knowledge in Explaining Variance in Post-Test Scores

The fact that prior knowledge has been demonstrated to be a potentially important educational variable in the sense of contribution to post-test variance has been shown in several investigations. Knowledge measured prior to a course, explained, on the average, no less than 50% of the variance in the post-test scores (ranging from 20 to 80 %). Comparable results were reported by Bloom (1976) who found correlations of 0.50 to 0.90 between pre-test and post-test scores. Dochy's work (1992), conducted in ecologically more valid settings (real life classroom settings), and using prior knowledge state tests, revealed that up to 42 % of variance was explained by prior knowledge. These investigations into the effect of variables on study results lead us to the general conclusion that prior knowledge generally explains between 30 and 60 % (or more) of the variance in study results and that it overrules all other variables (see also Tobias, 1994).

The Role of Prior Knowledge as Shown in Research by Means of Causal Modelling Techniques

Attempts to explore causal models of educational achievement have resulted in complex models, with a good overall fit and a multitude of significant structural coefficients, which stress once more the importance of prior knowledge. Parkerson, Lomax, Schiller, and Walberg (1984), in an attempt to explore causal models of educational achievement, reached a substantially similar simple productivity model. However, this simple model seemed inadequate because of a general lack of fit and many nonsignificant structure coefficients. Nevertheless, their complex model (Figure 2), with a good overall fit and a multitude of significant structural coefficients, stressed once more the importance of prior knowledge. Striking is the strong path coefficient between prior knowledge and achievement. Caution is needed to interpret for example the negative coefficient within this causal path model, such as between quality of instruction and achievement (Figure 2), possibly caused by students who are critical of the instruction.

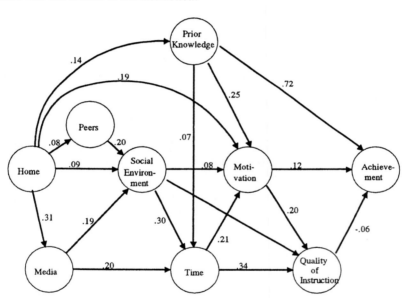

Figure 2. Complex Causal Model of Educational Achievement (free after Parkerson et al., 1984)

Körkel (1987) analyzed the relations among age, intelligence, metacognition, prior knowledge and performance through a structural equation model. Figure 3 gives the LISREL model representing the parameter estimations for the structural relationships. Again, the most important finding is the superior explanatory power of domain-specific prior knowledge, which is the most significant path in the model. In a replica of his former soccer study, Weinert (1989) found that domain-specific knowledge is a decisive prerequisite for good mathematics achievement. There is considerable evidence that the domain-specific prior knowledge is the type of prior knowledge that mostly affects the learning process and results. Above all, domain-specific prior knowledge should not be confused with the overall general ability called intelligence. In the fifties, the general belief was that more intelligent people could learn things that the less intelligent could not. A careful inspection of empirical findings makes this doubtful for several reasons. First, the correlation between intelligence and achievement is highly variable. Statistical meta-analyses have yielded overall coefficients that range between .34 and .51. Second, if one partials out the influence of prior knowledge, the correlation between intelligence and study result is drastically reduced to values ranging between .0 and .30 (Weinert, 1989).

Further, the results from studies on metacognition show remarkable parallels with the results from intelligence studies looking at predictors of learning outcomes (correlations was between .07 and .20). Contrary to expectations, past research has shown that motivational variables and instructional characteristics contribute very little to the prediction of study performance.

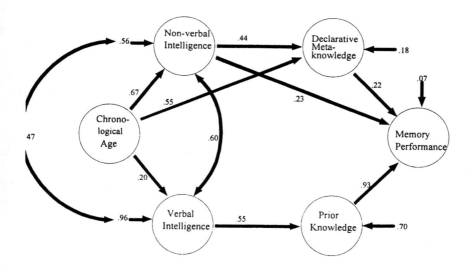

Figure 3. LISREL Model of Structural Relationships (after Körkel, 1987)

The correlations between prior knowledge and performance remained significant even with intelligence scores partialed out. It can also be concluded that domain-specific knowledge can compensate for low intellectual ability, but a high intellectual ability cannot compensate for a low prior knowledge (Weinert, 1990; Walker, 1987).

The most important finding resulting from causal models is the superior explanatory power of prior knowledge, i.e. it is the most significant path in the models. Overall, it is concluded that the past is in fact the best predictor for the future. Differences in the knowledge base are the main source of intra- and interindividual differences in cognitive achievement, irrespective of chronological age or the specific domain of knowledge.

THE STRUCTURE OF KNOWLEDGE: A CENTRAL ISSUE IN EDUCATIONAL SCIENCES

The structure of knowledge issue has been dealt with by a variety of theoretical disciplines: cognitive psychology, educational psychology, artificial intelligence, etc. From a pragmatic viewpoint, the issue has also been of prime importance in applied sciences such as instructional psychology, curriculum development theories and psychometrics.

Disciplines such as cognitive psychology, educational psychology, artificial intelligence, etc., have each highlighted the structure of knowledge, from their particular viewpoint, resulting in a puzzling variety of approaches, focuses, models, theories, research studies, etc. A representative sample of authors comprises e.g., Ausubel (1968), de Groot (1946), Mayer (1979), Reigeluth & Stein (1983). Following is a short outline of some of their specific theoretical contributions.

An early, cognitive-theoretical approach appears in the work of Ausubel (1968) who argues that new knowledge is only acquired to the extent that it is meaningfully related to existing knowledge. Ausubel maintains that knowledge is organized primarily in a hierarchical fashion, which implies that mastery of higher knowledge levels assumes mastery of all lower knowledge levels. In addition, Ausubel contends that the various pieces of information integrated within a particular knowledge structure are highly interrelated. Thus, the more structured the prior knowledge, the more flexible and easy the acquisition of new knowledge becomes.

Ausubel's conceptualization of learning as the assimilation of new knowledge into prior knowledge is echoed and extended in Mayer's (1979) schema theory. New knowledge is - according to Mayer - assimilated into a hierarchy of progressively more specific content within the learners cognitive store. Thus, the basic learning process can be described as the assimilation of new knowledge within hierarchically ordered schemata.

Another benchmark is set by the elaboration theory. According to this theory, multiple access avenues become available to the learner by the activation of alternate relational paths . This is also explained by the assumption that knowledge acquisition is facilitated to the extent that information is organized in a hierarchically integrated mode (Reigeluth & Stein, 1983). These theories are important since they stress the structured and hierarchical nature of knowledge, but they lack empirical support to ground their validity (Reigeluth & Stein, 1983). Additional support, especially for the hierarchical nature of the knowledge organization, should be sought.

The structure-of-knowledge paradigm should also be investigated in further detail from a more pragmatic, i.e., instructional-psychological, viewpoint in order to find more efficient ways for using instructional technology. Our attempts to find ways to manage prior knowledge indicate, for example, that different components of prior knowledge should be taken into account (e.g., along the content dimension) and that components of prior knowledge along other dimensions could be helpful to support and diagnose in educational settings.

If we summarize the variety of theoretical and pragmatic approaches, four main types of dimensions according to which knowledge is structured can be conceptualized: content-related dimensions, educational dimensions, epistemological dimensions, and item-characteristic dimensions. These dimensions will be presented in detail below.

PRIOR KNOWLEDGE AND THE STRUCTURE OF KNOWLEDGE

The quality and impact of prior knowledge has been a major issue in research about the role of prior knowledge at university level (Dochy, 1988; Dochy & Steenbakkers, 1988; Dochy, Bouwens, Wagemans, & Niestadt, 1991; Dochy, 1992). An important conclusion from this research body indicates that it may be fruitful to analyze the complex of components of prior knowledge in more detail. A first and promising attempt in this direction focused on the structure of prior knowledge along the content dimension (Dochy, Valcke, & Wagemans, 1991; Wagemans & Dochy, 1991). Three important concepts are introduced in the following paragraphs: prior knowledge, components of prior knowledge, and a complex of components. These three concepts refer to the value attached to a specific structure of prior knowledge. Our earlier research revealed that a structure could be indicated in prior knowledge, e.g., along the content dimension. We discriminated for instance between Optimal Requisite Prior Knowledge and Mathematics Knowledge. But it was also suggested that the differentiation of components of prior knowledge along other dimensions is needed to diagnose and support educational practice (Dochy, Valcke, & Wagemans, 1991).

KNOWLEDGE PROFILES AND A MULTI-PROFILE APPROACH

The concept of knowledge profiles as such is not found in the literature. Only student profiles (Wolf, Bixby, Glenn, & Gardner, 1991) and cognitive profiles (Letteri & Kuntz, 1982) have some similarity in meaning. This is certainly the case for the studies by Letteri (1980) and Letteri and Kuntz (1982). The concept of a profile is derived from the practice, common in educational research, of plotting the scores of a person (raw scores or standardized scores) as a graph or profile. In analyzing research findings, comparisons are made between persons or groups in terms of a set of measurements on specific related aspects. For each person or group a profile is obtained on a set of parameters. The comparison between profiles of persons is known by the generic term profile analysis.

Figure 4 shows the relationship between some key concepts. A dimension is used to construct a knowledge profile. Each dimension, consisting of several parameters, represents an approach towards the structure of knowledge. A student can get a profile on each dimension used, in which the parameters stay identical. From an instructional psychological point of view, knowledge profiles can provide practical indications of student achievement and learning in order to direct the learning process. In a recent overview of student assessment, Wolf, Bixby, Glenn, and Gardner (1991) advocate this approach. According to these authors, there is a need for a new brand of educational psychometrics capable of answering the much changed questions of educational achievement. These changes are the new premises: the multiple paths towards the prior knowledge state, more developmental oriented assessments and the ascertainment that students enter school with widely varying backgrounds. In our terms, we take these changes into account by trying to identify multiple components of the prior knowledge state, by implementing prior knowledge state tests and by intending to use these tests as progress tests administered several times a year. In this context it is necessary to agree on the relevant parameters that describe student performance and it is critical to develop ways of looking at student profiles. According to Wolf, Bixby, Glenn and Gardner (1991), it is difficult to envision student assessment ever informing, rather than merely measuring, the educational process, unless we develop these kinds of differentiated portraits of student performance within a domain.

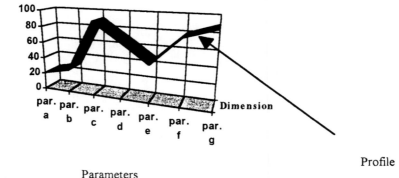

Figure 4. Example of a Profile on a Single Dimension

Figure 4 shows an example of a profile on a single dimension with 7 parameters. A *dimension* is the basis on which to construct a knowledge profile. Each dimension represents an approach towards the structure of knowledge since it introduces a related set of prior knowledge components. These components are called *parameters*.

As suggested above, our concept of *knowledge profiles* is related - to a certain degree - to Letteri's use of the concept. His work at the Center for Cognitive, Studies, University of Vermont, focuses on the development of an individual's cognitive profile. In Letteri's conception a profile is based on a continuum along which a variety of cognitive dimensions are put one next to the other. Letteri combines up to seven dimensions, such as scanning (focus), breadth of categorization, and cognitive complexity. An individuals cognitive profile is the diagram that results after positioning individual scores in relation to each of these dimensions along the continuum (Letteri & Kuntz, 1982). Letteri and Kuntz (1982) detected very high correlations between individuals' cognitive profiles and their performance on intellectual tasks, ability to learn and school performance. The results of the Letteri studies are impressive. His cognitive profiles can, for instance, help to divide seventh and eight grade students into significantly different achievement levels; they can account for up to 87 % of the variance in post-test scores and predict those scores at a significance level of .05 or better.

Moreover the results show that a cognitive profile is a basic determinant of academic achievement and can help to accurately identify specific learning deficits that significantly contribute to low academic achievement. Cognitive profiles seem to be reliable predictors of low/high academic achievement (Letteri, 1980).

Although the Vermont studies provide evidence for the potential of cognitive profiles, several critical remarks are needed. First, the work in Vermont concentrates on cognitive styles and characteristics of cognitive functioning, rather than on the structure of prior knowledge and using these prior knowledge components in learning. This is particularly obvious if we examine the dimensions used to construct the cognitive profiles in greater detail. Therefore, there is a clear distinction between their approach and ours. Our knowledge profile dimensions clearly consist of parameters referring to structure-aspects of knowledge. Second, the Letteri profiles do not seem to be appropriate for adult learners, as they are based on theories and research concerning child development. Third, we perceive profiles as diagrams based on a single dimension along which the parameters are clearly interrelated. The use of a set of such dimensions results in the construction of multiple knowledge profiles (i.e., one for each dimension). Letteri constructs only one profile, based on a variety of dimensions. His major focus is on the correlation between this profile and school performance. As a consequence, the remedial power of his profiles remains restricted. The Letteri profile can therefore be considered as an instrument for differentiating groups performing below or above average, taking into account the perceived correlations between the relative positioning on the profile and external measures of school performance. His remedial method is thus not based on the specific overall profile structure but on related external measures of school performance.

In contrast, our multi-profile approach generates *profile analysis*, an application of multivariate analysis of variance (MANOVA) in which several dependent variables are measured on the same scale (Tabachnick & Fidell, 1989). This profile analysis can provide relevant information with diagnostic and remedial value. In this way, the profiles help us to identify learning deficits which need to be treated.

OVERVIEW OF THE THEORETICAL DIMENSIONS OF THE PROFILES

In this paragraph, we review a representative sample of dimensions and parameters currently found in the literature. Each of these dimensions is based on a specific model or theory of knowledge structuring, which will only be discussed in short. Literature references are supplied for the reader looking for more information. As suggested earlier, the structure of knowledge issue has been dealt with from a wide variety of viewpoints, resulting in a number of dimensions.

One group of dimensions is classified according to common models of the economics domain. Other sets of dimensions are based on theories of knowledge representation, knowledge structure, learning theories, text representation models and psychometric theory. A first question in relation to each dimension is whether they are applicable as structures to identify components of prior knowledge. Secondly - and this will be discussed in the empirical part of this text - are these dimensions useful to differentiate groups of students. In this way we can scrutinize the descriptive, explanatory and remedial prospect of our knowledge profiles.

Content Dimensions

Economics Subdomain Dimension

Content is one of the most used dimensions in categorizing domain knowledge. Classification based on the parameter subdomain means that the domain of economics will be divided into common subject matter areas within the science of economics. One possibility, as implemented in the curriculum of the University of Maastricht, includes nine parameters: 1. Reporting; 2. Financing; 3. Organization; 4. Marketing; 5. Macroeconomics; 6. Microeconomics; 7. Public finances; 8. International economic affairs; 9. Behavioral and social sciences.

Curriculum Dimension

Certain contents of a science are expected to be mastered by the students at certain moments in the course of their studies. These moments are called the curriculum levels ((1) first and (2) second year level). A team of economists have helped to define these levels. These curriculum levels follow each other sequentially, but they are too broad to be considered as hierarchical.

Curriculum Accent Dimension

Within economics it is common to differentiate between two main streams, representing a different accent, i.e., (1) general economics and business administration on the one hand and (2) quantitative economics on the other hand.

Cognitive Psychological Dimensions

Propositional Dimension

Knowledge representation as used in schema theories (Dochy , Bouwens, et al., 1991) takes certain propositions or nodes as a starting point. A proposition is the smallest unit that can be qualified as true or false. According to most schema theories there are six kinds of nodes: (1) Physical State (PS, statement that refers to an ongoing state in the physical or social world), (2) Physical Event (PE, statement that refers to a state change in the physical or social world), (3) Internal State (IS, statement that refers to an ongoing state of knowledge, attitude, or belief in a character), (4) Internal Event (IE, statement that refers to a state change in knowledge, attitude or belief in a character), (5) Goal (G, statement that refers to an achieved or unachieved state that a person wants) and (6) Style (S, statement that refers to details about the style or manner in which an action or event occurred). Further examples and elaborations of these parameters are given in Dochy, Bouwens et al. (1991). These nodes are used in the representational theory of Graesser (1981) to represent knowledge as a network of labelled statement nodes that are interrelated by directed arcs (see below). As such, the nodes do not have any hierarchical relationship.

Node Relation Dimension

The node relation dimension is based on characteristics of the interrelations among the propositions presented above. Relations among propositions can be classified as node relations or arc parameters: (1) Reason (R, a Goal node is a reason for another Goal node), (2) Initiate (I, a State or Event initiates another Goal node), (3) Consequence (C, a State, Event or Goal node that has the consequence of another State or Event node), (4) Manner (M, an Event or Goal node occurs with some style), (5) Property (P, a person, object or entity has some property that is a State node) (see also Dochy, Bouwens et al., 1991). These arc parameters are not of a hierarchical nature. The following specific relations among the propositions have been identified: (1) G - G (REASON); (2) PS - G, IS - G, PE - G, IE - G (INITIATE); (3) PS - PE, IS - PE, PE - PE, IE - PE, G - PE, PS - PS, IS - PS, PE - PS, IE - PS, G - PS (CONSEQUENCE); (4) PE - S/G, IE - S/G, GE - S/G (MANNER); (5) PS - PS (PROPERTY).

Cognitive Complexity Dimension

Mc Daniel (1991) proposes five levels of cognitive complexity. These parameters are designed to measure thinking processes by determining the cognitive complexity apparent in written interpretations of complex situations.

Level 1: Unilateral Descriptions
The situation is simplified. It focuses on one idea or argument. Alternatives are not identified. No new information, meaning, or perspectives are brought in. Good-bad and either-or assertions are made. Appeals to authority or simple rules. Information is simply paraphrased, restated or repeated.

Level 2: Simplistic Alternatives
Simple and obvious conflicts are identified, but the conflicts are not pursued or analyzed. Develops a position by dismissing or ignoring one alternative and supporting the other with assertions and simple explanations rather than through deeper assessment of the situation.

Level 3: Emergent Complexity
More than one possible explanation or perspective is identified. Complexity is established and preserved. New elements are introduced. Supports position through comparisons and simple causal statements.

Level 4: Broad Interpretations
Broad ideas help define and interpret the situation. Ideas within the perspective established are manipulated. There is a clearly recognizable explanatory theme. Ideas are integrated into subassemblies each supporting a component of the explanation.

Level 5: Integrated Analysis
The situation is restructured or reconceptualized and the problem is approached from a new point of view. A network of cause-and-effect relationships is constructed. Ideas are integrated and extrapolated. Arrives at new interpretations by analogy, application of principles and generalizations. An organizing framework is constructed, connections are given and consequences are predicted.

Educational-Psychological Dimensions

Discussing the first two dimensions of this type, i.e., the behavioral and the content dimension, it is noteworthy to mention Component Display Theory (CDT,

Merrill, 1983) which makes use of related concepts. CDT can be described as a set of prescriptive relationships that can be used to guide the design and the development of learning activities. A basic assumption of CDT is that there is more than one type of learning and more than one kind of memory structure. Primary aspects of CDT are objectives, learning activities and tests. According to CDT, all objectives or test items can be classified in cells of a matrix, based on a content dimension and a performance one. The CDT content dimension differentiates between facts, concepts, principles and procedures. The CDT performance, dimension differentiates between remember, use and find. This also conforms to Gagné's tripartite : information, skills and strategies. CDT holds that this performance-content matrix can be considered as a taxonomy, thus suggesting a hierarchical base for the two determining dimensions in the matrix.

Behavioral Dimension

The much used distinction between declarative and procedural knowledge can be further operationalized as (1) to know, (2) to understand, and (3) to apply. These three concepts are considered as equivalent to recognition, reproduction and production (De Corte, Geerligs, Lagerweij, Peeters, & Vandenberghe, 1976). The concepts can also be related to the classification: appreciation, recognition and reproduction of information (= declarative) or production or applications (interpretative, convergent, divergent or evaluative production) which can be viewed as procedural (Keeves, 1988). The three parameters also correspond with the basic taxonomic levels proposed by several educationalists such as Bloom, Guilford, De Corte and De Block (see Keeves, 1988). Most researchers agree that these parameters are of a hierarchical nature which has also been supported by empirical evidence (Keeves, 1988). Research also suggests that there is some justification for treating Bloom's lower levels as being taxonomic. This should not be the case for the levels of synthesis and evaluation (Madaus, et. al., 1973).

Content Dimension

At the content level we can distinguish five parameters: facts, concepts, relations, structures and methods. This is in accordance with the work of Guilford in which he identifies several product parameters, and the work of other authors (Keeves, 1988). These parameters are widely accepted as being hierarchical (Keeves, 1988): (1) Facts, (2) Concepts, (3) Relations, (4) Structures, (5) Methods.

Epistemological Dimension

Based on the levels of knowledge representation of Brachman and Schmolze (1985), five levels can be distinguished along this dimension. These parameters can also be considered as the most appropriate combinations of behavior- and content parameters, as clarified between brackets : (1) knowledge identification (identifying facts and concepts), (2) knowledge conceptualisation (insight in concepts), (3) epistemological analysis (to know and understand relations and structures), (4) logical analysis (to know and understand methods), (5) implementational analysis (application of methods). These levels are considered as hierarchical since they are a combination of the hierarchical behavior and content dimensions.

Layers of Knowledge Dimension

A distinction can be made between: static knowledge (description of concepts and relations), knowledge of different types of inferences, knowledge representing elementary tasks (procedures), and strategic knowledge (Clancey, 1983).

(1)   The first layer consists of the static knowledge of the domain: domain concepts, relations and complex structures, such as models of processes or devices.

(2)   The second layer is the inference layer. In this layer we describe what inferences can be made on the basis of the knowledge in the static layer. Two types of entities are represented at the inference layer: meta-classes and knowledge sources. Meta-classes describe the role domain-concepts can play in reasoning. For example, a domain concept such as infection can play the role of a finding in a consultation process, but it may also play the role of a hypothesis. Knowledge sources describe what types of inferences can be made on the basis of the relations in the domain layer. Examples are the specification and the generalization of knowledge sources, which both make use of a subsumption relation in the domain layer.

(3)   The third layer is called the task layer. At this level the basic objects become goals and tasks. Tasks are ways in which knowledge sources can be combined to achieve a particular goal.

(4)   The fourth layer is the strategic layer wherein knowledge resides which allows a system to make plans - i.e., create a task structure - to control and monitor the execution of tasks, to diagnose when something goes wrong and to repair impasses.

Item-Characteristics Dimensions

Although these dimensions are of a completely different nature, they are of importance in the context of our research purposes. Items are used to measure the mastery of (prior) knowledge. Moreover, test items are clues to the activation of prior knowledge. The way the individual is instigated to show his mastery of knowledge and the way certain knowledge is (re)presented to the learner can also be related to the structure of knowledge issue.

Number of Propositions Dimension

A proposition is the smallest unit that can be considered as a separate statement that can be judged as true or false. In schema theories, propositions or nodes have a central function in the structure of schema. It is assumed that the amount of propositions determines the degree of structure needed to answer the item correctly. According to the mean amount of propositions in our items, we found that most items had 4 to 9 propositions. Three parameters have been identified in relation to this dimension : (1) < 5 propositions, (2) > 4 < 10 propositions, (3) > 9 propositions.

Information Level Dimension

The stem of an item is the general information which is given and which must not be evaluated as true or false. This correct information precedes the question(s) for which this information should be taken into account. Therefore we distinguish between (1) items with a stem   and (2) items without a stem. A stem can be connected to one or more subsequent questions. Therefore, the spatial and logical distance between the general information part of an item and the question part of the whole item is larger than for simple items without a stem.

Representation Level Dimension

Adhering to the representation structure used in the research of Boekaerts (1979), i.e., visual, verbal and symbolic representation, we used four parameters along this dimension. These parameters are also closely related to the four content levels in Guilfords structure of intellect model: figural, symbolic, semantic (the verbal factor) and behavioral (nonverbal information) and the Twyman (1985) categories : verbal, pictorial and schematic. Since test-items are always - in part - based on a textual representation of information, our dimension only distinguishes between parameters that are combinations of knowledge representation:(1) Textual-graphical, (2) Textual, (3) Textual-schematic, (4) Textual-symbolic.

Hierarchical and Non-Hierarchical Dimensions

In this theoretical discussion of the dimensions for the construction of knowledge profiles, the hierarchical or non-hierarchical nature of the dimensions is of importance. Empirical validation of the dimensions and their further application, has to take this particularity into account. Table 1 presents a summary. An asterisk (*) indicates that the dimension is considered to be of a hierarchical nature.

Table 1
Hierarchical and Non-Hierarchical Dimensions

Profile dimensions	Hierarchical
Economics Subdomains Dimension	-
Curriculum Dimension	-
Curriculum Accent Dimension	-
Propositional Dimension	-
Node Relation Dimension	-
Cognitive Complexity Dimension	*
Behavioral Dimension	*
Content Dimension	*
Epistemological Dimension	*
Layers Of Knowledge Dimension	*
Number Of Propositions Dimension	-
Information Level Dimension	-
Representation Level Dimension	*

RESEARCH METHOD

The main purpose of this study was to assert the relevance and validity of the knowledge profile dimensions. Two approaches will be adopted, based on data gathered during a study involving a sample of university students. First, an analysis of the extent to which the variables along the dimensions give information about different components of prior knowledge. Second, an analysis of the discriminatory power of the knowledge profile dimensions to discern prior knowledge differences between student sub-populations.

Subjects

627 students of the University of Maastricht (RL group) and the Dutch Open University (OU group) beginning their studies in economics were randomly selected.

Instruments: Considerations Underlying the Design of a Domain-Specific Knowledge State Test (DS KST)

There is evidence that learning is much more domain-specific than earlier learning theorists believed (Dochy, 1992). It is obvious that domain-referenced testing provides a reasonable possibility of measuring individuals knowledge status and of tracking their progress within a certain domain. Aside from this, there are additional arguments to account for extended applications of Domain-specific KS Tests.

First, it can be assumed that the learning process is also influenced by prior knowledge which is broader than strictly subject-specific prior knowledge. For this reason, a domain-specific test was developed covering the whole domain (up to a certain degree of difficulty of specialization). In our case we are concerned with the domain of economics.

Second, differences among students concerning specific subjects are sometimes rather large. A test at beginners level may not be able to reveal all of the differences among the students. The chance of this occurring is greater when using a test related to end terms, e.g., one whose level corresponds to the end of the second year of university studies.

Third, because some students have already gained a great deal of experience in their working environment or have already attained a relatively high educational level (some higher vocational education or university degree), a test at beginners level (final secondary level) would not be capable of measuring part of the prior knowledge state.

Fourth, the recent trend known as flexible learning which uses flexibility as a key concept, is strongly related to the use of domain-specific tests. *Flexible learning* tries to take the students prior knowledge into account and allows them to study at their own place and pace. Students have a large degree of freedom in choosing educational media and objectives. A sudden openness of objectives and other choices requires an appropriate assessment instrument, such as domain-specific tests. Other instruments tend to neglect these primary conditions of flexible learning. Domain-specific tests not only yield measurement results, but also information and guidelines to deal with deficiencies. Testing should serve the learning process.

A fifth argument is the psychometric quality of the item bank for domain-specific tests. The amount of available items for a course is often restricted and does not allow the removal of items on the basis of insufficient psychometric quality (validity, reliability, difficulty level). This problem disappears when using the larger item banks for domain-specific tests.

A sixth reason in favor of domain-specific tests is the possibility of using them for different purposes (i.e. assessment functions), e.g., assessment of entrance level, of progress and certification. Further, it allows to focus on different dimensions that extend beyond the content level.

Finally, there is the trend towards internationalization of higher education and co-operation between European universities. In this respect, domain-specific tests enable comparisons of individual students and comparisons of institutions to be made.

The Economics DS-KST

A domain-specific knowledge state test (DS-KST) was administered to the research sample. This test consists of 154 items. The test covers the whole domain of economics to be studied in the university courses. This test consists of multiple-choice questions which can be answered with true/false or 'I don't know'(?). The ?-alternative is taken as a third alternative in order to prevent guessing. The test was developed by a team of domain experts who made sure the test clearly represents - to a very large extent - the domain. The test can be considered reliable since its alpha-coefficient is .93. This high reliability level (Cronbach's α-coefficient) indicates that the test is homogeneous at the content level. The University of Maastricht has a wealth of experience in constructing tests, especially tests associated with end terms. Our DS Knowledge State Test was constructed as a representative random test of items selected from the item bank of the Economics Faculty of the University of Limburg. The items in the data bank are classified in nine subject areas: reporting, financing, organization, marketing, macro-economics, micro-economics, public finances, international economic affairs, and behavioral and social sciences. The 154 items were reviewed - separately - by the members of the research group. In reviewing the items, the researchers attempted to classify each item along each of the 13 dimensions, discussed earlier.

In relation to three dimensions the researchers encountered too many difficulties (Table 2) :

- The Propositional Parameters dimension could not be applied since all items consist of more than one node. But this dimension was helpful as a base to determine the Node Relation parameter of an item.
- The parameters along the Cognitive Complexity dimension were too vague and not defined at an operational level to be applied consistently. Moreover, they implied a reformulation of the items, which was not possible.
- The Layers of Knowledge dimension was felt to be a duplicate of the Behavioral Level dimension.

Table 2
Applying Profile Dimensions - Success or Failure

Profile Dimensions	Success / Failure
Economics Subdomains Dimension	+
Curriculum Dimension	+
Curriculum Accent Dimension	+
Propositional Dimension	-
Node Relation Dimension	+
Cognitive Complexity Dimension	-
Behavioral Dimension	+
Content Dimension	+
Epistemological Dimension	+
Layers Of Knowledge Dimension	-
Number Of Propositions Dimension	+
Information Level Dimension	+
Representation Level Dimension	+

+ = application successful, inter-rater reliability >.8
- = application failed, inter-rater reliability >.8

In relation to the other ten dimensions an inter-rater reliability $> .8$ ($p < .01$) was obtained. If there was a discussion in relation to the categorization of a specific item along a dimension, the discussion resulted in a consensus on the final classification of the item. In the remainder of this chapter, only the ten dimensions which seemed to be useful and reliable will be used for further analysis. Grouping the items along the knowledge profile dimension helped to calculate specific subscores. To compare the mean total subscores, the individual subscores were calculated as %-scores. The test, which covered the whole domain of economics, was set at a level which should be attained by the end of the second year of university studies. The heterogeneity of the examinees is so great that a test at beginners level would not reveal all the differences between the students. After all, it can be assumed that students with years of working experience in, for instance, the financial sector, or students who have obtained other academic (WO) or higher vocational education (HBO) diplomas will have advanced further than the beginners level in certain areas, and may achieve a score approximating the final economist level. In other words, because some students have already gained a great deal of experience in a working environment or have already attained a relatively high educational level, a test set at beginners level (final VWO level) would not be able to measure some of the prior knowledge state.

Data Collection

A test - consisting of 154 items and called the Domain-Specific Knowledge State Test (DS KST) - was administered to the 627 economics students of the University of Maastricht and the Dutch Open University, starting to study economics.

Data Analysis

After screening and reorganizing the items, the raw item scores were used as the base for calculating new subscores for each parameter along each dimension. To be able to compare the parameter subscores, mean percentage scores were calculated. Further screening of the data reveals that:
- There are no missing data.
- The large standard deviations might imply that the distribution of the scores is not normal (Skewness, Kurtosis) and that the distributions are influenced by outliers. The Kurtosis-values vary between -.63 and .98. Skewness-values vary between .08 and .88. Both measures suggest acceptable distributions of the data. To check multi-variate normality, box-plots of the data have been screened. They reveal there are extremes and outliers, but their number remains restricted. Moreover, outliers are expected (given the fact that we measure mastery of prior knowledge) and considered part of the particular distribution of our data. They are properly part of the population from which we intend to sample.
- Analysis of the correlation matrix reveals high r-values, but never > .8 which implies that all distinctive variables are non-redundant and do not measure comparable issues[i]. Multi-collinearity is therefore not a problem.
- Homogeneity of variance-covariance matrices is a necessary assumption if we compare the subscores along the different dimensions. Calculation of Cochran's C and Bartlett-Box F and their respective significance-levels, indicate that this assumption is not violated.

When validating the different knowledge profile dimensions, two approaches will be adopted : (1) an analysis of the extent to which the variables along the dimensions provide information about different components of prior knowledge; (2) an analysis of the discriminatory power of the dimensions to make apparent prior knowledge differences between student sub-populations.

In view of the first approach, a distinction is to be made between hierarchical and non-hierarchical dimensions. Hierarchical dimensions imply consecutive intercorrelations between the variables. This will be evaluated by applying multiple linear regression techniques. Non-hierarchical dimensions imply low correlations between the dimension variables. This will be evaluated by analysis of the correlation matrix.

THE VALIDITY OF THE NON-HIERARCHICAL DIMENSIONS

Economics Subdomain Dimension

The economics-subdomains reflect a rather practical subdivision of the economics domain in view of educational purposes. It is therefore to be foreseen that the mean percentage scores for the different economics subjects correlate to a certain extent (all r-coefficients are statistically significant at the 1% level)[ii], since this subdivision does not (and cannot) reflect an absolute and objective split-up of the economics domain (Table 3).

The data in Table 3 confirm our expectations. The different economics subtopics are intercorrelated. If we concentrate only on the r-coefficients > .6, we get the following picture (Figure 5).

Table 3
Correlation Matrix Subdomain-dimension

	1	2	3	4	5	6	7	8	9
1. Report	1.0	.63	.58	.55	.42	.47	.37	.35	.44
2. Finance		1.0	.68	.63	.55	.52	.50	.50	.51
3. Organ			1.0	.68	.49	.48	.47	.44	.48
4. Market				1.0	.54	.51	.49	.47	.50
5. Macro					1.0	.66	.56	.57	.51
6. Micro						1.0	.48	.54	.52
7. Public							1.0	.56	.45
8. International								1.0	.47
9. Behavior									1.0

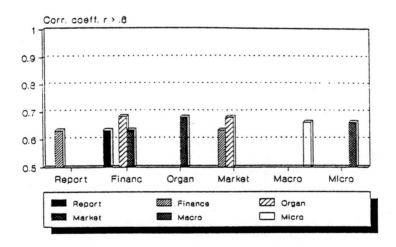

Figure 5. Correlation Structure Economics Subdomain-dimension

The six following subtopics are highly intercorrelated : Report, Finance, Organ, Market, Macro & Micro. This can be due to a high degree of content-links between these economics subdomains or the fact that mastery of a particular subdomain explicitly builds on the mastery of another domain. This is particularly important in relation to the subdomains Finance and Marketing.

A linear stepwise regression analysis[iii] of Finance on Report, Macro and Organ, using the mean percentage scores of these subdomains, indicated that 50.3 % of the variance in the Finance is accounted for by these three subdomains. Similarly, stepwise regression from Organ & Finance on Marketing reveals that 51.6 % of the variance in the Marketing mean score is accounted for by the scores of Organ & Finance. The interdependence among the subdomains can be taken into account when setting up learning activities or guidance initiatives for students.

An alternative interpretation of the correlation coefficients links the mastery of the different economics subdomains to students' previous experiences with the particular subtopics in their secondary education. A subpopulation of beginner university students may have received an introduction to certain economics domains, such as micro- and macro-economics and reporting (accountancy). The subsequent high scores for these subtopics in the prior knowledge test are therefore expected to correlate to a certain extent.

Curriculum Dimension

In the prior knowledge test, the test items were subdivided into two course level sets : Level 1 grouping items that evaluate mastery at the first year level and Level 2 that evaluate the mastery at the second year level. The mastery of both the level 1 (M = 30.64) and the level 2 (M=22.31) items is restricted. As expected, the level 2 total subscore is the lowest, indicating the higher difficulty level of this set of items. Content experts indicate that mastery of level 1 items is, to a certain degree, related to mastery of level 2 items since part of the level 2 course content builds on the mastery of level 1 items. This is confirmed by linear regression analysis. This analysis indicates that the level 2 mean % score of the students helps to explain 38.2 % of the variance in the level 2 mean percentage scores[iv].

Curriculum Accent Dimension

A generally accepted subdivision in economics is splitting up the domain into general economics and quantitative economics. Our prior knowledge test, reflects this subdivision only to a very limited extent since only 15 items can be classified as quantitative economics questions whereas 139 items concentrate on the mastery of general economics knowledge. It is therefore predictable that the test results along this dimension will not be very useful. Analysis of the mean scores (M_{quant} = 24.36; $M_{general}$= 28.20) and standard deviations (SD_{quant} = 13.77; $SD_{general}$ = 12.80) indicates that the students master the two types of economics knowledge to a comparable extent. Moreover, the intercorrelation between both measures is rather high (r =.62**). The subdivision between quantitative and general economics does therefore not sufficiently separate knowledge components.

Node Relation Dimension

The correlation display in Figure 6 clearly indicates that most parameters along this dimension can be clearly separated from each other. The property parameter is highly correlated with the initiate (r =.64**) and the consequence (r =.85**) parameter.

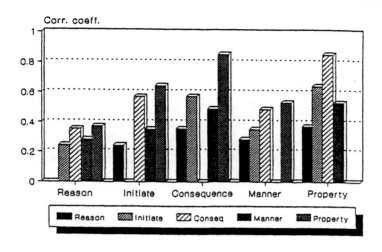

Figure 6. Node Relation Dimension - Correlation Structure

Number of Propositions Dimension

Since the number of propositions in test items can be considered as a measure comparable to difficulty levels, a gradual decrease in the mean scores for the three variables on this dimension is expected. The data confirm our expectations ($M_{propos1}$=27.18; $M_{propos2}$=13.63; $M_{propos3}$=6.93). Analysis of the correlation matrix reveals striking results (all r-coefficients are statistically significant, $p < .001$).

Table 4
Correlation Matrix : Number of Propositions

	1	2	3
1. <5 propositions	1.0	.76	.80
2. >4<10 propositions		1.0	.76
3. >9 propositions			1.0

The results in Table 4 and Figure 7 can be interpreted as follows: Students who are able to solve items, consisting of >9 propositions (3) are able to solve items consisting of a number of proposition > 5 < 10 (2) and are certainly able of solving items consisting of < 5 propositions (1). This is confirmed by a linear regression analysis: The scores for items with > 9 propositions explain 64.3 % of the variance in the scores of items with < 5 propositions. If we add the scores for items with > 4 < 9 propositions to the regression equation, up to 70 % of the variance is accounted for.

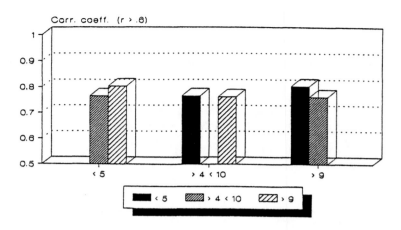

Figure 7. Intercorrelation Between Mean Percentage Scores for Number of
Propositions

Information Level Dimension

As explained earlier, items with a stem are similar in that the spatial and logical
distance between the basic information and the question part of the item is greater
than in items without a stem. To a certain extent, this dimension can be compared to
the number of propositions dimension.

It is expected that items with a stem are more difficult for students than those
without a stem. This is confirmed by the data when comparing the mean percentage
scores and SD ($M_{with\ stem}$ = 29.92; $M_{without}$ = 39.32; $SD_{with\ stem}$ = 13.45;
$SD_{without}$ = 19.67). This is also confirmed by the analysis of the correlation
matrix. Both variables are highly correlated (r = .82**). This can be explained as
follows: The students able to solve items with a stem are, to a great extent, able to
solve items without a stem. Linear regression confirms this hypothesis: The mean
percentage scores for the items with a stem explain 68% of the variance in the scores
for items without a stem.

VALIDATING HIERARCHICAL DIMENSIONS

Six dimensions have been identified as being hierarchical (Table 1) and four of
these seemed to be applicable (Table 2). As explained above hierarchical dimensions
imply consecutive intercorrelations between the parameters along the dimensions.
This can be evaluated by applying multiple linear regression techniques.

Behavioral Dimension

Figure 8 clearly indicates features of the hierarchical nature of this dimension,
although the highest correlations are observed in relation to items measuring the
mastery of items at insight-level (insight-apply = .72**; insight-know = .79**). The

latter fact is consistent with earlier validations of this dimension as done by Bloom, i.e., the taxonomic classification of Bloom: knowledge - comprehension - application - analysis - synthesis and evaluation. Keeves (1988, p. 346), for example, refers to a validation by Ebel, Hill and Horn.

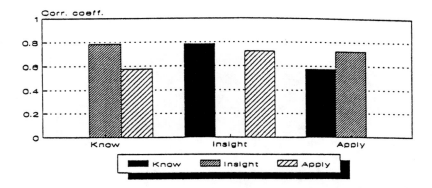

Figure 8. Behavioral Dimension - Correlation Structure

The three lowest levels, knowledge, comprehension and application, are comparable to our three first behavioral levels and are found to be hierarchical. Higher up in the hierarchy a branching takes place. If we extend our analysis to a regression analysis in which we evaluate the interrelations between the three consecutive behavioral levels, we get the following picture as presented in Table 5.

Table 5
Regression Analysis Behavioral Dimension

Independent Variable	Dependent Variable	% Variance Explained
Know	Insight	61%
Know , Insight	Apply	52.2%

When entering the parameters know and insight in the regression equation, the contribution of the parameter know is considered too low[v] and therefore excluded from the regression equation.

The results in Table 5 help to confirm the assumptions about the hierarchical nature of this dimension since the preceding parameter(s) always help to explain the major part of the variance in the mean percentage scores for the subsequent parameter along the dimension.

Content Dimension

From Figure 9, it can be concluded that the correlation coefficients increase along the consecutive parameters of this dimension. This can be considered as a first indicator to support the hierarchical nature of this dimension. Only in relation to the parameter methods is there a minor decrease in the *r*-values.

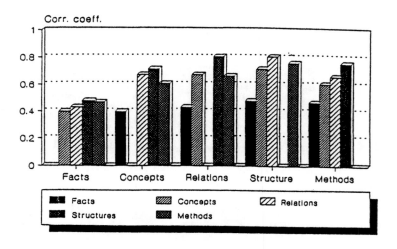

Figure 9. Content Dimension - Correlation Structure

The results in Table 6 are very consistent. At the consecutive levels, the hierarchy between facts - concepts - relations and structures is followed. In the second column the letters and their order of appearance refer to the pattern in which the independent variables help to explain the variance in the dependent variable. This order always follows the supposed hierarchy. Only at the skills-level, is there a deviant structure. This suggests that skills might be of a more general and complex nature than facts, concepts, relations and structures.

Table 6
Regression Analysis Content Dimension

Independent Variables	Dependent Variables	% Variance Explained
(F)acts	Concepts	15.5% F
(F)acts - (C)oncepts	Relations	47.9% C F
(F)acts - (C)oncepts - (R)elations	Structures	71.0% R C F
(F)acts - (C)oncepts - (R)elations - (S)tructures	Methods	59.6% S F C R

Epistemological Dimension

As explained earlier, this dimension can be considered as a combination of the behavioral and content dimension. The structure is especially based on the assumption that lower behavioral parameters tend to be linked with lower content parameters (e.g., knowledge of a fact) and that higher behavioral parameters tend to be linked with higher content parameters (e.g., application of a theory). This mixture of two hierarchical dimensions might impose difficulties in recognizing in terms of their interaction. The correlation matrix, for example, is not helpful in recognizing - at first sight - the hierarchical structure. As can be seen in Figure 10, there are several high correlations between the lower and higher parameters along this dimension. Nevertheless, the highest correlations are observed when the distance between a high parameter and another one along the dimension is small (e.g., between implem and logical) and the lowest correlations are observed when the distance between a high parameter and another one is large (e.g., between implem and kident). A regression analysis in which the parameters are evaluated in terms of their explanatory power for the consecutive parameters yields the following picture as presented in Table 7.

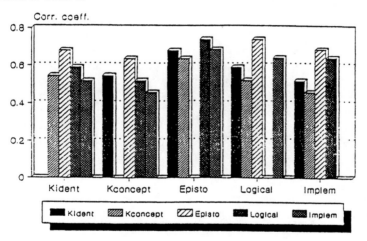

Figure 10. Epistemological Dimension - Correlation Structure

Table 7
Regression Analysis - Epistemological Dimension

Independent Variables	Dependent Variable	% Explained Variance
(Ki)dent	(Kc)oncept	29.7%
(Ki)dent - (Kc)oncept	(E)pisto	56% KiKc
(Ki)dent - (Kc)oncept - (E)pisto	(L)ogical	56% EKi
(Ki)dent - (Kc)oncept - (E)pisto - (L)ogical	(I)mplem	50.7% EL

The regression analysis confirms the former preliminary conclusions. The hierarchy is disturbed but still present. The proportion of the variance in the consecutive parameters is always explained by the former parameters with the shortest distance along the dimension. Moreover, the proportion of explained variance is >50%. Lower level parameters are sometimes excluded from the regression equation.

Representation Level Dimension

Figure 11 reveals high intercorrelations between all parameters and the text parameter. This is to be expected since the test items are never based solely on concrete, schematic or symbolic information. The items are a priori based on textual information which is supported, enhanced, enriched or supplemented with information of another nature. Nevertheless it is remarkable that the mean percentage scores for the subsequent parameters decrease from 36.58% to 22.47%, suggesting higher difficulty levels for the items based on higher order representation levels.

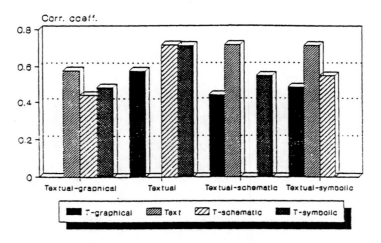

Figure 11. Representation Level Dimension - Correlation Structure

Table 8 confirms the expected disturbance of the hierarchical nature by the predominance of the textual representation mode in most items. The text parameter is always the parameter responsible for the highest proportion of the variance in the subsequent parameter.

Table 8
Regression Analysis Representation Level Dimension

Independent Variables	Dependent Variable	% Explained Variance
(C)oncret	(T)ext	33.0 %
(C)oncret - (T)ext	(Sc)heme	51.0 % T
(C)oncret - (T)ext - (Sc)heme	(Sy)mbol	51.6 % T C

THE DISCRIMINATORY POWER OF THE KNOWLEDGE PROFILE DIMENSIONS: DIFFERENCES BETWEEN STUDENTS STUDYING IN DIFFERING UNIVERSITY CONTEXTS

To validate the ten knowledge profile dimensions according to our second approach, their power to make explicit differences in prior knowledge between subpopulations of students was tested. Students studying the same course in differing university contexts, all part of the earlier mentioned sample, were investigated.

Students have an option to choose from a variety of university contexts and educational approaches at university level (e.g., problem centered approach, experiential learning, distance education, etc.). A relatively new development (since 1985) in this perspective is the provision of open and distance university education by the Dutch Open University (OU). The question can be raised whether this new university setting is just another higher education institution enriching the variety of already existing provisions or whether the Open University answers the need of (a) specific student population(s); e.g. second chance, older students, female students, handicapped people, foreign students, post-university students. A way to look for answers to this question is to analyze - by interviews, questionnaires, etc. - demographic variables of the actual student population of the OU.

Another approach goes beyond these surface variables and analyzes the prior knowledge of the students opting for the OU in more detail. The research question resulting from this approach is whether the prior knowledge of the students, opting for this study context, is different from students studying at a regular university. Making use of the ten knowledge profile dimensions, an extensive analysis has been executed on research data of students studying economics at the Dutch Open University (OU) and students studying economics at the University of Maastricht (RL) where a problem centered approach towards education is adopted.

When comparing knowledge profiles from different student samples, a comparison of the mean results for the different parameters along a dimension is not possible using univariate statistics. A univariate analysis of variance (see Dochy, 1992) does not take into account the intercorrelations between the different parameters along the profile dimensions. These intercorrelations are important (although not making the specific variables redundant) and can be explained at the theoretical level as clarified elsewhere. A multivariate analysis of variance is needed to refine our analysis and to look for more conclusive information about the differences in prior knowledge state between OU and RL students. A multivariate analysis can take these intercorrelations into account. Profile analysis[vi] is an extension of multivariate analysis and is especially appropriate and helpful to evaluate the parameter structure in relation to each profile dimension when comparing subpopulations. Several tests are available in profile analysis. Of principal interest - for our purposes - is the parallelism test which helps to answer the question whether the profiles of two subpopulations are parallel or not. At the theoretical level, the flatness test might be relevant too, since this test controls the similarity of responses for the different parameters along one dimension, independent of groups or subgroups. This test helps to support the validity of the different dimensions since the results indicate whether or not the dimensions/parameters are helpful to specify differences in the mastery of different components of the prior knowledge state. A profile analysis will be performed on the complex of parameters in relation to each dimension. The grouping variable for this analysis is university.

The SPSS-PC+ MANOVA procedure was used for our profile analysis.

Before the profile analysis was executed, a control of underlying assumptions was done. Profile analysis implies that specific assumptions about the quality of the research data are met [no missing data, comparable sample sizes, (multivariate) normal distributions, no outliers, homogeneity of variance-covariance, multicollinearity]. Therefore, data were screened to reveal missing data, control of sample sizes was done, an evaluation of the homogeneity of variance-covariance matrices based on Cochran's C and the Bartlett-Box F test was performed, an evaluation of assumptions about multivariate normality took place, boxplots of the mean submeasures for each dimension were screened, and finally multicollinearity was tested with the Bartlett test of sphericity. In general we concluded that assumptions were met in order to execute a profile analysis on the research data available. The main hypothesis of this analysis is: OU students and RL students differ in terms of parameters along the knowledge profile dimensions.

Profile Analysis: Parallelism Test

Table 9 presents an overview of the results for the parallelism test. This helps to answer the question whether the two different student groups have parallel or non-parallel profiles. Parallelism is the primary question addressed by profile analysis. Figure 12 represents the knowledge profiles of both university populations for the content dimension.

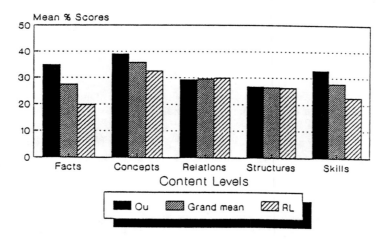

Figure 12. Content Knowledge Profile (Comparison OU & RL)

In relation to each profile dimension, Wilks' Lambda (Λ) was calculated and p-level determined. In Table 9, Wilks' Λ is not reported in relation to three dimensions (marked with *). This is because these dimensions only contain two variables; in these cases a test of significance for Hotelling's T using the unique sums of squares was calculated, checking the interaction of the independent variable (university) and the two dependent variables on the specific dimensions. The data in Table 9 are helpful to detect specific significant differences between OU and RL-students. The intermediate conclusion of non-significant differences between OU-students and RL-students, based on analysis of the overall economics-score (F= 3.75, p= .054), can be revisited by the refined breakdown of the profile analysis results. There are seven knowledge profile dimensions which are helpful to illuminate significant differences between both student populations.

Table 9
Profile Analysis Data for the Parallelism Test

Profile Dimension	Wilks' Λ	or F	p
Economics subdomains	.59		.00
Curriculum level*		44.24*	.00
Curriculum accent*		0.13*	.72
Node relation	.78		.00
Behavioral	.89		.00
Content	.67		.00
Epistemological	.75		.00
Information level*		0.00*	.98
Number of propositions	.98		.16
Representation level	.83		.00

A further analysis of non-parallel profiles can help to identify those parameters along the specific dimensions that contribute most to the differences between the two subpopulations (RL and OU). In Table 10 the results of the discriminant analyses are shown. Wilks' Λ can, in this context, be interpreted as the proportion of variance not explained by the group differences. In the fourth column of the table, we derived from this value the proportion of variability explained ((1-Λ) * 100) by the group differences resulting from the independent variable university.

Table 10
Results of the Discriminant Analyses

Profile Dimension	Wilks' Λ	p	% explained
Economics subdomains	.54	.000	46%
Curriculum level*	.80	.000	20%
Node relation	.75	.000	25%
Behavioral	.85	.000	15%
Content	.63	.000	37%
Epistemological	.71	.000	29%
Representation level	.80	.000	20%

The discriminant analysis can be completed by calculating structure coefficients to determine the discriminatory power of the separate parameters along a knowledge profile dimension. Since the subvalues on each profile dimension are highly intercorrelated, we cannot use raw or standardized discriminant function coefficients. The highly correlated variables share the discriminant weights. Therefore, our interpretation is based on the structure coefficients which are less likely to be influenced by these intercorrelations. The results of this analysis are shown in Table 11.

Table 11
Overview of Structure Coefficients

Dimension	Parameter	Structure Coefficient
Economics subdomains	Reporting	.49
	Financing	.30
	Organization	.40
Curriculum level	Level 2	.64
Node relation	Initiate	-.76
	Property	-.29
Behavioral	Apply	.74
Content	Factual	.51
	Methods	.45
Epistemological	Implementational analysis	-.51
	Kident	-.40
Representation level	Textual-symbolic	-.44
	Textual-graphical	.42

A structure coefficient indicates the correlation between a parameter and the discriminant function. High values (> .35) indicate important discriminant effects (only the relevant ones are given). Table 11 demonstrates that some parameters have structure coefficients >.5 . If we combine these results with those dimensions that are statistically sufficiently significant to differentiate between populations, we can conclude that the two university populations can especially be differentiated along the following two knowledge profile dimensions: the content level dimension and the epistemological level dimension.

Profile Analysis: Flatness Test

Is the mastery of the prior knowledge state, as defined by the parameters along a dimension different, independent of the groups, i.e., is there a within-subjects main effect? In other words, do students master the prior knowledge state in a similar way as defined by the different parameters along a dimension? This question is especially relevant for parallel profiles, since in non-parallel profiles at least one parameter is not flat. If the flatness test is non-significant, then the profiles are not helpful to clarify or detect differences in the mastery of different components of the prior knowledge state. The results of the flatness test are therefore also relevant in determining the validity of the knowledge profile dimensions. The results of the flatness test can be found in Table 12. For each dimension Wilks' Λ has been calculated, with the exception of the three dimensions where only two parameters are available; there the F-value is reported (marked with *).

All dimensions result in non-flat knowledge profiles. This implies that all dimensions are helpful to identify a specific structure in the mastery of the prior knowledge state. Following this structure, mastery of certain components[vii] of the prior knowledge state is better than that of other components.

Table 12
Results of the Flatness Test in Profile Analysis

Profile Dimension	Wilks' Λ or	F	p
Economics subdomains	.39		.000
Curriculum level*		34.14*	.000
Curriculum accent*		23.36*	.000
Node relation	.69		.000
Behavioral	.83		.000
Content	.63		.000
Epistemological	.58		.000
Number of propositions	.19		.000
Information level*		111.54*	.000
Representation level	.74		.000

Although the overall prior knowledge mean percentage score for the economics domain does not significantly differ between the OU- and the RL-student sample, a univariate analysis of the knowledge profiles sheds light on obvious and significant differences in the complex composition of components of prior knowledge. These results are confirmed and reinforced by the results of the profile analysis (multivariate analysis of variance). The results of the profile analysis (parallelism test and discriminant analysis) help to reveal specific and significant differences between the profiles of both student populations. Seven of the ten knowledge profile dimensions appear to be of relevance (Table 11). The content dimension and the epistemological dimension were particularly helpful to describe these differences. A further extension of our profile analysis (flatness test) yields additional evidence to support the validity of the knowledge profile dimensions, since all profiles are non-flat. This implies that all dimensions are helpful in identifying a specific structure in the mastery of prior knowledge. When using this structure, the mastery of certain components of prior knowledge is better than that of other components.

CONCLUSIONS

In this chapter we have introduced knowledge profiles in the form of graphs of scores of a group or individuals on a prior knowledge state test. We defined several dimensions on which knowledge profiles can be based and tried to look beyond the subject-matter level. The first goal of this analysis was to find out the extent to which the variables along the dimensions are informative about different components of prior knowledge. A second goal was to determine the discriminatory power of the knowledge profile dimensions to make apparent prior knowledge differences between student sub-populations.

To validate the different knowledge profile dimensions, the parameters were related to the knowledge state test items and we analyzed the extent to which the parameters along the dimensions are informative about the components of the prior knowledge state. The non-hierarchical dimensions suggest that they do relate to different components of the prior knowledge state. This is further supported by the profile analyses (flatness tests) when comparing different populations. The other five dimensions were indeed shown to be hierarchical, although to different extents. Moreover, we searched for other evidence to validate our knowledge profiles by looking at the discriminatory power of the dimensions in detecting the prior knowledge state differences between student populations. RL and OU students do not differ in their mean percentage scores, but profile analyses revealed significant differences on the knowledge profiles. Knowledge profile dimensions that are especially promising in these terms seem to be curriculum level dimension, representation level dimension, epistemological dimension, content dimension, economics subdomain dimension, as well as the behavioral dimension, curriculum accent dimension, information level dimension and the number of propositions dimension.

The results show that there are specific and significant differences between knowledge profiles of student sub-populations. A further extension of our profile analysis, i.e., the flatness test, offers further evidence to support the validity of the knowledge profile dimensions, since all profiles are non-flat. This implies that all dimensions are helpful in identifying a specific structure in the mastery of prior knowledge.

These findings are of importance since they model and operationalize a new and promising approach towards the analysis of prior knowledge. We believe that in situations where there are significant differences in the prior knowledge state of specific subpopulations, the profile dimensions can be helpful in detecting and analyzing the strengths and weaknesses of the students involved. This might be a promising starting point for differentiated diagnostic and guidance approaches.

NOTES

i   Tabachnik & Fidell (1990, p. 87) use a limit of $r > .9$ to distinguish redundant variables.

ii   When indicating significance levels in the next part of this text ** indicates $p < .01$ and * indicates $p < .05$.

iii When regression analysis is executed, the residuals too are analyzed in order to detect violations of regression assumptions (linearity, normality of the distribution of the dependent variable, constant variance). When violations were detected, they are reported.

iv   When executing linear regression analysis, basic assumptions have been checked. No violations have been detected, for instance the distribution of the residuals is normal.

v   The limit of PIN=.05 is reached.

vi   When using profile analysis as a substitute for univariate repeated measures ANOVA, the parallelism test is the test of interaction.

vii The concept components refers to a specific parameter along a knowledge profile dimension.

REFERENCES

Alexander, P. A. (1992). Domain knowledge: Evolving issues and emerging concerns. *Educational Psychologist, 27,* 33-51.

Alexander, P. A., & Dochy, F.J.R.C. (1994). Adults views about knowing and believing. In R. Garner & P.A. Alexander (Eds.), *Beliefs about text and about instruction with text.* Hillsdale, NJ: Lawrence Erlbaum Associates.

Alexander, P. A., & Judy, J. E. (1988). The interaction of domain-specific and strategic knowledge in academic performance. *Review of Educational Research, 58,* 375-404.

Alexander, P. A., & Kulikowich, J. M. (1992, April). *Learning from physics text.* Paper presented at the annual meeting of the American Educational Research Association, San Francisco.

Alexander, P.A., Kulikowich, J.A., & Schulze, S.K. (1992, July). *How subject-matter knowledge affects recall and interest.* Paper presented at the XXV International Congress of Psychology, Brussels.

Alexander, P. A., Pate, E. P., Kulikowich, J. M., Farrell, D. M., & Wright, N. L. (1989). Domain-specific and strategic knowledge: Effects of training on students of differing ages or competence levels. *Learning and Individual Differences, 1,* 283-325.

Alexander, P. A., Schallert, D. L., & Hare, V. C. (1991). Coming to terms: How researchers in learning and literacy talk about knowledge. *Review of Educational Research, 61,* 315-343.

Ausubel, D.P. (1968). *Educational Psychology: A cognitive view.* New York: Holt, Rinehart and Winston.

Bloom, B.S., (1976). *Human characteristics and school learning.* New York: McGraw-Hill.

Boekaerts, M. (1979). *Towards a theory of learning based on individual differences.* Ghent: Communication and Cognition.

Brachman, R.J., & Schmolze, J.G., (1985). An overview of the KL-ONE Knowledge Representation System. *Cognitive Science, 9,* 171-216.

Carey, S. (1985). *Conceptual change in childhood.* Cambridge, MA: MIT Press.

Chase, W. G., & Simon, H. A. (1973). Perception in chess. *Cognitive Psychology, 4,* 55-81.

Chi, M. T., Glaser, R., & Rees, E. (1982). Prior knowledge in problem solving. In R. J. Sternberg (Ed.), *Advances in the psychology of human intelligence* (pp. 7-76). Hillsdale, NJ: Erlbaum.

Clancey, W.J. (1983). The epistemology of a rule-based expert system - a framework for explanation. *Artificial Intelligence, 20,* 215-251.

De Corte, E., Geerligs, T., Lagerweij, N., Peeters, J., & Vandenberghe, R. (1976). *Beknopte didaxologie.* Groningen: Wolters-Noordhoff.

De Corte, E. (1990). Acquiring and teaching cognitive skills: A state-of-the-art of theory and research. In P.J. Drenth, J.A. Sergeant, & R.J. Takens (Eds.), *European perspectives in psychology* (Vol. 1, pp.237-263). London: John Wiley.

De Corte, E., Lodewijks, H., Parmentier, R., & Span, P. (1987). *Learning and instruction: European research in an international context.* Oxford: Pergamon.

Dochy, F.J.R.C. (1988). *The Prior Knowledge State of students and its facilitating effect on learning.* OTIC research report 1.2. Heerlen :Center for Educational Technology and Innovation.

Dochy, F.J.R.C. (1992). *Assessment of prior knowledge as a determinant for future learning: The use of knowledge state tests and knowledge profiles.* Utrecht/London: Lemma B.V./Jessica Kingsley Publishers.

Dochy, F.J.R.C. (1993, April). *An alternative to the assessment of domain-specific knowledge: Profile analysis.* Paper presented at the Annual Conference of the American Educational Research Association, Atlanta.

Dochy, F. (1994). Prior knowledge and learning. In T. Husen and N. Postlethwaite (Eds.), *International encyclopedia of education,* second edition (pp. 4698-4702). London/New York: Pergamon.

Dochy, F. (1995). Investigating the use of knowledge profiles in a flexible learning environment: Analysing students prior knowledge states. In S. Vosniadou , E. De Corte & H. Mandl (Eds.), *Psychological and educational foundations of technology-based learning environments.* NATO ASI Series F, Special Programme AET. Berlin/New York: Springer-Verlag.

Dochy, F.J.R.C., & Alexander, P.A. (1995). Mapping Prior Knowledge: a Framework for Discussion among Researchers. *European Journal for Psychology of Education, 10* (2), 123-145.

Dochy, F.J.R.C., Bouwens, M.R.J., Wagemans, L.J.J.M., & Niestadt, D.W. (1991). *The role of subject-oriented prior knowledge. A study of the impact of personal and contextual variables on success in an economics course as indicators of prior knowledge.* Ex post facto research 2. OTIC research report 25. Heerlen : Center for Educational Technology and Innovation.

Dochy, F.J.R.C., & Steenbakkers, W.H.L. (1988). *Students views on prior knowledge.* OTIC research report 3.2. Heerlen : Center for Educational Technology and Innovation.

Dochy, F.J.R.C., & Valcke, M.M.A. (1992). *Knowledge profiles of economics and law students: An in-depth analysis of the prior knowledge state.* OTIC research report 34. Heerlen: Centre for Educational Technology and Innovation.

Dochy, F., Valcke, M., & Wagemans, L. (1991). Learning economics in higher education: An investigation concerning the quality and impact of prior knowledge. *Higher Education in Europe, 4,* 123 - 136.

Duffy, T.M., & Waller, R. (1985) (Eds.). *Designing usable texts.* Orlando: Academic Press.

Ennis, R. (1989). Critical thinking and subject specificity. *Educational Researcher, 18*(3), 4-10.

Ennis, R. (1990). The extent to which critical thinking is subject-specific: Further clarification. *Educational Researcher, 19* (4), 13 -16.

Glaser, R. (1984). Education and thinking: The role of knowledge. *American Psychologist, 39,* 93-104.

Glaser, R., & De Corte, E. (1992). Preface to the assessment of prior knowledge as a determinant for future learning.   In Dochy, F. J. R. C. (1992). *Assessment of prior knowledge as a determinant for future learning.* Utrecht/London: Lemma B.V./Jessica Kingsley Publishers.

Graesser, A.C. (1981). *Prose comprehension beyond the word.* New York: Springer-Verlag.

Groot, A.D. de (1946). *Het denken van den schaker* (Thinking of the chess player). Amsterdam: Noord-Hollandse Uitgeversmaatschappij.

Haertel, G.D., Walberg, H.J., & Weinstein, Th. (1983). Psychological models of educational performance: A theoretical synthesis of constructs. *Review of Educational Research, 53* (1), 75-91.

Keeves, J.P. (Ed.). (1988). *Educational research, methodology and measurement: An international handbook.* Oxford/New York: Pergamon.

Körkel, J. (1987). *Die Entwicklung von Gedächtnis- und Metagedächtnisleistungen in Abhängigkeit von bereichsspezifischen Vorkenntnissen.* Frankfurt: Peter Lang.

Lesgold, A. M., Feltovich, P. J., Glaser, R., & Wang, Y. (1981). *The acquisition of perceptual diagnosic skill in radiology.* Pittsburgh, PA: University of Pittsburgh, Learning Research and Development Center.

Letteri, C.A. (1980). Cognitive profile: Basic determinant of academic achievement. *The Journal of Educational Research, 4,* 195-198.

Letteri, C.A., & Kuntz, S.W. (1982, March). *Cognitive profiles: Examining self-planned learning and thinking styles.* Paper presented at the Annual American Educational Research Association Meeting, New York City.

Madaus, G.F., Woods, E.N., & Nuttal, R.L. (1973). A causal model analysis of Bloom's taxonomy. *American Educational Research Journal, 10,* 253-263.

Mayer, R.E. (1979). Twenty years of research on advance organizers. *Instructional Science, 8,* 133-167.

Mc Daniel, E. (1991). *Levels of cognitive complexity: A framework for the measurement of thinking.* Paper presented at the annual meeting of the AERA, Chicago.

Merrill, M.D. (1983). Component display theory. In Reigeluth, C.M. (Ed.), *Instructional-design models: An overview of the current status.* Hillsdale, N.J.: Erlbaum.

Parkerson, J.A., Lornax, R.G., Schiller, D.P., & Walberg, H.J. (1984). Exploring causal models of educational achievement. *Journal of Educational Psychology, 76* (4), 638-646.

Reigeluth, C.M., & Stein, F.S. (1983). The elaboration theory of instruction. In C.M. Reigeluth (Ed.), *Instructional-design models: An overview of the current status.* Hillsdale, N.J.: Erlbaum.

Shuell, T. J. (1986). Cognitive conceptions of learning. *Review of Educational Research, 56,* 411-436.

Sternberg, R. (1985a). *A triarchic theory of human intelligence.* Cambridge: Cambridge University Press.

Sternberg, R. (1985b). *Human abilities: An information processing approach.* New York : Freeman.

Tabachnick, B.G., & Fidell, L.S. (1989). *Using multivariate statistics.* New York: Harper & Row.

Tobias, S. (1994). Interest, prior knowledge and learning. *Review of Educational Research, 64* (1), 37-54.

Tuma, D.T., & Reif, F. (1980). *Problem solving and education: Issues in teaching and research.* Hillsdale, NJ: Erlbaum.

Twyman, M. (1985). Using pictorial language: A discussion of the dimensions of the problem. In T.M. Duffy, & R. Waller (Eds.), *Designing usable texts.* Orlando: Academic Press.

Voss, J.F., Greene, T.R., Post, T.A., & Penner, B.C. (1983). Problem-solving skill in the social sciences. In G.H. Bower (Ed.), *The psychology of learning and motivation: Advances in search and theory.* (pp. 165-213). New York: Academic Press.

Voss, J.F., Blais, J., Means, M.L., Greene, T.R., & Ahwesh, E. (1986). Informal reasoning and subject matter knowledge in the solving of economics problems of naive and novice individuals. *Cognition and Instruction, 3,* 269-302.

Wagemans, L.J.J.M., & Dochy, F.J.R.C. (1991). Principles in the use of experiential learning as a source of prior knowledge. *Distance Education, 12*, 85-108.

Wagemans, L.J.J.M., Valcke, M.M.A., & Dochy, F.J.R.C. (1992). *Comparing knowledge profiles of students at a distance teaching university and a regular university.* OTIC Research Report 36. Heerlen: Center for Educational Technology and Innovation.

Walker, C. H. (1987). Relative importance of domain knowledge and overall attitude on acquisition of domain-related information. *Cognition and Instruction, 4*, 25-42.

Weinert, F. (1989). The impact of schooling on cognitive development: One hypothetical assumption, some empirical results, and many theoretical implications. *EARLI News, 8*, 3-7.

Wolf, D., Bixby, J., Glenn, J., & Gardner, H. (1991). To use their minds well: investigating new forms of student assessment. *Review of Research in Education, 17*, 31-74.

How General are the Effects of Domain-Specific Prior Knowledge on Study Expertise as Compared to General Thinking Skills ?

Alexander Minnaert and
Piet J. Janssen

INTRODUCTION

Entrance selection of freshmen is not customary in Belgium. Due to this fact, failure rates of freshmen are relatively high (De Neve, 1991): 60% in Human Sciences, 51% in Biomedical Sciences, and 49% in Exact Sciences. In non-university higher education the outcomes are as dramatic. Apparently these freshmen do not appropriately assess their potentialities in starting their career at the higher education level. To improve psychological and educational insights into this so called "threshold" of the first year in higher education, a structural model of studying is designed that may explain these individual differences in academic achievement. It was applied in a specific department of a Belgian university.

To imitate the study task of a first year student, we designed a test which was presented as "an excursion into the domain of my future studies". The underlying theoretical framework was derived from Janssen's (1989) theory of studying as *the integration of learning and thinking on the basis of motivation.* We briefly outline the five constituent processes involved in studying as described by Janssen. The starting point is students' understanding of what is presented to them. This presupposes sufficient (domain-specific) prior knowledge. What is understood can be restructured, i.e., either the presented information has to fit into the available cognitive structures, or the structure has to be restructured, or a new structure has to be developed. Only in this way effective functioning becomes possible, leading to a more complete and deeper understanding of the study contents. The thinking involved in developing understanding can be serial, holistic, or both (versatile). The motivational component does not only integrate learning and thinking dynamically and efficiently in the stage of restructuring the knowledge base (because it ought to be done, or because it is in line with the student's personal values) but also controls and directs studying in order to master the study contents and to become an expert.

To enhance insight into the process of studying, this excursion was designed as an imitation of a first year student's task (Minnaert & Janssen, 1992a). A brief description of that study situation follows as far as this is relevant to the objectives of this contribution. Within a limited amount of time, students have to study a large amount of new information within their chosen domain. Depending on the curriculum completed in high school, on the domain-specific knowledge and on their intrinsic motivation, the acquisition of new information will be more or less successfully (accurately and rapidly) related to the cognitive structure already built. Its elaboration (transformation, in Ausubel's [1977] description of learning) implies a process of goal-oriented restructuring of the already available knowledge into a new, more complex structure. At this stage especially the learning process has to be integrated with two distinct thinking processes: serial thinking - a deep, stepwise analysis of one problem after another (hereafter called "analysis") - and holistic thinking, i.e., the search for a broad synthesis of different elements from distinguished themes ("synthesis"). Thinking and learning should be integrated on the basis of motivation in order to develop real expertise in subject matter. To evaluate the quality of the expertise obtained as a result of studying, an oral and/or written examination of the different courses in the study program takes place at the end of the academic year.

The information processing system has three stages: the acquisition stage in terms of speed of processing, the transformation stage, characterized by the goal-oriented control of processing, and the consolidation or master stage in terms of long-term expertise. Demetriou, Efklides and Platsidou (1993) already indicated in the architecture of the developing mind that the three components in the information processing system are interrelated. Their research results prove that the the speed of processing enhances the goal-oriented control of processing. In turn, the speed and control of processing facilitate the consolidation and retrieval of stored information. Translated to the process of studying, the theory of the processing system implies that the faster students act as processors, the more information they will be able to process within a limited amount of time, and consequently, the more efficient they will become in serial and holistic thinking, in analysis and synthesis. The more efficient they are in terms of speed and control of information processing, the better they will be in using the acquired and transformed information being consolidated in memory.

By implementing this study task on a small scale at the beginning of an academic year, we intend to examine the relative importance of study skills (analysis, synthesis, goal-oriented restructuring, etc.), domain-specific knowledge, domain-related interest, the curriculum completed in high school, and degree of general thinking skills, as determinants of success and progress in higher education. We assume that academic performance in higher education is influenced directly and/or indirectly by a combination of cognitive and motivational variables (see Figure 1). As a result, students should be able to realistically evaluate their future outcomes.

The focus of this chapter is on the duality of domain-specificity versus general heuristics theorems. In the literature of higher education we find evidence about the impact of domain-specific prior knowledge on problem solving and study behavior (Chi, Feltovich & Glaser, 1981; Decruyenaere & Janssen, 1989; Dochy, 1992; Glaser, 1984; Vosniadou & Brewer, 1987). This effect is also demonstrated in different study contexts (open university, regular courses) and fields of study (e.g., astronomy, economics, physics, psychology). Scepticism about the impact of general thinking skills (that would improve the ability to learn across many curriculum areas) without anchoring into domain-specific knowledge has already been expressed by many researchers (e.g., Alexander & Judy, 1988; Resnick, 1987; Weinert, Schrader & Helmke, 1990).

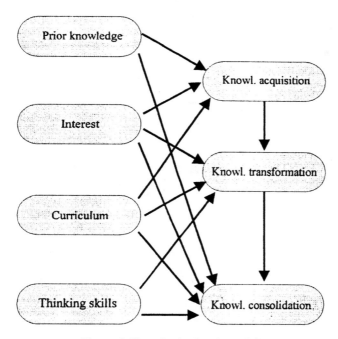

Figure 1. Hypothesized path-model.

When trying to unravel the duality, different hypotheses can be formulated. If domain-specificity refers to the same "general" information-processing components that intelligence tests appear to measure (Sternberg, 1985), the covariation of the variances between domain-specific prior knowledge and general thinking skills should be very high. If they have no information-processing component in common, we postulate that the correlation will not significantly differ from zero. In line with the sceptical view, we expect a moderate correlation between both factors, indicating a common as well as a specific source of determination. In light of this we predict a different effect of domain-specific prior knowledge and general thinking skills on study skills, according to our theoretical framework: prior knowledge facilitates the acquisition (assimilation) of new knowledge, while thinking skills enhance the transformation/restructuring of the knowledge base.

Domain-specific prior knowledge refers to structures of knowledge in terms of concepts, rules and algorithms within a specified field of knowledge. The acquisition of domain-related knowledge involves not only knowledge related to domain-specific names, concepts, symbols, data, formulas and their interrelations, but also to formal schemata in a specific domain (e.g., physical laws, grammar) and to a specific curriculum (facility to progress and to change one's study project, dissertation, work field). These knowledge structures should be developed over time and retrieved during each process of problem solving.

METHOD

Sample

In the first week of the 1986-1987 academic year, 169 freshmen in the Department of Psychology at the University of Leuven (i.e., 83% of the freshmen psychology population in that academic year) participated in our three-hours study skill test, and 158 of them also participated a few days later in a general thinking test within the context of another research project. In September 1991, 40% of these students graduated in time, 39% had dropped out and 21% were at that point lagging behind by one to three academic years. The structural model was tested on a sample of 150 students (40 men and 110 women) who participated in all the final exams at the end of their first year at the university.

Instruments

Our study skill test involves three different tests. A hierarchical *silent reading test* - ten texts on topics in the psychology study program plus appropriate multiple choice questions to be answered immediately after reading each text - was designed to measure speed of acquisition of new information and at the same time probed the thinking processes in deep-level learning: serial (analysis) and holistic thinking (synthesis). In order to reach a maximum of content validity in this silent reading test, we selected and adapted text fragments of different courses from the study program for the first two years. The variety in study program contents (courses on psychology, philosophy, statistics, physiology, etc.) is proportionally represented by different topics in our silent reading test. This variety demonstrates the content and face validity of the instrument. The students were also asked to evaluate their domain-related interest regarding each text separately.

Next, a *general information test* was presented to measure domain-specific prior knowledge in psychology, supposed to be incidentally picked up during the process of vocational choice. Recent media information about psychology (breadth of previous knowledge), domain-related information in the literature suggested as preparation before the start of the academic year (depth of previous knowledge), and curriculum information at students' disposal (previous knowledge related to structure), were the sources from which these domain-specific prior knowledge questions were constructed and formulated. The absence of explicit prerequisites about the amount, quality and content of prior knowledge in the field of psychology is due to the fact that almost no Belgian high schools offer courses on psychology.

Finally, all students took an *unannounced closed book exam* about the content of the silent reading texts studied before. This exam measures the domain-related expertise as developed while studying the hierarchical text contents. This latter implies a process of goal-oriented restructuring of the acquired new information into the cognitive structure already built up.

Procedure

We constructed reliable measurement scales within each test on the basis of principal factor analysis with varimax rotation of the items, followed by the application of a Gulliksen item analysis program (Verhelst & Vander Steene, 1972) thus for each of the scales.

To evaluate the measurement models and the structural equation model by the parameter estimation method of Maximum-Likelihood (ML), the computer program LISREL 7.20 was used (Jöreskog & Sörbom, 1989). Note that a direct effect in this equation model can be interpreted as a partial correlation coefficient. None of the observed variables used in the model did significantly depart from normality.

Variables

Three measurement scales were developed within the *silent reading test*. We pinpointed the two a priori defined problem solving thinking processes, namely analysis (n=18; KR-8=.70) and synthesis (n=13; KR-8=.67). In the rotated factor matrix the items for the third scale are all located at the end of the test; more specifically the questions of the last three texts load highly on it. The resemblance of the test to an academic year reveals the typicality of the limited time and speed related character of the study situation of students in Belgium. Therefore, we denominated this scale as speed and accuracy of information processing during silent reading (n=17; KR-8=.86).

The *general information test* generates three scales that each register a different aspect of domain-specific prior knowledge. The general prior knowledge scale (n=14; KR-8=.70) measures the understanding of common knowledge (spread via newspapers, television) about psychology (breadth of previous knowledge). We registered also the understanding of difficult scientific notions (n=9; KR-8=.65) in psychology (depth of previous knowledge). The third scale measures prior knowledge about the choice of domain, curriculum and university in general (n=8; KR-8=.70). Those items reflect the acquired information schemes that precede a responsible and efficient choice of course (previous knowledge as related to structure).

Two scales within the *closed book exam* were developed. The first reflects the speed and accuracy of information processing during the (re-)production (n=8; KR-8=.77). The second registers the long-term expertise (n=14; KR-8=.73) as developed in studying the texts. All of the questions in the exam were variants of the items used during the reading test to measure students' analysis and synthesis behavior.

Two *interest ratings* in the subject matter, as elicited by the content of the study material in the texts on social and differential psychology, were inserted in the model. These elicited motivation ratings were not only prototypical for psychology, but all students were able to study and evaluate both texts within the two hours time.

The quantification of the variable *curriculum completed in high school* is borrowed from a follow-up of 6000 Belgian school-leavers (Stinissen, 1987). We used the standardized loadings of each curriculum in high school on the function of discriminating the succesful from the non-succesful Human Sciences students in higher education as a whole.

A traditional *intelligence test* with verbal-numerical problem solving tasks (the Group Test of High-grade Intelligence by Alice Heim (1968)) was used as measure of general thinking skills. The results of this measure are taken from the ISSAD research project about problem solving in physics (Vanderlocht & Van Damme, 1990).

We inserted two measures of academic performance into the model. The *percentage of points obtained at the end of the first exam period in the first year* is considered as an index of academic success in the first year of higher education. Study progress in psychology is specified by the *study output after five academic years*. This variable takes into account the degrees obtained (special distinction; distinction; successful without distinction; failed), the time needed to get that degree (first or second exam period; after an extra year) and the stage of studies reached after five academic years (fifth, fourth, or third course year in psychology; drop out after the first, second, third or fourth academic year).

STATISTICAL ANALYSIS

Statistical Analysis of the Measurement Models

We tested the hypothesis of a simple structure matrix with unconstrained correlations between the latent factors *domain-specific prior knowledge, domain-related interest, curriculum completed in high school* and *general thinking skills*. The first model fits the data well (Table 1), indicating that the model cannot be rejected. Note the absence of a substantial correlation between domain-specific prior knowledge and domain-related interest, stressing the importance of both factors.

Measurement model II (Table 2) represents the hypothesis of a simple structure matrix with unconstrained correlations between the latent factors *speed and accuracy of study behavior, goal-oriented study skills* and *academic success and progress*. The ML-solution of measurement model II indicates that the model cannot be rejected on the basis of our data.

Statistical Analysis of the Structural Equation Model

The hypothetical model consists of four latent exogenous variables (domain-specific prior knowledge, domain-related interest, curriculum completed in high school, and general thinking skills) which are not explained by the model. The other variables are endogenous. The two measurement models were now combined into one model with structural relations between the latent factors.

According to our theory about studying (Janssen, 1989), the factors speed and accuracy in study behavior and goal-oriented study processes are influenced by the latent exogenous variables. The factor goal-oriented restructuring is also influenced directly by the speed factor. We considered success and progress in higher education to be determined by all the motivational and cognitive exogenous variables. We further hypothesized that goal-oriented restructuring has a direct effect on this academic performance.

The ML-solution of the LISREL model fits the observed data and cannot be rejected (χ^2=73.23, df=66, p=.253). The other indices of goodness-of-fit are also satisfactory: GFI=.936, AGFI=.898, RMSR=.050.

Table 1
ML-Solution of Measurement Model I (N=150)

| | Λ | | | | Θδ | | Φ | | |
	ξ1	ξ2	ξ3	ξ4			ξ1	ξ2	ξ3
Domain-specific prior knowledge									
general	.516	0*	0*	0*	.734	ξ2	.103		
difficult notions	.348	0*	0*	0*	.879	ξ3	.415	.223	
course, curriculum	.396	0*	0*	0*	.843	ξ4	.368	.361	.238
Domain-related interest in									
social psychology	0*	.712	0*	0*	.492				
differential psychology	0*	.531	0*	0*	.718				
Curriculum completed in									
high school	0*	0*	1*	0*	.000				
General thinking skills	0*	0*	0*	1*	.000				

Indices of Goodness-of-fit	χ^2=3.97	df=10	p=.949
	GFI=.993	AGFI=.979	RMSR=.030

Note. The values in italics are statistically significant: p<.05.   * : Fixed values

Table 2
ML-Solution of Measurement Model II (N=150)

| | Λ | | | Θδ | | Φ | |
	ξ1	ξ2	ξ3			ξ1	ξ2
Speed and accuracy							
during silent reading	.774	0*	0*	.400	ξ2	.476	
during (re)production	.855	0*	0*	.268	ξ3	.390	.610
Goal-oriented study processes							
analysis	0*	.595	0*	.646			
synthesis	0*	.276	0*	.924			
long-term expertise	0*	.842	0*	.291			
Study success and progress							
after the first year	0*	0*	.902	.186			
after five years	0*	0*	.932	.131			

Indices of Goodness-of-fit	χ^2=9.74	df=11	p=.554
	GFI=.982	AGFI=.954	RMSR=.034

Note. The values in italics are statistically significant: p<.05.   * : Fixed values

RESULTS AND INTERPRETATION

The structural equation model explains 56% (R=.748) of the variance in study success and study progress after five years (Figure 2). The structural equation parameters confirm the hypothesized effects of domain-specific prior knowledge, domain-related interest, curriculum completed in high school, general thinking skills, and goal-oriented restructuring study skills on study success and progress in psychology. About 57% of the variance in goal-oriented restructuring study skills are explained by the model.

Furthermore, the results (see also Table 3) confirm the significant direct effect of domain-specific prior knowledge on the speed and accuracy of study behavior ($p<.001$) and an indirect effect on goal-oriented restructuring ($p<.01$). So the hypothesis that the amount of present knowledge (schemata for understanding) is an important determinant of fluent, accurate and goal-oriented restructuring in studying new information cannot be rejected (Minnaert & Janssen, 1992b). This finding is perfectly in line with the expert-novice paradigm according to which experts learn more when studying new information in their domain of expertise than do novices in that domain (Voss, Fincher-Kiefer, Greene, & Post,1986). Glaser (1984) already pointed out that the amount of initial problem solving representations influences the efficiency and accuracy of thinking and learning within that specific domain. According to Sternberg (1985) expertise develops largely from the increasingly greater take-over of information processing by local processing and knowledge systems.

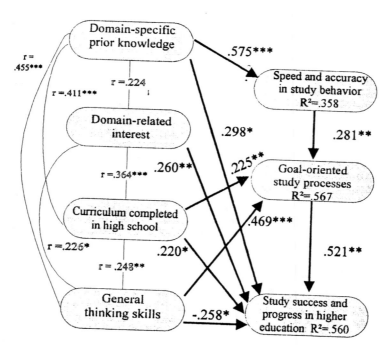

Figure 2. ML-Solution for the Structural Equation Model of the Latent Variables
(N=150; *** p<.001 ; ** p<.01 ; * p<.05)

Table 3
*Total (TE), Direct (DE) and Indirect (IE) Effects of the Latent Variables on the
Endogenous Latent Variables (N=150)*

		Prior know-ledge	Domain-related interest	Curricu-lum in high sch.	General thinking skills	Speed and accuracy	Goal-or. study processes
Speed and	TE	.575***					
accuracy in	DE	.575***					
study behavior	IE	0					
Goal-oriented	TE	.162**		.225**	.469***	.281**	
study	DE	0		.225**	.469***	.281**	
processes	IE	.162**		0	0	0	
Study success	TE	.382**	.260**	.337**	-.014	.146*	.521**
and progress in	DE	.298*	.260**	.220**	-.258*	0	.521**
higher educat.	IE	.084*	0	.117*	.244**	.146*	0

*** p<.001; ** p<.01; * p<.05

The importance of both declarative and procedural knowledge has already been stressed by other researchers (Anderson, 1982; Decruyenaere & Janssen, 1989; Weinert, 1987). The total effects of domain-specific prior knowledge on the latent endogenous variables are very substantial (p<.01). The effects of the studying processes on the curriculum outcomes are very striking too. Even after correction for general thinking skills, study processes, domain-related interest and curriculum completed in high school, domain-specific prior knowledge explains a substantial amount of the variance in study success and progress. Although the influence of general thinking skills on the goal-oriented study processes is very substantial (p<.001), the total effect on study success and progress into the equation turns out to be of no (statistical) importance (Table 3). The indirect effect via study processes of general thinking skills on the curriculum output compensates for the negative path of general thinking skills to study success and progress. This means that general thinking skills have a slightly negative mathematical influence on curriculum output when all the other latent factors in the equation model (domain-specific prior knowledge, domain-related interest, curriculum completed in high school and study processes) are taken into account for the explanation of the variance in study success and progress. A high level of general thinking skills without influence on study processes, results in a lower performance level in study success and progress. This effect can partly explain the astonishing finding that one out of three highly intelligent students did not succeed in their first year of higher education (Stinissen, 1987). The contribution of general thinking skills is predominantly in their direct effect on the study skills that transform the knowledge base (analysis, synthesis and the transformed long-term knowledge base as estimator of study expertise).

In this chapter we also consider the estimated correlation between domain-specific prior knowledge and general thinking skills (r=.455; p<.001). These factors have an estimated common variance of 20.7%, which corresponds to 79.3% of factor specific variance and error variance. The common variance between curriculum completed in high school and domain-specific prior knowledge in the structural equation model is estimated at 16.9%.

Domain-specificity, general thinking skills and the curriculum completed in high school have some striking heuristic features in common which likely form part of transferable knowledge structures or information-processing components. However, the limited amount of common variance demands the utmost deliberate guidance and monitoring for teaching transferable knowledge structures (Salomon & Perkins, 1987) as well as for designing powerful learning environments (De Corte, 1993). So we find a moderate correlation between domain-specific prior knowledge and general thinking skills. This means that a common as well as a specific source of determination exists. Besides, the results confirm our hypothesis that domain-specific prior knowledge facilitates the acquisition of new knowledge and that general thinking skills enhance the transformation or restructuring of the knowledge base.

Student Differences in Forms of Prior Knowledge

We distinguished three a posteriori levels (low, medium and high) in each of the domain-specific prior knowledge measures. As concerns the forms of understanding (Entwistle & Entwistle, 1991) we investigate the relationship between level of domain-specificity to study skills and study success and progress. MANCOVA (multiple analysis of covariance) models were used with speed and accuracy, goal-oriented study processes and study success and progress as the three dependent measures; general thinking skills acted as covariate effect. Given the results of the univariate and multivariate homogeneity of variance tests, there appears to be no reason to suspect the assumption of homogeneity of the variance-covariance matrices.

* General domain-specific prior knowledge (breadth of previous knowledge) has no significant main effect on the dependent measures (Table 4). The univariate tests were not significant either. Only the multivariate test for the covariate effect of general thinking skills was substantial; Wilks' Λ=.714, S=1, M=1/2, N=71, $F(3.144)$=19.20, p<.001. To illustrate this effect, we report that the proportion of explained variance in goal-oriented study processes increased astonishingly from 1.3% to 29.3% when the covariate effect is added to the non-significant mean effect of general domain-specific prior knowledge.

* A significant main effect of domain-specific prior knowledge in terms of difficult notions (depth of previous knowledge) was found (Table 5); Wilks' Λ=.905, S=2, M=0, N=71, $F(6.288)$=2.43, p=.026. The univariate tests showed that the level of previous knowledge in depth had a significant mean effect on goal-oriented study processes $[F(2.146)$=3.60, p=.030] and on study success and progress $[F(2.146)$=5.20, p=.007]. In these results the significant covariate effect was also taken into account; Wilks' Λ=.709, S=1, M=1/2, N=71, $F(3.144)$=19.63, p<.001. The proportion of explained variance in goal-oriented study processes grows from 5.6% to 32.6% when the covariate effect is added to the significant main effect of the depth of previous knowledge. The extent to which the student is able to provide an explanation of difficult but domain-related notions facilitates not only the performance of transformation or restructuring of the knowledge base while studying new, domain-related information but also the study output performance on the exams.

Table 4
Mancova And Manova Models for Student Differences in General Domain-Specific Prior Knowledge (N=150)

	Wilks' Λ	df	F	R^2	R	R cov	t
Multivariate effects							
main effects (S=2; M=0; N=71)	.982	(6.288)	0.43				
covariate effects (S=1; M=1/2; N=71)	.714	(3.144)	19.20***				
Univariate effects on							
speed and accuracy							
main effect		(2.147)	2.23	.029	.172		
covariate effect and		(1.146)	10.78**	.083	.288	.235	2.92**
main effect		(2.146)	1.22				
study processes							
main effect		(2.147)	0.96	.013	.114		
covariate effect and		(1.146)	60.53***	.293	.541	.532	7.60***
main effect		(2.146)	0.01				
success and progress							
main effect		(2.147)	0.60	.008	.090		
covariate effect and		(1.146)	10.32**	.068	.260	.245	3.05**
main effect		(2.146)	0.14				

*** p<.001;   ** p<.01;   * p<.05

Table 5

Mancova And Manova Models For Student Differences in Domain-Specific Prior Knowledge About Difficult Notions (N=150)

	Wilks' Λ	df	F	R^2	R	R cov	t
Multivariate effects							
main effects (S=2; M=0; N=71)	.905	(6.288)	2.43*				
covariate effects (S=1; M=1/2; N=71)	.709	(3.144)	19.63***				
Univariate effects on							
speed and accuracy main effect		(2.147)	2.08	.028	.166		
covariate effect and		(1.146)	10.88**	.091	.302	.255	3.19**
main effect		(2.146)	1.88				
study processes main effect		(2.147)	4.39*	.056	.238		
covariate effect and		(1.146)	63.51***	.326	.571	.534	7.64***
main effect		(2.146)	3.60*				
success and progress main effect		(2.147)	6.04**	.076	.276		
covariate effect and		(1.146)	11.03**	.128	.358	.237	2.95**
main effect		(2.146)	5.20**				

*** p<.001;   ** p<.01;   * p<.05

Table 6

Mancova And Manova Models For Student Differences in Domain-Specific Prior Knowledge About Course And Curriculum (N=150)

	Wilks' Λ	df	F	R²	R	R cov	t
Multivariate effects							
main effects (S=2; M=0; N=71)	.878	(6,288)	3.19**				
covariate effects (S=1; M=1/2; N=71)	.703	(3,144)	20.19***				
Univariate effects on							
speed and accuracy							
main effect		(2,147)	6.68**	.083	.289		
covariate effect and		(1,146)	11.51**	.141	.376	.251	3.14**
main effect		(2,146)	6.26**				
study processes							
main effect		(2,147)	2.89	.038	.195		
covariate effect and		(1,146)	62.77***	.318	.564	.539	7.75***
main effect		(2,146)	2.70				
success and progress							
main effect		(2,147)	6.26**	.079	.280		
covariate effect and		(1,146)	11.12**	.135	.368	.248	3.09**
main effect		(2,146)	5.86**				

*** p<.001;   ** p<.01;   * p<.05

*   The multivariate tests revealed a very substantial main effect of domain-specific prior knowledge in terms of curriculum information (previous knowledge as related to structure) on the dependent measures (Table 6); Wilks' $\Lambda=.878$, $S=2$, $M=0$, $N=71$, $F(6.288)=3.19$, $p=.005$. The univariate tests showed that the level of previous knowledge as related to structure had a significant main effect on speed and accuracy in study behavior [$F(2.146)=6.26$, $p=.002$] and on study success and progress [$F(2,146)=5.86$, $p=.004$]. The main effect on goal-oriented study processes was not significant. In these results too the significant covariate effect was taken into account; Wilks' $\Lambda=.703$, $S=1$, $M=1/2$, $N=71$, $F(3.144)=20.19$, $p<.001$. The proportion of explained variance in speed and accuracy in study behavior increases from 8.3% to 14.1% when the covariate effect is added to the significant main effect of previous knowledge as related to structure. According to Entwistle and Entwistle (1991) this form of understanding (previous knowledge as related to structure) being interrelated with both breadth and depth of previous knowledge, marked the main differences between students.

This kind of prior knowledge seems to optimize the relevance and clarity of study contents and the accurate use of study time. Dochy (1992) evaluates these effects as indirect, which is highly congruent with the significant indirect effects of domain-specific prior knowledge in the structural equation model.

CONCLUSION AND DISCUSSION

Domain-specific prior knowledge as well as domain-related study skills are necessary prerequisites to accomplish study success and progress in psychology studies at the university. Besides this differences in curriculum outcomes are also significantly ($p<.01$) influenced by differences in domain-related interest. The non-significant correlation between domain-specific prior knowledge and domain-related interest turns out to be congruent with findings in the literature about text-based interest (Hidi, 1990). Futhermore, the hypothesis that interest in subject matter might increase learning by affecting the depth of information processing, has to be rejected. Nevertheless, the total impact of domain-related interest on study success and progress encourages further research on this topic and shows that text-based interest has a profound effect on the academic performance in higher education. Unraveling the complexity of cognitive-motivational relationships turns out to be very difficult but worth investigating because of its implications for learning and instruction.

Although many researchers have already demonstrated the importance of domain-specific prior knowledge on problem solving, even at the level of higher education (cf. Chi, Feltovich, & Glaser, 1981; Decruyenaere & Janssen, 1989; Dochy, 1992; Vosniadou & Brewer, 1987), none of them have reported research on the direct and/or indirect effects of domain-specific prior knowledge on the quality of graduating (in time, late, not at all, with or without a degree) in the relevant domain. The important role of prior knowledge in studying from texts was empirically pinpointed in this contribution.

The results of this research on studying in higher education, defined as the integration of learning and thinking on the basis of motivation, lead us into further investigations on the acquisition of structures of domain-specific knowledge in relation to domain-related study skills. Even after correction for general thinking skills, the depth of understanding and understanding as related to structure significantly influence study skills as well as study success and progress. This does not account for the breadth of understanding. Given its content and nomological validity, our instrument possibly has the necessary predictive validity - when applied at the right stage - to promote better vocational choices of entering freshmen. The developed "excursion" can help future students in the evaluation of their knowledge base and their capacities with respect to a specific study programme.

Finally, the results call for two concluding comments. A very interesting research topic in the educational field is a longitudinal approach of testing the variation in validity coefficients. Although yearly fluctuations in validity coefficients can easily be explained by sampling variations and institutional trends, research into real variations in validity coefficients over time still remains a challenge for the future. In this perspective Ramist and Weiss (1990) discovered in the USA that the correlation (after correction for restriction of range) between the Scholastic Aptitude Test and the freshmen grade-point average (GPA) decreased in the period between 1973-1976 and 1985-1988 from .56 to .52, while the correlation of high school record with GPA stayed the same (.58) during this period. They also found that the total mean and the standard deviation on the Scholastic Aptitude Test decreased over the years and that the high school record remained stable. Results like these may hold important implications and guidelines for educational practice and counseling projects.

So far, most studies based on the expert-novice paradigm have emphasized the role of domain-specific prior knowledge in explaining text recall, ignoring possible influences of metacognitive knowledge and metacognitive activities (Voss et al., 1986). The opposite also occurs, namely, neglecting the importance of domain-specific prior knowledge while exploring the effects of metacognition on memory for text (Garner, 1987). The few studies that integrated both prior knowledge and metacognition in their research lack ecological validity (Körkel & Schneider, 1991) and/or any valid long-term criterion, such as study success and progress, to explore the indirect effects of prior knowledge and metacognition (Elen, 1992). We are working on this project as well as on the replication of our structural equation model. As soon as the necessary (longitudinal) data are collected, we will be able to investigate the intriguing (causal) relationships between domain-specific prior knowledge, domain-related interest, general thinking skills, study skills, metacognitive factors and curriculum outcomes.

REFERENCES

Alexander, P.A., & Judy, J.E. (1988). The interaction of domain-specific and strategic knowledge in academic performance. *Review of Educational Research, 58*, 375-404.

Anderson, J.R. (1982). Acquisition of cognitive skill. *Psychological Review, 89*, 369-406.

Ausubel, D.P. (1977). The facilitation of meaningful verbal learning in the classroom. *Educational Psychologist, 12*, 162-178.

Chi, M.T., Feltovich, H., & Glaser, R. (1981). Categorization and representation of physics problems by experts and novices. *Cognitive Science, 5*, 121-152.

De Corte, E. (1993, July). *On the design of powerful environments for fostering cognitive development*. Paper presented at the third European Congress of Psychology, Tampere, Finland.

Decruyenaere, M., & Janssen, P.J. (1989). A structural model for individual differences in academic performance of freshmen. In H. Mandl, E. De Corte, N. Bennett, & H.F. Friedrich (Eds.), *Learning and instruction. European research in an international context: Volume 2.1* (pp. 481-495). Oxford: Pergamon.

Demetriou, A., Efklides, A., & Platsidou, M. (1993). The architecture and dynamics of developing mind: Experiential structuralism as a frame for unifying cognitive developmental theories. *Monographs of the Society for Research in Child Development*, 58 (Serial number 234).

De Neve, H. (1991). *Studierendementen aan de K.U.Leuven in de Periode 1984-85 tot en met 1988-1989* [Study outputs at the K.U.Leuven in the period 1984-85 up to 1988-89]. Leuven: Dienst Universitair Onderwijs.

Dochy, F.J.R.C. (1992). *Assessment of prior knowledge as a determinant for future learning*. Utrecht/London: Lemma/Jessica Kingsley.

Elen, J. (1992). *Toward prescriptions in instructional design: A theoretical and empirical approach*. Unpublished doctoral dissertation, Centre for Instructional Psychology and Technology, University of Leuven, Leuven.

Entwistle, N.J., & Entwistle, A. (1991). Contrasting forms of understanding for degree examinations: The student experience and its implications. *Higher Education*, 22, 205-227.

Garner, R. (1987). *Metacognition and reading comprehension*. Norwood, NJ: Ablex.

Glaser, R. (1984). Education and thinking. The role of knowledge. *American Psychologist*, 93, 93-104.

Heim, A. (1968). *Manual for the AH5 Group Test of High-Grade Intelligence* (Rev. ed.). Windsor (UK): NFER-Nelson.

Hidi, S. (1990). Interest and its contribution as a mental resource for learning. *Review of Educational Research*, 60 (4), 549-571.

Janssen, P.J. (1989). Task, development and process in student learning: Toward an integrated theory of studying. *European Journal of Psychology of Education*, 4, 469-488.

Jöreskog, K.G., & Sörbom, D. (1989). *LISREL 7 User's Reference Guide*. Mooresville, IN: Scientific Software.

Körkel, J., & Schneider, W. (1991). Domain-specific versus metacognitive knowledge effects on text recall and comprehension. In M. Carretero, M. Pope, R.-J. Simons, & J.I. Pozo (Eds.), *Learning and instruction. European research in an international context: Volume 3* (pp. 311-323). Oxford: Pergamon.

Minnaert, A., & Janssen, P.J. (1992a). Success and progress in higher education: A structural model of studying. *British Journal of Educational Psychology*, 62, 184-192.

Minnaert, A., & Janssen, P.J. (1992b, June). *The causal role of domain-specific prior knowledge on study skills and curriculum outcomes after five academic years*. Paper presented at the European Conference on Educational Research, Enschede, The Netherlands.

Ramist, L., & Weiss, G. (1990). The predictive validity of the SAT, 1964 to 1988. In W.W. Willingham, C. Lewis, R. Morgan, & L. Ramist (Eds.), *Predicting college grades: An analysis of institutional trends over two decades* (pp. 117-140). Princeton, NJ: Educational Testing Service.

Resnick, L.B. (1987). Instruction and the cultivation of thinking. In E. De Corte, H. Lodewijks, R. Parmentier, & P. Span (Eds.), *Learning and instruction. European research in an international context: Volume 1* (pp. 415-442). Oxford/Leuven: Pergamon/Leuven University Press.

Salomon, G., & Perkins, D.N. (1987). Transfer of cognitive skills from programming: When and how? *Journal of Educational Computing Research, 3,* 149-169.

Sternberg, R.J. (1985). *Beyond IQ. A triarchic theory of human intelligence.* Cambridge: Cambridge University Press.

Stinissen, J. (Ed.). (1987). *De overgang van secundair naar hoger onderwijs. Een follow-up van 6000 abituriënten - Rapport 3: Doorstromen en slagen* [The transition from high school to higher education. A follow-up of 6000 school-leavers - Report 3: Move up and succeed]. Leuven: Acco.

Vanderlocht, M., & Van Damme, J. (1990). Knowledge and problem solving in physics. *Pedagogische Studiën, 67,* 70-81.

Verhelst, N., & Vander Steene, G. (1972). A Gulliksen item analysis program. *Behavioral Science, 17,* 491-493.

Vosniadou, S., & Brewer, W.F. (1987). Theories of knowledge restructuring in development. *Review of Educational Research, 57,* 51-67.

Voss, J.F., Fincher-Kiefer, R.H., Greene, T.R., & Post, T.A. (1986). Individual differences in performance: The contrastive approach to knowledge. In R.J. Sternberg (Ed.), *Advances in the psychology of human intelligence* (Vol. 3, pp. 297-334). Hillsdale, NJ: Erlbaum.

Weinert, F.E. (1987). Developmental processes and instruction. In E. De Corte, H. Lodewijks, R. Parmentier, & P. Span (Eds.), *Learning and instruction. European research in an international context: Volume 1* (pp. 1-18). Oxford/Leuven: Pergamon/Leuven University Press.

Weinert, F.E., Schrader, F.W., & Helmke, A. (1990). Quality of instruction and achievement outcomes. *Learning and Instruction, 13,* 895-914.

The Revised Inventory of Learning Processes: A Multifaceted Perspective on Individual Differences in Learning

Elke Geisler-Brenstein and
Ronald R. Schmeck

INTRODUCTION

Today's educators are faced with the growing information explosion on the one hand and declining student performance on the other. Students not only have to learn more but also must be able to adapt to changing realities at an increasingly fast pace. It has been shown that the "training approach" to education is no longer a viable one as it produces "experts" who demonstrate competence in the classroom but are unable to apply their expertise to real-life tasks (Mandl, Gruber, & Renkl 1993; Sternberg, 1989). Instead of falling prey to the intellectual tunnel-vision which results from accumulating "inert knowledge," students need to become self-motivated and self-regulated independent thinkers who can approach ill-defined real-world problems with their complex ramifications. They need to be able to apply their skills and know-how in novel situations for which pat solutions don't exist (Dörner, 1989). There are numerous approaches designed to teach students how to be critical thinkers (Baron & Sternberg, 1987) or "good strategy" users (Pressley, Borkowski, & Schneider, 1989). While these approaches are generally effective, students have been found to differ in the extent to which they can benefit from such educational interventions (Sternberg & Martin, 1988). Many training programs do not address the fact that students may approach educational experiences in qualitatively different ways (Schmeck, 1988b). The recent concern with student "diversity" has prompted a growing awareness of differences among people and resulted in greater acceptance of different ways of functioning, socially and intellectually. Still, there is little concern for the more subtle manifestations of differences among learners, and their impact on the learning process and learning outcomes (Geisler-Brenstein, Schmeck, & Hetherington, in press).

Toward a More Diverse Conceptualization of Individual Differences in Learning

In the last decade, there have been encouraging efforts toward more diversity in conceptualizations of learner characteristics and their effects on learning processes and outcomes. For example, Sternberg's triarchic theory of intelligence (Berg & Sternberg, 1985) and Gardener's theory of multiple intelligences (Gardner, 1983; Granott & Gardner, 1994) recognize diversity in aptitude. Current models of learning behavior and learner characteristics have also become more diverse in that they present a more holistic view of the learner and the learning process which includes affective and conative dimensions (Boekarts, 1994; Snow, 1989, 1994; Sternberg, 1994) and consideration of the roles of prior knowledge and situational and task variables (Schneider & Weinert, 1990). For example, the aptitude-by-treatment interaction (ATI) framework of analysis originated by Cronbach and Snow (1977) substantiates that students with different levels of prior knowledge, abilities, skills, or personality traits may differentially benefit from instructional "treatments" (Jonassen & Grabowski, 1993; Snow, 1994). The increasing diversity in methodologies and approaches to the study of learning, and the new interactionism are providing a richer, more ecologically valid account of student learning. However, the discussion of the impact of individual difference dimensions is usually limited to the consideration of levels of ability or motivational factors - with some notable exceptions (e.g., Miller, 1991). Too little is still known about other dimensions of interpersonal variability.

The lack of information about origins, nature, and practical implications of individual differences in learning can be traced back to several problems that have plagued the empirical study of individual differences in general. Individual differences are often viewed as tangential given that basic research is generally aimed at specific content areas. Moreover, cognitive psychologists have displayed "a marked reluctance to take individual differences seriously" (Eysenck & Keane, 1990). Thus researchers focus on developing general models or theories of reading comprehension, or creative problem solving, for example, rather than exploring how people with different cognitive styles read or solve problems in different ways (Schneider & Weinert, 1990). As Sternberg (1989) puts it, "hard-nosed cognitive psychologists have treated style more as a nuisance variable, something that cannot always be suppressed, but that is not worthy of a theory in its own right" (p.119). Often it is a matter of not wanting to introduce yet another level of complexity by asking which variables may moderate observed effects. However, in many cases, it is simply that researchers don't know how to chose among the multitude of proposed dimensions.

Certainly, there is no shortage of instruments measuring cognitive and learning styles (Jonassen & Grabowski, 1993). However, the lack of consensus among the multitude of often contradictory taxonomies creates a dilemma for researchers and practitioners as to which measures to consider. The result is a vicious cycle where the exclusion of individual differences from research and practice leads to theories and findings that fail to take these variables into account.

Also, cognitive and learning style variables present several methodological problems. Since they don't necessarily affect *how much* is learned but may make a difference in *how* the information is encoded and processed (Sternberg, 1989), there has been weak support for predictive validity involving performance criteria. In many cases, the nature of cognitive style concepts (some of which have their roots in perception research and were developed in lab settings) have made it difficult to validate the constructs in educational settings -- to the point that Tiedeman (1989) concluded that there is no convincing evidence for the majority of cognitive style constructs. This criticism is partially justified because many cognitive style dimensions are too vague and all-inclusive to be of practical utility. Many of the relationships don't yield main effects but only emerge in ATI designs. Moreover, a person's standing on only one cognitive style variable does not provide a valid representation of his or her overall way of functioning. Usually, there are several variables to be considered simultaneously. This is rarely done as most taxonomies provide at best a two-by-two model that is not comprehensive enough to have explanatory and predictive power (see discussion below). Another complication in research on stylistic dimensions is that having functional *preferences* does not necessarily mean that they are *expressed* in a given task/situation context (Wakefield, 1989). This implied distinction (similar to that between genotype and phenotype) further muddles the measurement issue.

Despite problems with the operationalization of styles, we feel that "the baby was thrown out with the bath water" as many concluded that there is little sense in looking for cross-situational consistency in learning behavior in light of so much situational variability. Our work, and that of others (see Schmeck, 1988a) has demonstrated the existence of reliable differences in the ways students approach learning. This chapter deals with an exploration of these subtle manifestations of individuality. While they represent only one side of the complex interaction of person and situation, we feel that knowing a student's self-perceived strengths and weaknesses expressed as a generalizable approach or orientation toward learning can be helpful in choosing appropriate teaching strategies and environments. At the same time, students can benefit from the metacognitive potential that grows with self-awareness.

In the following, we first look back on the development history of the Inventory of Learning Processes (ILP) and then discuss substantive and methodological improvements implemented in the recently revised version. We then discuss individual scale constructs in more detail, incorporating results from two recent studies as evidence for construct validity as well as providing specific suggestions for modifying study behavior and attitudes. Finally, we discuss underlying assumptions about the conceptual and behavioral stability of individual differences in learning with special emphasis on the role the self concept plays in the development of a viable learning style.

THE INVENTORY OF LEARNING PROCESSES THEN AND NOW

The ILP was first published in 1977 (Schmeck, Ribich, & Ramanaiah, 1977). It was constructed by factor analyzing student responses to statements concerned with academic studying, statements constructed by describing activities and beliefs suggested by cognitive psychology, memory, and information processing research. The factor analyses revealed four factors labeled Deep Processing, Elaborative Processing, Fact Retention, and Methodical Study. Deep and Elaborative Processing were both reflective study strategies (cf. McCarthy, Shaw, & Schmeck, 1986) differing in the extent to which personal experience was emphasized. Deep Processing was more abstract, logical, and theoretical (the "academic" style), while

Elaborative Processing was more experiential, episodic, and self-expressive (e.g., the "search for relevance" popular in the early seventies). Fact Retention was oriented toward retaining atomized bits of information required for success on many objective, multiple choice examinations. Methodical Study literally was method-oriented, seemingly based on the assumption that anyone can succeed in school if the "proper" trappings of studying are evident (e.g., using the library, recopying notes, outlining, reviewing regularly, keeping one's work-area clean and orderly, etc.).

Validation studies conducted since 1977 provided more detailed definitions of the nature of the original ILP dimensions and revealed various personality correlates (see Schmeck, Geisler-Brenstein, & Cercy, 1991, for a detailed review). For example, Schmeck and Ribich (1978) found that individuals who processed information "deeply" (abstractly and theoretically) were able to achieve either by conforming or by independent thought, as the situation warranted, whereas those who focused on facts and those who emphasized study methods tended to achieve only via conformity (Gough, 1957). Similar relations between information processing styles and personality were found for self-efficacy, self-esteem, self-assertion, locus of control, anxiety, and fear of failure (see below). In several cases, personality variables acted as moderators of the relationship between information processing and actual performance variables. For example, Schmeck and Spofford (1982) found that neuroticism moderated the usual tendency of deep processors to attend to abstract cues, with the neurotic/worried deep processor giving more attention to superficial aspects of information.

In addition to the original four ILP scales, Schmeck (1988b) reported two dimensions of efficacy (with regard to thought and memorization) and two dimensions of cognitive style (holistic versus serialist). Subsequent research substantiated the findings regarding the holist-serialist dimension (Beyler & Schmeck, 1992) and the two efficacy dimensions (MacGregor, 1989). Furthermore, anxiety (Schmeck & Spofford, 1982) and self-esteem (Schmeck & Meier, 1984) were found to predict ILP scores and moderate their effects. Similarly, as noted above, a conforming and conventional attitude toward cultural values (Tracy, Schmeck, & Spofford, 1980; Schmeck & Ribich, 1978) related to ILP scales in predictable ways. Finally, achievement motivation and locus of control were regular correlates of the original ILP dimensions (Meier, McCarthy, & Schmeck, 1984). As a result of these types of findings, the item pool was expanded in 1987 to include motivational and learning-related personality statements (Geisler-Brenstein, 1987). The Revised Inventory of Learning Processes (Schmeck, et al., 1991) incorporated self-concept and motivational scales. The expanded 180 item pool was later factor-analyzed with a large sample from which bogus responses had been eliminated (Geisler-Brenstein, 1993). The result was an improved factor structure with good convergent and discriminant scale validity. The instrument has subsequently undergone minor revisions in an attempt to refine a hierarchical scoring key which allows us to assess individual facets as well as higher-level constructs (Geisler-Brenstein, Schmeck, & Hetherington, 1995; Schmeck & Geisler-Brenstein, 1995).

Despite slight variations due to changes in the item pool, certain consistencies have continually emerged over the last few years. Personality and cognitive process items and scales have consistently grouped in meaningful ways to produce a hierarchical model of individual differences in learning behavior and attitudes (see Figure 1). Academic Self-Efficacy, Self-Esteem, Self-Assertion, and Motivation consistently appear as non-cognitive or "personality" dimensions. Deep, Elaborative,

Agentic, and Methodical Learning continually emerge as separate learning dimensions (Schmeck, Geisler-Brenstein, & Cercy, 1991; Geisler-Brenstein, 1993). The ILP-R currently includes several major dimensions (higher-order factors) assessed in terms of empirically derived facets. Self-Efficacy is assessed in reference to cognitive organization, critical thinking and fact retention. As for Motivation, three aspects are considered: intrinsic interest, personal responsibility, and effort. With regard to the learning scales, routes to achievement include reflective and agentic learning. Reflective Learning is characterized by a preference for dialectical, meaning-oriented learning which can either have an abstract emphasis on theoretical knowledge or emphasize more applied and experiential forms of knowledge. Agentic Learning, on the other hand, is a more pragmatic approach to learning that is highly purposive, directed toward completion of tasks, and responsive to external contingencies. A third dimension labelled Methodical Learning describes a very strategic approach to learning which focuses on utilizing "proper" techniques over content/substance.

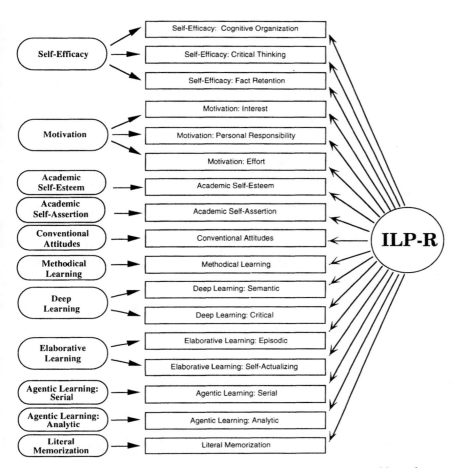

Figure 1. Confirmatory Factor Analysis Model for the Inventory of Learning Processes-Revised

Recent Developments

We have recently taken several steps to improve the practical usefulness of the inventory. For example, a special effort has been made to improve the content validity of the item pool. In a recent pilot study, the content validity of existing ILP-R items was examined by asking students to rate how clear and understandable each item was. Students were asked to paraphrase inventory items which they had rated as not very clear, and provide an example from their experience. As a result, several items were reworded and some deleted from the inventory. Also, factor analyses of the item pool as well as correlational data with other instruments had consistently identified some items with low commonalities. Similarly, item analyses have identified items which can be dropped due to lack of convergent or discriminant validity or extremely skewed item distributions. At the same time, several items were newly written to improve the content saturation of some of the constructs. Over the years we have attempted to shorten the instrument for practical reasons without sacrificing validity and adequate content coverage. The latest version has 150 items including 12 maintenance items (the Random Response and Impression Management scales).

The maintenance scales were added in order to help us assess the validity of the responses. The Impression Management scale consists of items that describe "socially desirable" but somewhat unlikely behaviors or opinions. A high score (1 SD above the mean) is used to alert us to responses that are affected by social desirability as perceived in a learning context. The Random Response scale was added in order to help identify bogus responses in research settings. It is part of a more elaborate system developed to identified invalid responses on the basis of several criteria (e.g., acquiescent response style, missing data). Somewhat to our surprise, we have found that in a variety of student samples totalling 2000, the average number of bogus responses was 30%. Looking more closely at subgroups, we found that the percentage of presumably invalid data ranged from 57% in some introductory psychology subject pools to 7% in an upper level psychology class taught by one of the test authors. Not surprisingly, the percentage of valid responses was significantly higher for women than for men. Furthermore, chances for obtaining valid data also increased with grade level: upper-level students provided over 10% more valid responses than freshmen and sophomores (Geisler-Brenstein, 1993). We have continually found that the elimination of bogus responses had a significant impact on analyses examining the structural relationships among scale constructs in that it provided clearer factor structures with less "noise".

The academic self-concept scales have also proven useful as indirect indicators of validity. Our moderator analyses have consistently shown that people with high self-esteem and a well developed academic self-concept are more likely to be able to provide an accurate assessment of their learning behaviors and attitudes (see also Campbell & Lavallee, 1993). Thus, our interpretation of individual profiles differs for those high or low in self-efficacy variables and academic self-esteem (see discussion below).

Finally, the facet approach to learning style assessment has proven useful because we have found considerable differences in how individual subscales relate to other ILP-R scales as well as to other instruments. While the subscales share a common element which makes them "hang together" in factor analyses and item analysis, they have been shown to have differential validity in several validation studies (see also Geisler-Brenstein, et al., in press).

We have found the detailed information presented in individual profiles to be very informative in counseling students with regard to their learning styles. We have observed distinct response patterns that don't appear in overall analyses which aggregate individual profiles into group tendencies. For example, the episodic subscale (reflecting a random-access type of organization) is negatively related to the serial subscale (reflecting sequential orderliness). However, a number of student profiles show high scores on *both* scales. We have found that such students often have high self-efficacy, indicating that they have found a way to manage their random, exploratory style by making a conscious (almost defensive) effort to sequentially organize their actions.

Future developments of the ILP-R will include Item-Response scoring as well as an attempt to identify a limited set of commonly occurring profiles that would simultaneously indicate students' scores on several dimensions, rather than simplistically characterizing a student as being high or low on individual scales only. Moderator analyses performed in different studies (Schmeck et al., 1991; Geisler-Brenstein et al., in press) have demonstrated how different the interpretation of a particular score can be, depending on what other statements the student has endorsed. To facilitate counseling students on a one-on-one basis, we have developed a computerized version of the ILP-R which provides customized narrative feedback which will eventually include moderator considerations.

Reliability and Construct Validity

Table 1 shows internal consistency reliabilities and intercorrelation coefficients for the ILP-R subscales. The intercorrelations among subscales are in agreement with theoretical predictions. For example, the Deep and Elaborative Learning subscales, which we have termed reflective learning scales, are positively related to each other (especially the Semantic and Episodic subscales) and also relate positively to Self-Efficacy and Motivation: Interest subscales. Notably, the Critical Learning subscale relates highest to Self-Efficacy: Critical Thinking. The Deep Learning subscales also relate positively to the Methodical Learning scale. On the other hand, high scores on Literal Memorization are related to high scores on the Analytic subscale and *low* scores on Self-Efficacy: Cognitive Organization and Self-Efficacy: Critical Thinking (not Self-Efficacy: Fact Retention), Motivation: Interest and Motivation: Personal Responsibility (not Motivation: Effort), Academic Self-Esteem, and the two Deep Learning subscales. Serial and Analytic Strategies are positively correlated with the Methodical Learning scale. Serial Learning is also characterized by high Motivation: Effort.

The two studies reported below provide further evidence for the construct validity of the ILP-R subscales by relating them to interview statements (Study 1) as well as measures assessing serialist, holist, and integrated information processing tactics (Study 2). The ILP-R has recently been examined via confirmatory factor analysis (see Figure 1). The proposed structure was validated and proved robust with a second, independent cross-validation sample (Geisler-Brenstein et al., 1995). The inventory has also been related to the five-factor model of personality (Digman, 1990). In a hierarchical regression analysis (Geisler-Brenstein et al., in press), we found that differences in learning behavior and attitudes share a significant amount of variance

Table 1

Number of Scale Items, Internal Consistency Reliabilities, Means, Standard Deviations, and Intercorrelation Coefficients For ILP-R Subscales.

Subscale	n	α	Mean	SD	1	2	3	4	5	6	7	8	9	10	11	12	13	14	15	16
Self-Efficacy	28	.87																		
1 Cog. Organization	12	.83	6.61	10.14																
2 Critical Thinking	7	.71	5.65	5.99	.57**															
3 Fact Retention	9	.75	5.11	8.98	.52**	.44**														
Motivation	23	.84																		
4 Interest	12	.82	7.03	11.25	.35**	.12	.15													
5 Pers. Responsibility	4	.58	3.16	3.04	.23*	.18	-.08	.31**												
6 Effort	7	.71	5.02	6.80	.16	.01	.12	.57**	.27*											
7 Self-Esteem	9	.80	-3.26	10.16	.48**	.42**	.22*	.22*	.20	.03										
8 Self-Assertion	10	.72	3.85	9.01	.23*	.30**	.38**	.17	.07	.01	.41**									
9 Conventional Attitudes	4	.75	-1.44	5.20	-.19	-.25*	-.27*	-.08	-.08	.01	-.32**	-.30**								
10 Methodical Learning	12	.83	-4.26	12.37	.12	.09	.24*	.46**	-.04	.43**	-.15	.08	.08							
Deep Learning	18	.83																		
11 Semantic	9	.80	6.24	8.06	.33**	.36**	.12	.42**	.02	.05	.20	.22*	.01	.30**						
12 Critical	9	.68	6.63	7.25	.45**	.48**	.16	.44**	.10	.08	.40**	.38**	-.12	.31**	.75**					
Elaborative Learning	17	.73																		
13 Self-Actualizing	9	.68	14.27	4.83	.27*	.11	.24*	.34**	.15	.43**	.01	.22*	-.14	.25*	.33**	.32**				
14 Episodic	8	.73	7.48	7.43	.09	.25*	.01	.05	-.03	-.13	-.00	.12	-.18	-.06	.52**	.41**	.30**			
Agentic Learning	12	.78																		
15 Serial	8	.77	4.98	8.66	.22*	-.05	.28*	.40**	.05	.53**	-.14	.10	.05	.44**	.14	.15	.34**	-.16		
16 Analytic	4	.75	3.03	4.75	-.16	-.21	.00	.08	-.21	.11	-.36**	-.14	.21	.43**	.06	-.03	.00	-.29*	.50**	
17 Literal Memorization	5	.66	1.11	5.39	-.55**	-.33**	.02	-.34**	-.34**	-.05	-.41**	-.13	.10	.00	-.41**	-.48**	-.01	-.16	.02	.33**

** Coefficients are significant at p < .001 (one-tailed)
* Coefficients are significant at p < .05 (one-tailed)

with Costa and McCrae's (1985) *Big Five* personality dimensions (Neuroticism, Extraversion, Openness to Experience, Agreeableness, and Conscientiousness). Furthermore, an exploratory factor analysis meaningfully grouped ILP-R and NEO-PI facet scales (see Table 2) in terms of six orthogonal factors with good simple structure, providing evidence for the convergent and discriminant validity of ILP-R constructs. In addition to two NEO-PI-related factors, one ILP-R factor emerged, grouping Academic Self-Concept and Motivation subscales. The remaining three factors combined ILP-R and NEO-PI scales in meaningful ways. The first two corroborated Schmeck, Geisler-Brenstein, and Cercy's (1991) distinction between reflective and agentic approaches to learning. The reflective approach, defined by emphasis on theoretical concepts and critical evaluation as well as experiential "knowing" and personal relevance (the ILP-R Deep and Elaborative scales), is characterized by intellectual curiosity and interest in intellectual pursuits, as well as appreciation for fine arts and beauty (NEO-PI Openness: Ideas and Aesthetics). The Agentic approach is highly task- and goal-oriented and marked by a preference for high-structure, step-by-step procedures, attention to detail, and organized study methods (ILP-R Serial, Analytic, and Methodical scales; NEO-PI Conscientiousness; ILP-R Motivation: Effort, and a negative loading from the NEO-PI Openness: Fantasy subscale). Finally, the NEO-PI Assertiveness and Activity facet scales combined with the ILP-R Self-Assertion subscale to form an Assertiveness factor. In summary, the Deep and Elaborate Learning scales related to different aspects of the Openness to Experience scale, while the Agentic Learning scales were strongly characterized by the construct of "conscientiousness" which implies a preference for organized, orderly, structured, sequential functioning. The self-esteem scale was significantly related to the Neuroticism factor, and Self-Assertion was related to the assertiveness component of Extraversion. These findings support the claim that common latent factors underlie variability in learning and personality.

Group Differences

Scale means and patterns of intercorrelations of ILP-R subscales have been found to differ by sex and grade level, as well as for different majors (Schmeck & Geisler-Brenstein, 1995; Geisler-Brenstein et al., 1995). Differences between males and females were found for several of the dimensions. For example, males were found to score higher on Academic Self-Esteem, the Semantic subscale of the Deep Learning scale, and the Random Response scale. Females on the other hand, had higher scores, on average, on all motivation subscales. They also scored significantly higher on the Self-Actualizing subscale of the Elaborative Learning scale as well as the Agentic Learning: Serial and the Literal Memorization scale.

Many researchers have discussed developmental trends in students' learning-related behaviors and conceptualizations (e.g., Perry, 1970). We have also found that mean scores differ over time, i.e., during the first four years of students' college experiences. Surprisingly, only few trends were discernible. Seniors had significantly higher scores on all three self-efficacy dimensions, suggesting that students became more confident with regard to their abilities to cope with the demands of school over time. Interestingly, the levels of Academic Self-Esteem remained essentially unchanged. Also, the more advanced students were less likely to respond randomly to the ILP-R questions.

Table 2
Joint Factor Analysis of ILP-R and NEO-PI Subscales

NEO-PI and ILP-R subscales		F1	F2	F3	F4	F5	F6
E1	Warmth	.77					
E6	Positive Emotions	.75					
A	Agreeableness	.66					-.38
O3	Feelings	.58					
E5	Excitement-Seeking	.55					
E2	Gregariousness	.52					
O6	Values	.45					
N3	Depression		.77				
N1	Anxiety		.70				
N2	Hostility		.64				
N4	Self-Consciousness		.63				
N6	Vulnerability		.58				
N5	Impulsiveness	.38	.51				
ILP-R	Self-Efficacy: Cognitive Organization			.75			
ILP-R	Motivation: Interest			.63	.41		
ILP-R	Academic Self-Esteem		-.44	.58			
ILP-R	Motivation: Personal Responsibility			.58			
ILP-R	Self-Efficacy: Fact Retention			.43			
ILP-R	Self-Efficacy: Critical Thinking			.42			
ILP-R	Literal Memorization			-.39			
ILP-R	Semantic				.77		
ILP-R	Critical				.77		
ILP-R	Episodic				.61		
ILP-R	Self-Actualizing				.49		
O5	Ideas				.48		
O2	Aesthetics				.44		
ILP-R	Serial					.66	
ILP-R	Motivation: Effort			.42		.63	
C	Conscientiousness					.58	
ILP-R	Methodical Learning					.55	
ILP-R	Analytic					.46	
ILP-R	Conventional Attitude					.44	
O1	Fantasy	.36				-.36	
O4	Actions						
E3	Assertiveness						.69
E4	Activity						.49
ILP-R	Self-Assertion			.35			.47

Note:

Loadings < .30 omitted
Prefixes refer to individual NEO-PI or ILP-R subscales: N= Neuroticism, E= Extraversion, O= Openness, A= Agreeableness, C= Conscientiousness.

ILP-R SCALES

In the following we briefly describe each ILP-R subscale (see Appendix 1 for sample items). We have included samples of specific suggestions for modifying learning strategies that are given to students as part of the customized feedback in individual counseling sessions. Furthermore, we discuss some recent findings supporting the construct validity of the scales and subscales. The data presented come from two unpublished studies which are referred to as Study 1 and Study 2 (see Appendix 2 for details concerning methods). The purpose of Study 1 was to examine the construct validity of the ILP-R by relating inventory scale and subscale scores to individuals' open-ended statements obtained via guided interviews. Specifically, we wanted to gain more insight into how students' attitudes, approaches, and learning outcomes differ in different contexts, how these differences come about, and to what extent maladaptive strategies might be amenable to change. This is part of an on-going effort to formulate a comprehensive model of individual differences in learning which not only describes differences along conative and cognitive dimensions statically but also addresses origins, interrelationships, and possibilities for change. Unfortunately, low cell frequencies obtained due to the large number of response categories did not allow us to quantitatively assess the significance of all the findings. However, the qualitative analyses provided evidence for construct validity. For the interview questions which directly assessed ILP-R scale content, close correspondence was observed between inventory scores and ratings of interview responses by independent raters (cf. McCarthy, Shaw, & Schmeck, 1986). The interviews also provided valuable insights into how subscale scores combine to form distinct learner profiles. In the following, we provide brief descriptive summaries of some of the findings.

The correlational study (Study 2) examined information processing tactics employed by students scoring high and low on the various ILP-R learning strategy scales: Deep (conceptualizing), Elaborative (personalizing), Agentic (task-oriented and effortful), Methodical (formalizing), and Literal Memorization (repeating literally) as well as the Conventional Attitudes subscale (see Table 3). Three main types of processing tactics were assessed (Beyler & Schmeck, 1992): serialist, holist, and integrated. Serialist information processing tactics tend to be rule-based, and marked by temporal-sensitivity and attention to the constituent properties of stimuli, while holist tactics tend to be impressionistic and involve attention to "global relations of overall similarity" (Kemler-Nelson, 1984). Beyler and Schmeck (1992) examined commonly available instruments that might be used to assess serialist versus holist tactics. These were the Human Information Processing Survey (HIPS) (Torrance, Taggart, & Taggart, 1984) and the Myers-Briggs Type Indicator (MBTI) (Myers & McCaulley, 1985). Beyler and Schmeck (1992) reported that certain subscales of this test battery converged to reflect serialist, holist, and integrated tactics. Specifically, the HIPS Left Brain subscale (HIPS-LB) combined with the MBTI Sensing and Judging scales (MBTI-S and MBTI-J) to indicate the presence of serialist tactics. On the other hand, the HIPS Right Brain subscale (HIPS-RB) combined with the MBTI Intuition and Perceiving scales (MBTI-N and MBTI-P) to indicate holist tactics. A third dimension was assessed by the HIPS Integrated subscale (HIPS-I). Torrance et al. (1984) refer to this third dimension as "whole-brained" functioning since it involves flexible combination of serialist ("left-brain") and holist ("right-brain") tactics. The findings of Linn and Petersen (1985) suggested that the Differential Aptitudes Spatial Relations subtest (DAT-S) (Bennett, Seashore, & Wesman, 1989) similarly involves use of integrated tactics; this test was therefore included in the present study to help triangulate the dimension of integrated processing. Also, the correlational study used the sum of the three ILP-R Self-Efficacy scales plus the Academic Self-Esteem scale as a moderator while examining relationships between ILP-R Learning scales and information processing tactics (with the subject sample thus split into high and low self-concept groups).

Table 3

ILP-R Scale Correlations with Other Instruments for Students with High or Low Academic Self-Esteem

ILP-R Scale	Self-Concept Split Group	MBTI				HIPS			DAT Spatial	AAT	MBTI		Marlowe Crowne
		E	N	F	J	LB	RB	I			Worry	Com	
Deep Learning	high	.08	.18	.04	.12	-.57**	.03	.53**	.63**	-.44**	-.08	-.18	.04
	low	.49**	.51**	.11	-.29*	-.36**	.06	.16	.14	-.31**	-.34**	-.08	.11
Elaborative Learning	high	.52**	.45**	.15	-.18	-.50**	.35**	.35**	.51**	-.42**	-.09	-.20	-.19
	low	.14	.25*	.30*	-.24*	-.58**	.06	.05	.22*	-.29*	-.43**	.14	.03
Agentic Learning	high	.11	-.66**	.06	.75**	.36**	-.57**	-.08	-.39**	.53**	.21*	.41**	.37**
	low	.04	-.50**	.00	.61**	.16	-.31**	-.04	-.34**	-.09	.43**	.58**	.26*
Methodical Learning	high	.00	-.09	.16	.44**	-.05	-.13	.14	-.18	-.03	-.01	.06	.23*
	low	.43**	.25*	.05	.15	-.05	-.05	.21	.12	.16	-.03	-.07	.09
Literal Memorization	high	.05	-.16	.32**	.34**	-.17	-.17	.02	.06	.18	.52**	-.26*	.11
	low	.03	-.24*	-.14	.21*	.10	-.05	.13	-.22*	.12	.00	.27*	.25*
Conventional Attitudes	high	.23*	-.65**	.11	.73**	.31**	-.31**	-.04	-.43**	.28*	.16	.45**	.41**
	low	.14	-.58**	.06	.60**	.34**	-.46**	-.05	-.27*	-.04	.47**	.58**	.28*

Note:
MBTI subscales: E = Extraversion, N= Intuition, F= Feeling, J = Judging, Com= Compliance.
HIPS subscales: LB= Left Brain, RB= Right Brain, I = Integrated.

** Coefficients are significant at p < .001 (one-tailed).
* Coefficients are significant at P < .05 (one-tailed).

Academic Self-Concept and Motivational Subscales

Self-Efficacy

In factor analyses of the ILP item pool, items now grouped on the Self-Efficacy scale have repeatedly formed the first factor explaining a large percentage of the common variance. Many of these items had previously been part of the various learning scales. However, rather than actually describing learning processes, they are of an evaluative nature and concern students' perceptions of personal competence with regard to academic tasks. This overall level of confidence enables students to discover and express school abilities rather than inhibiting them. The scale consists of three facets.

Self-Efficacy: Cognitive Organization assesses students' confidence in their information management potential, i.e., putting knowledge into an orderly, functional, structured hierarchy including using facts as evidence, seeing how one fact relates to another, knowing which fact is more important, and why certain facts are grouped together while others are separated. This includes the ability to plan and schedule information processing activities. The second efficacy subscale, *Self-Efficacy: Critical Thinking*, is concerned with confidence in one's ability to reason, argue, or discuss information with self and others. Finally, *Self-Efficacy: Fact Retention* assesses confidence in one's memory for particulars (the lower part of an information hierarchy which anchors and evidentially supports the general ideas).

In the interview study, students classified as having high academic self efficacy on the basis of their ILP-R scores, stated that they were attending university for personal reasons, had higher confidence in their ability to earn high grades, avoided literal memorization of class notes and textbook material, and had high self esteem independent of their success or failure in school. Students high on Self-Efficacy also stated that they preferred essay over objective tests. When asked "How do you feel about yourself as a student?" those scoring high on the ILP-R Self-Efficacy scales reported feeling "good" about themselves as students, while those scoring low were rated as feeling "O.K." or "bad." Students with high scores on Self Efficacy: Fact Retention rated themselves as not creative, while those scoring low indicated that they *did* feel creative. In a blind rating of interview protocols of students scoring high and low on ILP-R Self-Efficacy, all students were correctly classified based on comments they made during the interview. Their statements indicated that they have confidence based on high ability ("I do very well in my classes"). and ability to motivate self ("I can do anything I put my mind to"). They also reported being interested in challenges.

Motivation

This scale measures academic motivation in terms of three interrelated but very different subscales. The first one, *Motivation: Interest*, reflects curiosity about and enjoyment of school work, including creatively imagining how material may be useful, finding reasons for studying rather than simply waiting for a teacher or textbook to "turn on" enthusiasm. In short, it assesses intrinsic academic motivation. The second subscale *Motivation: Personal Responsibility* assesses the degree to which students are willing to take the initiative and not overestimate power others have over their lives. It is directly related to the concept of locus of control. The third subscale, *Motivation: Effort* reflects firm educational goals and a cooperative attitude toward school which are manifested in students' efforts to excel through frequent and intense studying.

While all three motivation subscales are theoretically related, many different combinations of subscale scores are conceivable. For example, a student may be highly "motivated" by personal interest in a subject matter, but fail to energetically apply him or herself to specific academic tasks (low effort). Evidence for discriminant validity was provided by the fact that the three motivation subscales related differentially and predictably with other learning style scales as well as with personality scales. For example, the Interest subscale related most strongly to reflective learning strategies, while the Effort subscale related to the Agentic Learning scales (Geisler-Brenstein et al., in press).

In the interview study, students scoring high on ILP-R Motivation: Interest were predominantly rated as having an intrinsic motivation based on responses to the question "What made you decide to go to college?" Students with low scores were predominantly rated as having an extrinsic motivation. Similar to the efficacy subscales, those scoring high on the motivation subscales stated that they felt "good" about themselves as students.

Academic Self-Esteem

This scale measures positive self-regard and self-respect. It is related to a tendency to decide for oneself whether criticism of others is warranted or not. The student scoring low on this scale worries excessively about the opinions of others and indicates an excessive need to receive direction from others. Schmeck et al. (1991) report that this scale is significantly related to the Self-Esteem Inventory (Coopersmith, 1981), an established instrument for assessing self-esteem. Geisler-Brenstein et al. (in press) also observed a significant negative relationship between ILP-R Academic Self-Esteem and the NEO-Personality Inventory (NEO-PI) Vulnerability facet of the Neuroticism scale (Costa & McCrae, 1985). As expected, the interview study indicated that students who scored high on ILP-R Academic Self-Esteem felt good about themselves as students.

Self-Assertion

The Self-Assertion scale assesses a student's willingness to express and assert him or herself in school, including a willingness to get involved in group discussions, openly express opinions, and challenge authority figures. Schmeck et al. (1991) report that self-assertion is positively related to both Deep and Elaborative Learning. Geisler-Brenstein et al. (in press) report that the ILP-R Academic Self-Assertion scale is significantly related to the Assertiveness subscale of the Extraversion scale of the NEO-PI . Students identified as assertive by the ILP-R were rated as confident and outspoken in the interview study.

Conventional Attitudes

Students scoring high on this scale are likely to have attitudes and principles that are traditional, orthodox, and conformist and tend to cooperate with rules and conventions by demonstrating a hesitancy to question authority. When interviewed, students scoring high on this scale reported having traditional values and looking up to authority figures.

In the correlational study (see Table 3), the Conventional Attitudes scale was consistently and positively correlated with serialist information processing tactics regardless of self concept status (r = +.34 and +.31 with HIPS-LB) and equally consistently and negatively correlated with holist tactics (r = -.46 and -.31 with HIPS-RB). Conventional Attitudes was not related to HIPS-I, but DAT-S suggested a specific *absence* of integrated information processing tactics especially when self concept was high (r = -.27 and -.43 with DAT-S). The presence of serialist tactics and absence of holist tactics was confirmed when the MBTI was examined, with Conventional Attitudes relating very positively to MBTI-S and MBTI-J, especially when self concept was high. Beyler and Schmeck (1992) report that the S-J profile on the MBTI suggests reliance upon serialist tactics.

It can also be seen in Table 3 that the correlation between the MBTI-Compliance subscale and Conventional Attitudes was high regardless of self concept (r = +.58 and +.45), suggesting an emphasis upon conformity as a tactic. Similarly, the Marlow-Crowne Social Desirability scale indicated an emphasis upon being socially acceptable. When self concept was low, the correlation between Conventional and M-C Social Desirability was +.28; the corresponding correlation was +.41 when academic self concept was high. It should be noted that similar relationships involving Compliance and Social Desirability were obtained with the ILP-R Agentic Learning scale.

Learning Subscales

Deep Learning

This scale assesses what might be called the *traditional academic* learning style characterized by intellectual understanding, striving for theoretical and logical perspective, and comparing and contrasting of theories. It is made up of two facets: *Deep Learning: Semantic* is a subscale which assesses preference for semantic rather than episodic memory. One might say it involves knowing *about* things rather than knowing things directly from practical experience. It involves comfort with use of language and other symbol systems to think abstractly while studying. The other Deep subscale, *Deep Learning: Critical*, involves judging and critically evaluating theories. Students scoring high on this subscale determine whether and why they agree with a theory and whether they can find fault with its logic or find a better theory to replace it.

The following is a sample of suggestions given to students as part of the computerized feedback. They are meant to provide students with specific tactics for increasing or decreasing the use of particular strategies or changing attitudes which constitute a given learning style.

> If you do not habitually use Semantic or Critical strategies, you may want to try the following. Academic learning requires quite a lot of abstract information processing. Take time to compare one explanation or theory with another rather than just memorizing them as they are given by a textbook or teacher. See how they are similar and how they are different. If the textbook presents only one theory or explanation, see if you can think of one of your own. Make yourself understand the logic of a theory and take

time to agree or disagree with it. If more than one explanation is provided, choose between them and think of arguments in favor of the one you choose much as you would if you were in a debate with someone else. If you received a high score on the Semantic or Critical subscales, you may also want to consider the practical implications of what you study, and think of concrete examples. Also, you might want to relate ideas to your personal experiences so as to "round out" your approach.

Elaborative Learning

This scale measures a way of studying that is not so much logical and theoretical as it is personal and creative. It involves common sense more than abstract thinking and intuition more than logic. It also includes personal memories and feelings. It involves figuring out what the self is and making the most of it by discovering likes and dislikes from the inside, from the heart, with one's feeling and intuition. It is concerned with use of concrete real-life experiences when studying, seeing how information relates to personal memories and expressing and discovering oneself in the process. This scale includes two subscales. *Elaborative Learning: Episodic,* concerns using one's imagination to apply bits and pieces of personal memory, including past classes in school, T.V. shows, movies, and actual personal experience; it is related to common sense, letting one's mind wander to related memories which are consonant with, or call into question, that which is being studied, and asking oneself how ideas in books and lectures can be applied in the "real world." The second subscale, *Elaborative Learning: Self-Actualizing,* assesses a view of learning which emphasizes self-expression and personal development, relying on intuition rather than logic, and respecting one's personal thoughts and ideas as basis for decision making.

Suggestions for students:

> Here are some suggestions, if you want to increase your use of Episodic and Self-Actualizing strategies. Ask yourself how the information relates to your own personal experience, choose courses to match your interests or take a course that is not related to your major. Take a class just for fun. Apply the things you study in school to developing as a person. Use your imagination. Ask yourself how the concepts you are studying might relate to the "real world." When you learn facts, ask yourself personal questions about these facts. Don't be afraid to let your mind wander to related memories which either agree with or call into question what you are studying. If you use Episodic and Self-Actualizing strategies a lot, you may want to remind yourself that it is important to maintain a healthy balance between your need for personal exploration and task accomplishment by being more task-oriented than people-oriented at certain times. Also, there is value in being able to see things objectively and theoretically from a distance without emotional involvement.

In the interview study, students classified as deep and elaborative indicated that they critically and logically evaluate information they study, bring in personal experiences and examples where relevant, and are willing to assert their opinions. McCarthy et al. (1986) obtained similar interview results with regard to the original ILP Deep and Elaborative Processing scales. When asked "If you could change one thing about your high school or college experience, what would you change?" students high on Elaborative Learning: Self-Actualizing more often named social/personal issues rather than academic ones. Self-Actualizing is related to the "changing as a person" conception of learning (Marton, Dall'Alba, & Beaty, in press).

In general, the ILP-R Deep and Elaborative Learning Scales are more reflective than work-oriented (compare Agentic Learning below). Thus, it was no surprise when the correlational study revealed that they involve similar information processing tactics. Both of these reflective strategies related negatively to preference for serialist tactics. Table 3 reveals that the coefficients of correlation between Deep Learning and HIPS-LB were -.36 for those with a low self concept and -.57 for students with a high self concept. The corresponding coefficients for Elaborative Learning were -.58 and -.50. Furthermore, both reflective strategies showed an increasingly positive relationship to the use of integrated tactics as self concept improved. The coefficients of correlation between Deep Learning and HIPS-I are +.16 for students with a low self concept and +.53 for those with a high self concept. The corresponding coefficients for Elaborative Learning are +.05 and +.35. Thus, the relationships between the reflective strategies and integrated tactics are positive, and this is most clearly true when self concept is high. As shown in Table 3, this was also true when DAT-S was used as a measure of integrated information processing.

A major difference between Deep and Elaborative Learning appeared to concern the use of *holist* tactics. While neither Deep nor Elaborative Learning involved holist tactics when academic self concept was low, Elaborative Learning involved increased use of such tactics as academic self concept increased. Specifically, coefficients of correlation between Elaborative Learning and HIPS-RB increased from zero with low self concept to +.35 with high self concept, while Deep Learning remained uncorrelated with use of holist tactics regardless of self concept status. In the case of the Myers-Briggs Type Indicator, there was an increased correlation between Elaborative Learning and MBTI-Intuition as academic self concept increased ($r = +.25$ when self concept was low and +.45 when self concept was high). The *reverse* was true of Deep Learning as the coefficients went from +.51 when self concept was low to +.18 when it was high. Since Table 3 suggests that as self concept improves the use of integrated tactics increases more in the case of Deep than of Elaborative Learning, it may be the case that integrated tactics are supplanting holist tactics in the case of Deep Learning.

Also, Elaborative Learning involved a component of extraversion (MBTI-E) when self concept was high ($r = .14$ with low self concept and .52 when it was high), while Deep Learning seemed to involve extraversion when self concept was low ($r = .49$ when self concept was low and .08 when it was high). Finally, Table 3 indicates that regardless of whether academic self concept was high or low, both Deep and Elaborative Learning related negatively to test anxiety or fear of failure as assessed by the Achievement Anxiety Test (Alpert & Haber, 1960), with r's ranging between -.29 and -.44.

Agentic Learning

The Agentic Learning scale assesses an orientation toward work and task completion. It tends to be associated with effortful processing. It is detail-oriented and involves seeing the smaller tasks that make up a bigger task (the parts that make up the whole) and seeing the order in which they have to be completed in order to reach a goal. Two subscales address specific aspects of Agentic Learning. *Agentic Learning: Serial* emphasizes proceeding step-by-step, one thing at a time, with a dislike for switching from one task to another until the first one is completed. It also includes attention to temporal sequencing of activities (scheduling or programming). It involves making lists of things to do and checking them off as they are completed. The other subscale, *Agentic Learning: Analytic* includes logical decomposition of the constituent components of tasks and it seems to assess tactics which are rule-based.

Suggestions for students:

> You can improve your agentic skills by making to-do-lists, scheduling your activities and sticking to the schedule, making a detailed plan for writing your next term paper, and outlining the specific steps you will follow when studying for your next test. If you are too worried about task completion (too focused) you can achieve balance by paying more attention to the "big picture" and general ideas in addition to focussing on specific facts and details, relying on feelings and intuition at times, letting your mind wander from time to time to see how information is interrelated or how it relates to your personal experience. Playfulness should balance seriousness. Proceeding sequentially is good when there is a deadline to meet. In order to get jobs done, we often have to stick to a time table. However, changing from one task to another or taking things as they come sometimes stimulates creativity and can make work interesting.

In the interview study, high Agentic students (along with those low on Deep and Elaborative Learning) expressed a preference for objective rather than essay tests. Also the majority of high Agentic students reported feeling organized (not so for Methodical learners, see below). This was reflected in how they go about writing a paper in that the strategies of high Agentic students were classified as systematic while those employed by low Agentic students were rated as intuitive. Furthermore, high Agentic students indicated in the interviews that they preferred to conform to conventions, do one thing at a time in serial order, and strived to remember as much as possible factual data to support the main ideas they were studying.

The correlational study explored the relationships between ILP-R Agentic Learning and information processing tactics using HIPS-LB, HIPS-RB, and HIPS-I. We found that students dedicated to agentic learning seemed to rely upon serialist tactics and avoid holist tactics. This tendency was most evident when self concept was high, suggesting that the students who specialized in agentic learning were comfortable with their serialist emphasis. As Table 3 indicates, the coefficient of correlation between Agentic Learning and HIPS-LB was $r = +.16$ when self concept was low and $r = +.36$ when self concept was high. These same students demonstrated an avoidance of holist tactics, with r's ranging from -.31 with HIPS-RB when self concept was low to -.57 when self concept was high. This pattern is the reverse of that obtained above with the reflective learning scales (Deep and Elaborative). When the results from the MBTI were examined, agentic learning again involved serialist tactics and avoidance of holist tactics. For example, the Agentic Learning Scale was consistently related to MBTI-J regardless of self concept (+.61 with low self concept and +.75 when self concept was high); similarly the relationships with MBTI-N were negative, ranging from -.50 to -.66 and indicating that the agentic student is high on MBTI-S. The avoidance of holistic tactics might well stem from the fact that such tactics can delay the completion of a task, and task completion is the primary goal of agentic learning (e.g., when working on a deadline).

The relationships between the Agentic Learning scales and integrated information processing tactics were either zero or negative depending upon the assessment device used, suggesting either low integration or the absence of a relationship with integrated processing. As can be seen in Table 3, correlation with HIPS-I was essentially zero; the corresponding relationships with the DAT-S ranged from -.34 to -.39 as self concept increased.

Agentic Learning was more highly correlated to fear of failure when academic self concept was high, suggesting that agentic students feel better about themselves when they are anxious. When self concept was low, the correlation between Agentic Learning and test anxiety (AAT) was -.09, but when academic self concept was high the correlation increased to +.53. It should be noted that, in general, results from the correlational study suggested that study strategies which rely more upon use of serialist information processing tactics tended to be energized by anxiety or worry. This statement was supported by positive correlation coefficients between HIPS-LB and both the Achievement Anxiety Test and the MBTI-Worry subscale ($r = +.55$ with AAT and +.33 with MBTI-Worry). It would be interesting to determine whether individuals are worrisome because they use serialist tactics or whether they worry *in order to* engage serialist tactics. In other words, worry itself may be a tactic for managing information processing.

Methodical Learning

The Methodical Learning scale assesses a self-proclaimed adherence to traditional "good" study methods such as recopying notes, reviewing frequently, outlining, making charts and diagrams, using the dictionary, maintaining regular study hours, and preparing a list of questions expected to be on an exam. These study methods should generally be effective, but it has been our experience that many students who score high on this scale often have low or average scores on measures of achievement such as course grades.

Suggestions for students:

> Sometimes you can learn more by thinking about information than you can by 'studying' it in the traditional way. Go for a walk and think about what you were reading, find personal significance in the information you study, don't put too much faith in 'methods' alone. Looking up a word in a dictionary or recopying your notes doesn't necessarily mean that you will remember the information. Sometimes it's very helpful to discuss material with other students or argue with your teachers about a topic you are trying to learn. If you feel you could benefit from a more methodical approach to studying, you may want to try to pace yourself and work out a system that works for you. But remember that no method can replace true interest and understanding of a subject.

In the interview study, those with high scores on ILP-R Methodical Learning seemed concerned with issues involving discipline and study habits. Interestingly, many students scoring high on the Methodical Learning scale, reported not feeling good about themselves as students. When asked "What do you dislike about yourself?", people high on Methodical Learning listed lack of "control" and "will power" twice as frequently as those with low scores on this scale. High Methodical students also indicated that they used a "systematic strategy" when writing papers.

The correlational study revealed few relationships between the ILP-R Methodical Learning Scale and information processing tactics. However, the MBTI revealed some interesting differences between Methodical students with high and low self concepts. Methodical Learning in the case of a student with a low self concept evidences extraversion while that of a student with a high self concept involves an orientation to task completion. Methodical Learning related to MBTI-E for low self-concept students ($r = .43$), but with high self-concept students it related to MBTI-J ($r = .44$). In the past, we were confused because some students who used methodical learning seemed sincere and extremely conscientious while others were somewhat dissimulating and manipulative. It appears from this data that one variable dividing these two groups might be self concept. When self concept was low, there was no relationship between Methodical Learning and MBTI-J, but when self concept was high this relationship was substantial. Similar results were reported by Geisler-Brenstein et al. (in press) involving the NEO-PI Conscientiousness scale (which is highly correlated with the MBTI-J scale). It should be added that Methodical Learning showed no relationship to test anxiety.

Literal Memorization

As the name suggests, this scale assesses an emphasis upon committing information to memory literally, typically by repeating it over and over instead of agreeing or disagreeing with it. It can be a useful strategy where necessary, but our experience suggests that students who emphasize it are excessively driven by fear of failure. This was supported by the interview study which seemed to indicate that students high on Literal Memorization cared about their grades but were troubled by insecurity and low self-esteem.

Suggestions to students:

> Memorization is necessary to pass examinations in certain courses. If you want to improve your memorization skills there are some excellent books available to help you improve your memory. As usual, balance is important. You can often remember material by just thinking about it instead of only repeating it. People who always memorize often don't trust their ability to remember just by thinking about information. If you want to increase your confidence that you can do this, try studying for some of your tests by thinking about the material instead of repeating it. Draw some pictures or diagrams connecting and comparing and contrasting the ideas, think about class material like a lecture you just heard or part of a textbook you just read. Since you want to be successful and raise your confidence, be sure to spend extra time preparing for these particular tests. Remember, you are not only trying to pass the particular test but you are also trying to practice thinking about material as a way of studying it, and you are trying to raise your confidence that you can do it that way. You'll be

accomplishing several goals all at once so be prepared to invest some extra time.

In the correlational study, there were no relationships between ILP-R Literal Memorization and information processing tactics as assessed via the HIPS or the DAT. However, there were some interesting relationships with MBTI-J suggesting an emphasis upon task completion, and there was a relationship with MBTI-F suggesting a tendency to avoid disapproval. Among students who had a good self concept, Literal Memorization related positively to MBTI-J ($r = .34$) and to MBTI-F ($r = .32$); these relationships were less evident in students with a low self concept. It appears that the student who is committed to literally memorizing the words of text and lecture (high self concept) is taking school seriously, cares about the outcome and defines success in terms of the completion of class assignments (i.e., meeting the demands of instructors). The correlation coefficients between ILP-R Literal Memorization and the AAT (test anxiety) measure were small and insignificant ($r = +.12$ and $r = +.18$, respectively) regardless of the status of the student's academic self concept. However, results with the MBTI-Worry subscale were more striking. There was a clearly positive correlation with MBTI-Worry as self concept increased (from 0 when self concept was low to $+.52$ when self concept was high).

STABLE THREADS, DIVERSE PATTERNS

Ideally, students should be able to use the above strategies to the best of their advantage, choosing whichever strategy best fits the demands of the situation and the task at hand. However, some students have been shown to continually adhere to a limited set of strategies *regardless* of situational requirements. For example, students who habitually focus on surface characteristics (high on Literal Memorization) have been shown to be unwilling/unable to attend to stimuli at a deeper level of understanding. On the other hand, students who seek to *understand* material instead of memorizing isolated facts (high on the Deep Learning scales) are also able to focus on details when required to do so. Their more elaborate network of associations is hierarchically organized and actually facilitates recall of pieces of information (Wenestam, 1980; Schmeck & Ribich, 1978). We argue that memorizing literally in a habitual way is indicative of more profound issues (e.g., low self-esteem and resulting fear of failure) which cannot be addressed without looking at the underlying dynamics of the person as a whole.

We recently examined the psychological mechanisms underlying learning behavior in more detail by relating ILP-R scales and subscales with facet scales of the NEO-Personality Inventory (Geisler-Brenstein, 1993; Geisler-Brenstein et al., in press) and found that differences in learning behavior and attitudes share a significant amount of variance with Costa and McCrae's (1985) *Big Five* personality dimensions (Neuroticism, Extraversion, Openness to Experience, Agreeableness, and Conscientiousness). While these findings may be taken to suggest simply that personality differences are related to learning behavior, we argued that both may be expressions of the same underlying dimensions of cognitive and affective organization (Geisler-Brenstein et al., in press). In a recent article on manifestations of personality in cognition, learning and teaching, Messick (1994) similarly proposes a new perspective on stylistic dimensions by suggesting "not to treat styles as cognitive variables that are related to personality variables but to view them as bridging variables that embody cognition and personality simultaneously" (p. 133). He calls for a guiding personality theory and says "If this theory illuminates the nature of form-giving structures in personality development, then styles can be treated not as cognitive or affective or behavioral variables related to personality but as the manifestations of form-giving personality structures in cognition, affect, and behavior" (p.133).

As we have demonstrated in our research (Geisler-Brenstein, 1993; Geisler-Brenstein et al., in press), the five factor model shows promise for providing an integrative, descriptive framework for the discussion of individual difference observed in a learning context. In a similar vein, in their research on critical thinking, Facione et al. (1993) have identified "a *characterological profile*, a constellation of attitudes, a set of intellectual virtues, or, if you will, a group of habits of mind which we refer to as the overall disposition to think critically" (p. 2; italics added). This profile comprises seven specific aspects: open-mindedness, truth-seeking, analyticity, systematicity, confidence in critical thinking, inquisitiveness, and cognitive maturity. Thus, research suggests that we can identify a limited set of higher-order dimensions of variability with regard to how students approach learning tasks and situations. The question remains to what extent idealized characterizations reflect the reality of student learning. Mulaik (1987) discusses the *average man fallacy* which refers to the reification or objectification of a mean value as a statistical artifact with no objective referent. Likewise, in research on learning and cognition, the average (or for that matter, the "ideal") perceiver, problem solver, or text processor is likely to be a statistical and theoretical artifact rather than being representative of any individual's true performance. Instead, all learners exhibit a unique *constellation* of preferences in the ways they approach learning tasks and in the ways they perceive and process information.

Researchers need to be concerned *both* with low-level operationalizations and with general dimensions of individual variability in order to examine the complex manifestations of higher-order preferences in context. As Briggs (1989) pointed out, "our success in reducing the trait language to its basic dimensions should not be taken to mean that these dimensions are optimal for description or prediction" (p. 251). In a similar vein, Allport (1958) has questioned the ideographic utility of nomothetic models like the five factor model of personality:

> Factors are simply a summary principle of classification of many measures... [they] offer scalable dimensions; that is to say, they are common units in respect to which all personalities can be compared. None of them corresponds to the cleavages that exist in any single personality. (pp. 251-252)

We therefore advocate the use of profile analysis and typological groupings of student profiles which indicate a person's standing on a number of specific dimensions simultaneously (Geisler-Brenstein et al., in press). We have found that the information gathered at the facet-level of individual profiles provides valuable information regarding interactive effects among subscales which is lost in correlational analyses of aggregate data. Similarly, John and Robins (1993) describe the benefits of looking at actual combinations of scores:

> nomothetic dimensions do not constitute a model of personality structure if we mean by structure the particular configuration, patterning, and dynamic organization of the individuals' total set of characteristics. Idiographic

analyses are needed to elucidate the ways in which [...] factors combine within particular individuals; although not strictly idiographic, typological analyses represent a person-centered approach that can identify groups or subsets of individuals who have similar configurations of characteristics and share the same basic personality structure. (p. 229)

Although some educational researchers acknowledge the existence of general cognitive, attitudinal, and motivational preferences, many are reluctant to accept the deterministic connotations of the style concept. Thus proponents of style constructs are often accused of being narrowly focused on the nature-side of the age-old nature-nurture debate (Biggs, 1993). However, change and stability are not mutually exclusive. Instead, the evidence from behavior genetics and personality research (Digman, 1990; Neubauer & Neubauer, 1990; Tellegen et al., 1988) suggests that people have a certain range of potential which can be shaped and expanded as individuals take advantage of the opportunities the environment provides. Thus, "traits are not repetitive habits, but inherently dynamic dispositions that interact with the opportunities and challenges of the moment" (McCrae & Costa, 1994, p. 175).

As the constructivist perspective implies, conceptualization does not occur without context (thinking is always thinking about something). By the same token, objective reality does not exist separately from people's constructions of that reality. Thus constructivism indirectly reintroduces person variables in that people's constructions are necessarily influenced by their prior knowledge and cognitive and affective biases. As Snow (1994) states,

abilities are affordances-properties of the union of person and environment that exhibit the opportunity structure of a situation and the effectivity structure of the person in taking advantage of the opportunities afforded for learning. Particular persons are tuned or prepared to perceive particular affordances in a situation that invites the particular actions they are able to assemble. (p. 31)

While abilities may increase over time through practice, stylistic preferences are supposed to be stable across time and situations. However, as Facione et al. (1994) point out with regard to the disposition toward critical thinking, styles and skills (or abilities) are likely to be related in a complex interactive feedback loop where a style or disposition encourages the use of the corresponding skill and success experiences are then likely to reinforce the disposition (see also Perkins, Jay, & Tishman, 1993). As Sternberg (1994) puts it, "a style is not a level or even kind of ability, but rather a way of utilizing an ability or set of abilities. In other words, it is a proclivity, not a talent" (p. 225). Thus, stylistic preferences come about through a crystallization process based on adaptive utility. Schmeck & Geisler-Brenstein (1989) describe the process as follows:

In the process of adapting [...] the person is changed further by new experience in a sort of "crystallization" process that operates to establish identity, individuality, and predictability (i.e., individual differences). Learning style becomes more and more "crystallized" as we approach subsequent school settings with perceptual category systems and interpretations developed in past encounters with school. (p. 102)

The terms *orientation, disposition, learning style* or *preference* used in learning research capture the notion that individuals (some more than others) tend to develop certain habitual ways of perceiving, processing, and acting upon information which show some stability across situations and time. In our thinking, styles are by no means "neither negotiable nor sensitive to context, being static in-built features of the individual" (Biggs, 1993). Instead, as Riding and Cheema (1991) point out, a style can be understood in terms of its more stable structural elements or as a process or a combination of both:

> if cognitive style is viewed as a process, then the focus is on how it changes; as such, trainers may even try to foster that change. Style areas can be built upon and can be used to compensate for or strengthen weaknesses. Style is seen as dynamic, not 'frozen forever'. For others, cognitive style is viewed as both process and structure. It may be relatively stable, not changeable like liquid with no form on its own, yet at the same time always in flux. In such a view, style structure is continually modified as new events influence it directly or indirectly. (p. 195)

AWARENESS AND CHOICE

At the highest level of development, learners should be able to use a number of opposing strategies in flexible alternation as required by situational demands. As the concept of learning *strategies* implies, learning behavior should be goal-directed and involve conscious selection of a course of action from a range of possible alternatives based on awareness of one's capabilities and the requirements of the situation. However, few individuals achieve a level where they can use different cognitive functions with equal ease and skill. Therefore, students' inherent cognitive and affective preferences and strengths may place limitations upon what they can/want to learn and how they learn it (cf. Schmeck, 1988a/b). It has been our experience that only few learners have reached a level of self-awareness and self-regulation required for truly *strategic learning*.

Messick points out that the same phenomenon can be strategy or style (e.g., risk taking vs. cautiousness) depending upon how much *choice* the individual has. Learning style research has shown that the more developed an individual is, the more he or she is likely to have a certain degree of meta-awareness and acquired flexibility so that an informed judgement of the situation can be made and the appropriate strategies can be chosen in flexible alternation. Learning researchers have extensively discussed the benefits of versatility (e.g., Biggs, 1985; Entwistle & Ramsden, 1983; McCarthy et al., 1986; Pask, 1988; Schmeck, 1988; Torrance & Rockenstein, 1988) as well as the dangers of one-sided functioning. For example, Pask (1988) discusses two "pathologies" which result when an individual's preference has developed *at the expense of* another function. While a certain inherent preference for one or the other style is considered normal, the exclusive reliance on one mode can be considered a pathology. Thus, a general global orientation may range from an extremely "globetrotting pathology" to a more integrated form of processing which, in the case of the global processor, requires more analytic functioning. Likewise, the extremely analytic processor falls victim to the "improvidence pathology" if he or she overrelies upon focussing and atomizing and a more global component is needed for more integrated functioning. Since an integrated level of functioning is not easily achieved, students may show a global or analytic cross-situational bias.

While many strategy instruction programs are quite optimistic about the ability to change students' behaviors, attitudes, and self-efficacy beliefs, others have argued that some of the obtained effects are short-lived and superficial. By analogy, Schmeck (1988a/b) has pointed out that assertiveness training may teach students to say "no" and yet not change the fact that someone does not "want" to say no (i.e., is inherently shy). By the same token, a student who has learned to mimic the behavior of a reflective student is not necessarily better off than one who has learned to face the underlying issues which prevent him or her from approaching school as a reflective learner. Therefore, some have warned against excessive optimism on the part of clinicians, counselors, and educational practitioners who believe that maladaptive styles of functioning can easily be changed or modified to lead to better emotional health and increases in performance:

> wholesale attempts to encourage stylistic versatility in all students is not only a waste of time, but also can be psychologically damaging. Extremely specialised students should be left alone, secure within the confines of their dominant modes. Certainly, attempts should be made to adjust teaching to suit these styles, but not to change them. It follows that versatility is a reasonable goal for those who are already predisposed to it. [...] Secondly, it would seem that treating learning styles as cognitive styles, bereft of affective, motivational and defensive implications, is naive. Thirdly, many ethical questions are raised by attempts to modify styles, personality, or otherwise. Separating out relatively flexible students for special treatment smacks of elitism and would be controversial. Finally, a genuine concern for personality development as a goal of education would require that teaching becomes a form of counseling over and above the mere transmission of information. This is unlikely to happen since the traditional separation of 'intellect' from 'personality' is too entrenched in academic circles. However, versatility is, I believe, an eminently sensible educational goal, one that is achievable, perhaps in isolated pockets where there are teachers who have the necessary understanding and commitment to their students. (Miller, 1991, pp. 235-236)

Fundamental changes are not easily accomplished, since by the time a person has reached adulthood, personality and other styles of functioning have become deeply ingrained. Research has shown that a person's "operating system" exerts a powerful influence on the acquisition of new knowledge in that it processes information which is congruent with existing thought structures more quickly, accurately and deeply than incongruent information (Campbell & Lavallee, 1993). Thus change can usually only come about via gradual accommodation. Only major counseling interventions are likely to have a more profound effect, that is, if they succeed in bringing about a true rearrangement of established belief structures.

So where does this leave us? What is the contribution of an instrument such as the ILP-R? Perhaps the most fundamental and yet most overlooked benefit to be gained from a self-report instrument is that of simple mirroring and simply raising consciousness. Counselors report that a client who has come to acknowledge a personal characteristic will frequently ask "What am I supposed to *do* with that knowledge?" not realizing that the insight alone is an important outcome in itself. Being aware of one's strengths and shortcomings and accepting them for what they are is an important first step toward becoming a mature, self-directed learner. Knowledge about stylistic preferences is valuable in that it makes inherent biases transparent (for students and teachers), thus allowing them to capitalize on strengths and concentrate on improving (or living with) weaknesses. As the saying "you have to reach them to teach them" implies, knowledge of individual differences is also a prerequisite for successful communication and teaching.

> Educators need to become aware of their own teaching styles and intellectual preferences and of those of their students, and of the possible consequences of such preferences. They should remain flexible and experimental in their use of teaching styles so as to select a given style on the basis of what works best in a particular situation. (Sternberg, 1988, pp. 564-565)

Although student-teacher interaction is likely to be easier, more successful and pleasant when both are "on the same wavelength" (i.e., have similar preferences), the benefit of matching is debatable because it can lead to the one-sided reinforcement of stylistic tendencies. Pask's (1988) concept of stylistic pathologies illustrates this point. Likewise, we need to avoid "robbing Peter to serve Paul," i.e., perhaps unknowingly discriminating against some students while teaching to other students' styles. Preferably, an instructor should consider a variety of approaches with regard to giving assignments, types of tests, presentation of information, student participation, time-lines, etc., and be aware of his or her own biases as well as considerate of students' preferences.

SELF-CONCEPT: GROWING AS LEARNERS

Little is known about how to influence students to achieve more integrated functioning or why some students seem to be "stuck" within a particular style or preference as suggested by Pask's (1988) pathologies. Instructors wonder why some students fail to integrate facts and details into higher-level personal and conceptual schemata and, in fact, seem to actively resist any attempts to induce "deeper" forms of information processing. As suggested above, it is our position that in order to achieve higher levels of complexity and differentiation of cognitive resources, a person has to achieve higher levels of development as a person through increasing awareness.

As McCarthy & Schmeck (1988) point out, the "self" is a very powerful schema for encoding, organizing and elaborating individual experience. Self-reference has been shown to be a powerful process for improving retention (Schmeck & Meier, 1984). Since the self-concept is an emotionally loaded schema, information that is congruent with this network of self-knowledge is processed faster and retained better than incongruent information. Self-esteem and self-concept are integrally related. People with low self-esteem have been shown to have a self-concept which is fragmented and confused. The prototypical low self-esteem person is also "highly susceptible to and dependent on external self-relevant cues and their social perceptions and behaviors reflect a cautious and conservative orientation" (Campbell & Lavallee, 1993, p. 15). Kohut (1984) maintains that self-esteem is the "glue" that holds together the self and all of its cognitive functions. Also, our research has demonstrated very clearly that students with a high score on the ILP-R Academic Self-Esteem scale have a more coherent and developed self-concept (Geisler-Brenstein, et al., in press) and are therefore more *consistent* in stating their learning *preferences*, while at the same time, exhibiting *more flexibility* in their *behavioral and attitudinal responses*.

The data presented earlier suggest that the tactics which make up a strategy vary somewhat depending upon self concept variables. For example, the conceptual and personal strategies of deep and elaborative individuals integrate serialist and holist tactics to a greater extent when academic self concept is high. Furthermore, as self concept increases, the personal strategy of elaborative students increasingly involves holist tactics. On the other hand, the effortful strategy of students high on Agentic Learning involves increasing avoidance of holist tactics as academic self concept increases. Furthermore, their strategy involves a larger component of fear and worry when self concept is high, perhaps suggesting that for these students fear and worry are instrumental in generating effort, e.g., engaging serialist focus and avoiding holist distraction. If we were counseling an agentic student troubled by fear of failure, it might be helpful to point out that they may worry in order to help them avoid distractions. Just pointing out that worry is a *tactic* perhaps employed with *intent* might decrease the agentic student's feeling of being helplessly accosted by worry.

Healthy self concept development includes the ability to integrate opposites, and see others and oneself as complex beings as well as the development of a variety of self concepts for different roles (Marsh, 1993). Complexity of self-roles is an important factor in coping with blows to self esteem in a particular domain since the differentiated person still has other positive self images to rely upon. A poorly integrated self-concept, on the other hand, limits cognitive development by interfering with perception and information processing. Splitting and fragmentation make it impossible to perceive information accurately (e.g., a negative self-concept encourages selective attention), remember information accurately (distortions occur over time) and thus severely limit the ability to develop the information base and confidence necessary for sound judgment which requires weighing the pros and cons in light of an established value system (be it objective or subjectively based). While high self-esteem leads to open exploration, low self-esteem brings other agendas (e.g., need for approval) into the forefront and thus prevents optimum functioning.

The above suggests reasons why the normal developmental sequence from dualistic conceptions of reality and truth to more relativistic positions of personal commitment discussed by Perry (1970) and Riegel (1973) may be disrupted. As Riegel points out in his discussion of neo-Piagetian stages of intellectual development, the highest level of cognitive development implies a type of thinking that lies above formal reasoning. This type of *dialectical* reasoning involves contrasting opposing points of view or perceptions to arrive at probabilistic rather than absolute truths and requires a tolerance for ambiguity and uncertainty as well as acceptance of the possibility that ultimately there are only differing perspectives that are more or less useful rather than absolutes that will hold regardless of the circumstances. If one has a need to see things a certain way in order to fortify self-esteem, tolerance for ambiguity will be low and limits will be placed on integrative associations.

SUMMARY AND CONCLUSIONS

In this chapter, we have presented an empirically derived hierarchical and multifaceted conception of student learning in terms of learning styles and strategies as well as motivational and self-concept factors as it evolved from our research with the recently revised Inventory of Learning Processes (ILP-R). We have discussed student learning from a developmental perspective since a student's meta-cognitive abilities to adapt to changing instructional demands is greatly dependent upon awareness of personal vulnerabilities, preferences, and strengths. Moreover, the relative "maturity" of a style affects the effectiveness and cross-situational consistency of learning styles and strategies. One of our goals has been the development and application of an instrument that raises students' awareness so as to increase freedom of choice in selecting appropriate learning strategies.

While we agree with other researchers that cognitive and non-cognitive aspects should be separated conceptually, we have found that non-cognitive factors such as a student's overall academic self-concept, (i.e. level of self-esteem and feelings of self-efficacy with regard to different components of the learning process) as well as different aspects of motivation (interest, personal responsibility, effort) play a fundamental moderating role in the development, expression, and effective utilization of a learning style or strategy, thus forming an integral part of a student's approach to learning.

We have presented some findings which support the construct and discriminative validity of individual ILP-R facets. Descriptive data from an interview study provided some insights into how individual scales combine to form distinct learner profiles. Generally, we have argued for bringing research on individual differences in learning back to the level of the individual, rather than solely examining relationships among aggregate scores. Since many possible combinations among high or low scores on different dimensions may be lost at the level of group analyses, looking at profiles of individual students or subgroups of students allows for a more differentiated discussion of different constellations of scores instead of simplistically characterizing a student as scoring high or low on individual scales. Profile analysis thus provides researchers and practitioners with a means for incorporating concerns with moderator effects and interactions among dimensions at different levels of development.

Individual differences in learning behavior can be examined in terms of personal characteristics or situational affordances (similar to the old nomothetic versus ideographic distinction). Concrete acts of learning occur of course at the interface of the person, the situation, and the task. Thus, lower-level manifestations of individual difference dimensions may vary in context because they are likely not to be static, but dynamic and changing as an individual grows and matures and acquires new knowledge about the world and the self (Wakefield, 1989). Yet, we feel that it is possible to create a taxonomy of person characteristics at a higher level of abstraction which does contribute to an understanding of learner motivations and behavior.

The fact that we have chosen to examine variability in learning behavior as a function of person-characteristics rather than situational factors does not mean that we deny the importance of situational variables or the ability of individuals to adapt and change in response to situational demands. On the contrary, we have stressed the importance of an integrated self-concept as a moderating agent which negotiates the transition from stylistic fixation on one way of functioning (pathology) to versatility and integration of complementary preferences. Although the beneficial impact of a positive self-concept and sense of efficacy is well known to educators, discussions of individual differences in learning styles often fail to differentiate among manifestations of a "style" for those with a low or high academic self-concept and also fail to take different levels of personal and cognitive development into account.

As we learn more about qualitative differences in mental and affective organization, it becomes apparent that maturation takes different forms for different people. Self-concept and personal identity can only be achieved when the reality of these fundamental differences which affect the way people perceive information, think, solve problems and relate to others are acknowledged and nurtured. Our work has addressed these considerations in the hope of facilitating the formulation of successful interventions. As a result, we have become interested in raising academic self-awareness as a way of opening up opportunities to *choose* one's approach to learning rather than repeating old habits. While it is difficult to change deeply-rooted beliefs and habits, it is possible to affect students' self esteem by placing the individual in an environment which is consonant or harmonious with their learning style. By permitting several paths to achievement in a course, we may in a sense provide a "place for everyone" and thereby raise their esteem while simultaneously exposing them to alternative strategies that may enrich their repertoirs of learning behavior. We feel, that the recognition of individual differences and the understanding of their role in achievement are important elements in providing meaningful learning experiences that are both challenging and fair.

ACKNOWLEDGMENTS

We would like to express our appreciation to Kimberly Spurling for her assistance with qualitative data analysis.

REFERENCES

Allport, G.W. (1958). What units shall we employ? In G. Lindzey (Ed.), *Assessment of human motives* (pp. 238-260). New York: Reinhart.

Alpert, R., & Haber, R.N. (1960). Anxiety in academic achievement situations. *Journal of Abnormal and Social Psychology, 61*, 207-215.

Baron, J.B., & Sternberg, R.S. (Eds.). (1987). *Teaching thinking skills.* New York: W.H. Freeman.

Bennett, G.K., Seashore, H.G., & Wesman, A.G. (1989). *Differential aptitude tests: Perceptual abilities test.* New York: The Psychological Corporation.

Berg, C.A., & Sternberg, R.J. (1985). A triarchic theory of intellectual development during adulthood. *Developmental Review, 5*, 334-370.

Beyler, J., & Schmeck, R.R. (1992). Assessment of individual differences in preferences for holistic-analytic strategies: Evaluation of some commonly available instruments. *Educational and Psychological Measurement, 52* , 709-719.

Biggs, J.B. (1985). The role of metalearning in study processes. *Journal of Educational Psychology, 55*, 185-212.

Biggs, J. (1993). What do inventories of students' learning processes really measure? A theoretical review and clarification. *British Journal of Educational Psychology, 63,* 3-19.

Boekaerts, M. (1992). The adaptable learning process: Initiating and maintaining behavioral change. *Journal of Applied Psychology: An International Review, 41 (4)*, 377-397.

Boekaerts, M. (1994). The interface between intelligence and personality as determinants of classroom learning. In D.H. Saklofske, & M. Zeidner (Eds.), *Handbook of personality and intelligence*. New York: Plenum Press.

Briggs, S.R. (1989). The optimum level of measurement for personality constructs. In D.M. Buss, & N. Cantor (Eds.), *Personality psychology: Recent trends and emerging directions*. New York: Springer Verlag.

Campbell, J.D., & Lavallee, L.F. (1993). Who am I? The role of self-concept confusion in understanding the behavior of people with low self-esteem. In R.F. Baumeister (Ed.), *Self-esteem: The puzzle of low self-regard* (pp. 3-20). New York: Plenum Press.

Coopersmith, S. (1981). *SEI: Self-esteem inventories. A manual for administration, scoring, and interpretation*. Palo Alto, CA: Consulting Psychologists Press.

Costa, P.T., & McCrae, R.R. (1985). *The NEO Personality Inventory manual*. Odessa, FL: Psychological Assessment Resources, Odessa, FL: Psychological Assessment Resources.

Costa, P.T., & McCrae, R.R. (1992). *The Revised NEO Personality Inventory (NEO-PI-R) and NEO Five-Factor Inventory (NEO-FFI) professional manual*.

Cronbach, L.J., & Snow, R.E. (1977). *Aptitudes and instructional methods: A handbook for research on interactions*. New York: Irvington.

Crowne, D., & Marlowe, D. (1964). *The approval motive*. New York: Wiley.

Digman, J.M. (1990). Personality structure: Emergence of the five-factor model. *Annual Review of Psychology, 41*, 417-440.

Dörner, D. (1989). *Die Logik des Mißlingens: Strategisches Denken in komplexen Situationen*. Reinbek: Rowohlt Verlag.

Entwistle, N., & Ramsden, P. (1983). *Understanding student learning*. London: Croom Helm.

Eysenck, M.W., & Keane, M.T. (1990). *Cognitive psychology: A student's handbook*. Hillsdale, NJ: Erlbaum.

Facione, P.A., Sanchez, C.A., Facione, N.C., & Gainen, J. (1994). *The disposition toward critical thinking*. Paper presented at the American Educational Research Association, New Orleans, LA.

Gardner, H. (1983). *Frames of mind: The theory of multiple intelligences*. New York: Basic Books.

Geisler-Brenstein, E. (1987). *Cross-cultural measurement of cognitive / learning styles and related personality traits*. Unpublished Master's thesis, Southern Illinois University, Carbondale, Illinois.

Geisler-Brenstein. (1993). *An integrative approach to the study of individual differences in learning: Convergent and discriminant validity of learning style and personality constructs*. Unpublished doctoral dissertation. Southern Illinois University, Carbondale, Illinois.

Geisler-Brenstein, E., Schmeck, R.R., & Hetherington, J. (1995). *Confirmatory Factor Analysis of the Revised Inventory of Learning Processes*. Unpublished manuscript, Southern Illinois University, Carbondale, IL.

Geisler-Brenstein, E., Schmeck, R.R., & Hetherington, J. (in press). An individual difference perspective on student diversity. *Higher Education*.

Gough, H.G. (1957). *Manual for the California Psychological Inventory*. Palo Alto, CA: Consulting Psychologists Press.

Granott, N., & Gardner, H. (1994). When minds meet: Interactions, coincidence, and development in domains of ability. In R.J. Sternberg, & R.K. Wagner (Eds.), *Mind in context* (pp. 171-201). New York: Cambridge University Press.

John, O.P., & Robins, R.W. (1993). Gordon Allport: Father and critic of the Five-Factor Model. In K.H. Craik, R. Hogan, & R.N. Wolfe (Eds.), *Fifty years of personality psychology*. New York: Plenum Press.

Jonassen, D.H., & Grabowski, B.L. (1993). *Handbook of individual differences, learning, and instruction*. Hillsdale, NJ: Erlbaum.

Kemler-Nelson, D.G. (1984). The effect of intention on what concepts are acquired. *Journal of Verbal Learning and Verbal Behavior, 23*, 734-759.

Kohut, H. (1984). *How does analysis cure?* Chicago: The University of Chicago Press.

Linn, M.C., & Petersen, A.C. (1985). Emergence and characterization of sex differences in spatial ability: a metaanalysis. *Child Development, 56*, 1479-1498.

MacGregor, L. (1989). *The impact of self-assessment on implicit and explicit memory performance*. Unpublished Master's thesis. Southern Illinois University, Carbondale, Illinois.

Mandl, H., Gruber, H., & Renkl, A. (1993). Das träge Wissen. *Psychologie Heute, 20 ,* 64-69.

Marsh, H. (1993). Academic self-concept: Theory, measurement, and research. In J. Suls (Ed.), *Psychological perspectives on the self*. Hillsdale, NJ: Erlbaum.

Marton, F. (1993). Towards a pedagogy of awareness. Paper presented at the 5th European Conference of the European Association for Research on Learning and Instruction, Aix-en-Provence, France.

Marton, F., Dall'Alba, G., & Beaty, E. (in press). Conceptions of learning. *International Journal of Educational Research*.

McCarthy, P.R., Shaw, T., & Schmeck, R.R. (1986). Behavioral analysis of client learning style during counseling. *Journal of Counseling Psychology, 88*, 249-254.

McCarthy, P.R., & Schmeck, R.R. (1988). Students' self-concepts and the quality of learning in public schools and universities. In R.R. Schmeck (Ed.), *Learning strategies and learning styles* (pp. 131-158). New York: Plenum Press.

McCrae, R.R., & Costa, P.T. (1994). The stability of personality: Observations and evaluations. *Current Directions in Psychological Science, 3*, 173-175.

Meier, S., McCarthy, P.R., & Schmeck, R.R. (1984). Validity of self-efficacy as a predictor of writing performance. *Cognitive Therapy and Research, 8*, 107-120.

Messick, S. (1994). The matter of style: Manifestations of personality in cognition, learning, and teaching. *Educational Psychologist, 29* (3), 121-136.

Miller, A. (1991). Personality types, learning styles, and educational goals. *Educational Psychology, 11*, 217-238.

Mulaik, S.A. (1987). A brief history of the philosophical foundations of exploratory factor analysis. *Multivariate Behavioral Research, 22*, 267-305.

Myers, I.B., & McCaulley, M.H. (1985). *Manual: A guide to the development and use of the Myers-Briggs Type Indicator*. Palo Alto, CA: Consulting Psychologists Press.

Neubauer, P.B., & Neubauer, A. (1990). *Nature's thumbprint*. Reading, MA: Addison-Wesley.

Pask, G. (1988). Learning strategies, teaching strategies, and conceptual or learning style. In R.R. Schmeck (Ed.), *Learning strategies and learning styles* (pp. 83-100). New York: Plenum Press.

Perkins, D.N., Jay, E., & Tishman, S. (1993). Beyond abilities: A dispositional theory of thinking. *The Merrill Palmer Quarterly, 39,* 1-21

Perry, W. F. (1970). *Forms of intellectual and ethical development in the college years: A scheme.* New York: Holt, Rinehart & Winston.

Pressley, M., Borkowski, J.G., & Schneider, W. (1989). Good information processing: what it is and how can education promote it? *International Journal of Educational Research, 13,* 857-867.

Pressley, M., Harris, K.R., & Marks, M.B. (1992). But good strategy instructors are constructivist. *Educational Psychology Review, 4,* 3-31.

Riding, R., & Cheema, I. (1991). Cognitive styles - an overview and integration. *Educational Psychology, 11,* 193-215.

Riegel, K. F. (1973). Dialectic Operations: The final period of Cognitive Development. *Human Development, 16,* 346-370.

Saunders, D. (1987). *Type Differentiation Indicator.* Palo Alto, CA: Consulting Psychologists Press.

Schmeck, R.R. (1983). Learning styles of college students. *Individual Differences in Cognition,* 233-279.

Schmeck, R.R. (Ed.). (1988a). *Learning strategies and learning styles.* New York: Plenum Press.

Schmeck, R.R. (1988b). Individual differences and learning strategies. In C. Weinstein, P. Alexander, & E. Goetz, E. (Eds.), *Learning and study strategies: Issues in assessment, instruction, and evaluation* (pp. 171-192). New York: Academic Press.

Schmeck, R.R., & Geisler-Brenstein, E. (1989). Individual differences that affect the way students approach learning. *Learning and Individual Differences, 1,* 85-124.

Schmeck, R.R., & Geisler-Brenstein, E. (1995). *The Revised Inventory of Learning Processes Manual.* Carbondale, IL: Individuation Technologies.

Schmeck, R. R., Geisler-Brenstein, E., & Cercy, S. P. (1991). Self-concept and learning: The Revised Inventory of Learning Processes. *Educational Psychology, 11,* 343-362.

Schmeck, R.R., & Meier, S. (1984). Self reference as a learning strategy and a learning style. *Human Learning, 3,* 9-17.

Schmeck, R.R., & Ribich, F. (1978). Construct validation of the Inventory of Learning Processes. *Applied Psychological Measurement, 2,* 551-562.

Schmeck, R.R., Ribich, F., & Ramanaiah, N. (1977). Development of a self-report inventory for using individual differences in learning processes. *Applied Psychological Measurement, 1,* 413-431.

Schmeck, R.R., & Spofford, M. (1982). Attention to semantic versus phonetic verbal attributes as a function of individual differences in arousal and learning strategy. *Contemporary Educational Psychology, 7,* 312-319.

Schneider, W., & Weinert, F.E. (Eds.), (1990). *Interactions among aptitudes, strategies, and knowledge in cognitive performance.* New York: Springer-Verlag.

Snow, R.E. (1989). Aptitude, instruction, and individual development. *International Journal of Educational Research, 13,* 869-879.

Snow, R.E. (1994). Abilities in academic tasks. In R.J. Sternberg, & R.K. Wagner (Eds.), *Mind in context* (pp. 3-37). New York: Cambridge University Press.

Sternberg, R. J.& Martin, M. (1988). When teaching thinking does not work, what goes wrong? *Teachers College Record, 89,* 555-577.

Sternberg, R. J. (1989). Domain-generality versus domain-specificity: The life and impending death of a false dichotomy. *Merrill-Palmer Quarterly, 35,* 115-130.

Sternberg, R. J. (1994). PRSVL: An integrative framework for understanding mind in context. In R.J. Sternberg, & R.K. Wagner (Eds.), *Mind in context* (pp. 218-232). New York: Cambridge University Press.

Tellegen, A., Lykken, D.T., Bouchard, T.J., Wilcox, K.J., Segal, N.L., & Rich, S. (1988). Personality similarity in twins reared apart and together. *Journal of Personality and Social Psychology, 54,* 1031-1039.

Tiedeman, J. (1989). Measures of cognitive styles: A critical review. *Educational Psychologist, 24,* 261-275.

Torrance, P., & Rockenstein, Z. (1988). Styles of thinking and creativity. In R.R. Schmeck (Ed.), *Learning strategies and learning styles* (pp. 275-290). New York: Plenum Press.

Torrance, E.P., Taggart, B., & Taggart, W. (1984). *Human information processing survey.* Bensenville, Illinois: Scholastic Testing Service.

Tracy, K., Schmeck, R.R., & Spofford, M. (1980). *Determiners of vocational interest: Sex, spatial-verbal abilities, and information processing style.* Paper presented at the annual meeting of the Midwestern Psychological Association, St. Louis, Missouri, U.S.A..

Wakefield, J. C. (1989). Levels of explanation in personality theory. In D.M.C.N. Buss (Ed.), *Personality psychology: Recent trends and emerging directions.* New York: Springer Verlag.

Wenestam, C.G. (1980). *Qualitative differences in retention.* Goteborg: Acta Universitatis Gothoburgensis.

APPENDIX 1

ILP-R Subscales- Sample items

Self-Efficacy: Cognitive Organization
> I have trouble keeping the information that I remember organized in my mind.
> I am often confused by what I study.

Self-Efficacy: Critical Thinking
> I have trouble drawing logical conclusions.
> I find it difficult to answer questions requiring critical evaluation.

Self-Efficacy: Fact Retention
> I am very good at learning facts (names and dates).
> I am good at picking the correct answer on a multiple choice test.

Motivation: Interest
> I go to school because I have to (answered "disagree").
> I get excited about learning new things.

Motivation: Personal Responsibility
> It's the teacher's job to tell me the answers.
> My life is mainly determined by other people.

Motivation: Effort
> I spend less time studying than most of my friends (answered "disagree").
> I carefully complete all class assignments.

Academic Self-Esteem
> If I am left to do things on my own, I worry whether I am doing the right thing.
> I usually feel very bad when someone criticizes me.

Academic Self-Assertion
> I express and assert myself in school.
> In a group, I'd rather sit back and listen to others than talk myself (answered "disagree").

Conventional Attitude
> I don't like when people go against the norm.
> I think it is bad to go against the laws of society.

Methodical Learning
> When I am studying I prepare a list of questions and answers that I expect to be on the exam.
> I always outline a paper thoroughly before I begin to write.

Deep Learning: Semantic
> Scientific explanations fascinate me.
> I like to compare different theories.

Deep Learning: Critical
> I often criticize the things that I read.
> I often find myself questioning things that I hear in lectures or read in books.

Elaborative Learning: Episodic
> I often seem to think in pictures.
> Ideas in books often make my mind wander to other topics not necessarily related to what I am reading.

Elaborative Learning: Self-Actualizing
> In my heart, I feel that experience is as important as school instruction.
> I am interested mainly in self-development, in becoming.

Agentic Learning: Serial
> When doing homework, I usually finish one task completely before starting something new.
> I like to jump around from one task to another (answered "disagree").

Agentic Learning: Analytic
> The best approach to any kind of problem is systematic and logical thinking.
> I generally prefer to work on each part of a problem i order, working out one part at a time.

Literal Memorization
> I usually memorize a lot of what I have to learn word for word.
> I usually don't have time to think about the implications of what I read.

APPENDIX 2

Study 1

Subjects and Procedure
Subjects were undergraduate college students (N=48, 43% male) representing different majors at a large midwestern university. Students received course credit for research participation. They first took the ILP-R in small group sessions and were subsequently interviewed via a guided interview protocol by a trained interviewer (who did not know students' ILP-R scores) in individually scheduled sessions. The interviewer followed a semi-formal protocol. Students were encouraged to respond freely, but probed to provide details or elaborate on specific aspects where necessary. The video-taped protocols were first content-analyzed to identify relevant issues for each of the topics. A categorization system was then developed for classification of the responses along the identified dimensions. Protocols were rated by two independent raters along each of the dimensions (interrater agreement was high for all questions > 85%). The coded interview data were examined via frequency and crosstab analysis. The construct validity of the ILP-R scales was assessed by relating scores on the inventory to the ratings of the interview responses.

Materials
The Inventory of Learning Processes-Revised (ILP-R) (Schmeck & Geisler-Brenstein, 1995) measures general preferences in learning styles: Deep Learning (Semantic, Critical), Elaborative Learning (Episodic, Self-Actualizing), Agentic Learning (Serial, Analytic), Methodical Learning, and Literal Memorization. It also assesses related motivational, attitudinal, and personality aspects of school learning: Academic Self-Efficacy (Cognitive Organization, Critical Thinking, Fact Retention), Academic Motivation (Interest, Personal Responsibility, and Effort), Self-Assertion, and Conventional Attitudes. The 150-item self-report questionnaire takes 20-30 minutes to complete. Responses are recorded on custom computer-scorable answer sheets and scored on a 6-point Likert scale with response options ranging from strongly disagree to strongly agree. Internal consistency reliabilities (Cronbach's a) range from .72 to .87 for the main scales, and from .58 to .83 for the subscales.

Study 2

Subjects and Procedure
Subjects were 70 undergraduate students enrolled in a 400-level individual differences course in psychology. Students participated on a voluntary basis as part of a self-exploration class project. Student responses were divided into high and low self-concept groups (one STD above or below the mean). Scale scores for different instruments were intercorrelated separately for both groups.

Materials
Myers-Briggs Type Indicator (MBTI) Form J. The MBTI (Myers & McCaulley, 1985) was originally designed to classify individuals on the basis of the psychological functions originally proposed by C.G. Jung. The version employed in the present study provides overall MBTI scores as well as five subscale scores for each of the four traditional MBTI indices (Extraversion/Introversion, Sensing/Intuition, Thinking/Feeling, and Judging/Perceiving). It also provides an overall score and seven subscale scores for a fifth dimension labelled Comfort/Discomfort. Overall scale reliabilities are comparable to the MBTI scoring; subscale reliabilities range from .38 to .72 (Thomson's Pooling Square). This inventory was used to measure serialist vs. holist information processing tactics as well as several personality dimensions including compliance (conformity) and worry. Beyler and Schmeck (1992) found that MBTI Judging and Sensing converged to measure serial tactics. Similarly, MBTI Perceiving and Intuiting converged to measure holist tactics.

Human Information Processing Survey (HIPS). The HIPS employs 40 multiple-choice items to measure differences which the authors (Taggart & Torrance, 1984) labeled "cerebral hemispheric preferences" (left-brained, right-brained, and integrated). Beyler and Schmeck (1992) reported that the left-brain scale assesses serialist information processing tactics while the right-brain scale assesses holist tactics. The Integrated scale of the HIPS loaded on a factor by itself; therefore, the DAT-Spatial Relations scale was included as an additional measure of integration.

Differential Aptitude Test: Space Relations (DAT-S). The DAT-S (Bennett, Seashore, & Wesman, 1989) assesses spatial visualization, a process which Linn and Petersen (1985) describe as flexible adaptation of a repertoire of solution strategies reflecting integrated functioning. The tasks on the DAT-S can be answered with a combination of rule-based and global tactics.

Social Desirability Scale (SDS). The SDS (Crowne & Marlowe, 1964) was designed to measure the need for social approval. It reflects the degree to which individuals use the tactics of impression management to achieve success.

Achievement Anxiety Test (AAT). The AAT (Alpert & Haber, 1960) assesses fear of failure. It asks students a series of questions regarding the degree of anxiety they experience when confronted with evaluative situations such as tests and class presentations.

Assessing Students' Motivation and Learning Strategies in the Classroom Context: The Motivated Strategies for Learning Questionnaire

Teresa Garcia and
Paul R. Pintrich

Current research on student classroom learning stresses the importance of considering both motivational and cognitive components of academic performance (Garcia & Pintrich, 1994; Pintrich & De Groot, 1990). Motivational components include students' perceptions of the classroom environment as well as their self-related beliefs such as personal goals, self-efficacy, interest, and value beliefs. Cognitive components include students' content knowledge as well as various cognitive learning strategies such as rehearsal, elaboration, and organization, and metacognitive strategies such as planning, monitoring, and regulating learning (Garcia & Pintrich, 1994). Research in both experimental and field settings has consistently shown that positive motivational beliefs such as perceptions of high self-efficacy, a focus on mastery goals, high value and interest in the task or content, and low levels of test anxiety are positively related to greater cognitive engagement in terms of the use of cognitive and metacognitive strategies as well as actual academic performance (see Pintrich & Schrauben, 1992 for a review).

Given that both motivational and cognitive components are important for classroom learning, how can we assess them in the classroom context? Of course, in laboratory studies there are a number of techniques that can be used, including reaction time or think-aloud protocols to measure strategy use, and actual experimental manipulations to induce certain types of motivational goals (cf. Ericsson & Simon, 1993; Graham & Golan, 1991). Although these types of techniques can provide good construct validity and high internal validity, they do sacrifice some external validity and generalizability to the classroom setting. For example, students have self-efficacy beliefs for most academic tasks based on their past history of success and failure with similar tasks, while the laboratory task may be relatively unfamiliar to them. Students also have differing levels of personal interest and value for classroom academic tasks. In contrast, most laboratory tasks probably have low value for the typical student, as the artificiality of certain tasks (e.g., ring-tossing; puzzle completion) may make the activity seem unimportant or not meaningful to "real" life (however, the novelty of certain laboratory tasks can make them very interesting to students). Accordingly, if students' motivational beliefs for laboratory tasks may be qualitatively different from their motivational beliefs for classroom academic work, and if experimental settings may not adequately tap into the complex and multifaceted nature of students' beliefs regarding their classroom academic work, how might we realistically assess these beliefs in the classroom and link them to students' cognitive and metacognitive learning strategies? For researchers who aspire to study the interaction of motivation and cognition in a classroom setting, this presents a serious problem with no one "correct" solution, just tradeoffs among the strengths and weaknesses of various methods.

ASSESSING MOTIVATION AND LEARNING STRATEGIES IN THE CLASSROOM

As regards the methods that can be used in a classroom setting, reaction time and think-aloud protocols are rather difficult to use in terms of pragmatic concerns and may also limit ecological validity. However, observations, stimulated recall, interviews, and questionnaires can all be used in classroom settings. Of course, observations (both high and low inference quantitative observational schemes as well as more qualitative and ethnographic techniques) can be used to assess students' motivation and cognition. In fact, many indicators of motivation are behavioral in nature, such as choice of tasks, level of effort on tasks, and persistence at tasks. These three behaviors are all good indicators of a student who is motivated for the task. However, in most current motivational models, simple observation of the behaviors of choice, effort, and persistence is considered inadequate for characterizing student motivation. Both attribution theory (Weiner, 1986) and goal theory (Ames, 1992) suggest that students' perceptions of the task and themselves, as well as their achievement behaviors, have implications for future cognition, motivation, and affect. For example, in goal theory, two students may both demonstrate high levels of effort and persistence on an academic tasks, but if one is mastery-oriented and the other is performance-oriented, then these qualitative differences in goal orientation can have a dramatic effect on subsequent cognitions, attributions, motivation, and affect (Ames, 1992).

Accordingly, from this general constructivist perspective, it is very important to also collect data on students' perceptions and beliefs about the task and their behavior, not just the behavioral indices that can be generated from observational data. Of course, if the observational data include student speech and discourse in the classroom, the actual statements could be coded for indicators of student motivation (e.g., Thorkildsen & Nicholls, 1991) or actual strategy use (e.g., Corno, 1989). However, this type of observational data is not easy to collect or use. The collection and transcription of this type of data is very time-consuming. Moreover, the coding of the data is fraught with reliability and validity issues. In particular, it is not clear how to characterize the representativeness of the discourse and codes for other students or classrooms besides the ones actually in the sample (Carter, 1993).

Stimulated recall methods can provide the same type of rich descriptive data that is generated by observational methods, and can also supply measures of students' beliefs and perceptions of their behavior. By having students respond to a videotaped replay of their behavior from an earlier classroom session, researchers can ground students' self reports of their motivation and cognition in actual classroom behavior. This approach assists in limiting some of the validity problems with self-report data, provided that the time lag between actual behavior and stimulated recall of the behavior is not too lengthy (Ericsson & Simon, 1993). In particular, stimulated recalls may allow the researcher to assess students' beliefs and cognitions at a fairly small "grain size" (Howard-Rose & Winne, 1993), thereby providing data about microlevel cognitive and motivational processes that influence learning. Additionally, stimulated recall techniques can be used as classroom events unfold over time, unlike think-aloud protocols which could not be used in an actual classroom setting during instruction. Stimulated recall techniques also can be used with large numbers of students, although data collection is time-consuming. Stimulated recall methods may provide the best data in terms of reliability and validity, but have the disadvantages of being expensive, time-consuming, and impractical for researchers with limited resources.

SELF-REPORT MEASURES IN THE CLASSROOM

Other self-report methods such as interviews and questionnaires are often the most practical and easy to use in classroom settings. They can be administered relatively easily, and in the case of self-report questionnaires with closed-ended items, scored and prepared for complex data analyses fairly quickly. Most importantly, given their ease of use, questionnaires can be used with large and diverse samples which can increase the generalizability of the findings. Of course, there are reliability and validity problems with these types of self-report instruments as well.

Reliability of Self-Reports

In terms of reliability over time, Assor and Connell (1992) suggest that students' self-assessments of their competence may not be stable when they are quite young because in fact, children's perceptions of competence are changing quite rapidly as a function of development and experience. Nevertheless, these researchers note that children's perceptions of competence can show moderate stability, enough to meet basic psychometric requirements that allow for valid assessment (Assor & Connell, 1992). Indeed, this general issue of stability is pertinent not only to competence beliefs, but also to other motivational factors and to the use of cognitive strategies for learning. That is, it may be that the most adaptive or self-regulated learners do modify and change their beliefs and strategies as a function of the task or context. In this case, traditional estimates of stability over time are difficult to use.

Besides the stability issue, other researchers suggest that the internal consistency or coherence of factor structures generated from self-report questionnaires may vary with age (Pintrich & De Groot, 1990; Wigfield & Eccles, 1992). For example, in our own work, somewhat different factor structures emerge from our questionnaire data with junior high school and college students (cf., Pintrich & De Groot, 1990; Pintrich, Smith, Garcia, & McKeachie, 1993), but the results still fit within our general conceptual model. Future research needs to address whether these developmental differences in factor structures are a function of method variance or actually reflect developmental differences in cognition and motivation. Although these types of developmental differences make for interesting problems in building and elaborating theoretical models, they do not necessarily invalidate the use of self-report instruments as long as developmentally and methodologically appropriate factor structures are used.

Validity of Self-Reports

Besides these reliability issues, the overall validity of self-report questionnaires or interviews has been questioned throughout the history of empirical psychology. There are often concerns about the social desirability of students' responses. Although this is always a concern to keep in mind when using questionnaires or interviews, in our own work, when we have included measures of social desirability (e.g., the Crown-Marlowe social desirability scale), these measures of response bias did not account for any significant amount of variance and did not change our final results. In terms of motivational beliefs, there also is concern abut the inaccuracy of competence beliefs, in particular that students often overestimate their competence. However, Assor and Connell (1992) suggest that, although these beliefs may not reflect "reality" in terms of agreement with grades or achievement test scores, their longitudinal data shows that two years later, these inflated perceptions of competence actually do relate to achievement. Hence, these "overestimates" of competence are adaptive and help students who are not doing that well cope with the demands of the tasks and maintain their effort. In general, if one adopts a constructivist perspective regarding student motivation, then it is crucial to assess students' perceptions of their own motivation, not just "objective" measures of motivation such as observations and teachers' or parents' reports.

The validity of self-reports of cognitive strategy use is not so easily resolved, however. In this case, students' self-reports from interviews or questionnaires may not reflect actual strategy use. Actual observations or some behavioral indicator of strategy use provide better construct validity. In addition, these behavioral measures can be used to assess the smaller grain size of the more basic or microlevel cognitive processes that make up cognitive and metacognitive strategy use (Howard-Rose & Winne, 1993). These measures are very useful in helping us understand *which* of the many possible cognitive processes or strategies contribute most to self-regulated learning. However, at the larger grain size of more global indicators of strategy use or metacognition, self-reports such as interviews or questionnaires can be quite useful. These more global measures can help us decide if *any* cognitive or metacognitive strategy use is taking place. For example, in our own work with the Motivated Strategies for Learning Questionnaire (MSLQ), we have found over and over again that the three general aspects of metacognition-planning, monitoring, and regulating, do not load into separate factors in a factor analyses, but just load into one factor. From this questionnaire data we would not want to conclude that the theoretical distinctions between planning, monitoring, and regulating are not useful. We would leave the explication of the relations between the three aspects to more experimental studies where the processes could be examined in more microlevel detail. However, our results do suggest that when students engage in some aspects of metacognition, they tend to report doing all three aspects and they also do better in terms of actual achievement, which is in line with our general assumptions about self-regulated learning.

In addition, self-reports of strategy use can be improved when students are asked to report on concrete behaviors that they could engage in, not abstract cognitive operations. Accordingly, in our instrument development, we try to have items that ask students about actual behaviors they might use as they study their course material. For example, we ask students if they outline their course material or write short summaries of their readings and lecture notes to assess their use of cognitive strategies. For metacognition, we ask them if they reread course material when they can't understand it, not if they "monitor and regulate" their reading comprehension (see Appendix). Of course, some of our items are more global than those, but most students should be able to report if they engage in certain types of behaviors. However, there may be a lower developmental limit to young children's ability to use these type of self-report items. We have had success with the MSLQ with children as young as fifth and sixth graders, but in the early elementary grades these items may be difficult for them. It may be that they are not able to understand the items or lack the metacognitive awareness to even report on their own behavior. At the same time, it may not be just developmental, it may be that the nature of the context and the types of academic tasks in the early elementary grades do not provide affordances for the use of these strategies. In this case, lacking the opportunities to develop strategies, we would not expect young children to be able to report on their use of strategies very well.

In any event, carefully designed self-report instruments can probably be used with students in the upper elementary grades and beyond. They can provide a relatively efficient and practical measure of students' motivation and use of learning strategies. In addition, depending on how they are constructed, they can be used to assess motivation and learning strategies in a manner that is ecologically valid for the classroom setting. In the remainder of this paper, we outline the development of one such instrument - the Motivated Strategies for Learning Questionnaire. We discuss the development of the questionnaire, present some data on the reliability and validity of the scales, and discuss how we have used it in our own research program on motivation and cognition in the classroom.

DESCRIPTION AND DEVELOPMENT OF THE MOTIVATED STRATEGIES FOR LEARNING QUESTIONNAIRE

The Motivated Strategies for Learning Questionnaire (MSLQ) is a self-report instrument designed to assess college students' motivational orientation and their use of different learning strategies for a college course. The MSLQ is based on a general social-cognitive view of motivation and learning strategies, with the student represented as an active processor of information whose beliefs and cognitions are important mediators of instructional input and task characteristics. By focusing on the roles of both motivation and cognition in the classroom, the MSLQ also addresses recent advances in self-regulated learning, which emphasizes the interface between motivation and cognition (Schunk & Zimmerman, 1994; Zimmerman & Schunk, 1989). This theoretical framework distinguishes the MSLQ from many of the older study skill inventories (e.g., Brown & Holtzman, 1967; Christensen, 1968; Goldman & Warren, 1973), which have been criticized for being atheoretical (e.g., Weinstein & Underwood, 1985), and measures of learning styles, which proceed from an individual differences framework (e.g., Lockhart & Schmeck, 1984; Torrance, Reynolds, Riegel, & Ball, 1977). In contrast to another widely used self-report instrument, the Learning and Study Strategies Inventory (the LASSI, Weinstein,

Palmer, & Schulte, 1987), the MSLQ takes a more detailed view of the motivational processes involved in self-regulated learning, and contextualizes motivation and learning strategies by assessing them at the course level, rather than at a general level.

The MSLQ has been under development formally since 1986 when the National Center for Research on improving Postsecondary Teaching and Learning (NCRIPTAL) at the University of Michigan was funded and informally since 1982. During 1982-1986, self-report instruments to assess students' motivation and use of learning strategies (varying from 50 to 140 items) were used to evaluate the effectiveness of the "Learning to Learn" course offered at the University of Michigan (see McKeachie, Pintrich, & Lin, 1985; Pintrich, McKeachie & Lin, 1987). These measures were used with over 1000 University of Michigan undergraduates enrolled in the course. These early instruments were subjected to the usual statistical and psychometric analyses, including internal reliability coefficient computation, factor analysis, and correlations with academic performance and aptitude measures (e.g., SAT scores). The items have undergone continuous revisions on the basis of these results. The formal development of the MSLQ began in earnest when NCRIPTAL was founded in 1986. NCRIPTAL was funded for research on college populations excluding major research institutions like the University of Michigan. Accordingly, the MSLQ was administered at three collaborating institutions in the Midwest: a four-year public, comprehensive university; a small liberal arts college; and a community college. There were three major waves of data collection with previous versions of the MSLQ used with students from these three institutions: 1986, 1987, and 1988. The items on these previous versions of the MSLQ also underwent the usual statistical and psychometric analyses including internal reliability coefficient computation, factor analyses, and correlations with academic performance measures. The first wave of data collected in 1986 included 326 students; the second wave in 1987 included 687 students; and the third wave in 1988 included 758 students. After each of these waves the data were analyzed and items revised as the conceptual model underlying the instrument was refined.

The final version of the MSLQ presented in this paper reflects the past dozen years of work on these various waves of data collection (see the Appendix for a copy of the most current version of the MSLQ). The instrument is designed to be given in class and takes approximately 20-30 minutes to administer. There are two sections to the MSLQ, a motivation section and a learning strategies section. The 81 items on this version of the MSLQ are scored on a seven-point Likert scale, from 1 (not at all true of me) to 7 (very true of me). The motivation section consists of 31 items that assess students' goals and value beliefs for a course, their beliefs about their skills to succeed in a course, and their anxiety about tests in a course (see Figure 1). The learning strategy section includes 50 questions: 31 items regarding students' use of different cognitive and metacognitive strategies and 19 items concerning student management of different learning resources (see Figure 2).

The questionnaire as a whole and all items are designed to be answered in terms of the students' motivation and use of learning strategies for a specific course. Students usually take the questionnaire during the actual meeting time of the class and are asked to respond about their motivation and use of learning strategies for that specific course. By having them respond to the MSLQ while physically sitting in the classroom for the course with the instructor, the other students, and course books and materials actually present, we hope that these cues will stimulate the respondents to think about their actual beliefs and behavior for that course, thereby increasing

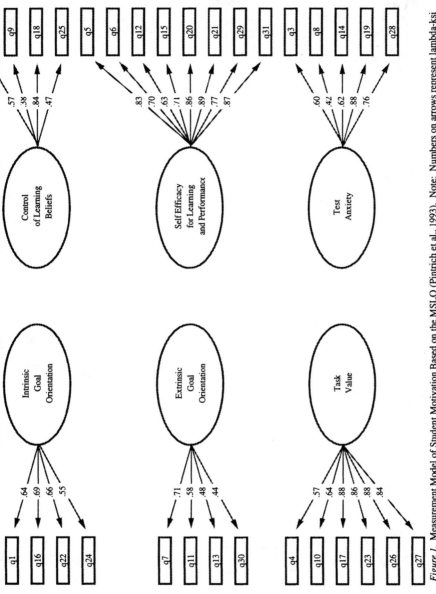

Figure 1. Measurement Model of Student Motivation Based on the MSLQ (Pintrich et al., 1993). Note: Numbers on arrows represent lambda-ksi estimates of the standardized solution.

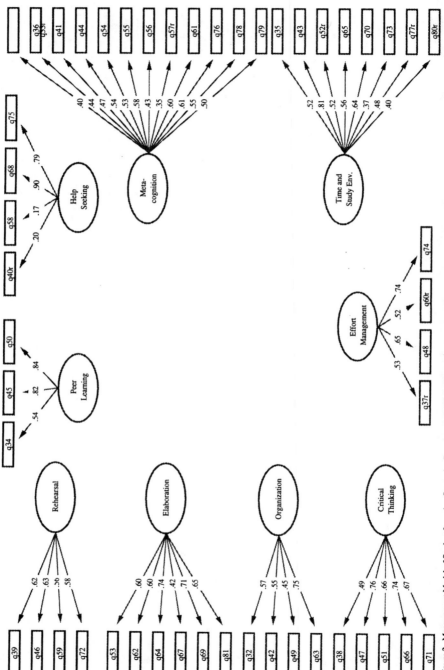

Figure 2. Measurement Model of Student Learning Strategies Based on the MSLQ (Pintrich et al., 1993). Note: Numbers on arrows represent lambda-ksi estimates of the standardized solution.

accuracy. In addition, our theoretical model assumes that students' motivation and learning strategies are contextualized and situation-specific, not generalized individual differences or learning styles. Accordingly, we did not operationalize the MSLQ at the general level of having students respond in terms of their general approach to all learning situations or all classroom learning (cf. the LASSI, Weinstein, Zimmerman & Palmer, 1988). We assume that students' motivation varies for different courses (e.g., more interest or value in an elective course vs. a required course; more efficacy for an easier course in psychology in comparison to a difficult math or physics course) and that their strategy use might vary as well depending on the nature of the academic tasks (e.g., multiple choice vs. essay exams). At the same time, in terms of practical utility, we did not think it useful to operationalize the questionnaire items in terms of all the various tasks and situations that a student might confront in one course (e.g., studying for a test; trying to understand one lecture; reading one chapter in a textbook; writing a final paper or studying for the comprehensive final exam). We chose the course level as an appropriate level for our items as a reasonable compromise between the very general and global level of all learning situations and the impractical and unwieldy level of every specific situation within one course.

Scale scores are constructed by taking the mean of the items that make up that scale. For example, intrinsic goal orientation has four items (see Table 1 and Appendix). An individual's score for intrinsic goal orientation would be computed by summing the four items and taking the average. There are some negatively worded items and the ratings should be reversed before an individual's score is computed, so that the statistics reported represent the positive wording of all the items and higher scores indicate greater levels of the construct of interest. The 15 different scales on the MSLQ can be used together or singly. The scales are designed to be modular and can be used to fit the needs of the researcher or instructor. The motivational scales are based on a broad social-cognitive model of motivation that proposes three general motivational constructs (Pintrich, 1988a, 1988b, 1989): expectancy, value, and affect. Expectancy components refer to students' beliefs that they can accomplish a task, and two MLSQ subscales are directed towards assessing perceptions of self-efficacy and control beliefs for learning. Our definition and measurement of self-efficacy is a bit broader than other measures (e.g., the LASSI, Weinstein, Zimmerman & Palmer, 1988), in that both expectancy for success (which is specific to task performance) and judgments of one's ability to accomplish a task and confidence in one's skills to perform a task are collapsed within the general term *self-efficacy*. Control beliefs for learning refer to students' beliefs that outcomes are contingent upon their own effort, rather than external factors such as the teacher or luck. Value components focus on the reasons why students engage in an academic task. Three subscales are included in the MSLQ to measure value beliefs: intrinsic goal orientation (a focus on learning and mastery), extrinsic goal orientation (a focus on grades and approval from others), and task value beliefs (judgments of how interesting, useful, and important the course content is to the student). The third general motivational construct is affect, and has been operationalized in terms of responses to the test anxiety scale, which taps into students' worry and concern over taking exams.

The learning strategies section of the instrument is based on a general cognitive model of learning and information processing (see Weinstein & Mayer, 1986). There are three general types of scales: cognitive, metacognitive, and resource management. Cognitive strategies include students' use of basic and complex strategies for the processing of information from texts and lectures. The most basic cognitive strategy subscale provides a measure of the use of rehearsal by students (e.g., repeating the words over and over to oneself to help in the recall of information). The use of more complex strategies are measured by two subscales concerning the use of elaboration strategies (e.g., paraphrasing, summarizing) and organization strategies (e.g., outlining, creating tables). In addition, a subscale on critical thinking is included, which refers to students' use of strategies to apply previous knowledge to new situations or make critical evaluations of ideas. The second general category is metacognitive control strategies, which is measured by one large subscale concerning the use of strategies that help students control and regulate their own cognition. This subscale includes planning (setting goals), monitoring (of one's comprehension), and regulating (e.g., adjusting reading speed depending on the task). The third general strategy category is resource management, which includes four subscales on students' regulatory strategies for controlling other resources besides their cognition. These strategies include managing one's time and study environment (e.g., using one's time well, having an appropriate place to study), as well as regulation of one's effort (e.g., persisting in the face of difficult or boring tasks). Finally, the remaining two subscales, peer learning (e.g., using a study group or friends to help learn) and help-seeking (e.g., seeking help from peers or instructors when needed) focus on the use of others in learning.

Table 1
Coefficient Alphas and Items Comprising the Fifteen MSLQ Scales

Scale	Items Comprising the Scale	Alpha
Motivation Scales		
Intrinsic Goal Orientation	1, 16, 22, 24	.74
Extrinsic Goal Orientation	7, 11, 13, 30	.62
Task Value	4, 10, 17, 23, 26, 27	.90
Control of Learning Beliefs	2, 9, 18, 25	.68
Self-Efficacy for Learning & Performance	5, 6, 12, 15, 20, 21, 29, 31	.93
Test Anxiety	3, 8, 14, 19, 28	.80
Learning Strategies Scales		
Rehearsal	39, 46, 59, 72	.69
Elaboration	53, 62, 64, 67, 69, 81	.75
Organization	32, 42, 49, 63	.64
Critical Thinking	38, 47, 51, 66, 71	.80
Metacognitive Self-Regulation	33r, 36, 41, 44, 54, 55, 56, 57r, 61, 76, 78, 79	.79
Time & Study Environment Management	35, 43, 52r, 65, 70, 73, 77r, 80r	.76
Effort Regulation	37r, 48, 60r, 74	.69
Peer Learning	34, 45, 50	.76
Help-Seeking	40r, 58, 68, 75	.52

PSYCHOMETRIC PROPERTIES OF THE MSLQ

Construct Validity.

In order to test the utility of the theoretical model and its operationalization in the final version of the MSLQ scales, we used data gathered from 380 Midwestern college students enrolled in 37 classrooms (spanning 14 subject domains and five disciplines: natural science, humanities, social science, computer science, and foreign language) to perform two confirmatory factor analyses: one for the set of motivation items and another for the set of cognitive and metacognitive strategy items (Pintrich, Smith, Garcia, & McKeachie, 1993). Structural equation modeling was used to estimate parameters and test the models. In contrast to exploratory factor analysis, confirmatory factor analysis requires the identification of which items (indicators) should fall onto which factors (latent variables). Parameter estimates for the model specified were generated using maximum likelihood, and tests for goodness-of-fit were made. The goodness-of-fit tests assessed how well correlations that were reproduced, given the model specified, "matched up" with the input set of correlations. In other words, confirmatory factor analysis allowed for a quantitative test of the theoretical model. For example, we have four items that are assumed to be indicators of a construct called Intrinsic Goal Orientation. The confirmatory factor analysis tested how closely the input correlations could be reproduced given the constraints that Items 1, 16, 22, and 24 fall onto one specific factor (Intrinsic Goal Orientation); that Items 7, 11, 13, and 30 fall onto another factor (Extrinsic Goal Orientation); that Items 4, 10, 17, 23, 26, and 27 fall onto another (Task Value), and so forth. Each item on the MSLQ was constrained to fall on one specific latent factor. The 31 motivation items were tested to see how well they fit six correlated latent factors: (1) intrinsic goal orientation, (2) extrinsic goal orientation, (3) task value, (4) control beliefs about learning, (5) self-efficacy for learning and performance, and (6) test anxiety (see Figure 1 for the measurement model). The 50 cognitive strategy items were tested to see how well they fit nine correlated latent factors: (1) rehearsal, (2) elaboration, (3) organization, (4) critical thinking, (5) metacognitive self-regulation, (6) time and study environment management, (7) effort regulation, (8) peer learning, and (9) help seeking (see Figure 2 for the measurement model). Therefore, the measurement models tested in the analyses followed the theoretical framework, and the structural models freely estimated the covariances between the latent constructs.

The goodness of fit indices generated by the LISREL program suggested that the general model of motivational components with six scales and the general model of cognitive components with nine scales were indeed reasonable representations of the data (Pintrich et al., 1993; cf. Garcia & Pintrich, 1991). Several omnibus fit statistics were calculated: the chi-square to degrees of freedom ratio (χ^2/df); the goodness-of-fit and adjusted goodness-of-fit indices (GFI and AGFI); and the root mean residual (RMR). A χ^2/df ratio of less than 5 is considered to be indicative of a good fit between the observed and reproduced correlation matrices (Hayduk, 1987); a GFI or AGFI of .9 or greater and an RMR of .05 or less are heuristic values that indicate that the model "fits" the input data well. The motivation model (see Figure 1) resulted in a GFI of .77, an AGFI of .73, an RMR of .07, and generated a χ^2/df ratio of 3.49 (Pintrich et. al., 1993). The six correlated latent factors model appears to be the best fitting representation of the input data, as the largest modification index provided by LISREL VI was 50.2, and making the modification did not substantively "improve" the overall fit indices for the motivation model (e.g., the GFI increased from .773 to .784; the RMR decreased from .074 to .072). Constraining the 50 learning strategies items to fall onto nine correlated latent factors generated a χ^2/df ratio of 2.26, a GFI of .78, an AGFI of .75, and an RMR of .08. The nine correlated latent factors model appears to be the best fitting representation of the input data, as the largest modification index provided by LISREL VI was 91.59, and modifying the model did not substantively "improve" the overall fit indices for the learning strategies model (e.g., the GFI increased from .779 to .789; the RMR decreased from .078 to .076). These results provide support for the soundness of the measurement and theoretical models for the two sections of the MSLQ.

On a more basic level, the correlations among the MSLQ scales suggest that the scales are valid measures of the motivational and cognitive constructs. The value and expectancy scales, intrinsic goal orientation, extrinsic goal orientation, task value, control of learning beliefs, and self-efficacy, were all positively correlated with one another, with rs ranging from .14 to .68 (see Table 2). Test anxiety was modestly correlated with the value and expectancy scales in the expected directions. Test anxiety was negatively correlated with the "positive" motivational beliefs of intrinsic goal orientation, task value, control of learning beliefs, and self-efficacy as would be expected theoretically. It was positively correlated with extrinsic goal orientation, a motivational belief that focuses on getting good grades and performing well, so it is not surprising that students who are concerned about grades would show more test anxiety (Garcia & Pintrich, 1991; Pintrich et al., 1993). As expected, all the cognitive strategy and resource management scales were positively related to one another, with rs ranging from .10 to .70 (see Table 2). Peer learning and help-seeking were generally more weakly correlated with the other scales: their correlations with cognitive strategies and other resource management strategies range from .10 to .28.

Table 2
Correlations Among MSLQ scales

	Intr	Extr	Tskv	Cont	Slfef	Tanx	Reh	Elab	Org	Crit	Mcg	Tstdy	Efft	Prlrn
Extr	.15													
Tskv	.68	.18												
Cont	.29	.14	.30											
Slfef	.59	.15	.51	.44										
Tanx	-.15	.23	-.14	-.10	-.37									
Reh	.10	.23	.12	.02	.10	.11								
Elab	.48	.13	.44	.22	.35	-.13	.36							
Org	.27	.09	.19	.02	.21	-.05	.49	.52						
Crit	.58	.06	.39	.18	.42	-.11	.15	.57	.31					
Mcg	.50	.07	.45	.17	.46	-.24	.39	.67	.55	.53				
Tstdy	.32	.13	.37	.00	.32	-.17	.38	.44	.44	.25	.58			
Efft	.43	.11	.47	.07	.44	-.21	.26	.44	.36	.25	.61	.70		
Prlrn	.13	.20	.09	-.03	.05	.10	.21	.19	.23	.25	.15	.10	.05	
Hsk	.10	.08	.16	.00	.08	.08	.18	.28	.22	.19	.25	.21	.18	.55

Note. Intr: Intrinsic Goal Orientation; Extr: Extrinsic Goal Orientation; Tskv: Task Value; Cont: Control of Learning Beliefs; Slfef: Self-Efficacy for Learning and Performance; Tanx: Test Anxiety; Reh: Rehearsal; Elab: Elaboration; Org: Organization; Crit: Critical Thinking; Mcg: Metacognitive Self-Regulation; Tstdy: Time and Study Environment Management; Efft: Effort Regulation; Prlrn: Peer Learning; Hsk: Help-Seeking.

Finally, the motivational and learning strategies scales were correlated in the expected directions. The positive motivational beliefs of intrinsic goal orientation, task value, self-efficacy, and control of learning were positively associated with the use of cognitive, metacognitive, and resource management strategies. At the same time, test anxiety was negatively related to the use of cognitive, metacognitive, and resource management strategies. Although some of the correlations are low, as a whole the relationships between the constructs are in the directions predicted by theory. Indeed, the low correlations may be interpreted as evidence for the orthogonality of these constructs: that the motivation scales are measuring different aspects of motivation, and that the learning strategies scales are measuring different classroom learning tactics.

With regard to the interface between motivation and cognition, we have found consistent patterns of relationships between students' motivational beliefs and their cognitive engagement. Self-efficacy, task value, and an intrinsic goal orientation are typically the motivational factors most highly correlated with higher-order strategies such as elaboration, organization, critical thinking and metacognitive regulation (average $r = .39$), as well as strategies involving the management of one's time, study space, and effort (average $r = .38$). These three factors are less strongly related to the use of rehearsal strategies (average $r = .10$) and to peer learning or help-seeking (average $r = .09$). The weak relationships to rehearsal strategies may be due to the widespread use of memorization across college courses (i.e., so that students at all levels of motivation would use rehearsal strategies to the same extent). In terms of the peer learning or help-seeking, the low correlations to self-efficacy, task value, and intrinsic goal orientation may be due to students' lack of opportunities to engage in collaboration with their peers, and to a commonly-seen reluctance to seek assistance for college-level courses. An extrinsic goal orientation and internal control beliefs for learning are less strongly related to cognitive engagement (average $r = .12$), but are in the expected directions. Finally, we have found that test anxiety is consistently negatively related to higher-order strategies such as elaboration, organization, critical thinking, and metacognitive regulation, as well as to the management of one's time, study space and effort (average $r = .15$). In contrast, test anxiety is positively related (albeit weakly) to the use of rehearsal strategies, peer learning, and help seeking (average $r = .10$). As a whole, these patterns of correlations indicate that positive, more desirable motivational beliefs (i.e., self-efficacy, task value, intrinsic goal orientation) are related to higher levels of cognitive engagement, whereas less desirable motivational beliefs (e.g., extrinsic goal orientation, test anxiety) are either weakly or negatively related to cognitive engagement.

Internal Consistency and Reliability

Internal consistency estimates of reliability (coefficient alphas) lend additional support for the strength of the psychometric properties of the MSLQ subscales (see Table 1). The coefficient alphas for the motivational scales are robust, demonstrating good internal consistency (Pintrich & Garcia, 1991; Pintrich, Smith, Garcia, & McKeachie, 1991; Pintrich et al., 1993). Task value beliefs concerning students' ratings about how interesting, useful, and important the course material is to them typically have a very high alpha (averaging .90 across our datasets), as do students' judgments of their self-efficacy for learning (averaging .93). The Test Anxiety and

Intrinsic Goal Orientation subscales yielded good internal consistency estimates (generally .80 and .74 respectively). Extrinsic goal orientation and control of learning beliefs tend to show more variability in students' responses, with coefficient alphas averaging at about .65. Similarly, the alphas for the learning strategies scales are reasonable, with most of the coefficient alphas averaging above .70. However, help-seeking typically has the lowest alpha (below .60). This scale asks about seeking help from both peers and instructors and it may be that students tend to seek help from only one of these sources. Taken together, however, the confirmatory factor analyses discussed above and alphas of each of the fifteen scales suggest that the general model of motivational components with six scales and cognitive components with nine scales are a reasonable representation of the data.

Predictive Validity

We have examined predictive validity in terms of the relations between the MSLQ scales and standardized course grades (course grades were standardized to control for instructor grading differences). The motivational subscales showed significant correlations with final grade, and were in the expected directions, adding to the validity of the scales. Students who approached their course with an intrinsic goal for learning, who believed that the material was interesting and important, who had high self-efficacy beliefs for accomplishing the tasks, and who rated themselves as in control of their learning were more likely to do well in terms of course grade (average $r = .29$). At the same time, students who reported being anxious about test overall were less likely to do well in the course (average $r = -.26$; e.g., Pintrich & Garcia, 1991; Pintrich et al., 1993).

Most of the learning strategy subscales also showed the expected correlations with course grade. Students who relied on deeper processing strategies like elaboration, organization, critical thinking, and metacognitive self-regulation were more likely to receive higher grades in the course (average $r = .21$). Students who successfully managed their own time and study environment, as well as their own efforts (persistence at difficult tasks) were more likely to perform better in their courses (average $r = .30$). Surprisingly, the use of rehearsal, peer learning and help-seeking strategies are not significantly related to grades; this may be due to the fact that both high and low achieving students engage in these strategies to the same extent.

Multivariate analyses have lent further support for the predictive utility of the MSLQ. For students in the computer and natural sciences, the fifteen subscales accounted for a total of 39% of the variance in final course grade; self-efficacy and time and study environment management were the strongest predictors, with betas of .35 and .49, respectively. For students in the social sciences, humanities, and foreign language classes, the fifteen subscales accounted for a total of 17% of the variance in final course grade; however, the two strongest predictors, test anxiety and effort management, were only marginally significant ($p < .10$), with betas of -.12 and .16, respectively. In other studies (e.g., Pintrich & De Groot, 1990) we found that a subset of these variables accounted for 22% of the variance in final course grade. Given that many factors can account for the variance in the grades that teachers assign, these modest amounts of explained variance seem reasonable.

Practical Utility

It has been our policy to provide students feedback on the MSLQ as a form of compensation for their participation in our studies. We have chosen nine scales of the MSLQ (Task Value, Self-Efficacy for Learning and Performance, Test Anxiety, Rehearsal, Elaboration, Organization, Metacognition, Time and Study Environment Management, and Effort Regulation) on which to give students feedback. The student's individual scores, the class scale means, and quartile information for that class are included in the feedback form. We provide descriptions of each scale and also offer suggestions to students on how to increase their levels of motivation and strategy use. Although we have not done any formal research on the effects of this feedback on students' motivation, use of learning strategies, and performance, students do tell us that they find the feedback quite helpful and informative. We have also provided instructors with feedback on their course's motivation and use of learning strategies (at the group level, not the individual student level), and instructors too have found this information helpful in adapting the content and pace of the class. Of course, the amount and type of feedback may be adapted to the researcher's or instructor's needs.

We have not provided norms for the MSLQ and have no plans to do so given our theoretical assumptions of situation-specificity. It is designed to be used at the course level. As noted previously, we assume that students' responses to the items might vary as a function of different courses, so that the same individual might report different levels of motivation or strategy use depending on the course. If the user desires norms for comparative purposes over time, we suggest the development of local norms for the different courses or instructors at the local institution. The 15 different scales on the MSLQ can be used together or singly. The scales are designed to be modular and can be used to fit the needs of the researcher or instructor. The instrument is designed to be given in class and takes approximately 20-30 minutes to administer. Because of its modularity, flexibility, ease of administration, and sound psychometric properties, the MSLQ has shown to be a practical and useful means for assessing college students' motivation and learning strategies.

CONCLUSIONS

Although the validity of self-report measures has been questioned (e.g., Nisbett & Wilson, 1977), the criticisms made are themselves flawed, as they stem from data on respondents' misattributions (inaccurate ascriptions to "why did X happen?") rather than respondents' reports about their behaviors (e.g., "I do X when I study") or attitudes (Ericsson & Simon, 1993). That is, direct articulation of information stored in memory (such as a behavior in which one engages or an attitude which one holds) has been shown to be accurate and veridical, whereas verbalizations which are products of intermediate processing, such as abstractions, inferences, or attributions, are more subject to distortion (Ericsson & Simon, 1993). According to Ericsson & Simon (1993), the issue for researchers then becomes one of methodology, and they provide ample evidence for the utility of verbal reports as data. Similarly, survey researchers, who use self-report methods almost exclusively, have an entire literature on question-writing (e.g., Converse & Presser, 1986) and response effects (e.g., Bradburn, 1983; Wentland & Smith, 1993). This body of work suggests that while certain information may be unavailable in memory, the degree of response accuracy and consistency (even to sensitive questions) varies according to specific attributes of questions such as wording or length, indicating that particular conditions and stimuli facilitate information retrieval (Wentland & Smith, 1993). Admittedly, the use of self-report questionnaires does trade some internal validity for external validity, but we are confident that given careful construction of questions and conscientious administration of the instrument, relatively high levels of accuracy may be maintained.

The results suggest that the Motivated Strategies for Learning Questionnaire has relatively good reliability in terms of internal consistency. The general theoretical framework and the scales that measure it seem to be valid given the results of the two confirmatory factor analyses. The six motivational subscales and the nine learning strategies subscales represent a coherent conceptual and empirically validated framework for assessing student motivation and use for learning strategies in the college classroom (Pintrich et al., 1993). The six motivational scales measure three general components of college student motivation that seem to be distinct factors. In addition, the learning strategy scales represent an array of different cognitive, metacognitive, and resource management strategies that can be reliably distinguished from one another on both conceptual and empirical grounds. Finally, the subscales seem to show reasonable predictive validity. The motivational scales were related to academic performance in the expected directions. In the same fashion, the learning strategies scales were positively related to course grade. These significant, albeit modest relations with course grade are reasonable, given the many other factors that are related to college course grade that are not measured by the MSLQ (individual course grades themselves are not very reliable measures of performance or learning). The MSLQ seems to represent a useful, reliable, and valid means for assessing college students' motivation and use of learning strategies in the classroom.

REFERENCES

Ames, C. (1992). Classroom: Goals, structures, and student motivation. *Journal of Educational Psychology, 84*, 261-271.

Assor, A., & Connell, J. (1992). The validity of students' self-reports as measures of performance affecting self-appraisals. In D.H. Schunk & J. Meece, (Eds.), *Student perceptions in the classroom* (pp. 25-47). Hillsdale, NJ: Erlbaum.

Bradburn, N. (1983). Response effects. In P. H. Rossi, J. D. Wright, & A. B. Anderson (Eds.), *Handbook of survey research* (pp. 289-328). New York: Academic Press.

Brown, W., & Holtzman, W. (1967). *Survey of study habits and attitudes.* New York: Psychological Corporation.

Carter, K. (1993). The place of story in the study of teaching and teacher education. *Educational Researcher, 22* (1), 5-12.

Christensen, F. A. (1968). *College adjustment and study skills inventory.* Berea, OH: Personal Growth Press.

Converse, J. M., & Presser, S. (1986). *Survey questions: Handcrafting the standardized questionnaire.* Newbury Park, CA: Sage.

Corno, L. (1989). Self-regulated learning: A volitional analysis. In B.J. Zimmerman & D.H. Schunk (Eds.), *Self-regulated learning and academic achievement: Theory, research, and practice* (pp. 111-141). New York: Springer-Verlag.

Ericsson, K. A., & Simon, H. A. (1993). *Protocol analysis: Verbal reports as data* (revised edition). Cambridge, MA: MIT Press.

Garcia, T., & Pintrich, P. R. (1991, April). *Student motivation and self-regulated learning: A LISREL model.* Paper presented at the annual meeting of the American Educational Research Association, Chicago, IL.

Garcia, T., & Pintrich, P. R. (1994). Regulating motivation and cognition in the classroom: The role of self-schemas and self-regulatory strategies. In D.H. Schunk & B.J. Zimmerman (Eds.), *Self-regulation of learning and performance: Issues and educational applications* (pp. 127-153). Hillsdale, NJ: Erlbaum.

Goldman, R., & Warren, R. (1973). Discriminant analysis of study strategies connected with college grade success in different major fields. *Journal of Educational Measurement, 10,* 39-47.

Graham, S., & Golan, S. (1991). Motivational influences on cognition: Task involvement, ego involvement, and depth of information processing. *Journal of Educational Psychology, 83,* 187-194.

Hayduk, L. A. (1987). *Structural equation modeling with LISREL: Essentials and advances.* Baltimore, MD: Johns Hopkins University Press.

Howard-Rose, D., & Winne, P. (1993). Measuring component and sets of cognitive processes in self-regulated learning. *Journal of Educational Psychology, 85,* 591-604.

Joreskog, K. G., & Sorbom, D. (1986). *LISREL: Analysis of linear structural relationships by the method of maximum likelihood: User's guide.* Mooresville, IN: Scientific Software.

Lockhart, D, & Schmeck, R. (1984). Learning styles and classroom evaluation methods: Different strokes for different folks. *College Student Journal, 17,* 94-100.

McKeachie, W. J., Pintrich, P. R., & Lin, Y. G. (1985). Teaching learning strategies. *Educational Psychologist, 20,* 153-160.

Pintrich, P. R. (1988a). A process-oriented view of student motivation and cognition. In J. Stark & L. Mets (Eds.), *Improving teaching and learning through research: New directions for institutional research* (Vol. 57, pp. 65-79). San Francisco: Jossey-Bass.

Pintrich, P. R. (1988b). Student learning and college teaching. In R. E. Young & K. E. Eble (Eds.), *College teaching and learning: Preparing for new commitments. New directions for teaching and learning* (Vol. 33, pp. 71-86). San Francisco: Jossey-Bass.

Pintrich, P. R. (1989). The dynamic interplay of student motivation and cognition in the college classroom. In C. Ames & M.L. Maehr (Eds.), *Advances in motivation and achievement: Motivation-enhancing environments* (Vol. 6, pp. 117-160). Greenwich, CT: JAI Press.

Pintrich, P. R., & De Groot, E. (1990). Motivational and self-regulated learning components of classroom academic performance. *Journal of Educational Psychology, 82,* 33-40.

Pintrich, P. R., & Garcia, T. (1991). Student goal orientation and self-regulation in the college classroom. In M. L. Maehr & P. R. Pintrich (Eds.), *Advances in motivation and achievement: Goals and self-regulatory processes* (Vol. 7, pp. 371-402). Greenwich, CT: JAI Press.

Pintrich, P. R., McKeachie, J. W., & Lin, Y. G. (1987). Teaching as a course in learning to learn. *Teaching of Psychology, 14,* 81-86.

Pintrich, P.R., & Schrauben, B. (1992). Students' motivational beliefs and their cognitive engagement in classroom academic tasks. In D.H. Schunk & J. Meece (Eds.), *Student perceptions in the classroom* (pp. 149-183). Hillsdale, NJ: Erlbaum.

Pintrich, P. R., Smith, D. A. F., Garcia, T., & McKeachie, W. J. (1991). *A manual for the use of the motivated strategies questionnaire (MSLQ)*. Ann Arbor, MI: University of Michigan, National Center for Research to Improve Postsecondary Teaching and Learning.

Pintrich, P. R., Smith, D. A. F., Garcia, T., & McKeachie, W. J. (1993). Reliability and predictive validity of the Motivated Strategies for Learning Questionnaire (MSLQ). *Educational and Psychological Measurement, 53*, 801-813.

Schunk, D., & Zimmerman, B. (1994). *Self-regulation of learning and performance: Issues and educational application.* Hillsdale, NJ: Erlbaum.

Thorkildsen, T., & Nicholls, J. (1991). Students' critiques as motivation. *Educational Psychologist, 26*, 347-368.

Torrance, E. P., Reynolds, C. R., Riegel, T., & Ball, O. (1977). Your style of learning and thinking: Forms A and B. *The Gifted Child Quarterly, 21*, 563-573.

Weiner, B. (1986). *An attributional theory of motivation and emotion.* New York: Springer-Verlag.

Weinstein, C. E., & Mayer, R. E. (1986). The teaching of learning strategies. In M. Wittrock (Ed.), *Handbook of research on teaching* (pp. 315-327). New York: Macmillan.

Weinstein, C. E., Palmer, D. R., & Schulte, A. C. (1987). *Learning and study strategies inventory.* Clearwater, FL: H&H Publishing.

Weinstein, C. E., & Underwood, V. L. (1985). Learning strategies: The how of learning. In J. W. Segal, S. F. Chipman, & R. Glaser (Eds.), *Thinking and learning skills: Relating instruction to research* (Vol. 1, pp. 241-258). Hillsdale, NJ: Erlbaum.

Weinstein, C. E., Zimmerman, S. A., & Palmer, D. R. (1988). Assessing learning strategies: The design and development of the LASSI. In C. E. Weinstein, E. T. Goetz, & P. A. Alexander (Eds.), *Learning and study strategies: Issues in assessment, instruction, and evaluation* (pp. 25-40). New York: Academic Press.

Wentland, E. J., & Smith, K. W. (1993). *Survey responses: An evaluation of their validity.* New York: Academic Press.

Wigfield, A., & Eccles, J. (1992). The development of achievement task values: A theoretical analysis. *Developmental Review, 12*, 265-310.

Zimmerman, B.J., & Schunk D.H. (1989). *Self-regulated learning and academic achievement: Theory, research, and practice.* New York: Springer-Verlag.

APPENDIX

The MSLQ Items

Part A. Motivation

1. In a class like this, I prefer course material that really challenges me so I can learn new things.
2. If I study in appropriate ways, then I will be able to learn the material in this course.
3. When I take a test I think about how poorly I am doing compared with other students.
4. I think I will be able to use what I learn in this course in other courses.
5. I believe I will receive an excellent grade in this class.
6. I'm certain I can understand the most difficult material presented in the readings for this course.
7. Getting a good grade in this class is the most satisfying thing for me right now.
8. When I take a test I think about items on other parts of the test I can't answer.
9. It is my own fault if I don't learn the material in this course.
10. It is important for me to learn the course material in this class.
11. The most important thing for me right now is improving my overall grade point average, so my main concern in this class is getting a good grade.
12. I'm confident I can learn the basic concepts taught in this course.
13. If I can, I want to get better grades in this class than most of the other students.
14. When I take tests I think of the consequences of failing.
15. I'm confident I can understand the most complex material presented by the instructor in this course.
16. In a class like this, I prefer course material that arouses my curiosity, even if it is difficult to learn.
17. I am very interested in the content area of this course.
18. If I try hard enough, then I will understand the course material.
19. I have an uneasy, upset feeling when I take an exam.
20. I'm confident I can do an excellent job on the assignments and tests in this course.
21. I expect to do well in this class.
22. The most satisfying thing for me in this course is trying to understand the content as thoroughly as possible.
23. I think the course material in this class is useful for me to learn.
24. When I have the opportunity in this class, I choose course assignments that I can learn from even if they don't guarantee a good grade.
25. If I don't understand the course material, it is because I didn't try hard enough.
26. I like the subject matter of this course.
27. Understanding the subject matter of this course is very important to me.
28. I feel my heart beating fast when I take an exam.
29. I'm certain I can master the skills being taught in this class.
30. I want to do well in this class because it is important to show my ability to my family, friends, employer, or others.
31. Considering the difficulty of this course, the teacher, and my skills, I think I will do well in this class.

Part B. Learning Strategies

32. When I study the readings for this course, I outline the material to help me organize my thoughts.
33. During class time I often miss important points because I'm thinking of other things. (REVERSED)
34. When studying for this course, I often try to explain the material to a classmate or friend.
35. I usually study in a place where I can concentrate on my course work.
36. When reading for this course, I make up questions to help focus my reading.
37. I often feel so lazy or bored when I study for this class that I quit before I finish what I planned to do. (REVERSED)
38. I often find myself questioning things I hear or read in this course to decide if I find them convincing.
39. When I study for this class, I practice saying the material to myself over and over.
40. Even if I have trouble learning the material in this class, I try to do the work on my own, without help from anyone. (REVERSED)
41. When I become confused about something I'm reading for this class, I go back and try to figure it out.
42. When I study for this course, I go through the readings and my class notes and try to find the most important ideas.
43. I make good use of my study time for this course.
44. If course readings are difficult to understand, I change the way I read the material.
45. I try to work with other students from this class to complete the course assignments.
46. When studying for this course, I read my class notes and the course readings over and over again.
47. When a theory, interpretation, or conclusion is presented in class or in the readings, I try to decide if there is good supporting evidence.
48. I work hard to do well in this class even if I don't like what we are doing.
49. I make simple charts, diagrams, or tables to help me organize course material.
50. When studying for this course, I often set aside time to discuss course material with a group of students from the class.
51. I treat the course material as a starting point and try to develop my own ideas about it.
52. I find it hard to stick to a study schedule. (REVERSED)
53. When I study for this class, I pull together information from different sources, such as lectures, readings, and discussions.
54. Before I study new course material thoroughly, I often skim it to see how it is organized.
55. I ask myself questions to make sure I understand the material I have been studying in this class.
56. I try to change the way I study in order to fit the course requirements and the instructor's teaching style.
57. I often find that I have been reading for this class but don't know what it was all about. (REVERSED)
58. I ask the instructor to clarify concepts I don't understand well.
59. I memorize key words to remind me of important concepts in this class.
60. When course work is difficult, I either give up or only study the easy parts. (REVERSED)

61. I try to think through a topic and decide what I am supposed to learn from it rather than just reading it over when studying for this course.
62. I try to relate ideas in this subject to those in other courses whenever possible.
63. When I study for this course, I go over my class notes and make an outline of important concepts.
64. When reading for this class, I try to relate the material to what I already know.
65. I have a regular place set aside for studying.
66. I try to play around with ideas of my own related to what I am learning in this course.
67. When I study for this course, I write brief summaries of the main ideas from the readings and my class notes.
68. When I can't understand the material in this course, I ask another student in this class for help.
69. I try to understand the material in this class by making connections between the readings and the concepts from the lectures.
70. I make sure that I keep up with the weekly readings and assignments for this course.
71. Whenever I read or hear an assertion or conclusion in this class, I think about possible alternatives.
72. I make lists of important items for this course and memorize the lists.
73. I attend this class regularly.
74. Even when course materials are dull and uninteresting, I manage to keep working until I finish.
75. I try to identify students in this class whom I can ask for help if necessary.
76. When studying for this course I try to determine which concepts I don't understand well.
77. I often find that I don't spend very much time on this course because of other activities. (REVERSED)
78. When I study for this class, I set goals for myself in order to direct my activities in each study period.
79. If I get confused taking notes in class, I make sure I sort it out afterwards.
80. I rarely find time to review my notes or readings before an exam. (REVERSED)
81. I try to apply ideas from course readings in other class activities such as lecture and discussion.

Development of an Inventory to Measure Learning Strategies

Carmen Vizcarro
Isabel Bermejo
Marta del Castillo
Carmen Aragonés

INTRODUCTION

The present work originated in the observation of a surprisingly high failure rate among first year university students who might have delivered a good performance while in secondary school. Many works have described the new demands in a broad range of areas of functioning faced by students when they enter university. At the same time, general dimensions of learning have been identified that seem to have a significant effect on learning in different academic levels and domains of knowledge (Bereiter & Scardamalia, 1989; Resnick, 1987). If learning strategies (LS) can be considered among these general dimensions, one of the reasons for the above mentioned failure might be that students rely on study strategies that are not well suited to the work they are asked to perform once they enter university. In fact, previous research has shown that students who do poorly at university courses use less effective LS than successful students (Weinstein, 1978). Thus, it seemed reasonable to suppose that new academic demands on entering university call for more efficient LS. Working from this hypothesis, we set out to identify the general factors of learning and knowledge acquisition related to academic level and achievement that could partly account for these results. If these general factors could be established, we reasoned, subjects could be trained in them in a second phase of our work, as a number of previous studies have shown (McKeachie, Pintrich, & Lin, 1985; Weinstein & Mayer, 1986; Weinstein & Underwood, 1985), to help them make this transition more smoothly.

A first step to put this idea to test would be to study these general dimensions in secondary and university students, in order to analyze whether and how these two groups differed. Thus, as an initial step in our attempt to help the transition of students from secondary education to university by enhancing LS that are better adapted to the new demands, we had to assess these strategies in a comprehensive, reliable and valid way. A method of assessment was needed that would cover the strategies that had to be eventually trained, incorporating suggestions grounded in cognitive and instructional psychology and LS research.

In order to select such a method, we started the revision and comparison of some existent questionnaires. A review of questionnaires that are used in our field and aim at measuring study habits, showed they did not encompass the full range of strategies which research on these topics suggests should be considered. Then, a revision was undertaken of questionnaires developed from a cognitive perspective in other contexts. Included were questionnaires developed by Biggs (1978), Entwistle and Ramsden (1983), Ford (1985), Kolb, Rubin, and Osland (1991), Sakamoto (1985), Schmeck (1983), Torrance, Reynolds, Riegel, and Ball (1977), Weinstein, Schulte, and Cascallar (1983) and Wrenn (1967). Two of these (Kolb, et al., 1991; Torrance, et al., 1977) were excluded from the analysis because they represented a different methodology. Comparison of the remaining questionnaires, in order to select the one(s) best suited to our purpose, was not easy due to the lack of a unified theoretical basis: the questionnaires are constituted by scales which broadly differ in number and content, thus making direct comparison impossible. In addition, some of the items did not seem to fit our academic system. Hence we decided to construct a new questionnaire.

DEVELOPMENT OF THE QUESTIONNAIRE

Cognitive Task Analysis of Learning Activities

The procedure we followed for the construction of the questionnaire included a combination of two approaches. First, we used a rational approach to obtain an initial item pool which comprehensively represented the main cognitive processes and activities involved in the more common academic tasks. In the second place, we resorted to an empirical approach for the selection of the items to be included in the questionnaire, subjecting this initial, comprehensive item pool to principal component analysis. In this way, we may feel confident of the appropriateness of the original item pool while using an empirical approach to bring the questionnaire to a workable size, retaining only those scales and items which explain the largest amount of variance. Below, these procedures will be explained in more detail.

Thus, the first phase of our work was to analyze the main tasks involved in academic learning as well as the different ways to perform them which are related to differences in the quality of learning. The theoretical basis for this analysis was formed by concepts derived from cognitive psychology. Related to this general framework, we considered LS as different ways of processing information along with the specific procedures that allow this to happen (Weinstein & Mayer, 1986).

Research on LS has repeatedly shown that various cognitive approaches to academic tasks are associated with differences in the quality of learning. On the other hand, it has also been established that support strategies such as motivation, self control or social interactions with peers and teachers significantly influence the processing of information (Pintrich, 1989). More specifically, we initially based our work on the LS taxonomy developed by Weinstein and Mayer (1986). These authors consider two categories of support strategies (affective and metacognitive) and six categories of cognitive strategies with a direct bearing on the processing of the information that has to be learned. These six categories reflect, in fact, three kinds of strategies (rehearsal, elaboration, and organization) when carried out in two kinds of tasks: basic and complex. Pintrich and García (1992) also provide a schema integrating these factors which differentiates motivational (value expectancy, affective), cognitive (rehearsal, elaboration and organization) and self-regulatory strategies (metacognitive and resource management). Although structured differently, the content of both taxonomies is quite similar.

Our analysis thus had three steps: first, the more common academic tasks and activities were identified (such as textbook studying, attending teachers' explanations or peers' discussions, doing different kinds of exercises or essays, solving problems or taking examinations). Then, the main basic cognitive processes involved were established (attention, perception, representation, memory, problem solving). Finally, the different ways in which the tasks could be performed were considered, thus introducing the different LS, namely rehearsal, elaboration and organization.

The result of this analysis was a set of heterogeneous categories that cannot be considered a taxonomy, since they belong to different levels of analysis, or even as discrete categories, since they often overlap and in many cases mutually imply each other. Finally, these categories do not even constitute a sequence, since they often are recurrent activities or processes. Rather, we considered them a framework with useful heuristic properties. Marzano et al. (1988) arrive at a similar framework, which we did not use, however, because we considered more narrow categories would be preferable in that they allow a more detailed analysis. On the other hand, we also felt more comfortable with categories more congenial to the realm of cognitive psychology. Our purpose was to arrive at a framework that would guide the next phase, that of item classification (and eventually generation) and selection. Table 1 displays the final framework that was used to guide our analysis and classification of the items.

As can be seen, we tried to keep our analysis at the simplest, yet psychologically most meaningful level possible. Although in the LS field there is a tendency to collapse these processes into a few broad categories, we felt there was not much to gain in doing so, taking into account the many advances and refinements that have been achieved on these concepts in the broader field of psychology. In this sense, we considered that keeping the analysis as fine-grained as possible was more convenient both to facilitate analysis in this first stage of our work, and later on for intervention-oriented applied work. So we opted to keep separate these well established categories. Of course, this denies neither the obvious interrelations among these variables nor the fact that our categories are still very general and heterogeneous. A working definition of each dimension was also elaborated, specifying as many facets as possible to guide the subsequent steps of item classification and selection.

On this basis, we proceeded to classify the items of 12 questionnaires selected because of their frequent use in our context or because they were firmly grounded in cognitive psychology and/or learning strategies research (Biggs, 1978; Caballero, 1972; Carretero & Pozo, n.d.; Entwistle & Ramsden, 1983; Ford, 1985; MEC, n.d.; Pozar, 1972; Sakamoto, 1985; Schmeck, 1983; Selmes, 1988; Touron, 1989; Weinstein, et al., 1983; Wrenn, 1967). A pool of new items was also created, to address those facets of learning activities that we felt were not adequately covered by items from the previously mentioned questionnaires. Finally, a number of items

Table 1
Framework for a Cognitive Task Analysis of Learning Activities

1.		**Support Strategies**
	1. 1.	Motivation (achievement, intrinsic, extrinsic)
	1. 2.	Self-efficacy
	1. 3.	Anxiety (inhibition, fear of failure)
	1. 4.	Control of working conditions (environment, time planning, preparation of learning material and physical conditions)
	1. 5.	Social interactions (with teachers, with peers)
	1. 6.	Intentions related to learning (as defined for the learning types by several authors, e.g., Entwistle and Ramsden, 1983).
2.		**Cognitive Strategies**
	2. 1.	Attention
	2. 2.	Text and language comprehension
	2. 3.	Previous knowledge (and eventually search for additional information)
	2. 4.	Establishing connections (internal, external)
	2. 5.	Representation (as internal activity or spatial strategies)
	2. 6.	Memorization
	2. 7.	Problem solving
	2. 8.	Expression (oral, written)
	2. 9.	Metacognition
	2.10.	Test taking (work in various test modalities)

was selected to represent each dimension. It should be pointed out that at this stage a strong emphasis was placed on the comprehensiveness of the description, leaving the reduction of the data to the subsequent statistical analysis. A sufficient number of items was retained for each scale so that the dimension they represented would be measured in a reliable way (at least ten items per scale). Several criteria guided this selection process, namely comprehensiveness of coverage of the different facets of learning, and clear referents and formulation of the items. Most selected items were reformulated to adapt to these criteria. An effort was also made to include positive as well as negative items in each of the original scales, although in no case were they perfectly balanced. An additional Sincerity scale was included to control for this response bias. In this way, we arrived at an experimental version of the inventory, comprising 302 items, which we called the IDEA (standing for Inventario de Estrategias de Aprendizaje or Learning Strategies Inventory). Next, this questionnaire was given to two samples of students.

Application of the Questionnaire

Samples

Questionnaire data were obtained from several samples. Here, the main sample, from which the first data were obtained, will be described. Other samples will be only briefly mentioned, although some of them are described in appropriate sections of the chapter.

Sample 1. The experimental version of the IDEA questionnaire was given to 878 students, 487 of them in secondary education and 391 in their first year at the university (enrolled in five different departments: Economics, Management, Mathematics, Liberal Arts and Psychology). Secondary education students represented the four options possible in our system (Sciences, Liberal Arts and two mixed, in-between options) (see Table 2).

Table 2
Sample 1. Subjects Participating in the First Experimental Application of the IDEA

	Secondary	University
Sciences	162	83
Biology & Health sciences	94	64
Social sciences	171	177
Liberal arts	59	66
TOTAL	486	390

Sample 2. Some months later, a group of university students participated in a program to train learning strategies. Their pre- and post-training IDEA protocols, along with those of a control group matched for sex and academic level were obtained and their results were also included to analyze some features of the questionnaire (see Table 5).

Sample 3. Finally, the IDEA was also given, as part of a study on gender-related learning processes, to a new sample of secondary school students (N=198).

Procedure

The questionnaire was administered in two halves which were balanced in order of presentation to control for fatigue. Grade point average, and academic level and option of the students were also obtained, to be used as criteria in the data analysis.

Results

Principal component analysis

A principal component analysis was used as a method of data reduction. The first 14 main components, which explained 42% of the total variance, were also meaningful from a theoretical point of view and, as gleaned from the previous analyses, seemed to hold coherent relations with each other and with other relevant variables. These factors include 153 of the original items and will be listed below (a brief description of their content and source is also included). Some examples of items belonging to these factors appear in the Appendix. A copy of the questionnaire can be obtained upon request from the first author.

I.   *Attention:* The eighteen items included represent different facets of focusing and sustained attention and explain 26.85% of the variance. The source of the items is our initial dimension of Attention with some additions from support strategies (feelings of burden or affective conditions interfering with attention).

II.   *Establishing Connections:* Different kinds of connections are included, internal as well as external, between: concepts within a content matter, different content matters, content matters and nonacademic information, situations, experiences or applications. These eighteen items explain 10.13% of the variance and come mainly from Establishing Connections, with some items from Comprehension and Representation.

III.   *Knowledge Representation:* Twelve items are included related to the use of charts, schemas, diagrams, syntheses or cues and explain 6.25% of the variance. The items' source is the initial Representation dimension, with some items from Attention and Memorization.

IV.   *Oral and Written Expression:* Availability of adequate vocabulary and basic skills to communicate acquired knowledge in different academic tasks requiring oral or written expression. This factor comprises eight items, all from Expression, and explains 4.2% of the variance.

V.   *Assertivity with Teacher:* These seven items represent asking for teachers' help in several academic difficulties commonly experienced and explain 3.65% of the variance. These demands for help, however, do not preclude, but rather enhance students' initiative and preference for own work and decisions. All of these items come from Social Interactions.

VI.   *Motivation-Effort:* The thirteen items cover interest in academic matters, with a strong representation of items reflecting a positive disposition to make the necessary effort to comply with various academic tasks. The source of these items is varied: Motivation, Self-efficacy, Intention and Attention. They explain 3.4% of the variance.

VII.   *Perception of Control:* These fifteen items represent the perception of external control as well as feelings of lack of control over academic situations with the concomitant experience of burden caused by academic tasks. They come from Academic Neuroticism, Motivation, Self-efficacy, Anxiety and Intention (2.90% of variance explained). Although this content may seem to contradict the name given to this component, it has to be kept in mind that the process of correction of the protocols reverses this factor's score.

VIII.   *Non-Repetitive Learning:* This includes nine items and explains 2.65% of the variance. All of them come from Memorization but their scoring has been inverted.

IX.   *Examinations:* Includes five items pertaining to attention given to formal characteristics in written examinations. They come mainly from Expression. This factor explains 2.08% of the variance.

X.   *Work Design:* These are eight items related to the ability to devise a scheme to comply with academic tasks throughout a given period of time and actually carrying it out. They come mainly from Control of Working Conditions. The factor explains 2.20% of the variance.

XI.   *Metacognition:* Includes several facets of metacognition, such as planning an activity, reflecting on different facets of a problem and the solutions proposed, use of comments by teachers on the subjects' work or trying to find out the reasons behind a given outcome. Explained variance is 2.08%. The original dimensions of Metacognition and Problem Solving are equally represented in these 12 items, all having to do with planning and monitoring.

XII. *Search for Additional Information:* Refers to recourse to additional information when the need arises or just in response to own interest. The main source of these nine items is Previous Knowledge and Use of Additional information (explained variance 1.98%).

XIII. *Physical and Environmental Conditions for Learning:* Managing to arrange the best physical and environmental conditions for learning. This factor includes seven items, all from Control of Working Conditions, and explains 1.96% of the variance.

XIV. *Reflective Learning:* These eight items encompass very diverse activities such as making internal connections, rereading, reflecting on the meaning of what has been read, questioning the internal coherence or establishing the best way to proceed. The items come from Representation, Memorization and Metacognition and explain 1.88% of the variance.

As can be seen, the Principal Components identified, although not identical, fairly mirror the theoretical dimensions initially included. A closer examinations of the items they comprise, however, also reveals some differences. This is especially true for the support strategies. Thus, the two resulting scales, which relate to motivational and emotional conditions of learning (Motivation-Effort and Perception of Control), are essentially a blend of items coming from the initial pool of items made up by Motivation, Self-Efficacy, Anxiety, Academic Neuroticism and Intention. Social Interactions in learning, on the other hand, is reduced to interactions with teachers and Control of Working Conditions splits into two different factors: Work Design, more directly related to control of behavior, and Physical and Environmental Conditions, related to external conditions.

As for the cognitive dimensions, the main differences are the combination of Metacognition and Problem Solving in one single component and the emergence of Reflective Learning as a composite of items of various sources. The initial items of Text and Language Comprehension disappear as a separate scale, with some of its items distributed in other scales (Establishing Connections, Motivation-Effort and Reflective Learning). Finally, Test Taking is limited to formal characteristics of written examinations, excluding items with a stronger cognitive accent.

These factors make up the scales of the IDEA. A computer program allows a quick and easy scoring of the questionnaire.

Correlations between the scales

Table 3 shows the correlations between the scales themselves, and between the scales, Sincerity and academic achievement. As can be seen, many of the correlations of the scales with Sincerity are significant and negative. In order to calculate the error that this response bias might be introducing, the correlation of each of them with academic achievement was obtained, partialling out the effects of Sincerity. The results are shown parenthetically in Table 3. Other specific analyses for Sincerity with a new sample instructed to fake are currently being performed. As can be seen, the strongest correlations obtained for the motivational scales (Motivation-Effort, Perception of Control and Work Design) and Metacognition. Among the cognitive scales, Establishing Connections and Knowledge Representation also show a high correlation.

Table 3
Correlations between IDEA Scales, Academic Grades and Sincerity

	ATT	CONCT	KNO REP	EXPR	ASSERT	MOT EFFORT	PERC CONTR	N REP LEARN	EXAM	WORK DSG	META COGN	SUPP INFO	PHYS COND	REF LEARN	SINC	GRADES
ATT	1.00															
CONCT	.23 **	1.00														
KNO REP	.24 **	.37 **	1.00													
EXPR	.41 **	.31 **	.24 **	1.00												
ASSERT	.26 **	.35 **	.24 **	.28 **	1.00											
MOT-EFFORT	.50 **	.51 **	.40 **	.40 **	.29 **	1.00										
PERC CONTR	.68 **	.17 **	.16 **	.45 **	.25 **	.46 **	1.00									
N REP LEARN	.37 **	.25 **	.07 *	.21 **	.20 **	.20 **	.42 **	1.00								
EXAM	.27 **	.19 **	.29 **	.31 **	.06	.37 **	.22 **	.04	1.00							
WORK DSG	.46 **	.34 **	.40 **	.25 **	.29 **	.62 **	.30 **	.08 *	.36 **	1.00						
METACOGN	.34 **	.58 **	.40 **	.31 **	.34 **	.59 **	.29 **	.18 **	.28 **	.47 **	1.00					
SUPP INFO	.32 **	.48 **	.46 **	.25 **	.31 **	.42 **	.20 **	.19 **	.29 **	.45 **	.47 **	1.00				
PHYS COND	.25 **	.16 **	.22 **	.20 **	.09 *	.31 **	.21 **	.04	.28 **	.30 **	.24 **	.18 **	1.00			
REF LEARN	.29 **	.55 **	.44 **	.31 **	.28 **	.53 **	.22 **	.13 **	.28 **	.41 **	.57 **	.37 **	.28 **	1.00		
SINC	-.51 **	-.17 **	-.03	-.17 **	-.15 **	-.31 **	-.43 **	-.21 **	-.11 **	-.34 **	-.19 **	-.27 **	-.10 **	-.10 **	1.00	
GRADES	.28 ** (.25 **)	.15 ** (.16 **)	.07 * (.06)	.29 ** (.30 **)	.11 ** (.14 **)	.36 ** (.37 **)	.36 ** (.34 **)	.12 ** (.13 **)	.08 * (.08 *)	.31 ** (.29 **)	.23 ** (.21 **)	.06 (-.003)	.08 * (.08 *)	.20 ** (.23 **)	-.15 **	1.00

** p < .01 ; * p < .05

PSYCHOMETRIC PROPERTIES OF THE SCALES

Several psychometric properties of the scale were analyzed that will be discussed below.

Reliability of the Scales

The internal consistency of these scales (Cronbach's alpha) is not very informative, due to the method by which the scales were obtained. Nevertheless, it is shown in Table 4. Also included in this table is the temporal consistency of the scales, obtained from the control group in Sample 2. This sample comprises 63 university students who took the training program on LS, and their counterparts in the control group (N=52) (see Table 5). A period of three months elapsed between test and retest.

As can be seen, both forms of reliability seem to be very satisfactory, except for Non Repetitive Learning and test-retest reliability for Sincerity, which are rather low.

Validity

The issue of validity of the scales was addressed in several ways, which we shall describe below.

Table 4
Reliability of the IDEA Scales

	Scales	Internal Consistency (Cronbach's α) (N = 878)	Test-Retest Reliability (N = 52)
I.	Attention	.91	.70
II.	Establishing Connections	.89	.75
III.	Knowledge Representation	.84	.78
IV.	Oral and Written Expression	.80	.74
V.	Assertivity with Teacher	.77	.61
VI.	Motivation - Effort	.83	.82
VII.	Perception of Control	.81	.78
VIII.	Non-Repetitive Learning	.58	.57
IX.	Examinations	.77	.77
X.	Work Design	.79	.81
XI.	Metacognition	.80	.74
XII.	Supplementary Information	.76	.72
XIII.	Phys. and Environ. Conditions	.67	.69
XIV.	Reflective Learning	.70	.82
	Sincerity	.63	.47

Table 5
Sample 2. Subjects Participating in the Training Program

School	Subjects	
	Experimental	Control
Management - Economics	9	7
Liberal Arts	9	6
Psychology	9	7
Law	13	9
Sciences	22	22
Medicine	1	1
TOTAL	63	52

Discriminant validity

Two studies will be described concerning the ability of the scales to discriminate groups of students or conditions which can be predicted to show differences in LS. First, the factors were tested for discriminant validity, taking academic achievement, academic level and academic option as criteria. With this purpose, three series of ANOVAs were calculated with data from Sample 1. The above mentioned criteria were taken as independent variables and the scales as dependent variables. These results can be gleaned from Tables 6 and 7 (for brevity only the means and standard deviations are included) and graphically from Figures 1 and 2. As can be seen, the discriminant validity for these criteria seems to be quite adequate. By contrast, the results for academic option are very inconsistent and for this reason not presented. Taken together, these results seem to show that the identified factors aptly differentiate academic level and achievement. On the other hand, the fact that academic option does not seem to introduce significant differences in the scales seems to point at the general nature of these factors.

Secondly, data relevant for discriminant validity were also obtained from sample 2 (see Table 5). IDEA protocols were obtained for the students who took the training (experimental group) as well as for a matched control group on two occasions: before the LS training and immediately after it. For the control group, who did not take the training, a similar period of time elapsed between the first and the second protocol.

An ANOVA was performed with these data with one between-subjects factor (experimental, control groups) and one within-subjects factor (pre, post occasion) to measure change. The interaction of group x occasion was of interest since a greater gain was expected for the experimental group in the pre-post comparison than for the control group. Table 8 shows the interactions of group (experimental, control) x occasion (pre, post) for the IDEA scales. As can be seen, the scales show a high level of significance except Non Repetitive Learning. Table 9, on the other hand, shows the mean differences for the comparisons of the experimental and control groups on the two occasions (pre and post), along with the corresponding least significant differences. As can be seen, the experimental and control groups differed in a number of scales at pretest, the control group showing higher scorings. These differences, however, disappear in the assessment taken after the training. Significant differences can also be observed in this case for all the scales in the experimental group, except for Sincerity, which, of course, was not intended to change. Interestingly, only one scale shows gains for the control group, in which differences were not expected. A graphic representation of these results is also shown in Figure 3.

Table 6

Scale Means and Standard Deviations for two Academic Levels (Secondary and University)

	Scales	M SD	Secondary	University	Level of Significance
I.	Attention	M	48.26	52.13	(p< .001)
		SD	10.34	9.13	
II.	Establishing	M	47.85	52.70	(p< .001)
	Connections	SD	10.12	9.17	
III	Knowledge	M	48.74	51.57	(p< .001)
	Representation	SD	10.27	9.43	
IV	Oral and Written	M	48.65	51.67	(p< .001)
	Expression	SD	10.20	9.49	
V.	Assertivity with	M	50.32	49.60	n. s.
	Teacher	SD	10.20	9.75	
VI.	Motivation - Effort	M	48.11	52.35	(p< .001)
		SD	10.27	9.14	
VII.	Perception of Control	M	49.30	50.85	(p< .05)
		SD	10.28	9.59	
VIII.	Non-Repetitive	M	47.56	53.03	(p< .001)
	Learning	SD	9.65	9.52	
IX.	Examinations	M	47.84	52.68	(p< .001)
		SD	10.45	8.71	
X.	Work Design	M	47.79	52.75	(p< .001)
		SD	10.01	9.29	
XI.	Metacognition	M	48.62	51.72	(p< .001)
		SD	10.50	9.07	
XII.	Supplementary	M	48.38	52.00	(p< .001)
	Information	SD	10.30	9.24	
XIII.	Phys. and Environ.	M	49.21	50.98	(p< .01)
	Conditions	SD	10.52	9.23	
XIV.	Reflective Learning	M	49.32	50.85	(p< .05)
		SD	10.53	9.23	
	Sincerity	M	50.11	49.86	n. s.
		SD	10.62	9.17	

These data address from a different angle the question of discriminant validity, or the sensitivity of the scales in reflecting changes following an intervention aimed at improving LS.

Table 7
Scale Means and Standard Deviations for Three Levels of Academic Achievement

Scales	M SD	High 1	Medium 2	Low 3	Level of Significance
I. Attention	M	55.25	50.47	44.57	1>2>3 (p<.01)
	SD	8.47	9.78	9.47	
II. Establishing	M	52.74	50.40	46.46	1>3 (p<.01)
Connections	SD	10.17	9.95	9.56	2>3 (p<.01)
III. Knowledge	M	50.49	50.67	47.80	2>3 (p<.05)
Representation	SD	10.13	9.97	9.64	
IV. Oral/Written	M	54.46	50.39	44.70	1>2>3 (p<.01)
Expression	SD	9.55	9.81	9.20	
V. Assertivity with	M	53.19	49.47	48.61	1>2 (p<.01)
Teacher	SD	10.25	9.76	10.27	1>3 (p<.01)
VI. Motivation -Effort	M	56.19	50.84	43.29	1>2>3 (p<.01)
	SD	8.57	9.34	8.96	
VII. Perception of Control	M	56.81	49.94	44.48	1>2>3 (p<.01)
	SD	8.21	9.81	8.82	
VIII. Non-Repetitive	M	52.92	50.25	46.73	1>2>3 (p<.05)
Learning	SD	9.51	10.00	9.68	
IX. Examinations	M	51.06	50.57	47.32	2>3 (p<.01)
	SD	10.43	9.92	9.59	1>3 (p<.05)
X. Work Design	M	54.90	50.54	44.51	1>2>3 (p<.01)
	SD	9.91	9.54	9.35	
XI. Metacognition	M	53.46	50.12	47.02	1>2>3 (p<.01)
	SD	9.39	9.78	9.59	
XII. Supplementary	M	50.68	50.51	48.55	n. s.
Information	SD	10.55	9.82	9.20	
XIII. Phys./Environ.	M	52.46	50.17	48.08	1>3 (p<.01)
Conditions	SD	9.32	9.73	10.92	
XIV. Reflective Learning	M	52.57	50.47	44.85	1>3 (p<.01)
	SD	9.70	9.79	9.99	2>3 (p<.01)
Sincerity	M	45.29	50.41	52.13	3>1 (p<.01)
	SD	9.91	10.04	9.28	2>1 (p<.01)

Table 8
F Values for the Interaction of Group (Experimental-Control) x Occasion
(pre-post) for the IDEA Scales

Scales	Group x Occasion Interaction F
I. Attention	22.04***
II. Establishing Connections	16.31***
III. Knowledge Representation	29.56***
IV. Oral and Written Expression	5.68*
V. Assertivity with Teacher	12.91***
VI. Motivation-Effort	20.56***
VII. Perception of Control	25.63***
VIII. Non Repetitive Learning	0.32
IX. Examinations	7.02**
X. Work Design	22.34***
XI. Metacognition	20.35***
XII. Supplementary Information	15.91***
XIII. Physical / Environmental Conditions	18.66***
XIV. Reflective Learning	28.89***
Sincerity	0.89

* p<.05; ** p<.01; ***p<.001

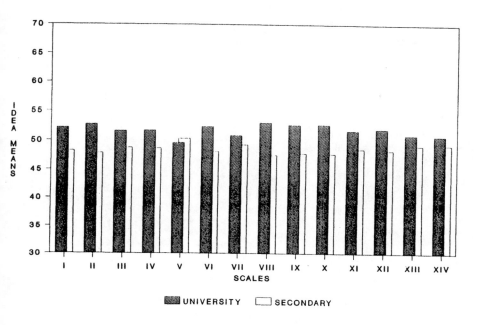

Figure 1. Scale Means for Two Academic Levels (University and Secondary)

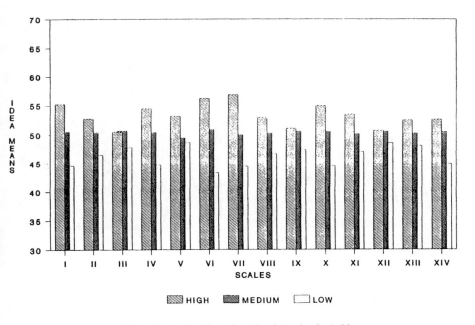

Figure 2. Scale Means for Three Levels of Academic Achievement

Table 9
Mean Differences for the Comparisons of the Experimental and Control Groups in Pre and Post Assessments

Scales		L.S.D.[1]	Pre Exp-Control M.D.[2]	Post Exp-Control M.D.[2]	Exp-Pre-Post M.D.[2]	Control Pre-Post M.D[2]
I.	Attention	2.90	-9.11 **	-1.76	- 8.70 **	-1.35
II.	Establishing Connections	2.96	-6.25 **	0.19	- 7.73 **	-1.29
III.	Knowledge Representation	2.69	-6.27 **	1.62	-10.17 **	-2.27
IV.	Oral/Written Expression	2.34	-4.15 **	-1.14	- 3.66 **	-0.65
V.	Assertivity with Teacher	2.95	-2.80	2.91	- 5.53 **	0.19
VI.	Motivation-Effort	2.65	-8.52 **	-2.04	- 6.32 **	0.16
VII.	Perception of Control	2.58	-8.23 **	-1.18	- 5.95 **	1.10
VIII.	Non-Repetitive Learning	2.92	-3.15 **	-2.26	- 2.97 **	-2.08
IX.	Examinations	2.52	-2.11	1.49	- 2.84 **	0.76
X.	Work Design	2.47	-7.52 **	-1.09	- 6.46 **	-0.03
XI.	Metacognition	2.96	-8.12 **	-0.91	- 7.42 **	-0.20
XII.	Supplementary Information	2.59	-4.21 **	1.36	- 6.91 **	-1.34
XIII.	Phys./Environmental Conditions	2.81	-4.25 **	2.30	- 4.88 **	1.67
XIV.	Reflective Learning	3.03	-8.47 **	0.32	- 7.82 **	0.97
	Sincerity	3.45	2.77	1.00	2.85	1.09

** p < .01
[1] Least Significant Differences
[2] Mean Differences

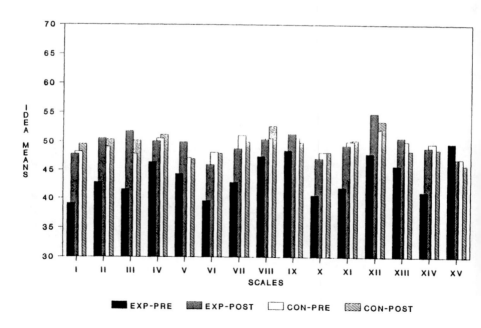

Figure 3: A Pre-Post Comparison for Experimental and Control Groups

Convergent validity

Although the development of the IDEA was in its origin conceptually driven, the scales, and of course their items, were obtained by statistical reduction of the initial items. Thus, it also seemed interesting to compare these scales with similar ones from a device aimed at the same purpose. The Motivated Strategies for Learning Questionnaire (Pintrich, Smith, Garcia & McKeachie, 1991) seemed to be a good choice to analyze these relationships, for two reasons: a) It was developed from a totally rational approach, and as previously mentioned, represents a very coherent picture of cognitive and support strategies for learning (Pintrich, 1989), and b) it was not included in the initial item pool, so the relationship will not be unduly inflated.

These two questionnaires were given to a sample of 198 secondary students (Sample 3) and the Pearson correlations among the scales that were supposed to be similar were calculated. Table 10 shows these correlations. As can be seen, they roughly adhere to the expected pattern: the correlations are higher within the three groups of scales (cognitive, motivational and resource use strategies). The value of these correlations, however, is only moderate. It is also interesting to note that both Metacognition scales present rather high correlations with all the cognitive strategies scales. However, with somewhat lower values, this is also true of Critical Thinking, on the one hand, and Reflective Thinking, on the other. Finally, and as should be expected from their definition (Pintrich, et al., 1991), the three cognitive strategies of Rehearsal. Elaboration and Organization have their highest correlations with Non Repetitive Learning (as expected, of negative value), Establishing Connections and Knowledge Representation.

As for Motivational variables, Effort Regulation shows its highest correlation with our three motivational scales: Work Design, Motivation-Effort and Perception of Control, Motivation-Effort also shows a moderate correlation with Task Value as does Perception of Control with Self-Efficacy. Perception of Control also shows negative correlations, as expected, with Test Anxiety and Extrinsic Goal Orientation.

Finally, Time and Study Environment shows its highest correlation, only moderate again, with Physical Conditions of Learning and the same is true for the correlation between Help Seeking and Assertivity with Teacher. Peer Learning, with no equivalent scale in our questionnaire, shows, nevertheless, a significant correlation with Assertivity with Teacher.

Criterion validity

Of course some correlation of the IDEA scales with academic achievement was expected, although grade cannot, by any means, be taken as a true criterion of learning strategies use. The best criteria for the validity of the scales as indicators of strategy use are observations based in more natural academic situations and experimental learning tasks, as we shall discuss later; data pertaining to this relationship are currently being collected. However, the relationship of the scales with academic grades had to be considered since it was the starting point of our research.

Table 3 shows the correlations of the scales with the students' average grade in the final exams previous to the application of the questionnaire (three months earlier). As can be seen, these correlations are all of a modest size but significant,

Table 10
Correlations between IDEA and MSLQ Scales

IDEA

MSLQ	COGNITIVE									MOTIVATION			OTHER	
	I	II	III	VIII	XI	XIV	XII	IX	IV	VI	VII	X	XIII	V
REHR	.09	.27***	.45***	-.36***	.41***	.34***	.31***	.25***	.09	.36***	.05	.37***	.26***	.18**
ELAB	.30***	.42***	.42***	.02	.43***	.42***	.36***	.17*	.21**	.45***	.24***	.45***	.24***	.32***
ORG	.12	.31***	.60***	-.08	.33***	.40***	.35***	.26***	.12	.38***	.04	.37***	.18**	.24***
CRIT	.10	.44***	.23***	.01	.36***	.27***	.39***	.11	.15*	.32***	.04	.26***	.10	.25***
MCG	.38***	.46***	.44***	.05	.52***	.44***	.40***	.38***	.33***	.56***	.27***	.39***	.34***	.29***
INTR	.18**	.23***	.16*	.18*	.19**	.18**	.27***	.21**	.12	.26***	.17*	.18*	.08	.16*
EXTR	-.10	.08	.20*	-.19**	.11	.06	.07	.02	-.16*	.05	-.17*	.01	.04	.02
TSKV	.45***	.20**	.28***	.11	.28***	.27***	.25***	.20**	.18**	.43***	.37***	.41***	.32***	.18*
CONT	-.05	.07	.07	-.01	.06	.03	.10	.07	.04	.07	-.01	.02	-.07	.13
SLFEF	.46***	.30***	.24***	.17*	.27***	.21**	.26***	.15*	.26***	.36***	.42***	.27***	.15*	.30***
TANX	-.24**	.00	-.05	-.14*	-.04	.09	-.02	-.02	-.23**	.07	-.30***	-.05	-.23**	.15*
EFF	.51***	.22***	.25***	.08	.32***	.25***	.22**	.12	.22***	.50***	.44***	.56***	.23***	.25***
HSK	.13	.30***	.25***	-.03	.30***	.32***	.16*	.21**	.24***	.33***	.13	.20**	.23***	.38***
TSDY	.48***	.06	.14*	-.02	.19**	.10	.18**	.09	.21**	.28***	.34***	.46***	.39***	.11
PRLN	-.02	.34***	.37***	-.19**	.26***	.29***	.35***	.24***	.07	.23***	-.14*	.27***	.07	.25***

*** p < .001
** p < .01
* p < .05

I.   Attention - Concentration
II.   Establishing Connections
III.   Knowledge Representation
IV.   Oral and Written Expression
V.   Assertivity with Teacher
VI.   Motivation - Effort
VII.   Perception of Control
VIII. Non-Repetitive Learning
IX.   Examinations
X.   Work Design
XI.   Metacognition
XII.   Supplementary Information
XIII. Physical and Environmental Conditions
XIV.   Reflective Learning
       Sincerity

M	REHR -	Rehearsal
	ELAB -	Elaboration
	ORG -	Organization
	CRIT -	Critical Thinking
	MCG -	Metacognitive Self-Regulation
S	INTR -	Intrinsic Goal Orientation
	ESTR -	Extrinsic Goal Orientation
L	TSKV -	Task Value
	CONT -	Control of Learning Beliefs
Q	SLFEF -	Self-Efficacy for Learning and Performance
	TANX -	Test Anxiety
	EFF -	Effort Regulation
	HSK -	Help Seeking
	TSDU -	Time and Study Environment
	PRLN -	Peer Learning

except for Supplementary Information. It is interesting to point out that the largest values belong to the Motivational and Metacognition scales. An all-possible-subsets regression analysis was performed with the scales as independent variables and grade as dependent variable. The best independent predictors were Perception of Control, Work Design, Attention, Motivation-Effort, Reflective Learning, Metacognition, Connections and Non Repetitive Learning. The best subset included Knowledge Representation, Perception of Control, Non Repetitive Learning, Examinations, Work Design, Supplementary Information, Organization, Motivation-Effort and Reflective Learning. The adjusted squared multiple correlation was .20 and the regression coefficients found were very small. Although the size of this relationship is very modest, it comes as no surprise. In the first place, it is similar to results found with other questionnaires (e.g., Pintrich, et al., 1993). On the other hand, as is well known, in the prediction of academic achievement other variables, such as prior knowledge or interest, to name a few, must be taken into account (see Alexander, Kulikowich, & Jetto, 1994; Dochy, 1992, and in this volume; Minnaert & Janssen, 1993, and in this volume; Tobias, 1994). In fact, we are currently conducting a study including these variables as additional predictors.

UTILITY OF THE QUESTIONNAIRE

In our program for LS training we have used the questionnaire as a starting point for reflection on the students' work habits. Giving them the questionnaire promotes their consideration of their practice, as well as alternative ways to proceed. After answering it, they receive graphic information comparing their individual results to those of an appropriate normative sample which gives them an objective estimation of their strengths and weaknesses. Additional information is given to them at this point explaining the meaning of the different scales to foster their reflection and understanding. As a result of this process they are prepared to select the specific modules in the program best suited to their needs. To better serve this purpose, we are currently preparing normative data derived, not from the general sample of a given academic level, but differentiating between those students who attain good and bad results in the appropriate academic level. In this way, students will hopefully be better prepared to judge their similarities and differences as compared to these two groups. Since our program is offered on a voluntary basis, this use satisfies our needs. However, another use of the questionnaire can be anticipated which might be adequate for other settings. It can be used to identify students with a special need for training, since it is economic enough to be administered to large groups of students for screening purposes. To this end, however, appropriate cutting points should be established.

CONCLUSIONS

As can be gathered from the results, the developed inventory fairly mirrors the rationally derived dimensions of learning and at the same time shows good psychometric properties. Its reliability seems adequate and its discriminant validity, as measured by several indices, is also satisfactory. Finally, it is not a costly procedure, which makes it suitable for use when rather large samples of students must be assessed.

Some of the results presented here deserve some comment. The empirical combination of items from the original scales of Problem Solving and Metacognition in one dimension in the principal component analysis is interesting. Since the questionnaire addressed the general student population, the items in Problem Solving were necessarily formulated in very broad and general terms, thus probably tapping general activities closely related to planning and monitoring the quality of work (and thus to metacognition).

At a broader level, it is also interesting to compare the dimensions identified by means of principal component analysis and the theoretical dimensions that guided our initial analysis. Although not equivalent, they can be considered very similar, the main difference being that the empirically identified dimensions are theoretically more heterogeneous. Otherwise, a content analysis of the items included in the inventory allows us to conclude that they fairly represent the main facets of the different LS our initial task analysis suggested should be included.

However, whereas a set of dimensions as well as the different facets of each theoretical dimension derived from rational analysis were included in the initial version of the questionnaire, only those items showing the greatest variability were retained, as an effect of the procedure used for item selection. To illustrate, Social Interactions, Oral and Written Expression and Test Taking were reduced to a few items, while Text and Language Comprehension disappeared as a discrete scale, with some of its initial items being included in other scales. Interindividual differences in consistent, but possibly opposed, patterns of responses to these scales may account, at least in part, for these results. For instance, students were consistently divided by their preference to study on their own or with fellow students. In this way, items or even scales that do not represent general dimensions of learning, but rather preferred styles of learning might have disappeared as Principal Components. While the procedure of item selection we followed is useful as a means to reduce the length of the questionnaire on an empirical basis thus making it more workable, idiographic information may be sacrificed that could be of interest for individual work. This leads us to consider working with a two-step measurement: The first one being useful for initial identification and description, as justified by its psychometric properties, the second one giving more idiographic and comprehensive information.

Only a subset of the relevant questions related to validity has been addressed to this point. This matter, however, is of interest especially since we are dealing with a self-report measure and questions could be raised regarding the disposition of the subjects to give the information or even its availability to them. Regarding the validity of data we presented, the thorny question of criteria could be raised. None of those we used can be taken as a true criterion. Rather, it is strongly felt that the only satisfactory approach to this question would be an independent analysis of the students' practices in natural learning situations (or analogic conditions). In this respect, the ecological validity of the inventory should be addressed in a direct fashion. We are indeed currently working on this analysis. As a first approach to this issue, several measures have been developed to be used in LS training seminars, which we feel will give an opportunity for extended observations of student behavior in academic settings in a variety of relevant academic tasks.

With the data at hand, and even maintaining a skeptical position regarding the used criteria, it should be pointed out that our index of academic achievement was a composite of all the academic subjects the students were taking. We feel this somewhat reinforces this particular criterion by averaging some of its biases. However, the problem remains that although a moderate and positive relationship is expected between effective learning strategies and academic achievement, these two cannot, by any means, be considered equivalent. If the intent is to help develop independent learners, it should be kept in mind that personal goals may or may not coincide with academic task performance. However, if these personal goals include academic progress, as usually is the case, a significant, although moderate relationship between the two should be expected, and was indeed found in our data.

Further analyses are needed to address some specific issues. For instance, a confirmatory factor analysis, preferably with a new sample of subjects should be performed in order to increase our confidence in the identified scales. A cluster analysis to identify discrete types of learners and their relationship to outcome measures would also be interesting.

Finally, a more general question could be raised in relation to the overall approach of LS assessment and training, as opposed to an infusion approach. While agreeing that the latter should be the preferred approach whenever possible, we also believe other ways which can be brought under his or her direct control, as an adult and independent learner, should remain open for the interested student. In fact, this is the philosophy underlying our training program, and we make it explicit from the very beginning.

To summarize, then, very general aspects of learning which might be applicable across different domains, have been described and we feel confident our inventory adequately taps some of them. For this reason, it might be of practical interest. Of course, this does not mean to imply that other more domain-specific factors, do not play a role. On the contrary, detailed work within different domains is also needed, as in fact we try to do in our training program.

ACKNOWLEDGMENTS

Studies discussed in this chapter were made possible by two research grants provided by CIDE (1990 and 1991). This work also benefited from a sabbatical leave of the first author supported by the Ministry of Education.

REFERENCES

Alexander, P.A., Kulikowich, J.M., & Jetton, T.L. (1994). The role of subject matter knowledge and interest in the processing of linear and nonlinear texts. *Review of Educational Research, 64,* 201-252.

Bereiter, C., & Scardamalia, M. (1989). Intentional learning as a goal of instruction. In L.B. Resnick (Ed.), *Knowing, learning, and instruction.* Hillsdale, New Jersey: Erlbaum.

Biggs, J.B. (1978). Individual and group differences in study processes. *British Journal of Educational Psychology, 48,* 266-279.

Caballero, A. (1972). *Diagnóstico de técnicas de trabajo intelectual. (ACH-73).* Madrid: INAPP.

Carretero, M., & Pozo, I. (n.d.). *Inventario de hábitos de estudio*. Madrid: UAM. Unpublished manuscript.

Dochy, F.J.R.C. (1992). *Assessment of prior knowledge as a determinant of future learning*. Utrecht, The Netherlands: Lemma.

Entwistle, N.J., & Ramsden. P. (1983). *Understanding student learning*. New York: Nichols.

Ford, N. (1985). Learning styles and strategies of postgraduate students. *British Journal of Educational Psychology, 1*, 65-77.

Kolb, D.A., Rubin, I.M., & Osland, J. (1991). *Organization behavioral. An experimental approach*. London: Prentice Hall.

Marzano, R.J., Brandt, R.S., Hughes, C.S., Fly Jones, B., Presseisen, B.Z., Rankin, S.C., & Suhor, C. (1988). *Dimensions of thinking: A framework for curriculum and instruction*. Alexandria, VA: The Association for Supervision and Curriculum Development.

McKeachie, W.J., Pintrich, P.R., & Lin, Y. (1985). Teaching learning strategies. *Educational Psychologist, 2*, 153-160.

MEC (n.d.). *Cuestionario EIDE de Hábitos de Estudio*. Madrid: Spanish Ministry of Education.

Minnaert, A., & Janssen, P.J. (1993, August-September). *How general are the effects of domain-specific prior knowledge on study expertise as compared to general thinking skills?* Paper presented at the 5th European Conference on Learning and Instruction. Aix-en-Provence, France.

Pintrich, P.R. (1989). The dynamic interplay of student motivation and cognition in the college classroom. In M. Maehr, & C. Ames (Eds.), *Advances in motivation and achievement* (vol.6. pp. 117-160). Greenwich, CT: JAI.

Pintrich, P.R., & Garcia, T. (1992). *An integrated model of motivation and self-regulated learning*. Paper presented at the American Educational Research Association convention, San Francisco.

Pintrich, P.R., Smith. D.A.F., Garcia. T., & McKeachie, W. (1991). *A manual for the use of motivated strategies for Learning questionnaire (MSLQ)*. Ann Arbor, MI: University of Michigan, NCRIPTAL

Pintrich, P.R., Smith, D.A.F., Garcia, T., & McKeachie, W. (1993). Reliability and predictive validity of the motivated strategies for learning questionnaire (MSLQ). *Educational and Psychological Measurement, 53*, 801-813.

Pozar, F.F. (1972). *Inventario de Hábitos de Estudio*. Madrid: TEA.

Resnick, L.B. (1987). *Education and learning to think*. Washington: National Academy Press.

Sakamoto, T. (1985). Characteristics of study skills in Japanese pupils (SMM). *Evaluation in Education, 9* (3), 243-251.

Schmeck, R. R. (1983). Learning styles of college students. In R. Dillon, & R.R. Schmeck (Eds.), *Individual differences in cognition*. New York: Academic Press.

Selmes, I. (1988). Inventario del estudio en la escuela: IDEE. In I. Selmes, *La mejora sobre las habilidades para el estudio*. Madrid: Paidos/MEC.

Tobias, S. (1994). Interest, prior knowledge and learning. *Review of Educational Research, 64*, 37-54.

Torrance, E.P., Reynolds, C.R., Riegel, T., & Ball, O. (1977). Your style of learning and thinking: Forms A and B. *The Gifted Quarterly, 21* (4), 563-573.

Tourón, J. (1989). *Métodos de estudio en las Universidad*. Pamplona: Eunse.

Weinstein, C.E. (1978). Elaboration Skills as a Learning Strategy. In H.F. O'Neil, Jr. (Ed.), *Learning Strategies*. New York: Academic Press.

Weinstein, C.E., & Mayer, R.E. (1986). The teaching of learning strategies. In M.C. Wittrock (Ed.), *Handbook of research on teaching* (pp. 315-327). New York: McMillan.

Weinstein, C.E., Schulte, A.C., & Cascallar, E.C. (1983). *The Learning and Studies Strategies Inventory (LASSI): Initial design and development.* Technical Report, U.S. Army Research Institute for the Social and Behavioral Sciences. VA: Alexandría.

Weinstein, C.E., & Underwood, V. (1985). Learning strategies: The how of learning. In J. Segal, S. Chipman, & R. Glaser (Eds.), *Thinking and learning skills: relating instruction to research.* Hillsdale, NJ: Erlbaum.

Wrenn, C.G. (1967). *Inventario de hábitos de estudio.* Madrid: Paidós.

APPENDIX

Following are some examples of the items included in the scales. The weight of the item in the principal component analysis and its number in the IDEA are also shown. For origin see references in parenthesis and at the end of this appendix.

Factor I - *Attention*

Weight	Item	TEXT
.81	9.	When I study, I often get distracted by matters I worry about. (5)
.79	10.	It is difficult for me to concentrate on what I have to study. (5)
.62	33.	I find it hard to concentrate on what I am reading, so that when I finish I do not know what I have been reading about. (13)
.80	80.	I am distracted from my studies very easily. (12)
.67	95.	My mind wanders a lot when I study. (12)

Factor II - *Establishing Connections*

Weight	Item	TEXT
.61	5.	I try to see how what I am studying would apply to my everyday life. (12)
.65	17.	I learn new terms or ideas by trying to imagine a situation in which they might occur. (9)
.73	45.	I try to relate what I am studying to my own experiences. (12)
.57	49.	Whenever it is possible, I try to relate among the ideas of different subjects. (4)
.61	89.	While I am studying, I often think of real life situations to which the material that I am learning would be useful. (1)

Factor III - *Knowledge Representation*

Weight	Item	TEXT
.79	4.	When I have to learn a new lesson, I usually make an outline with the main ideas. (3)
.70	61.	I usually make up charts and graphs showing the relationships between the ideas comprised in a lesson. (6)
.82	82.	I make charts, diagrams or tables to summarize material in my courses. (12)
.70	120.	When studying a lesson, I write down an abstract in my own words containing the main ideas I have underlined. (6)
.60	137.	When reviewing the material, I use the charts I have previously made. (11)

Factor IV - *Oral and Written Expression*

Weight	Item	TEXT
.63	16.	The terms I use in my oral or written presentations are properly used (they are fitted to the ideas I try to convey). (11)
.66	19.	I often have difficulties finding the right words to express my ideas. (9)
.65	53.	I have trouble in expressing my ideas, and for this reason I get poor grades in written exercises or exams. (5)
.57	65.	In oral and written expression I use my own terms. (11)
.64	121.	I am bad at exercises involving written expression. (5)

Factor V - *Assertivity with Teacher*

Weight	Item	TEXT
.82	23.	When there is something I do not understand, I ask the teacher. (8)
.56	50.	If I have trouble with some subject, I ask my teacher for help. (5)
.61	93.	I am able to ask relevant questions on the teacher's presentation addressed to myself or to others. (11)
.82	122.	When I do not understand something the teacher is explaining, I ask at once. (3)
.57	141.	I have a bad time whenever I have to speak out loud in class. (4)

Factor VI - *Motivation-Effort*

Weight	Item	TEXT
.44	60.	When study tasks are difficult, I leave them undone. (10)
.41	108.	Before trying to solve a problem, I read it carefully, trying to understand its terms and what I am asked to do. (11)
.52	133.	Generally, I try hard to understand things that initially seem difficult. (4)
.45	135.	I strive to understand the main line of reasoning in a text. Only in this way is it possible to remember significant details. (6)
.41	147.	I work steadily on a project, undaunted by the difficulties that might arise. (11)

Factor VII - *Perception of Control*

Weight	Item	TEXT
.48	12.	When I look back I wonder why I decided to study this courses. (4)
.39	13.	I often find myself wondering if my work is worthwhile. (4)
.44	38.	It is impossible for a student to do all the assignments. (5)
.49	88.	I do not have enough time to take the notes I need. (10)
.50	97.	I often feel like I have little control over what happens to me in school. (12)

Factor VIII - *Non-Repetitive Learning*

Weight	Item	TEXT
.61	68.	For my exams, I learn the material as it is presented in my textbooks or notes. (9)
.41	77.	I usually "cram" for my examinations. (9)
.68	98.	I often memorize things I don't understand. (9)
.49	112.	When I cannot understand something, it is better to learn it by rote than trying to find out its meaning. (3)
.69	123.	I learn some things by rote, going over and over them until I know them by heart. (1)

Factor IX - *Examinations*

Weight	Item	TEXT
.59	57.	In my written exercises, I do not worry much about my writing or making sure my teacher will understand what I am saying. (5)
.72	106.	I am careful to make sure that my written exercises are clearly presented. (11)
.73	107.	In an examination, I take care to write clearly. (6)
.28	127.	I reread my written exams before turning them in. (7)
.79	134.	When doing exercises or exams, I see that the presentation is adequate. (2)

Factor X - *Work Design*

Weight	Item	TEXT
.56	69.	I try to work consistently throughout the term and review regularly when the exams are close. (1)
.53	85.	I only study when there is the pressure of a test. (12)
.49	92.	I review my notes before the next class. (12)
.54	119.	I often go over what I have learnt so that I shall not forget it .(7)
.51	136.	I work steadily throughout the year. (2)

Factor XI - *Metacognition*

Weight	Item	TEXT
.57	14.	I solve a problem by focusing on its main point. (8)
.47	18.	When faced with practical problems, I systematically explore several ways to solve them until I find the one which seems more satisfying. (6)
.56	124.	Once I have solved a problem or practical exercise, I stop to think if my solution makes sense. (6)

Factor XI - *Metacognition* (cont.)

Weight	Item	TEXT
.45	126.	When faced with a difficult problem, I look at it from various aspects without giving up. (8)
.37	139.	If the results and my expectations differ, I try to find the cause of the difference. (8)

Factor XII - *Search for Additional Information*

Weight	Item	TEXT
.51	21.	When I study, I use all the aids that are necessary, such as maps, drawings or representations, etc. (2)
.42	55.	I spend a lot of my free time finding out more about interesting topics which have been discussed in different classes. (1)
.42	56.	I generally restrict my study to what is specifically said as I think it is unnecessary to do anything extra. (1)
.51	132.	I am able to find the book I need in the library for every occasion. (11)
.63	148.	I frequently use books from the library (9).

Factor XIII - *Physical and Environmental Conditions for Learning*

Weight	Item	TEXT
.73	28.	I have a usual place to study. (9)
.46	46.	I sleep enough time for people my age. (2)
.34	75.	I start to study when my physical conditions are optimal (when I am not sleepy, tired, etc.). (11)
.78	83.	I study in an adequate place without noise and people bothering me.(7)
.79	149.	I study in a comfortable place with an adequate table, airing, temperature and light. (7)

Factor XIV - *Reflective Learning*

Weight	Item	TEXT
.31	22.	When I am studying a topic, I try to make everything fit together logically. (12)
.45	58.	I stop periodically while reading and mentally review what was said. (12)
.36	84.	When I read things become gradually more coherent to me. (6)
.39	110.	I try to think through a topic and decide what I am supposed to learn from it rather than just read it over when studying. (12)
.34	114.	When I review the material I reflect on the relationships between different topics. (10)

Sincerity

Item	TEXT
41.	I wish my teachers were nicer to me. (7)
51.	At times, I think my teachers are not very understanding. (7)
113.	Even if I don't like a subject, I read it with pleasure. (7)
128.	Some days I feel more like working than others. (7)
146.	I study easily subjects I don't like. (7)

Appendix References:

(1) Biggs, 1978; (2) Caballero, 1972; (3) Carretero and Pozo, 1986; (4) Entwistle and Ramsden, 1982; MEC, undated; (6) New items; (7) Pozar, 1972; (8) Sakamoto, 1985; (9) Schmeck, 1983; (10) Selmes, 1988; (11) Touron, 1989; (12) Weinstein, Schulte and Cascallar, 1983; (13) Wrenn, 1967.

Identifying and Advising Students with Deficient Study Skills: An Integrated Computer-Based Package for Staff and Students

Noel Entwistle
Hilary Tait
Carol Speth

INTRODUCTION

The main theme of this book is assessment of achievement - a term which can be used in a number of different ways. In some of the other chapters, assessment refers to the assessment of a student's knowledge and understanding of a specific discipline. However, it is also important to discover how well students have developed their learning skills. Particularly during the first year at university, many students encounter difficulties which can lead to failure and dropout. And these difficulties are often attributable, at least in part, to ineffective study skills and strategies. This chapter reports a project which is using a computer package to identify and advise such students. It complements the chapters by Garcia and Pintrich, Geisler-Brenstein and Schmeck, and Vizcarro and her colleagues which also address the topic of study skills.

In a recent research study carried out for the Scottish Office Education Department (Wall, Macaulay, Tait, Entwistle, & Entwistle, 1991), it was found that many students believed that they entered higher education with inadequate study skills, and that their higher education institutions had made few provisions to help them acquire these skills. In a previous study (Entwistle, Hounsell, Macaulay, Situnayake, & Tait, 1989), working specifically with electrical engineering students, poor study skills were found to be related to difficulty or failure in the first year. With a rising number of students entering higher education, and in particular a higher proportion of students with unconventional entry qualifications, the need to provide adequate study skills training will become increasingly important.

While it will be important for each institution to develop an institution-wide policy on such provision (Entwistle & Tait, 1992), a key role will continue to be played by individual departments or faculties. It is impossible for any large institution to provide even a full induction programme including study skills due to the number of students involved. Such arrangements are more manageable at faculty, school, department or course levels. Although it is essential that all students are provided with at least a written introduction to the study skills needed in higher education, there may be no need to provide workshops for all students. As there is a wide range of study methods adopted by successful students, it is more economical of resources, and of students' time, to try to identify students encountering difficulties.

The traditional mechanism used for alerting departments to potential academic problems is the examination diet at the end of the first term or semester, but some of the deficiencies in study methods are not picked up by examinations at this stage, or by course work. While poor performance in initial assignments or examinations is one indicator, students doing badly may well not be aware that the difficulties they have in coping with the course have their origin in study behaviour, and thus it is not sufficient to leave the students themselves to come forward, at least without some prompting. In addition, some students can often "carry" ineffective study methods at least until the end of the first year without major effects on their results. Problems, however, do become evident in subsequent years. It thus seems more efficient to try to identify students whose patterns of studying are likely to cause problems.

There is growing evidence that it is possible both to identify students at risk of subsequent failure using questionnaire responses in combination with traditional indicators of academic progress, and also to intervene successfully to help students overcome those problems (Meyer, 1991). Often, simply being made aware of the nature of those potential problems can be a great help to a student. Inventories, which are carefully calibrated sets of questions with fixed-choice responses, have been developed to provide not just a way of identifying students at risk, but also of suggesting the specific nature of the difficulties. Research on student learning can now also be used to suggest ways of helping students to improve their learning and study strategies.

CURRENT PROJECT

The project described here involved three main areas of activity. The first aspect involved continuing work on the questionnaire designed to identify students whose study methods and strategies appear to be ineffective. The core of the questionnaire is an inventory on approaches to studying, but additional questions are used to collect information about preparation for higher education, difficulties with study skills, and influences on progress. The second part of the project involved further development of a computer-based visualisation tool - *StudentView* - to provide information to departments about the nature and extent of the difficulties their students experience, and to indicate the students who may need specific forms of support with their studying. The final aspect of the project involved developing another computer-based system which will provide advice to students on study skills and strategies. This *StudyAdvisor* can be linked to students' responses to the questionnaire on approaches to studying. The advice has the capability of being "customised" to guide students, in their first use of the package, towards advice which seems most appropriate to their existing patterns of studying. Each part of the project will now be described in turn.

Developing the Questionnaire

Research on student learning over the last twenty years has identified dimensions which describe the main differences in study behaviour. Although this research has followed contrasting theoretical perspectives, there is now substantial agreement about how to characterise the different ways of studying (Biggs, 1993). The main distinction is between, on the one hand, an approach to studying which uses shallow or surface processing (mainly memorising or routine procedures) leading to the reproduction of lecture or text-book content or to problem-solving using set routines and, on the other, an approach in which the student seeks a deep level of conceptual understanding through interacting with the course material, elaborating and so transforming it. The two approaches to learning have been called *surface* and *deep*, respectively, to indicate their links with the ideas of Marton and Saljo (1984). The other main dimension, on which there is substantial agreement, is described as *organised* or *strategic studying*.

The questionnaire had its origins in much earlier research which led to the development of the *Approaches to Studying Inventory* (ASI) (Entwistle & Ramsden, 1983; Ramsden & Entwistle, 1981). Factor analyses of that instrument usually produce three or four separable factors or *orientations to studying* with variations in the loading of sub-scales between different samples and subject areas. The three factors represent deep, surface, and strategic approaches to studying, with the fourth factor, where present, describing an apathetic approach, showing negative attitudes and disorganised study methods. Since the ASI was developed, there has been a wealth of research into student learning, some of it using one or other of the inventories (see Biggs, 1993; Entwistle & Tait, 1990; Meyer, 1991) while other studies have been based on the qualitative analysis of interviews (see Entwistle & Marton, 1989, 1994; Marton, Hounsell & Entwistle, 1984).

Examination of the literature on approaches to learning and studying suggested how best to update the original inventory through both conceptual clarification and redirecting the focus more directly towards the identification of study difficulties. The initial outcome of this revision was a pilot inventory which contained 60 items, organised within 15 sub-scales which were intended to fall within five main conceptual domains.

These domains were represented by composite scores on deep approach, surface approach, strategic approach, apathetic approach, and a sub-scale score on academic self-confidence. The fifteen individual sub-scales each contained only four five-point Likert items, with correspondingly low internal reliability, but the three composite scales all had Cronbach alpha values of above 0.75. Evidence of validity has accumulated over many previous studies (see Entwistle & Tait, 1990; Biggs, 1993).

Factor analysis of the inventory was carried out on a sample of 448 first-year university students (231 from psychology and 217 from engineering) using maximum likelihood with rotation to oblique simple structure. Initially, individual inventory items, rather than sub-scales, were entered into the factor analysis to confirm that there was empirical justification for the conceptual groupings of items into sub-scales and main dimensions.

Although broadly satisfactory, a detailed examination of the item analyses suggested that the inventory could be reduced in length without affecting its reliability or sacrificing content. This shorter version contained 38 items, again covering the three main approaches (deep, surface and strategic), and retaining the separate academic self-confidence scale, but this time replacing the apathetic approach with a more tightly defined "lack of direction" scale. Cronbach alpha coefficients of internal reliability were found to be satisfactory for these revised scales being 0.82 for deep approach, 0.79 for surface approach, 0.84 for strategic approach, 0.66 for academic self-confidence and 0.74 for lack of direction. The three main approaches each contained ten items, while 'academic self-confidence' and 'lack of direction' each contained four items. Since some of the sub-scales within the main dimensions had been reduced to just two items, it was not appropriate to calculate Cronbach alpha values for the sub-scales. Sample items from the inventory can be found in Appendix 1. Maximum likelihood item factor analysis was carried out on a new sample of 345 first-year students (199 from psychology, 68 from computer studies, and 78 from business and information technology). The eigenvalue criterion was used in conjunction with a scree plot to determine the number of factors to extract. Four factors accounting for 42% variance were extracted and it was found that items fitted well into their intended domains. A subsequent factor analysis was therefore carried out at sub-scale level which also included four separate items from the questionnaire asking students how well prepared they were for higher education in terms of entry qualifications, study skills, previous knowledge, and their ability to work independently. Three factors explaining 51% variance were extracted. The factor pattern can be seen in Table 1.

The three strongest factors described the expected main *approaches to studying* - deep, surface, and strategic - and it can be seen that two of the *preparedness on entry* items - ability to plan and organise studying and study skills - load on the strategic factor, while the other two - entry qualifications and knowledge - load negatively, and somewhat more weakly, on the surface approach factor.

While revising the inventory, it had been decided to extend the surrounding questionnaire by developing additional items which would pick up specific areas of difficulty both in study skills and in other aspects of students' lives which affect studying. Only in that way could there be a sufficiently close connection between the questionnaire and the advice on study skills and approaches to studying subsequently offered. Two main sections were therefore added to the revised questionnaire. The first, a study skills section, included questions on lectures and lecture notes, discussion classes, practicals or laboratory classes, reading, asking for help, writing essays, tackling set problems, organising studying, and revision. The other new section asked students to rate the extent to which various non-academic factors, such as family commitments or health problems, affected their ability to study. No particular relationships were intended among or between these various questionnaire sections - instead they were meant to capture the range of influences on studying which exists for students in higher education. It was anticipated that some students would report that their studies were being adversely affected by non-academic factors, others would have inappropriate approaches to studying, and others again would have study skills weaknesses. For some students, studying would be affected by a combination of the above factors.

Table 1
Factor Pattern Matrix for the Inventory Sub-scales. (N=345).

Factors	I	II	III
Preparedness on entry (in terms of)			
Entry qualifications		(-.25)	
Knowledge		-.34	
Study skills	.77		
Ability to study independently	.53		
Deep Approach			
• Looking for meaning			.62
• Active interest			.69
• Relating and organising ideas			.84
• Using evidence and logic			.68
Surface Approach			
• Relying on memorising	.33	.51	
• Difficulty in making sense		.52	
• Unrelatedness		.58	
• Concern about coping		.85	
Strategic Approach			
• Determination to excel	(.29)		.39
• Effort in studying	.62		
• Organised studying	.77		
• Time management	.68		
Apathetic Approach			
• Lack of direction	(-.24)	(.25)	
Academic Aptitude			
• Academic self-confidence		-.58	

Maximum likelihood extracted 51% of the variance; loadings below .30 have generally been omitted

Factor intercorrelations	II	III
Factor I	-.15	.50
Factor II		-.24

The revised questionnaire has subsequently been developed into an interactive computer-based version (Odor, 1994a) and is scored automatically to provide the data which feed into either of the two specially developed pieces of software (see below for further details). The interactive version presents a student with the questions one at a time, and the student indicates his or her desired response by using the mouse to point and click. Once a student has responded to a question, the next question is automatically presented, though the student can move forwards and backwards manually using the directional arrows to change responses if required. A horizontal bar at the bottom of the screen fills up as the questionnaire is completed. Figure 1 provides an example of a card from the interactive questionnaire.

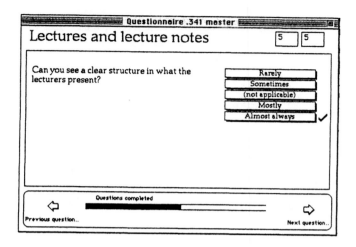

Figure 1. A Card from *Questionnaire*

Identifying Students at Risk

Based on the questionnaire responses, the self-reported study strategies of each student can be represented as a point within the three-dimensional space created by positioning the scores of a student within the three main axes formed by deep, surface, and strategic approaches to studying respectively. *Lack of direction* and *academic self-confidence* were not used to construct the axes because it was suspected, based on previous studies, that these short sub-scales would contribute to different main dimensions depending on particular student samples. *Lack of direction*, for example, sometimes loads positively on surface approach, and at other times loads negatively on strategic approach. Although for display purposes the axes are orientated at 90° to each other, this is not intended to have any conceptual or empirical basis, or to suggest any particular relationships between or among these main dimensions. All students from a particular class can be plotted together in the one space using the second piece of HyperCard-based software called *StudentView* (Odor, 1994b). *StudentView* accepts the scored data from the questionnaire, displays the positions of students within the plots, indicates which students appear to be at risk in terms of their self-reported patterns of study behaviour, and suggests simple sources of help for these students. Unlike most graphical displays of statistical data, the plots provided within *StudentView* are interactive, allowing individual students at risk to be easily identified either by clicking on a point within the space or on a student identifier in the adjacent scrolling bar, while retaining a global view of a whole class. An example of a three-dimensional plot can be seen in Figure 2 below. Since this is rather difficult to interpret where class sizes are large, two dimensional plots can also be obtained. An example of a two-dimensional plot can be seen in Figure 3.

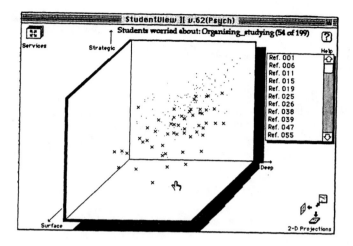

Figure 2. A Three-dimensional *StudentView* Plot

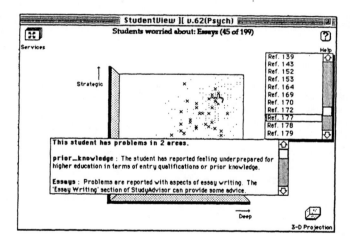

Figure 3: A Two-dimensional *StudentView* Plot

Students are identified as being 'at risk' in a number of different ways. Conceptually, there is an area within the three-dimensional space representing study strategies which are generally deemed to be inappropriate for higher education. This region is broadly defined by high surface approach scores combined with low strategic and low deep scores, though the particular shape and size of this region will vary by academic discipline and context. Students positioned within this area could be said to be employing approaches to studying which would be unlikely to lead to success.

A list of all the study skills which students have responded to on the questionnaire appears in a pull-down menu in *StudentView*. The user can then select a skill or task (e.g., essay writing), and any students who have reported having difficulty with this are then identified in the plot by an 'x'. A comments box is also available (as seen in Figure 3) which displays a list of all reported problems for any particular student, along with a summary statement of the number of reported problems. As the number of problems increases for any student, so too will the degree of being at risk, and the need for some support and advice to be offered.

Other types of problems besides study skills can also be identified using the questionnaire, and again these can be mapped on to the three-dimensional plot. For example, problems with course content, or those of a non-academic nature, can be identified. Each problem, of course, will require a different type of advice, but the remit of the project is limited to providing help with study strategies and skills. This is the potential power of the system - students experiencing problems which can best be addressed at local level (such as those relating to course content) will be made apparent to teaching staff through *StudentView* which in turn offers some suggestions as to how teaching staff can be of help through its accompanying documentation (with the course content example, suggestions might include simply producing back-up reading lists or materials, or providing remedial tutorials).

Mapping difficulties with study skills on to a study approaches plot implies an empirical relationship between the two. Intuitively though, it seems likely that some students will have problems with specific study skills but yet will be employing appropriate approaches to studying, while other students will be using study strategies which seem incongruent with the aims of higher education yet report no study skills difficulties. The original rationale for combining study skills and approaches on the same graphical plot within *StudentView* was based on the idea that students would be increasingly unlikely to perform well as the number of skills with which they reported having difficulty rose, or where skills difficulties and weaknesses in approach existed simultaneously. However, statistical analysis carried out on data gathered during the development stages of the questionnaire suggests that there are statistically significant negative correlations between the number of skills with which a student reports having difficulty and scores on both deep and strategic approaches, and that a positive correlation exists between the number of problematic skills and his or her score on the scale measuring lack of direction in studying. But correlations of this kind do not rule out the possibility of the pattern described above existing for at least some students and this could still be important.

StudentView therefore can provide valuable information for teaching staff about the ways in which their students study in general, and can also pinpoint specific problems that some of the students are experiencing. *StudentView* has two accompanying pieces of documentation: one that provides advice to staff on the best ways to deal with different kinds of difficulty; and a second that describes the student model which is being employed.

Providing Advice to Students

Initial discussions with teaching departments indicated that *StudentView* was considered to be a potentially useful tool in helping staff gain greater insights into the students in their classes. However, it was pointed out that the identification of students experiencing study skills and strategies difficulties was only half of the problem, the other half being what to do once these students had been identified. It was also emphasised that current workloads in most departments made additional work with individual students impossible to provide and, in any case, few members of staff felt confident in advising students on study skills. It was thus decided to develop a third piece of interrelated, though not interdependent, HyperCard-based software called *StudyAdvisor* (Odor, 1993) to offer advice and suggestions to students which some staff felt they had neither the knowledge, resources, or time to handle successfully entirely by themselves.

In designing this software, it was necessary to take account of continuing criticism in the literature about the ineffectiveness of traditional study skills training (Nisbet, 1979). While it is clear that students can be given useful information about the types of study skills they need in higher education, it is much less clear how to do it in ways which students will find useful. There are several problems with existing study skills manuals. They are often based on out-of-date ideas derived from mainstream psychology and suggest practices which are too demanding of time (Gibbs, 1981). Many such manuals are also patronising in tone, or go to the other extreme and reduce a serious enterprise into cartoon strips. There is also a tendency to give advice which is inappropriately didactic, giving the impression that there are "correct" ways of studying and trying to impose a particular method, say, of taking notes or reading, rather than inviting students to explore alternative approaches. And implying that there are correct methods can be damaging, if students decide to alter study methods which are working well. Students also find much of the advice idealised, implying a commitment to studying beyond what typical students can accept. And, finally, skills have to be practised within the everyday study context; to be effective any advice has to be converted into action and habit.

In writing advice for *StudyAdvisor*, it was attempted to take account of these criticisms. The most important step was to draw, not on mainstream psychology, but on the literature from student learning to provide an underpinning rationale (Entwistle & Tait, 1992). Recent research has suggested that the most effective studying depends on students developing a conscious awareness of their purposes and strategies in studying - what Biggs (1985) has called *metalearning*. However, Biggs (1987) has also argued that advice has to be tailored to the stage a student has reached. At the start of higher education, he suggests that the advice should be simple and didactic, introducing the basic skills and giving practical suggestions. Students who have particular difficulties may need to be persuaded that they would be able to cope with such advice. These students seem to take more notice of what other students say about what is feasible. Promising results have been achieved by presenting such students with videotaped discussions between other students who had experienced difficulties, but who overcame them by changing their study strategies (Van Overwalle, Segebarth, & Goldchstein, 1989). Once students have developed more confidence in their studying, Biggs (1987) suggests that they should be encouraged to become more reflective about their own studying, monitoring their success in relation to what they hope to achieve.

The advice for *StudyAdvisor* has therefore been provided at different levels of complexity and detail, starting with simple didactic advice and encouraging students to move on to more detailed advice in which comments from students, derived from research interviews, are also provided. The advice has been written with the need to encourage personal engagement with studying being built in from the very beginning, but this becomes apparent to the student only later in the sequence. We have also tried to develop a "tone" in writing which is conversational but serious, to explain the reasons for giving the advice, and to take into account the demands which any advice may make on the student.

StudyAdvisor contains a series of cards organised *horizontally* to progress through various different skills and contexts and *vertically* to allow students to explore advice about study skills at different levels of detail. Students may have been directed to *StudyAdvisor* on the basis of their responses to the questionnaire. In that case, they will bring with them, or have available on their computer desktop, a profile of their scores and self-ratings derived from the questionnaire. This profile is then used to direct the student to the most personally relevant advice, thereby cutting down the amount of reading that would otherwise be required. Students can opt not to use their profile, and browse freely if they wish.

Among the introductory set of cards, one card indicates what it takes, in general, to be an effective student. The components below have been drawn from the research on student learning and studying and these principles are then used to guide the advice offered in each of the main areas of study skills described subsequently. Within each of these areas, hypertext techniques are used to present advice at different levels of detail and sophistication. Below follow components used for the introductory cards:
- Reasons for taking your present course
- The extent to which you gear your learning to course requirements
- Your previous knowledge, skills, and underlying ability
- The extent to which you try to understand things for yourself
- How well you organise your study time
- The extent to which you think about study methods

At the simplest level, the advice stack presents hints and tips about thirteen different areas: types of university classes, managing tasks and time, learning from lectures, reading, taking notes from books, writing essays, using resources, making the most of tutorials, problem solving, taking practical classes, revising for examinations, sitting examinations, and influences on successful studying.

At the second level, more detailed advice is offered across all these areas, together with "pop-ups" through which relevant comments from students are presented. These comments are intended to bring the advice to life mainly through extracts from research interviews in which students explain their own approach to some aspect of studying. *StudyAdvisor* allows students to print out their own individualised study skills guide by selecting certain cards from the stack to save and print. Appendix 2 illustrates what some of the advice on essay writing would look like when printed out, including how the 'pop-ups' are displayed.

SUMMARY: HOW THE SOFTWARE ACTS AS A SYSTEM

Figure 4 summarises the interrelations between the three pieces of software and the supporting documentation which this project is developing to identify and advise students with deficient study skills.

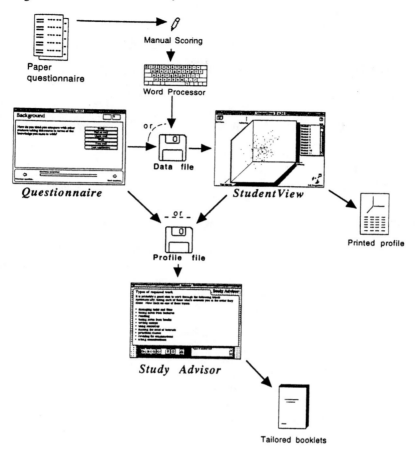

Paper
questionnaire

Manual Scoring

Word Processor

Questionnaire

Data file

or

StudentView

Printed profile

_ or _

Profile file

Study Advisor

Tailored booklets

Figure 4. Diagrammatic Representation of the Overall System

FUTURE WORK

Adaptation of the Software by Departments

Each piece of software has been designed in such a way that relatively easy modification of the content of the additional questions within the questionnaire, the functions used to define students at risk, and the advice offered, can be carried out. The main modifications that are currently envisaged would be the provision of study skills advice specific to particular departments or disciplines. *StudyAdvisor* has quite extensive editing tools provided and the manual will provide enough detail to allow staff to undertake such adaptations. Less modification is anticipated with *StudentView,* but again the manual will indicate what can readily be undertaken.

Evaluation Strategy

Although the evaluations will provide evidence of the value of the software as perceived by both staff and students, the research team has several remaining areas of concern about the uses to which the software will be put. First, the questionnaire and inventory are general instruments, which do not take account of differences between academic disciplines or institutions. It is envisaged that the current questionnaire and inventory would represent a core, with additional items being added to take account of local and disciplinary differences. *StudentView* could also be adapted to provide specific suggestions about the local arrangements for advice on study skills and personal problems.

The next issue relates to the nature of the advice that is being provided. That advice is based on the research on student learning, which encourages students to adopt a deep approach to learning and to be strategic in their studying. While being strategic will generally help students, there are some departments whose methods of teaching and assessment might make a deep approach counterproductive, at least in the short term (see Thomas & Bain, 1984). *StudentView*'s accompanying document consequently incorporates some suggestions for departments about the importance of ensuring that teaching and assessment do encourage students to develop personal understanding (Entwistle, Thompson, & Tait, 1992), but with only very limited expectations of any change in established practices. In those circumstances, there is a danger that if the advice presented in *StudyAdvsior* is followed too closely, it may weaken the assessment performances of students.

A final concern relates to the problem of encouraging students to practise the skills described in *StudyAdvisor*, particularly since there is a growing consensus that study skills advice is effective only if students are encouraged to try out the advice within their courses of study. The provision of such opportunities has thus been recommended to departments.

Since full trialling of the software has just begun, nothing can yet be said about resulting improvements in the quality of student learning. It is clear that any improvements will not be seen immediately, and that the effectiveness of the system in general, and *StudyAdvisor* in particular, could only be evaluated in a few years' time when it has become an integral part of a department's or institution's study skills provision.

ACKNOWLEDGMENTS

The project team is grateful to Mr J.P. Odor, computing consultant to the project, for designing and developing the software shells and for providing general help and support. It is also grateful to the *Scottish Higher Education Funding Council* for funding the project under its *Teaching and Learning Technology Programme*.

REFERENCES

Biggs, J.B. (1985). The role of metalearning in study processes. *British Journal of Educational Psychology, 55*, 185-212.

Biggs, J.B. (1987). *Student approaches to learning and studying.* Melbourne: Australian Council for Educational Research.

Biggs, J.B. (1993). What do inventories of students' learning processes really measure? A theoretical review and a clarification. *British Journal of Educational Psychology, 63,* 3-19.

Entwistle, N.J., Hounsell, D.J., Macaulay, C., Situnayake, G., & Tait, H. (1989). *The performance of electrical engineers in Scottish higher education.* University of Edinburgh: Centre for Research on Learning and Instruction.

Entwistle, N.J., & Marton, F. (Eds.). (1989). The psychology of student learning. *European Journal of the Psychology of Education ,* IV, (special issue).

Entwistle, N.J., & Marton, F. (1994). Knowledge objects: Understandings constituted through intensive academic study. *British Journal of Educational Psychology, 64* (1), 161-178.

Entwistle, N.J., & Ramsden, P. (1983). *Understanding student learning.* London: Croom Helm.

Entwistle, N.J., & Tait, H. (1990). Approaches to learning, evaluations of teaching, and preferences for contrasting academic environments. *Higher Education, 19,* 169-194.

Entwistle, N.J., & Tait, H. (1992). Promoting effective study skills. Module 8, Block A. *Effective learning and teaching in higher education.* Sheffield: Universities' Staff Development Unit.

Entwistle, N.J., Thompson, S., & Tait, H. (1992). *Guidelines for promoting effective learning in higher education.* University of Edinburgh: Centre for Research on Learning and Instruction.

Gibbs, G. (1981). *Teaching students to learn: A student centred approach.* Milton Keynes: Open University Press.

Marton, F., Hounsell, D.J., & Entwistle, N.J. (1984). (Eds.) *The experience of learning.* Edinburgh: Scottish Academic Press.

Marton, F., & Saljo, R. (1984). Approaches to learning. In F. Marton, D.J. Hounsell, & N.J. Entwistle (Eds.), *The experience of learning.* Edinburgh: Scottish Academic Press.

Meyer, J.H.F. (1991). Study orchestration: The manifestation, interpretation and consequences of contextualised approaches to studying. *Higher Education, 22,* 297-316.

Meyer, J.H.F., & Parsons, P.(1989). Approaches to studying and course perceptions using the Lancaster inventory - A comparative study. *Studies in Higher Education, 20,* 67-89.

Nisbet, J.D. (1979). Beyond the study skills manual. In P.J. Hills (Ed.), *Study courses and counselling.* London: SRHE.

Odor, J.P. (1993). *StudyAdvisor editor. Author handbook draft release 3.* University of Edinburgh: Centre for Research on Learning and Instruction.

Odor, J.P. (1994a). *Questionnaire - An interactive system for administering student questionnaires. Student and administrator handbook version 1.2* University of Edinburgh: Centre for Research on Learning and Instruction.

Odor, J.P. (1994b). *StudentView II - An interactive graphical system for analysing and exploring student questionnaire data. User handbook version b2.1.* University of Edinburgh: Centre for Research on Learning and Instruction.

Ramsden, P., & Entwistle, N.J. (1981). Effects of academic departments on students' approaches to studying. *British Journal of Educational Psychology, 51, 368-383.*

Thomas, P.R., & Bain, J.D. (1984). Contextual dependence of learning approaches: The effects of assessments. *Human Learning, 3,* 227-240.

Van Overwalle, F., Segebarth, K. & Goldchstein, M. (1989). Improving performance of freshmen through attributional testimonies from fellow students. *British Journal of Educational Psychology, 59,* 75-85.

Wall, D., Macaulay, C., Tait, H., Entwistle, D., & Entwistle, N. (1991). *The transition from school to higher education in Scotland.* University of Edinburgh: Centre for Research on Learning and Instruction.

APPENDIX 1

Examples of items from the 38-item *Revised Approaches to Studying Inventory:*

Deep Approach
Looking for meaning
I usually set out to understand for myself the meaning of what we have to learn.

Active interest/Critical stance
I'm not prepared just to accept things I'm told: I have to think them out for myself.

Relating and organising ideas
I try to relate ideas I come across to other topics or other courses whenever possible.

Using evidence and logic
When I'm reading, I examine the details carefully to see how they fit in with what's being said.

Surface Approach
Relying on memorising
I find I have to concentrate on memorising a good deal of what I have to learn.

Difficulty in making sense
I often have trouble in making sense of the things I have to remember.

Unrelatedness
Although I can remember facts and details, I often can't see any overall picture.

Concern about coping
Often I lie awake worrying about work I think I won't be able to do.

Strategic Approach
Determination to excel
It's important to me to feel I'm doing as well as I really can on the courses here.

Effort in studying
I work hard when I'm studying and generally manage to keep my mind on what I'm doing.

Organised studying
I think I'm quite systematic and organised in the way I go about studying.

Time management
I organise my study time carefully to make the best use of it.

Lack of Direction
I rather drifted into higher education without deciding for myself what I really wanted to do.

Academic Self-confidence
Generally, I find the set work easy to do.

APPENDIX 2

An illustration of printed text on essay writing:

Writing an essay

In higher education, essays are one of the most common ways of helping you learn. They are also used to assess your progress. It is important for you to recognise essays as opportunities for learning, while also keeping an eye on meeting assessment requirements.

An essay is usually intended to encourage you to develop your own understanding of the topic, and to demonstrate that understanding by giving a clear and direct answer to the specific question set.

There is a map available.

See fig.1

Why? How? What next?

For writing essays, you are expected to use a DEEP APPROACH. To do that you need to think WHY you are doing the essay - think about what you want to learn from it and the tutor's reason for setting that particular question. You need to think ahead - to HOW and when you are going to do it, how much time you will need, which books you will need to find. And WHAT NEXT - when you have finished the essay, decide how well it went and how you might do it better next time.

The academic essay

Most students come into higher education with a clear idea about writing essays. Unfortunately, it is often the wrong idea! At school there are rules about what makes a good essay, generally laid down by the English teachers. But an academic essay demands a different style, one you will be expected to develop gradually over the course as a whole. Tutors will be looking, not just for accurate grammar and clear expression, but also for:

* the choice of reading
* the organisation of material into a convincing argument or explanation
* the use of evidence to substantiate conclusions, and
* a critical stance toward what you are writing which shows you are trying to think it out for yourself.

We always have to back up the argument, and I use statistics, figures, data or quotes. It is really just a way of backing up what you are saying and showing you are not just drawing assumptions out of thin air.

Too little and too much

It may seem that we are telling you more about the process of writing an essay than you can use or absorb right now. Much of this advice comes from interviews with more advanced students about what they have learned from experience. Try not to be intimidated. You will not be able to do all this at first. It will take time.

Author Index

Page numbers in *italics* denote complete bibliographical information.

Subject Index

K

L

M

N

O

P

T

V

W